To Vermont College

Perry H Merrill
Sept 1975

# *Vermont*

## UNDER FOUR FLAGS

A HISTORY OF THE GREEN MOUNTAIN STATE
1635-1975

Perry H. Merrill

Montpelier, Vermont
Published by the Author
1975

Designed and printed by Northlight
Studio Press, Inc., Barre, Vermont U.S.A.
Designer: Cyndy M. Brady
Typeface: Times Roman 11 point

Montpelier, Vermont
Published by the Author
1975

# Table of Contents

# Preface

The *style* of this book is by subject matter rather than the usually chronologically written history. A reader can obtain the entire history of a subject in one chapter. The biography at the end of each chapter will lead one to more details if one so desires. A chapter of the book can be read and placed aside until one's interest is whetted to take up another chapter. In reading the usual history of one or more volumes all connection with events of similar nature, which may have happened years previous, is usually lost. As an example, there was a severe hail storm in Alburg in July 1813 which ruined all the crops of buckwheat, wheat and oats. As was the custom the town petitioned the legislature to have all their taxes abated which accordingly was done. A similar philosophy of government occurred in 1972 and 1973 when the federal government aided the farmers in the Champlain Valley, where they lost their corn crops due to unfavorable weather conditions. Under the chapter, Agriculture, these two philosophies are brought together to show their relationship.

The *subject matter* in this book is grouped under the following headings: Our Flags, Vermont A Dutch Colony, Early History, Arts and Sciences, Banks and Money, Industry, Communications, Education, Government, Health and Welfare, Immigration and Emigration, Indians, Labor, Morals and Ethics, Natural Resources, Societies, Transportation, Wars and Riots, and Woman's Suffrage. For the first time the state's history of skiing is published between the covers of one book. There are many other subjects which have never been covered in a Vermont history.

The *incentive* to write a new Vermont history, which brings up-to-date historical records and scientific records, that have transpired during the past thirty years was given encouragement by three persons. To Mrs. Vivian Bryan, State Law Librarian, goes my sincere gratitude for her untiring efforts in suggesting and locating publications valuable in my writing. The advice of Mr. John A. Williams, Editor of State Papers, has been a great help in the research and publishing of this book. Mrs. Laura Abbott, Vermont Historical Society's librarian, has been of untold assistance in directing me to works of historical value. I wish to recognize with deep appreciation the sound advice and aid which Mr. Alan H. Weiss, Deputy Commissioner of Education has given in the preparation of this volume. Miss Karlene Russell and Mrs. Madge Boardman of the same department have aided by reading and suggesting changes in the chapter on Education. The task in editing the manuscript by Mrs. Kathryn Breer is sincerely appreciated.

Pertinent subject matter chapters have been referred to members of several state departments and other individuals for comment. I wish to acknowledge the help of Dr. A. E. Janowicz, state veterinarian, Edward Knapp, retired commissioner of aviation, Charles Doll, state geologist and Lawrence Turgeon, court administrator. There are many other persons, too numerous to mention, who have given me assistance in one way or another. Those who have reviewed the chapter on skiing, are former state forester, Albert W. Gottlieb, Charles D. Lord who worked for me in the C.C.C. days in the layout of trails on Mt. Mansfield and other state forest areas, E. Huntley Palmer and Abner Coleman enthusiastic early skiers. Owners, operators and others connected with skiing have furnished information on skiing and ski jumping. To mention a few, they are Sepp Ruschp of Stowe, W. Albert Cole of Bradford, the late Harold White of Brattleboro, Fred Pabst of Manchester, Harold Haynes, jr. of North Troy, Walter Schoenknecht of Mt. Snow and Warren Warner, a former employee and now manager of a New Hampshire ski development. Mrs. Fred Harris of Brattleboro made available much information concerning her late husband Fred's pioneer activities in ski jumping. My familiarity through the direction of the development of skiing facilities on Mt. Mansfield and other state areas has aided me in the writing of the chapter on skiing.

Mr. James Mereness, executive vice-president of the Associated Industries of Vermont has furnished me with much information about Vermont industries. The following associations have been very helpful in the distribution of advertising slips about the book or carried the printed word in their publications. The 251 Club, Vermont Education Association, The Vermont Medical Society, Washington Electric Cooperative, Vermont Electric Cooperative, The Vermont Sunday News, The Vermont State Libraries, The Washington World, Vermont Life. To the persons responsible for these actions I am truly indebted.

I have searched for information from original sources, where possible. Some of these sources are: the session laws from 1778 to 1975, the eight volumes of the Governor and Council, Reports of Vermont state departments, Town Histories, Documentary reports of the Province and State of Nw York, New Netherland's reports, the Vermont State Papers. The publication, *The Public Papers of Governor Thomas Chittenden 1778-1797,* edited by John A. Williams, state historian has furnished the author with information, which otherwise would have taken much time of careful research to locate. I have not gone into details in my writings because I have tried to keep the book due to costs to as small a size as possible. Details may be found in publications listed in the bibliography. I have omitted the first constitution which may be found in the early 1800 publications.

"Shades of my ancestors! Not thus,
As you too fully know,
Spake ye unto our grandmothers,
One hundred years ago.
Still yielding to the high demands,
Of the present "high-toned" day.
I'll strive to answer his commands,
As briefly as I may."

from the *Sleeping Beauty*

# Foreword

Vermont, the Green Mountain State, is tucked away in the Northeastern corner of the United States. Its history, traditions, and contributions have become an integral part of this great country.

Settled well before the American Revolution, Vermont, it is important to understand, for a long period of time was largely an inhospitable wilderness. It was populated by a rough and hardy citizenry whose almost exclusive preoccupation was wrestling the barest subsistence from a reluctant and often hostile environment. To the everlasting credit of those poor and harassed people, considerations of education, morality, and religion were so compelling to them that the encouragement of these virtues was made a principal objective of their government.

In 1777, Vermont declared itself a Republic and stayed a Republic until its entry into the Union in 1791, as the fourteenth state, with a population yet to be in excess of a half-million citizens. Vermont has a well-deserved reputation for beauty and Vermonters for wit, ingenuity, independence, inventiveness, leadership and culture. These characteristics are best described, as in this case, by one who knows and appreciates them.

The author of this book, Mr. Merrill, is an adopted son who has dedicated his life to the State. Long before conservation and open-land preservation became national practices, as Director of Vermont's Forests and Parks, he acquired for Vermont many of its beautiful tracts. Those of us who are fortunate enough to enjoy the hills, valleys, lakes, and rivers, woodlots, pastures and the scenic views of four seasons are indebted to his foresightedness. Thank you, Perry.

And now please turn the pages and share with him the history of Vermont.

Alan H. Weiss
Vermont Deputy Commissioner of Education

# Our Flags

The flags of four countries on the jacket does not mean that this state was under the control of all these governments, or even settled to any great extent by them. The chapter under Vermont, a Dutch Colony, relates the claim of the Dutch. The French had their seigneuries along Lake Champlain for a short time. The English with their fleet from Quebec tried to wrest control of the Champlain Valley. Vermont was supposed to be controlled by the New Hampshire grants, or English.

The history of flags which were flown by Vermonters has been very ably researched and documented by John Williams, Editor of State Papers. Therefore, I am reprinting in part his description of such flags.

"Vermont differed from the thirteen original states which inherited their colonial history, seats of government in most instances, archives and flags." Vermont, as related elsewhere, was never a colony of another nation nor did she bow to either New York or the New Hampshire Grants. At Westminster, on January 15, 1777, Vermont declared her independence, calling herself New Connecticut; changing her name to Vermont the year following at Windsor, on June 4, 1777. "Vermont was a separate and independent state — in fact, a republic — not to be accepted into the Union as the 14th state until 1791. There was no capitol, constitution, assembly or governor, and no flag."

"Neither the Constitution nor the Council of Safety, the temporary government, mention a flag. There was no provision for a flag until October 31, 1803, when a state militia flag was created with seventeen stars and seventeen stripes with the word 'Vermont' in capitals above the stars and stripes. The first evidence of a Vermont flag was the Bennington Battle Flag, which was raised during the Battle of Bennington, when the Vermont, New

Hampshire and Massachusetts militia were attacking Burgoyne's Hessian troops on August 16, 1777.

"It should be recalled that the Continental Congress had just authorized the first United States Flag on the 14th of June, 1777, to include thirteen stars, white in a blue field, and thirteen stripes, alternate red and white. The Bennington Battle Flag met these specifications except for the numerals 76 in the lower center of the union or canton, just under a semi-circle of 11 stars, with two more stars being located in the upper left and right corners. The evidence is very strong that this flag was, indeed, the first Stars and Stripes Flag to wave in the victory over an enemy force, since there is no known evidence of an earlier use of the Stars and Stripes.

"The Bennington Battle Flag is not only the earliest United States Flag, it is also Vermont's first authentic flag, because it was fabricated at Old Bennington Village and presented to General John Stark by Lieutenant Nathaniel Fillmore of Bennington, one of the native sons and heroes of the battle, whose wife Hepzibah is believed to have helped in the fabrication of the flag. Stark had arrived at Bennington on August 9, 1777. His camp was established there in ample time to have received the news of the creation of a national flag, and for the completion of the Bennington Battle Flag prior to August 16th when the battle took place."

# Vermont, a Dutch Colony

Today Vermont might have been a Dutch Colony or state if the Dutch had in the early 1600's sent to America enough settlers and soldiers to hold the land that they claimed in America.

Henry Hudson in his attempts to find a northeast passage to the Pacific Ocean explored the Hudson River area in 1608. The Dutch made quite extensive settlements in New York, and in Connecticut as far north as the present city of Hartford.

The Dutch who first settled this colony, claimed the whole of the Connecticut River and Lake Champlain and all the country southward of the St. Lawrence River down to the Delaware River. This fact appears from many ancient maps (particularly from Blair's and Ogilby's) and from William Bleau's map of New Netherlands and New England which shows the Connecticut River as the boundary line between New England and New Netherlands, as shown on page 9.

The original colony of New Hampshire, as it was granted by the Council of Plymouth and confirmed by the Crown about 1635, lay altogether on the east side of the Connecticut River which it did not reach by twenty miles.

"In the year 1614 there appeared before the Assembly of the States General of United Netherlands, the deputies of the United Company of Merchants who have discovered and founded New Netherlands, situate in America between New France and Virginia, the seacoasts whereof lie in the latitude 40 to 45 degrees. They came to ask a grant of an exclusive right to settle and trade with countries and obtained a monoply for three years which afterwards was extended in favor of the Dutch West India Company for four years from 1621.[1]

1. E. B. O'Callaghan, *Documents Appertaining to Colonial History of New York, 1856,* Albany: Weed & Persons & Co., Vol. 1, p. 10.

The lands they purchased comprehended all that part of New England in America which lies and extends itself from a river then called Narragansett, the space of 40 leagues, upon a straight line near the seashore, toward the southwest, west and by south and west as the coast line lieth toward Virginia...and all...lands... being within the lands aforesaid, north and south in latitude...and in...longitude, of and within all breadth aforesaid throughout the main land thence from the western ocean to the south sea, and also all the Islands lying in America aforesaid in the said seas (or either of them) on the Western and Eastern coasts or parts of said tracts of land.[2]

The Dutch barely edged out the English from Plymouth for the primacy of settlement in the general Hartford area. The English from the Plymouth Colony, hearing from the Pequoit Indians about the fertility of the Connecticut River Valley lands, made an exploratory tour of the area in 1632. The English settled all around Hartford and northerly to Agawam.[3]

The Manuscript of Sir William Johnson to the New York Governor and Council states, "That his Majestie's Title to the Northern Continent of America appears to be formed on the discovery thereof first made, and the Possessions thereof first taken in 1479 under a Commission from Henry the Seventh of England to Sebastian Cabot.

That the French had possessed themselves of several parts of this continent which by treaties have been ceded and confirmed to them. That the right of the English to the whole seacoast from Georgia to the St. Lawrence River on the north - except the Island of Cape Breton, and the Islands on the Bay of St. Lawrence - remain plain and indisputable. That all the land and countries from the Atlantic Ocean to the South Sea between the 48 and 34 degrees north latitude were expressly included in the grant of King James the First to divers subjects, so long since the year 1606 and afterward confirmed in 1620.[4]

Minor disagreements between the Dutch and English occurred in Connecticut and New York. The Treaty of Hartford in 1650 between the Commissioner of the United Colonies and Governor Stuyvesant was designed to bring the controversies over jurisdiction to a close. It provided among other things that the dividing line between the English and the Dutch "upon the Main" should be fixed, "to begin on the west side of Greenwich Bay, being about four miles from Stamford, and to run a northerly line twenty miles up into the country; and after as it shall be agreed by the two Governments of

2. Ibid, pp. 275, 287.

3. Albert E. Van Dusen, *Connecticut*, (New York: Random House, 1961), p. 19.

4. E. B. O'Callaghan, *Documentary History of the State of New York*, (Albany: Weed Parsons & Co., 1850), Vol. III, p. 353.

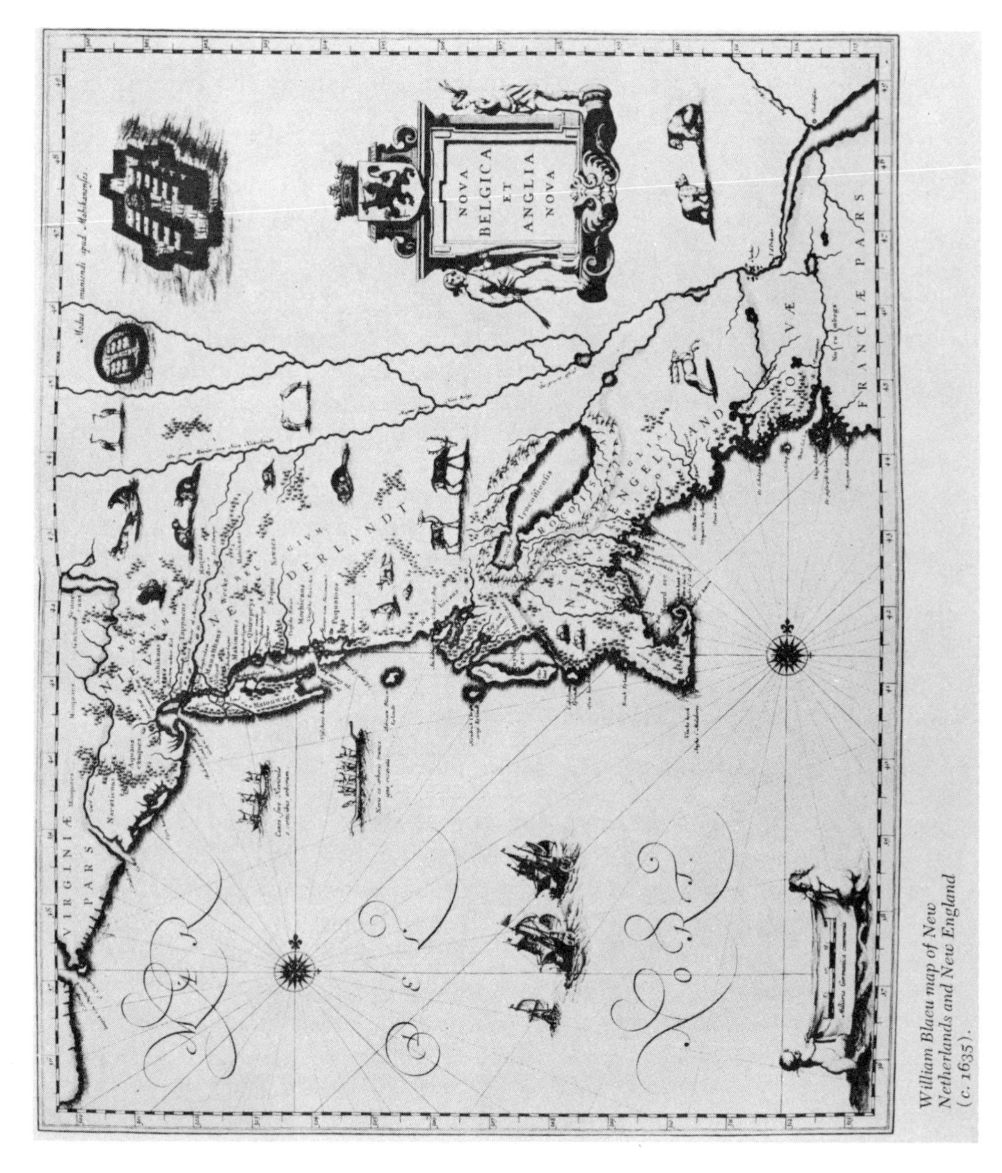


William Blaeu map of New Netherlands and New England (c. 1635).

*William Blaeu Map of New England - 1635*

the Dutch and New Haven (provided that the said line come not within ten miles of Hudson's River) and it is agreed that the Dutch shall not, at any time thereafter, build any house or habitation within six miles of said line; the inhabitants of Greenwich to remain (till further consideration be had) under the government of the Dutch. These bounds were to remain inviolate, until a full and final determination be agreed upon by mutual consent by the two states of England and Holland.[5]

Thus Vermont was saved eventually to become a free state and a part of the United States.

"In the year 1724 a few Dutch families squatted on the banks of the Hoosic River, without any title to the land. Who they were is not known, but some years afterwards the names Gregor, Van Orman, Anderson, Westerhouse, Forsburg, Voss and Sebastian Deal appear in connection with lands subsequently claimed under patents originating in New York and which titles on the measurements of their lands were extended into the town of Pownal about three miles on the western part (Allen's History)." It is reported elsewhere that there were Dutch "squatters" around Emerald Lake.[6]

The first settlers in Highgate were principally Dutch refugees who supposed that they had settled in Canada till after the establishment of the line between Canada and the States, and at the time there were no settlers found between Highgate and Burlington.[7]

Franklin - From Whitehall they proceeded on the ice (of Lake Champlain) to Mississquoi Bay, Canada, where there was a settlement, mostly of Dutch refugees of the Revolution, from the vicinity of Albany.[8]

*VERMONT, A DUTCH COLONY*
*SELECTED BIBLIOGRAPHY*

Hemenway, Abby Maria, *Vermont Historical Gazetteer,* Montpelier: Montpelier Watchman and State Journal, 1871.

O'Callaghan, E. B., et al., *Documentary History of the State of New York,* Albany, N.Y.: Weed and Parsons Co., 1856.

Van Dusen, Albert E., *Connecticut,* New York: Random House, 1961.

Wilbur, Lafayette, *Early History of Vermont,* Jericho: Roscoe Printing Company, 1899.

5. Lafayette, Wilbur, *Early History of Vermont,* (Jericho: Roscoe Printing Co., 1899), p. 68.

6. Abby Maria Hemenway, *Vermont Historical Gazetteer,* (Montpelier: Watchman and State Journal, C. W. Willard, 1871), Vol. I, p. 214.

7. Ibid, p. 225.

8. Ibid, p. 221.

# Chronology of Early Records

The Journals of the General Assembly of Vermont, from its first session, which was held at Windsor, Vermont, in March, 1778, to and including the October, 1783, session, are included in these volumes. Being authorized by the State and issued by the Secretary of State, they constitute, with the possible exception of some of the Journals for 1778, the first official printing of these records. To the late Secretary of State, Harry A. Black, is due the credit for having the necessary funds provided by the Legislature with which to continue the publication of State papers having to do with the early history of Vermont. Aaron H. Grout, the present Secretary of State, (1924) selected the material for publication and proposed the form in which the Journals appear. Edited by Vermont's historian, Walter H. Crockett, they become valuable historical records. No comprehensive and intelligent understanding can be had of the early history of this State, without the perusal of these Journals.

In the account presented by Judah P. and Alden Spooner, the State printers, in June, 1779, is an item dated November 10, 1778, for printing "200 Journals of Assembly, £45-0-0." This bill was paid by Ira Allen, State Treasurer, on June 3, 1779, so it may be fairly presumed that some of the Journals for that year were officially printed; however, no copy has ever been located. Owing to the fact that the "Votes," Resolves and Acts passed at the three sessions in 1778 were only temporary and also that during at least one of the sessions, representatives from several towns in New Hampshire voted on all questions, it is possible that all these Journals were destroyed between November 10, 1778 and February, 1779, when the "Union" between Vermont and sixteen towns in New Hampshire was dissolved. One other bill was paid to the Spooners by the State Treasurer, dated April 3, 1779, for "Printing 60 votes of Assembly, £10-0-0." It is my opinion that this charge was made for printing the proceedings of October 21, 1778, when the New Hampshire members of the Assembly were voted "out" and withdrew from the House. The Assembly voted October 21, 1778, to have the proceedings of that day printed. No other bills have been found for printing any other of the Journals herein contained.

In 1823, a volume of 567 pages, "Vermont State Papers," was compiled and published by William Slade, Jr., Secretary of State, who was born in 1786. This was authorized and paid for by the State. In his introduction, Slade wrote, "Every government, therefore, should possess and should place within the reach of the people, a complete history of its own legislation. ***The early institutions of a government are peculiarly liable to be lost sight of, in the progress of improvement. Superseded by new systems, they are supposed to have lost their value and are permitted to pass into oblivion. This has been in a peculiar sense true of the original Constitution and laws of Vermont[1]. Thirty-five years only have elapsed since that revision (1787) and not a single entire copy of the laws passed previous to that time is to be found." This is a remarkable statement as we have now located, with two minor exceptions (laws passed April, 1781, 2 pages, (first portion) and October 27, 1781, 1 page) all the laws printed from February, 1779, to 1791, the period ending Vermont's existence as a Republic. In these State Papers, Slade has published the Journals of 1778 only, so it is evident that at that early period, the printed Journals above referred to, were not known.

The manuscript records for the earlier sessions, if not the entire record, from which these Journals are printed, were undoubtedly written long after the holding of the sessions. They are in the handwriting of Dr. Roswell Hopkins, Clerk of the Assembly from 1779 to 1788 and Secretary of State from 1788 to 1802. Born in 1733, at this time he resided in Vergennes and lived to be ninety-seven years old.

He wrote a clear, legible hand and the only variation which can be noticed in it during all the years, is the difference caused by a good or bad goose quill, with which they are all written. His compensation, while Clerk, varied. The only instance, of which we know, in the records of the State, where the Legislature voted more than the amount recommended by the committee appointed to fix the compensation of the Clerk, occurred at the March session of 1780. The October session of 1779 had voted that the Clerk's pay be £ 6, about $20 lawful money, per day. The committee of the March, 1780 session reported that he should be paid $18 lawful money, per day. The Assembly refused to accept this report and voted him $46 lawful

1. Vermont did not possess a copy of its first Constitution until 1879, when it was purchased at the Brinley sale for $2.00. It is now (1924) worth about $1,000.

money, per day. It indicates that lawful money, at this time, was not on a specie basis. After 1780, his compensation ran from 7 to 12 shillings per day.

The early records lack detail and were copies from scraps of paper on which the minutes, resolutions and acts were written. Many blank spaces are left for resolutions and petitions that undoubtedly could not be found at the time of copying. Many of the reports of committees are omitted, if not lost; they were considered unimportant where no definite action was taken. Few of the remonstrances and petitions presented at the different sessions were copied. While many of them were dismissed with little consideration, they indicate the character of the people, and in some cases, expose conditions which, at that time, existed. Of special interest would be the charges brought against Ethan Allen, in the session of 1780, which induced Allen to resign as Brigadier General of the militia. The record of the first session held at Windsor, March 12, 1778 does not contain a list of members and at the bottom of the first page, Hopkins wrote: "A list of the representatives was not entered in the Journal and is not to be found."

The first compensation noted for copying Journals, in any of the proceedings is the following, which passed the Assembly, March 3, 1784:[2] A petition, signed, Roswell Hopkins, "Praying that he may have a Pay-table order (which he had obtained for recording the Journals of Assembly) paid, by giving him an order on the three penny tax was read and the prayer thereof granted, and thereupon it was resolved, that the Treasurer be, and is hereby directed to give an order, for the sum of four pounds, one shilling and three pence, (specie) etc., order to be dated, February 24, 1784." This sum must have been paid for copying Journals previous to this session. The first provision in any Journal providing for printing the Journal of Assembly, is a resolution passed at the February, 1784, session,[3] directing the Secretary, "as soon as may be after the rising of each session of the Legislature, to revise, and record the Journals of the proceedings, make a fair copy for the press, *** when printed, etc." Many of the laws passed from 1779 to 1783 during these sessions, are not mentioned in these Journals nor in "Governor and Council," edited by E. P. Walton and published in 1874[4], in eight volumes, by authority of the State. To indicate how incomplete the records were, on request of Hopkins, on October 27, 1781, it was "Resolved, that he have liberty to record the Journals of this House and make such amendments as he shall judge proper without altering the sense of the House."

2. Journal, Feb. 1784, p. 37.
3. Journal, Feb. 1784, p. 9.
4. The Vermont State Library still has (1924) a few of these volumes for sale.

As a further illustration of the slight regard for the preservation of the early records during this time when the State was surrounded by her enemies, attention may be called to the fact that at the 1782 session, (5) it was "Resolved, that the Secretary of State is directed to leave a blank in the record in order to record such laws as are mislaid and cannot, at present, be found and to record, from the printed copies where he is not possessed of the original acts, and where acts have been printed, to record them although the titles of them may not be entered on the Journals as having passed the General Assembly." Only at the end of the Journals of the February and June, 1782, sessions, did Hopkins attest their correctness, by stating "The foregoing are a true copy of the original Journals of the Assembly from the 31st of January to the 28th of March, 1782. Recorded by Roswell Hopkins, Clerk," and "The foregoing are a true record of the Journals of Assembly from the 13th to the 21st of June, 1782."

Notwithstanding these omissions, the present volumes complete the printed records of the Assemblies of the Republic of Vermont, which began the publication of its Assembly Journals in February, 1784. When the Assembly desired to go into executive session, it was "ordered that the doors be shut." Members were fined when absent without leave and because one member exchanged the State's "bills of credit" with another member for specie, at one quarter discount, both were expelled; "the crime being acknowledged." When any town refused to send in its grand list for taxing, it was "doomed," which meant that the officers of the town were subject to arrest and imprisonment.

These records disclose that the Assembly considered it was the supreme authority; overruling the courts, and also the executive, at times.

The members were a hardy, independent lot of men and generally with little or no experience in legislation. If the Journals are studied carefully, one will discover that the important acts and resolves were usually prepared in advance and it can easily be discovered that Ira Allen was in control during most of the period covered by these Journals. He was Treasurer and Surveyor General, two positions that alone would give control. Running an independent State required a talent for negotiation, diplomacy and compromise. In the last resort, it required steady courage and fighting power. Ira Allen had all these attributes and it was his master mind which guided the State during this critical period.

The merest outline of the great struggle Vermont made for its independence is sketched in the pages of these Journals. During

5. Journal, Feb., 1782, p. 106.

this time, the State confronted its greatest difficulties. After the treaty of peace in 1783, which included Vermont in the territory relinquished by Great Britain, the task of establishing the government of the State and regulating the internal affairs occupied the attention of those men who had gained independence for Vermont. The first serious mistake made by its legislators occurred when they annexed to Vermont the sixteen towns east of the Connecticut river, in 1778. This was done against the judgment of Ira Allen, but it was the first session of the Assembly and "some members contiguous to the Connecticut river threatened to withdraw from the Vermont Legislature, and unite with the people east of the said river, and form a State." [6] There was much debate and to prevent the first Assembly from breaking up in a violent manner, it was voted to refer the entire matter to the people and allow them to decide by electing members for or against the proposition.

As by far the greater part of the population of Vermont, at this time, was east of the mountain range which divided the State, a majority was returned in favor of annexation; and at the June session, the sixteen towns in New Hampshire were invited to send representatives to the October session of the Assembly. As Allen and others anticipated, this brought a storm of protest from the Governor and Council of New Hampshire, who took the matter to the Continental Congress which had guaranteed to each of the thirteen colonies, the territory included within the boundary lines established before the Revolution. Ethan Allen, who had been captured by the British in 1775, returned home to Vermont the last of May, 1778, and, in September, was sent to Philadelphia to ascertain how the members of Congress felt about the annexation. At the October session, Ethan Allen reported that Congress was strongly opposed to it.

The New Hampshire partisans had a majority in the Assembly so it was something of a task to dissolve this Union. It was done in a very clever way, on October 21, 1778, by submitting three questions to the members. First, "whether the counties in this State shall remain as they were established by this Assembly, at their sessions in March, last." This seemed an innocent question and it was carried in the affirmative by a vote of thirty-five for to twenty-six against. Those men who voted against, gave as their reason that the division of Vermont into two counties only was made before the union with the towns east of the river and "consequently, they never have been annexed to any county in the State, etc," and secondly, "because the affirmative of the question is in direct opposition to the report of the committee of both houses (of the 19th inst) on the

6. Allen, Ira, *History of Vermont*, page 114.

subject, which was confirmed by a resolve of Assembly yesterday, etc." Then the second and third questions were put together and voted upon, "Whether the towns, east of Connecticut river, included in the union with this State, shall be included in the county of Cumberland?" and "Whether the towns on the east side of Connecticut river, who are included, by union, within this State, shall be erected into a distinct county by themsleves?"—yeas, twenty-eight; nays, thirty-three. Only two deserted to the New Hampshire party on this vote. These questions were skillfully worded and the argument which assisted in putting them through, was "how much of New Hampshire's share of the debt of the thirteen States, will be assessed against these sixteen towns." "The members from the New Hampshire towns withdrew from the Assembly and were followed by the Lieutenant Governor, three members of the Council and fifteen members of the Assembly, who lived near Connecticut river," in Vermont. "The object was, to break up the Assembly as the Constitution required two-thirds of the members elected, to form a House for business"[7] The leaders, who had engineered this action, had foreseen this difficulty and were able to proceed with exactly a quorum. Ira Allen, who was selected to handle the matter with New Hampshire, exposed the design of the New Hampshire towns which had been to put Vermont and New Hampshire into one State, and locate its capital, at Hanover. This would secure the title under the New Hampshire Grants to the settlers in Vermont and New Hampshire would get the benefit of all the vacant lands remaining. Defeat of the plan was difficult but Allen effected it.

New Hampshire soon put in a claim before Congress, as did New York, to all, as did Massachusetts to a large part, of the territory of Vermont which was surrounded by these three claimants and the British on the North. These records disclose little of the bitter conflict that raged for over five years. Ira Allen, as agent to Congress in the fall of 1780, discovered that New York had made combinations with some of the Southern States and that Vermont would be turned over to New York, if some aggressive action was not taken at once. He decided to put New York and New Hampshire on the defensive by annexing a part of each State to Vermont. This, he returned home and accomplished. The sixteen New Hampshire towns were again put into Vermont at the February, 1781, session of the Assembly and in May, a union was formed with all that part of New York, lying between the Hudson river and a boundary line twenty miles east of the Hudson. This almost brought on civil war between Vermont and these two States but Allen managed affairs so adroitly that

7. Allen, Ira, *History of Vermont*, p. 116.

hostilities were avoided. He also, by negotiation, kept the British army in Canada from invading Vermont from 1780 to 1783.

While Ira Allen and Jonas Fay, as agents to Congress in the winter of 1781-1782, were endeavoring to have Congress admit Vermont as the fourteenth State, the Legislature of Vermont met in February, 1782. Governor Chittenden had received a letter from George Washington, dated January first, which was submitted to the Assembly. It strongly urged that Vermont relinquish this newly acquired territory and intimated that Congress, under certain resolutions that body had passed, would admit the independence of Vermont. This letter had a powerful effect and with the effort of some in the Assembly who would have done anything to discredit Allen and place themselves in power, the unions were dissolved.

The Assembly broke its agreement with the towns annexed under the terms of the two unions. Four agents were elected to go at once to Congress and arrange for Vermont to join the federation. They were authorized to take their seats as delegates in Congress. Ira Allen heard of this on his way home and gave himself and horse no rest until he reached Bennington, to find the Legislature adjourned and the agents waiting to receive £100 which the Assembly had voted that he, as Treasurer, should give to them. What he said to these people would be interesting though possibly not printable.

The agents went to Philadelphia, receiving scant attention from Congress, and returned home, wiser if not better men. This was the first session of the Assembly that Allen had not attended and directed and it came near wrecking Vermont's independence. Allen always excused it by quoting Washington's letter to Chittenden, and years afterwards wrote: "The universal confidence that the people of America placed in their Commander-in-chief from the firm, steady, persevering and able manner he had conducted the war; his known integrity, wisdom and virtue gave him more influence over the Legislature of Vermont than any other man in existence." Congress did not hesitate to sacrifice the honor Washington, for some of its members had induced him to write the letter. These occurrences, together with Allen's negotiations with General Haldimand, which had kept a large army idle in Canada and had enabled Washington to withdraw his troops from the north and take them to Yorktown to defeat Cornwallis, compose the great dramas enacted during the sessions whose records contain but a hint of their importance and the many difficulties encountered. The very men who took part in these sessions, with a few exceptions, were like privates in an army and they had little knowledge or appreciation of the ability, tact and diplomacy required successfully to contend against all the forces that were trying to bring about the elimination of Vermont. With the three surrounding States and Great Britain endeavoring to annex the territory comprising the State, undoubtedly New York and New Hampshire would have succeeded in their plan of dividing Vermont between them, had it not been for Ira Allen and a few associates. These Journals, if analyzed carefully, will supply rich material for research that if thoroughly made, will produce volumes of instructive and interesting contributions to history.

James Benjamin Wilbur

Manchester, 1924.

## *STATE OF VERMONT*

### *Windsor, Thursday March 12th 1778*

The Representatives of the freemen of the several Towns in this State, met at the meeting house in said Windsor, agreeable to the Constitution, and formed themselves into a House[8].

8. A list of the Representatives was not entered in the Journal. Using Comstock's revision of Deming's Vermont Officers, and checking the names of members mentioned in the Journal, the following list has been compiled for the March session of 1778.

| | | | |
|---|---|---|---|
| Arlington | Thomas Chittenden | | John G. Bayley |
| Barnard | Edmund Hodges | Pawlet | Zadock Everest |
| Barnet | Alexander Harvey | Pittsford | Johnathan Fassett |
| Bennington | Nathan Clark | Pomfret | John W. Dana |
| | John Fassett | Pownal | Thoms Jewett |
| Bradford | Benjamin Baldwin | Rockingham | Joshua Webb |
| Brandon | Thomas Tuttle | Rupert | Moses Robinson |
| Castleton | Zadock Remington | Rutland | Joseph Bowker |
| Cavendish | John Coffeen | | John Smith |
| Chester | Thomas Chandler, Jr. | Shaftsbury | John Burnam |
| Danby | Peter Lewis | | Gideon Olin |
| Dorset | Cephas Kent | Sharon | Daniel Gilbert |
| Dummerston | Thomas Amsden | Springfield | John Barrett |
| Guilford | Benjamin Carpenter | Thetford | Timothy Bartholomew |
| | John Shepardson | Tinmouth | Charles Brewster |
| Halifax | Edward Harris | Townshend | Samuel Fletcher |
| | Hubbell Wells | Wallingford | Abraham Jackson, Jr. |
| Hartland | William Gallup | Westminster | Nathaniel Robinson |
| Londonderry | Edward Aiken | Wilmington | Elijah Alvord |
| Manchester | Stephen Washburn | Windsor | Ebenezer Curtis |
| | Gideon Ormsby | | Thomas Cooper |
| Marlboro | Samuel King | Woodstock | John Strong |
| Newbury | Jacob Kent | | Joseph Safford |

The text of the Journal indicates that the following men, not mentioned in Deming, were members at the March session of the General Assembly:

Jacob Burton of Norwich.

Reuben Jones of Rockingham.

Thomas Rowley of Danby.

See Vermont Historical Society Proceeding (1878) for "The First Legislature of Vermont," by E. P. Walton.

The Assembly then chose Capt. Joseph Bowker[9], Speaker of the House, and Major Thomas Chandler, Clerk.

After the House was formed, the Reverend Mr. Powers preached a sermon[10] on the occasion, from the 28th Chapter of Matthew, 18th verse—Divine service being ended, proceeded, agreeable to the Constitution

9. For biographical sketch of Joseph Bowker see Governor and Council, Vol. 1, p. 190.

10. It was customary for many years for members of the Legislature to attend religious services at the opening of the session and the discourse preached on such an occasion was commonly known as the election sermon. This sermon was published in Newburyport, Mass., in 1778 and is a rare book.

# Early History
# (1724-1791)

The *first settlement* within the territory now known by the name of Vermont was made at Fort Dummer (in the present county of Windham) in the year 1724 under a grant from the provincial government of Massachuetts.

The boundary controversy between New Hampshire and Massachusetts continued until 1740 when the King decided: "That the northern boundary of the Province of Massachusetts be a similar curve line, pursuing the course of the Merrimack River, at three miles distance, on the north side thereof, beginning at the Atlantic Ocean, and ending at a point due north of Patucket Falls; and a straight line drawn from thence, due west, till it meets with his Majesty's other governments."[1]

By the settlement of the boundary between New Hampshire and Massachusetts, as well as by other Acts of the British Government, it was understood that the jurisdiction of the former Province was established as far west as Massachusetts had claimed and exercised; that is, to a line twenty mile east of Hudson's River.

Benning Wentworth was commissioned as Governor of New Hampshire in 1741. Governor Wentworth then immediately made a grant of the town of Bennington in his own name, which was six miles square and twenty miles east of Hudson's River.

### *NEW YORK NEGOTIATIONS*

Now began the voluminous correspondence between Governor Wentworth and the Province of New York. Governor Wentworth brought to the attention of the Governor of New York the premise that he was simply following out his Majesty's claim of the extension of Massachusetts to a point twenty miles east of Hudson's River;

1. William Slade Jr., *Vermont State Papers*, Middlebury, J. P. Copeland, 1823, p. 10.

and that New York had acquiesced in the act of Massachusetts in settling and developing the area.

Governor Clinton of New York replied to Wentworth that the Province of New York was bounded eastward by the Connecticut River, based upon letters from King Charles II to the Duke of York, expressly granting "all the lands from the west side of the Connecticut River to the east side of Delaware Bay."[2]

Governor Wentworth then raised the question as to why New York had acquiesced when both Connecticut and Massachusetts had extended their western boundary to within twenty miles of Hudson's River. To this Governor Clinton replied that an agreement had been reached with Connecticut in 1684, and the boundaries were marked in 1725, all being confirmed by King William. He admitted that Massachusetts had extended her holdings by intrusion and that New York, by negligence, had allowed the bounds to remain.

Talks and correspondence continued. Governor Wentworth however, proceeded in 1750 to make about 134 township grants. Following this action, Lieutenant Governor Colden of New York issued a proclamation in 1763 directing the Sheriff of Albany County to obtain the names of all persons who had taken lands under the New Hampshire Grants, contrary to the grantees of the Duke of York. Wentworth then issued a counter proclamation to the New Hampshire grantees that they should diligently work their grants and exercise jurisdiction over them.

Not wishing to stand on the grant of the Duke of York alone, the Province of New York then made an application to the Crown, which purported to be signed by a large number of the New Hampshire grantees. To this application, the Crown reiterated New York's claim to the west bank of the Connecticut River.

Following its own interpretation of the Crown's letter, the Province of New York proceeded to extend its jurisdiction over the New Hampshire grants by the establishment of four counties in the grants (which are treated under a separate heading: COUNTIES). The settlers were called upon to accept New York grants in lieu of the New Hampshire grants; most of them premptorily refused to comply with this order.

The settlers on the west side of the mountains met and formed an organization. Samuel Robinson of Bennington was appointed to go to the British Court and present the true feeling of the citizens. After considering the report, His Majesty notified the Governor of New York that, for the time being, no new charters should be made by that state. Governor Clinton nevertheless continued to make grants, and writs of ejectment.

2. Ibid., p. 11.

The citizens, enraged by this, called a meeting and formed a military association, of which Ethan Allen was appointed commandant. The Governor of New York immediately offered a reward of 150 pounds for the apprehension of Ethan Allen and others. In answer, Ethan Allen issued a proclamation offering five pounds for the apprehension of the Attorney General of the Colony of New York.

This exchange was followed by a letter from Governor Tryon of New York stating that his Majesty had finally fixed the Connecticut River as the boundary between New York and New Hampshire. A delegation led by Captain Stephen Fay called upon Governor Tryon and cited many incidents of maltreatment by the New York sheriff. The Governor approved the request of the committee that all civil suits be stopped. While negotiations were being carried on, however, the Green Mountain Boys proceeded to eject certain settlers from Otter Creek. Upon hearing of the ejection, Governor Tryon requested that the settlers be repossessed of their property.

Ethan Allen then replied that perhaps the Governor was not familiar with the circumstances: that a New York surveyor had first dispossessed the owners of a sawmill and then turned over the place to a Yorker; therefore, no action would be taken to give repossession to the Yorker.

Although His Majesty's government made suggestions as to how an amicable settlement to these disagreements between New York and the New Hampshire Grants might be made, Ethan Allen and his followers called several meetings. The members of the committees (which met frequently) adopted the following measures: 'all inhabitants of the New Hampshire grants are forbidden to hold, take or accept any office of honor or profit under the Colony of New York; and all civil and military officers who had acted under any authority of the Colony of New York should suspend their functions.'

New York proceeded with the passage of a law which denied the right of assembly to three or more persons in opposition to the demands of New York-all offenders to be arrested, tried and imprisoned; and provided for the arrest of Ethan Allen and others. The passage of this law terminated every prospect of peace or submission to the claims of New York.

## *WESTMINSTER RIOTS*[3]

During this controversy, the fear of war between Great Britain and the American Colonies had reached such an alarming pitch that any minor occurrence might provoke a major cirsis. The interruption of

3. William Slade, Jr., *Vermont State Papers*, Middlebury, J. P. Copeland, 1823, p. 55.

the action of the Cumberland County Court of the Colony of New York, which occurred at Westminster on the 13th of March, 1775, proved to be an influencing factor on future events.

In southern Cumberland County there were many New York sympathizers. The people of the Grants had certain actions against them that they wished to have considered by the court. So, early on the morning of the 13th, about a hundred of them — unarmed — stormed into the courthouse. Soon there appeared at the courthouse door an armed mob which demanded that the men of the Grants leave the courthouse. This they refused to do until the mob *entered* the courthouse, unarmed. Finally a gun was fired, and in the resulting melee several were wounded and killed. A band of 200 men from the New Hampshire government arrived the next day. More arrived on the 15th, and finally on the 16th when a critical examination was held, those found guilty were taken as prisoners to Northhampton, Massachusetts for safe confinement. Bonds were accepted for those who were considered less guilty, and they were released.

As a result of the massacre, the citizens on the east side of the state became incensed. At a meeting held in Westminster on April 11, 1775, it was voted that as a result of the malicious treatment by the Yorkers, and the imminent danger of having their property confiscated, the settlers should resist the administration of the government of New York. A committee which included Ethan Allen among others was selected to prepare a remonstrance to the Colony of New York. However, with the commencement of war with Great Britain, the attention of New York was suddenly diverted to the independence of the entire American colony.

The capture of the Fort at Ticonderoga on the 9th of May, 1775, gave the inhabitants of the Grants a realization of their increased national importance. They were deeply concerned with the protection of their frontier, which was now exposed to attack by the mother country. Still, the inhabitants did not wish to have any immediate dealings with New York, not even in the common defense.

Accordingly, a remonstrance was sent to Congress citing all the incidents which had occurred with New Yorkers, in answer to which Congress suggested that they submit to New York for the present, and contribute their assistance against Great Britain with the understanding that such action would not be construed to affirm or admit the jurisdiction of New York. Thus, when Congress on July 4th, 1776, announced to the world the memorable Declaration of Independence, the New Hampshire grantees were left in a peculiar position. They had purchased their lands under Royal grants from the Governor of New Hampshire, the same lands over which New

York also claimed jurisdiction. The settlers, who had petitioned the Crown for redress when the trouble between the colonies and Great Britain arose, now had nowhere to go for a superior party to decide upon the rights involved in the many controversies.

## *VERMONT STATEHOOD*[4]

At a meeting held at Dorset on July 24th, 1776, the delegates (chiefly from the west side of Vermont), with Jonas Fay of Bennington as Clerk, met and adopted a petition to the Continental Congress. The remonstrance cited how the settlers had received their lands under the New Hampshire Grants, and that New Yorkers were claiming said lands in the name of New York. They also cited many critical and unhappy disputes between the New York traders and the petitioners.

In September, it was voted that a committee be selected to form a statehood convention of compact, and to report as soon as may be. Captain Ira Allen and Colonel William Marsh were appointed to go into Cumberland and Gloucester counties to explain the proceedings of the convention, and to gain support therefor. Doctor Jonas Fay, Doctor Reuben Jones and Colonel Marsh were appointed a committee to draw up a remonstrance or petition to send to the Continental Congress then assembled in Philadelphia, and to report back to the Convention.

At the same meeting, it was voted "to build a gaol in the town of Manchester, twenty foot by thirty inside; Sd gaol to be built of logs and earth, and appoint a committee to treat the inhabitants of New Hampshire Grants on the east side of the Green Mountains relative to their associating with the west side body".

The Dorset group was beset with troubles and problems on every side. They were involved in a conflict with New York over land grants. There were tories in their midst who wished to be associated with New York or Great Britain. Others wished to be associated with New Hampshire, or Massachusetts.

Then there was the Province of Canada to the north which had its eye on the New Hampshire Grants. There was also the problem of Indian raids. Thus it was necessary to establish committees to deal with each of these problems, as well as to gain the support of the central government in Washington to furnish aid in the protection of the New Hampshire Grants.

## *FREE AND INDEPENDENT STATE*[5]

At an adjourned session of the convention held at Westminster on

4. William Slade, Jr., *Vermont State Papers*, Middlebury, J. P. Copeland, 1823, p. 67.
5. William Slade, Jr., *Vermont State Papers*, Middlebury, J. P. Copeland, 1823

January 15, 1777, many actions were taken. It was voted "that the district of land commonly called and known by the name of New Hampshire Grants, be a new and separate state; and for the future conduct themselves as such." A committee was formed to prepare a draught for a declaration for a new and separate state; and report to the convention as soon as may be. The convention voted to accept the name of *New Connecticut* for the state.

A committee of five was selected to carry the remonstrance and petition to the Continental Contress. A *Commitee of War* of nine persons was elected to act in conjunction with the Committee of War already chosen. Tories from Cumberland county were forbidden to act as delegates.

At a convention held at Windsor on June 4, 1777, the members were informed that a district of land lying on the Susquehanna river had been given the name New Connecticut. Thus it was voted that instead of New Connecticut, the district should ever be known by the name of *Vermont.* With this minor change the convention confirmed the former vote taken at Westminster in January last.

The 1777 constitution (except the preamble and less than fifty lines of the "Declaration of Rights" and the "Plan of Government") is a copy of the first Constitution of the State of Pennsylvania.[6] Vermont's constitution differs from all others except Pennsylvania and Georgia in that it established a single body called the "General Assembly" with exclusive and supreme legislative powers, giving to the Governor and Lieutenant Governor, and Council, only advisory power in the preparation, enactment, and amendment of bills, and executive power over laws and orders enacted by the General Assembly.

Before adjournment, the convention established a Council of Safety.

## *Council of Safety*[7]

The Council of Safety looked after the affairs of the new state during this time of trying circumstances. Of this period, Ira Allen wrote "The Council of Safety then attended to the affairs of the government, but their situation was very unpleasant, as the constitution had only declared the district to be a free state; but the Government was not organized, as the Constitution was not fully completed, and three quarters of the people on the west side of the Green Mountains were compelled to remove, and the rest were in great

6. John A. Williams, ed., *The Public Papers of Governor Thomas Chittenden, 1778-1789, & 1790-1797,* Barre, Modern Printing Co., Vol. XVII, 1969, p. 53.

7. John A. Williams, ed., *Public Papers of Governor Thomas Chittenden 1778-1789 & 1790-1797,* Barre, Modern Printing Co., Vol. XVII, 1969, p. 61.

danger. It was the western settlers who principally supported the title of the New Hampshire Grants, against the unjust claims of New York, and their removal would expose the settlers of the east side of the Green Mountains to an invasive war, both from the Savages and the British; besides the late proceedings of Congress had been partial towards New York, and against Vermont; the people of the new state had reason to expect no favor from the Committee of Safety of New York, as its members were in fact composed of the old sycophants of the last government, which they prudently deserted. Gain and dominion were objects of first consequence to some of the Committee of New York, and the citizens of the New State were conscious that this Committee would take every sinister and possible step to divide the people, and would not be dissatisfied with any misfortunes which befell them, even by the common enemy."

"The Council of Safety had no money or revenue at command, their powers and credit were not extensive, and all expresses were supported at their own expense: yet in this situation, it became necessary to raise men for the defense of the frontiers, with bounties and wages; ways and means were to be found out."

One duty of the Council (upon the suggestion and effort of Ira Allen) was to appoint Commissioners of Sequestration with authority to seize goods and chattels of all persons who had or should join the common enemy, all such seized property to be sold by the Council of Safety.

With the election of Thomas Chittenden as President, Jonas Fay as Vice-President and Ira Allen as Secretary, the membership of the Council of Safety became organized.

## *GENERAL SCHUYLER'S PROCLAMATION*[8]

The following document issued on July 13, 1777, by General Philip Schuyler was a cause of great alarm in the grants; "To the inhabitants of Castle Town, of Hubbardton, Rutland, Tinmouth, Pawlet, Wells, Granville (NY.) with neighboring districts ****. You are hereby directed to send from your several townships deputations of ten persons or more from each township, to meet Colonel Skene at Castleton, on Wednesday, July 15th at ten in the morning, who will have instructions not only to give further encouragement to those who comply with the terms of my late manifesto, but to communicate conditions upon which the persons and the properties of the disobedient may yet be spared."

Governor Chittenden wrote a letter to the inhabitants of the eastern part of Vermont expressing to them his surprise that they

8. John A. Williams, ed., *Public Papers of Governor Thomas Chittenden, 1778-1789 & 1790-1797,* Barre, Modern Printing Co., Vol. XVII., p. 66.

should feel in danger because they were so far away from the plundering of the enemy from the north, and that it was such a large country that they could obtain the necessities of life without going into the western sections. He informed them that the enemy had taken Castleton and were advancing, and that the Vermont troops would make a stand at Bennington. (See War and Riot section for details). It appeared that the Continental store of supplies at Bennington was their objective. At this time General Philip Schuyler made a request for all possible help to thwart General Burgoyne. Ira Allen, as secretary of the Council, sent a letter to the New Hampshire Council requesting aid, saying "Our good dispositions to defend ourselves and make a frontier for your state with our own, cannot be carried into execution without your assistance." A similar letter was sent to the Massachusetts Council.

## *BOARD OF WAR*

The Council of Safety's business was evidently closed out on March 12, 1778 when the first General Assembly of the State of Vermont was convened on this date. The Board of War was appointed by Governor Thomas Chittenden at the termination of the Council of Safety on February 25, 1779 to carry on the military operations for the Independent State of Vermont. The Board of War consisted of Governor Chittenden, President, Matthew Lyon, Secretary, Joseph Bowker, Timothy Brown, Jonas Fay, Moses Robinson, and Ira Allen. On October 27, 1779 the Board of War was separated from the Governor and Council with Timothy Brown chosen as President and Ira Allen as Secretary. Upon the completion of the war the Board of War was dissolved by 1783.*

*John A. Williams, ed., *State Papers of Vermont* (Barre: Modern Printing Co., 1969), Vol. XVIII., pp. 257 et. seq.

## *GENERAL STARK TO THE RESCUE*[9]

The President of the New Hampshire Council then informed Allen that General Stark would be dispatched with troops to Number Four Fort at Charlestown, N.H. by Thursday, to be advised in regard to the disposition of the New Hampshire troops and given information in regard to the manoeuvers of the enemy!

One of the important supplies needed was lead, and quite frequently there is a letter from the Council to the citizens to procure and send - as quickly as possible - a certain quantity of lead.

9. James Benjamin Wilbur, *Ira Allen, Founder of Vermont, 1751-1814,* Cambridge, Massachusetts, Riverside Press, 2 Vol., 1928, p. 102.

There was a shortage of shoes for our soldiers so a supply ot leather was stored at warehouses, where it was issued out to make moccasins until shoes could be procured.

Letters of instruction were sent by the Council secretary to members of the Committee of Sequestration to take cattle, horses and supplies from the Vermont tory citizens who had trafficked with the enemy.

### *TORY TREATMENT*

Many persons were found guilty of assisting the enemy by disarming the inhabitants of the state. They were punished in various ways. One person by the name of John Munro who lived in Shaftsbury near the New York line, joined the enemy upon its approach, so his property was confiscated. In one case, a man by the name of Francis Breckenridge was permitted to return home to his father's farm, and if found off to expect 39 lashes of the Beech Seal. The Council had a list of New Yorkers who were confined on suspicion that they were enemies of the United States. After hearings, some of the Tories were placed in the gaol at Westminster, while others were released on parole.

Another example of how a Tory was treated is shown in the case of a doctor in Bennington who held his land under the New Hampshire grants. He urged citizens in 1774 to dissent from the policies of the Green Mountain Boys. At this time many were holding grants under New York, and were considering taking titles out under the New Hampshire Grants. He advised them not to do so, and urged those with New Hampshire grants to purchase New York titles. He was very offensive to the Vermonters and they asked him to be silent and threatened him with violence. He was finally arrested and convicted as an enemy of the government; suspended for some time from the Catamount sign post. In 1777 he raised a company in the Arlington environs to cooperate with Burgoyne. He later fled to Canada, his property was confiscated and his family was sent behind the enemy lines.

Although Burgoyne surrendered on October 17, 1777 (See section WAR and RIOTS), there was still a need to protect the young state from tories within and enemies without. Since the state was considered a frontier to northern enemies, a line was drawn where the people could defend themselves. The north line of Castleton and the west-north lines of Pittsford to the foot of the Green Mountains was established, and all citizens living north of this line were ordered at once to move their families and effects south thereof.

Mount Independence was evacuated on November 8, 1777, and the fort there was destroyed. In recent years (1963-4) the bounds of the old hospital and other buildings and earthworks have been accurately located from maps found in the Canadian archives, John Caster Brown Library in Providence, and Fort Ticonderoga, New York. Mt. Independence has now been designated as a Vermont Historic Site.

The Commissioners of Sequestration had much work to do even after the British had surrendered. In the winter of 1778 there were many citizens who had been driven from their lands. They had not been able to raise any crops, so the Council through Thomas Chittenden directed that no wheat, rye or Indian corn meal or flour should be transported outside of the state, nor sold to any person not residing in the state unless a permit was first received from the Council.

New York appointed her Commissioners of Sequestration from among the citizens of the Grants. The Council accordingly issued an order that for the future no Commissioner of Sequestration would be allowed to transact business in the Grants if the Council of Vermont had already appointed one for the area.

At times, the Council acted as a court in settling cases where one party owed another. The Council took notice of the sale of small quantities of spiritous liquor being sold at exorbitant prices, causing drunkenness, idleness and quarrels. The Council resolved that until the General Assembly was established to act, the local officers be authorized to issue licenses at six shillings each.

## *NEW HAMPSHIRE RELATIONSHIPS*[10]

The Vermont Declaration of Independence led to other unforeseen difficulties. The original territory of New Hampshire consisted of sundry grants from the Council of New England to John Mason, made between the years of 1621 and 1623. This group of nobility which was known as the Council of New England, had been granted "All the land in America, lying between the degrees of 40 and 48 north latitude" to be known by the name of New England.

This grant was bounded on the west by a line sixty miles from the sea. The territory between this grant (as it was called) and the Connecticut River was subsequently granted to the governor of New Hampshire.

A group of towns in New Hampshire did not like to be governed from Exeter, which they felt was too far away, and so they were interested in joining with Vermont. There were sixteen townships lying adjacent to the Connecticut River which petitioned to be joined with Vermont: Cornish, Lebanon, Dresden, Lime, Orford, Piermont,

10. William Slade, Jr., *Vermont State Papers,* Middlebury, J. P. Copeland, 1823, p. 99.

Haverhill, Bath, Lyman, Apthorp, Enfield, Canaan, Cardigan, Landaff, Gunthwaite and Morristown. The General Assembly voted to accept the sixteen towns by a vote of 37 to 12.

Consequently the sixteen towns requested the government of New Hampshire to have a division line drawn, and a friendly feeling kept up. Upon receipt of the notice of the State of Vermont (accepting the sixteen towns), President Weare of New Hampshire dispatched a letter to the New Hampshire delegate in Congress, and to Governor Chittenden. In these remonstrances he argued why New Hampshire felt that Vermont should relinquish every connection, as a political body, with the sixteen towns.

## *CONFLICTING CLAIMS*[11]

Ethan Allen was requested by the Governor to repair to Philadelphia to learn the feelings of Congress on this matter, and he made his report to the Governor and the General Assembly on October 10, 1778. Over this matter, the pot really boiled — not only in Washington, but also in New York, New Hampshire and Vermont! Some representatives of the New Hampshire Grants refused to attend the meetings of the General Assembly. After many very close votes, the General Assembly on February 12, 1779 voted to dissolve the Union with the sixteen New Hampshire towns. A rump session attended by only eight Vermont towns voted to be connected and confederated with the State of New Hampshire.

This committee reported the action to the New Hampshire legislature which, on June 2, 1779, voted to accept claim to all the New Hampshire Grant territory. Between the claims of New Hampshire on the one hand, and the demands of New York on the other, Vermont was now in an exceedingly embarrassed situation.

To climax this situation, a group of representatives - New York sympathizers - in the towns of Brattleborough, Hinsdale, Guilford, Fulham, Putney, Westminster, Rockingham, Springfield and Weathersfield of Cumberland County, now directed a petition to his Excellency Governor George Clinton of the State of New York. In their petition they considered injustices to the loyal sympathizers of the State of New York, and asked for protection, even during the continuance with the war with Great Britain.

The Governor of New York directed a request to Congress to take notice of the situation, which was done by the appointment of a committee of five to make an investigation. Since only two of the committee met, Congress voted to appoint another committee to meet with the States of New York, New Hampshire and Massachu-

11. William Slade, Jr., *Vermont State Papers*, Middlebury, J. P. Copeland, 1823, p. 106.

setts Bay to determine all disputes existing between the several states. Vermont chose a committee of five (headed by Ethan Allen) to transact on behalf of Vermont any political affairs with the United States.

Realizing that Vermont was not succeeding very well so far in her dealings with the United States, a bolder attempt was adopted. Although in the past Vermont had acquiesced in allowing the sixteen towns east of the Connecticut River to rejoin the State of New Hampshire, a new petition was approved (by a committee voted by the delegates representing Cumberland, Grafton and Gloucester counties) for a union of the grants on both sides of the river.

## *PETITIONS FROM NEW YORK TOWNS*[12]

At about the same time, a petition was received from sundry inhabitants of northeastern New York, requesting to be admitted to the union with Vermont. The representatives of the New York towns informed the General Assembly that they were ready to take their seats according to the Articles of Union. Representatives, elected at a convention held at Cambridge, N.Y., were selected from the following districts: Hoosack, Scorticook, Cambridge, Saratoga, Upper White Creek, Black Creek, Granville, Skenesborough, Greenfield, Kingsbury, Fort Edward and Little Hoosack. By a vote of 53 to 24, the representatives from the western district were accepted, and after swearing the necessary oaths, took their seats in the House.

These actions exhibited the peculiar genius of Vermont statesmen and strengthened her fight to sustain her independence.

## *NEGOTIATIONS WITH CANADA*[13]

No people were more firmly attached to the cause of American Independence than were the people of Vermont. Their claim to independence had been treated with indifference; nevertheless, they were able to overlook this in their loyalty to the national cause.

Meetings were carried on in secrecy, so records are few; however, the most complete record of what transpired is found in Ira Allen's publication entitled "The Natural and Political History of Vermont", published in London, A.D. 1798, and Vermont Historical Society Collections, VII, 1871.

Ethan Allen received a letter from a British agent, Colonel Beverly Robinson of New York, on March 30, 1780. The letter - to which no reply was sent - suggested that Allen take an important

12. William Slade, Jr., *Vermont State Papers*, Middlebury, J. P. Copeland, 1823, p. 138.
13. William Slade, Jr., *Vermont State Papers*, Middlebury, J. P. Copeland, 1823, p. 141.

part in the formation of a separate state government, under the King and Constitution of England. A second letter dated February 2, 1781, about a year later, from Colonel Robinson stated that the opinion was held of an "inclination by Vermont to join the King's cause and restore America to her former peaceful and happy constitution." The two letters - without answer - were sent to Congress. Allen in his letter stated that he was "as resolutely determined to the independence of Vermont, as Congress are that of the United States, and rather than fail, will retire with the hardy Green Mountain Boys into the desolate caverns of the mountains, and wage war with human nature at large".

## *HALDIMAND NEGOTIATIONS*[14]

"Stimulated by the treaties between France and the United States, of amity, commerce, and defensive alliance against Great Britain, which were signed at Paris on 6 February, 1778, the British Government immediately resolved to adopt a conciliatory policy toward the United States." "Commissioners were appointed for the purpose, with power to offer to the colonies at large, or *separately,* a general or separate peace."

The negotiations with Vermont resulted from this policy instituted by Sir Henry Clinton, who became chief commissioner when he succeeded Sir William Howe in the command of the British forces in America. His headquarters were at the city of New York, and from thence the first attempt was made upon Vermont in the letter from Colonel Robinson mentioned above.

General Frederick Haldimand was a subordinate to Clinton, but in this business he appears as the principal actor in behalf of the British Government, having been specially authorized by Lord George Germain by reason of his readier access to Vermont, - and the position of his army which hovered on the norther frontier, ready to advance upon New York and Vermont.

Portions of the letter from Governor Chittenden to the President of Congress, dated at Bennington July 25, 1780, are of interest.

"Vermont as before mentioned, being a free and independent state, has denied the authority of Congress to judge of their jurisdiction. Over the head of all this, it appears that Congress, by their resolutions of the 9 ult. have determined that they have the power to judge the cause; which has already determined the essence of the dispute; for, if Vermont does not belong to some of the United States, Congress could have no such power, without their consent,

14. John A. Williams, ed., *Public Papers of Governor Thomas Chittenden, 1778-1789 & 1790-1797,* Barre, Modern Printing Co., Vol. XVII., p. 323-387.

so that consequently determining that they have such a power has determined that Vermont has no right to independence; for it is utterly incompatable with the rights and prerogatives of an independent state to be under the control or arbitrament of any other power. Vermont has therefore no alternative; they must either submit to the unwarrantable decree of Congress, or continue their appeal to heaven and to arms".

"The cloud that had hovered over Vermont, since the ungenerous claims of New Hampshire and Massachusetts Bay, has been and its motions carefully observed by this government; who expected that Congress would have averted the storm; but, disappointed in this, and unjustly treated as the people over whom I preside, on the most serious and candid deliberation, conceive themselves to be in this affair; yet, blessed by heaven with constancy of mind and connexions abroad, as an honest, valiant and brave people are necessitated to declare to your excellency, to Congress, and to the world, that, as life, liberty and the rights of the people, intrusted them by God, are inseparable, so they do not expect to be justified in the eye of Heaven, or that posterity would call them blessed if they should tamely surrender any part."

"Without doubt, Congress have, previous to this, been acquainted that this state has maintained several posts as frontiers, at its own expense; which are well known to be the only security to this quarter, of the frontier inhabitants of Massachusetts Bay and New Hampshire."

"..... if the United States have departed from the virtuous principles upon which they first commenced the war with Great Britain, and have assumed to themselves the power of usurping the rights of Vermont, it is time-high time-for her to seriously consider what she is fighting for, and to what purpose she has been, more than five years last past, spilling the blood of her bravest sons."

Governor Chittenden went on to state that Massachusetts Bay had not laid any claim on Vermont; nor had New Hampshire—which had previously conceded to the independence of Vermont. However, he stated that New Hampshire, following New York's claim to the west bank of the Connecticut River, had enacted laws to allow Congress to judicially determine the merits of their claim. Copies of this letter were sent to the governors of New Hampshire, Rhode Island and Massachusetts.

"Notwithstanding the usurption and injustice of neighboring governments toward Vermont", Governor Chittenden went on, "and the late resolution of Congress, this government from the principle of virtue and close attachment to the cause of liberty, as well as a thorough examination of their own policy, are induced once more to offer union with the United States of America, of which

Congress are the legal representative body. Should that be denied, this state will propose the same to the legislature of the United States separately, and take such other measures as self preservation shall justify."

"I do hereby in behalf of this state, demand your legislature that they relinquish their claim to jurisdiction over any and every part of this state; and request them to join in a solid union with Vermont; against the British forces which invade the American States."

Governor Haldimand's instructions to the Commissioners to negotiate with Vermont (written on December 20, 1780) were: "Having been given full power in my name to negotiate in conjunction with (Major Dundas) with the people of Vermont for the exchange of prisoners ...... I now instruct you in what you may assure and promise them as a means of accommodation, and their return to their allegiance. Sensible to the injustice which individuals in the New York government attempted against them, in soliciting and obtaining grants of lands which had in consequence of grants from New Hampshire been cultivated by the labour and industry of the inhabitants of the Green Mountains, I always regretted the measures which were taken by the Government of New York and feel compassion for the unhappy people who were the objects of them. I always have been of the opinion that a people who during the last war were so ready on every occasion to oppose the enemies of Great Britain, (would) never have been prevailed upon to separate themselves from a Country with which they were intimately connected by religion, laws and language, had their properties been secured to them. It is therefore with great cheerfulness that I authorize you to give these people the most positive assurances that their country will be erected into a separate province independent and unconnected with every government in America, and will be entitled to every prerogative and immunity which is promised to other provinces in your (copy of the) proclamation of the King's Commissioners (to the people of the colonies, October 3, 1778)."

To soft soap the Green Mountain Boys, Haldimand proposed to raise two Battalions, with Messers Allen and Chittenden as Commandants with the ranks of Lieutenant Colonel, and of which he would be Colonel with the right to appoint officers. They were also promised the same pay as his provincial troops This proffer was of course rejected.

Governor Chittenden had asked General Washington to produce some captives that could be exchanged for Vermonters; to which the General stated that he could give no countenance to such a deal.

In the exchange of correspondence between Haldimand and Ira Allen, Haldimand continually insisted that the citizens of Vermont would be much better off under the flag of Britain; but since his offers did not seem to be making much headway, he decided to take another course. He wrote to Sir Henry Clinton that he would show a strong detachment upon the frontier about the first of October, as well as strong parties sent to the Mohawk River and the frontier of Pennsylvania. As a result of this ravage of the frontier, he figured that many loyalists would side with Great Britain.

### *COLONEL ALLEN TO TREAT WITH THE BRITISH*

In April 1781, Colonel Ira Allen was appointed by the Governor and Council to settle a cartel with the British of Canada for the exchange of Prisoners, and also to procure an armistice between Vermont and the British. It was felt that an armistice was necessary for Vermont, since their militia of only 7,000 men could not contend against 10,000 British troops.

Since spies of the adjoining states and Congress were about, everything had to be carried on in secrecy, the information being known to only about eight persons. Colonel Allen met the British Commandant at *l'Isle Aux Noix* after a favorable boat trip. After seventeen days of negotiations in May of 1781, a cartel for the exchange of prisoners was completed, and a verbal agreement that the cessation of hostilities should not occur until after the session of the Vermont legislature. After listening to the Colonel, a committee of the whole of the legislature was held to consider the armistice and return of prisoners. Major Fay and Ira Allen were appointed as Commissioners of Prisoners and went on board the Royal George, obtaining the exchange of prisoners and further extension of the armistice.

The agents of the British government in Canada passed back and forth from Canada to Ethan and Ira Allen's common house in Sunderland without detection by anyone who would inform against them, even though party spirit ran high against tories.

Jonas Fay, Ira Allen and Bezabel Woodward were appointed at the June session of the Assembly as agents to Congress. On the arrival of the committee in Philadelphia, they read in a newspaper a letter written at Whitehall (NY) by the British, and intercepted by the French, sent to Paris and forwarded to Congress by Benjamin Franklin. The letter purported that Vermont should throw its allegiance to His Majesty, which would make an avenue for British troops to take possession of the upper parts of the Hudson and Connecticut river valleys and cut off communication between Albany and the Mohawk country.

The British Commissioners insisted that Vermont become a British colony, and offered to put one Brigidier General, two colonels and other officers on the British establishment; to which Col. Allen objected.

All of these officers were be to named by certain men in Vermont, with other advantages and lucrative offers; the British proposing an expedition against Albany. The British insisted that something definite must be settled before they parted, or the armistice must cease. The Vermont agents treated the matter with candor, and reflected upon the situation in which Vermont faced an exposed frontier, and the action of the adjoining state (and the United States) government. The Vermont agents explained that due to the lateness the year, such military action against Albany was not practical. After further discussion, the Agents and Commissioners separated on terms of mutual friendship.

In September of 1781, Colonel Allen and Major Fay renewed their negotiations at Skenesborough. The British suggested that they send scouts into Vermont and take prisoners who were opposed to the negotiations with their government.; this action was opposed by Allen.

Again on October 5, 1781, Haldimand - in a proclamation to the inhabitants of Vermont - promised free trade with Canada, protection of the people of Vermont, and sharing of the Vermont troops with those of the King's Army.

At about this time the British Army had reached Ticonderoga. (See section on War and Riots). General Enos in command of the troops at Castleton was familiar with the negotiations with the British in Canada. He suggested to the General Assembly that Vermont should raise 1500 men to be continued in service for three years. The General had established scouting parties to watch the enemy, and while on such a trip to Lake Champlain, one of the Vermonters was shot by Colonel St. Leger's patrol. The clothes of Sergeant Tupper, the man who was killed, were sent back with an apology by St. Leger. The General immediately dispatched a letter to the Governor in regard to the episode, which caused the Governor to call together the Board of War.

Colonel Allen and Major Fay dispatched a letter to the British Commissioners who were with Colonel St. Leger, explaining the change in the membership of the legislature, and the impending fall of Lord Cornwallis. With this news, the British returned to Canada, signaling the end of the 1781 campaign, with only one casualty. No further interviews took place with the British. However, a letter in 1782 queried what effect the fall of Lord Cornwallis had had upon the attitude of Vermonters.

The letter from General Haldimand in the summer of 1782 read as follows: "You may rest assured that I shall give such orders as will effectually prevent hostilities of any kind being exercised in the district of Vermont, until such time as a breach on your part, or some general event, may make the contrary my duty. And you have the authority to promulgate in such manner as you shall think fit, this my intentions to the people of said district, that they may, without any apprehension continue to encourage and promote the settlement and cultivation of that new country, to the interest and happiness of themselves, and their posterity.''

So Vermont by her own actions - though abandoned and exposed - was protected from a powerful enemy, while at the same time Congress listened to the requests for a hearing on her claims of independence.

## *JOINING THE UNION*[15]

With the threat from Canada removed, Vermont could now actively pursue negotiations for her admission into the Union. On the 22nd of June, 1781, the legislature appointed Jonas Fay, Ira Allen, Bezabel Woodward, as delegates; they were to repair to Congress with full power to propose to, and receive from them, terms for a union of Vermont with the United States, and to take a seat in Congress as delegates from Vermont, as soon as terms of union could be agreed upon and ratified.

On August 7, the subject was brought before Congress, and a resolution was adopted authorizing a committee of five to be appointed, to confer with representatives of the New Hampshire Grants immediately at Philadelphia, with full power to agree upon and ratify terms and articles of union and confederation with the United States of America.

## *NEGOTIATIONS WITH THE UNITED STATES*

On the 18th of August, a conference took place between the committee of Congress and the agents of Vermont. Many questions were raised by the Committee, which two days later made its report to Congress. As a result of this meeting and report, Congress passed a resolution which was very unsatisfactory to both New York and Vermont. This resolution stated that before Congress could give any preliminary recognition to Vermont and its admission to the Union, that it should relinquish all demands of lands or jurisdiction on the east side of the west bank of the Connecticut River.

The Vermont legislature (meeting at Charleston, N.H. on October 16, 1781) received the report of its committee, and three days later adopted the report. This adopted report suggested that when any boundary dispute should arise between New Hampshire and

15. William Slade, Jr., *Vermont State Papers*, Middlebury, J. P. Copeland, 1823, p. 154-193.

Vermont, that the two states settle the dispute through the selection of a committee of five by each state. A similar proposal was made in regard to the New York boundary disputes. A committee of nine was chosen, and Congress was informed of their action.

The legislature of New York on the 19th of November, 1781, considered the proposal of Congress, and resolved that Congress had no authority by the Articles of Confederation to carry out their assumption of power.

Governor Chittenden - probably more than any other early statesman - was particularly watchful and wise in the protection and interests of Vermont. On the 14th of November, 1781, he directed a communication to General Washington, stating that affairs were approaching a dangerous crisis.

The legislature met at Bennington on February 19, 1782, considered the conditions embraced in the resolution of Congress, and voted to comply with them. A committee comprised of Jonas Fay, Moses Robinson, and Isaac Tichenor was appointed to represent the state in Philadelphia as soon as possible. However, high hopes were soon dashed when they read the report of the April 27, 1782 four-member Committee of Congress. Congress refused to consider the report. Vermont sent a letter to Congress expressing disappointment for the delay of their request for consideration.

On April 14, 1782, the New York legislature passed two acts: one granted a pardon for certain offences of persons living in the New Hampshire Grants; the other provided that all grants and charters made by the New Hampshire Grants before April 14, 1782, and made prior to any New York grant to the same tract of land, be ratified and confirmed to the respective grantees.

Notwithstanding the unsettled and embarrassing state of external affairs, Vermont was maturing with an internal tranquility. New York had not interferred with Vermont's government - although she had not relinquished any jurisdictional claims - but had opposed in Congress Vermont's admission to the Union. Vermont now found it necessary to enact a draft law to increase its militia, since the federal government had withdrawn its troops on the Canadian frontier. With the encouragement of Governor Tryon, this draft was resisted in southeastern Vermont. Five of the principal persons who opposed Vermont's authority were arraigned before the Supreme Court, sentenced to banishment, and their property sequestered, which caused a remonstrance to be forwarded to Congress. Immediately, Congress passed a resolution condemning Vermont for the highhandedness of her actions, and sent a letter to Governor Chittenden. This action by Congress presumed to control the legislative action rights of Vermont, even to the control of her internal police power.

Congress, on the 5th of December, 1782, stated that it would take effectual measures to require that the citizens of southeastern Vermont be given back their property and allowed to return to their homes unmolested. Governor Chittenden replied by citing the previous resolutions of Congress to which Vermont had reluctantly agreed; and to the inaction of Congress in recognizing Vermont as a state of the Union; and its other several actions. "At no time had measures been adopted, aiming at a more fatal blow at the independence of Vermont, than those embraced in the act of Congress of the 5th of December, 1782; and never had the people of Vermont felt a more unshaken determination to maintain the independence, or a more decided and settled hostility toward those who aimed to destroy it."

The effect upon Vermont was directly opposite to that Congress had expected. The faith in Congress of the Green Mountain Boys had been nearly destroyed. With the signing of the peace treaty between Great Britain and the United States, the fear of attack on their northern border was lessened. With the heavy debt, and other matters in Congress, Vermonters did not see an immediate need now to join the Union. They had learned how to operate a government for which the taxes were not too severe. They had plenty of fertile land to sell. It now appeared that the federal congress had a desire to retire its debts, and treat all states in a diplomatic manner. Virginia, who had been the first state to lead opposition to the British Crown, now led the way in calling a convention to form a new constitution. Upon the adoption of the new constitution, a new Congress, furnished with competent powers, met in New York City on the third of March, 1789.

Vermont sensed that a saner and wiser atmosphere was taking place in Congress, which seemed to abate the fear of Vermonters, and developed a desire to join the Union. The difficulties with New York over land grants, however, had not yet been settled. The New Yorkers observed the increase in value of Vermont lands, and the continued reluctance of Vermont to acknowledge the validity of the New York grants.

Conditions favorable to Vermont's joining of the Union were finally acknowledged by New York, when it was found necessary in order to keep New York City instead of Philadelphia as the seat of the Federal Government. It was realized that Vermont's support in this matter would be of greater value to New York than the retention of the New York grants.

# Early History

*COUNCIL OF CENSORS*

*Sec. XLIV. Constitution.*

"In order that the freedom of the Commonwealth may be preserved inviolate, forever, there shall be chosen by ballot by the Freemen of the State, on the last Wednesday in March, in the year one thousand seven hundred and eighty-five, and on the last Wednesday in March in every seven years thereafter, thirteen persons who shall be chosen in the same manner the Council is chosen - except they shall not be out of the Council or General Assembly - to be called the Council of Censors; who shall meet together on the first Wednesday of June next ensuing their election; the majority of whom shall be a quorum in every case, except as to calling a convention, in which two-thirds of the whole number elected shall agree; and whose duty it shall be to enquire whether the constitution has been preserved inviolate in every part; whether the legislature and executive branches of government have performed their duty as guardians of the people; or assumed to themselves, or exercised other or greater powers, than they are entitled to by the constitution. They are also to enquire whether the public taxes have been justly laid and collected, in all parts of the Commonwealth - in what means the public monies have been disposed of, and whether the laws have been duly executed. For these purposes, they shall have power to send for persons, paper and records; they shall have authority to pass public censures - to order impeachments, and to recommend to the legislature the repealing of such laws as appear to them to have been enacted contrary to the principle of the constitution. These powers they shall continue to have, for and during the space of one year from the day of their election, and no longer. The said Council of Censors shall also have the power to call a Convention, to meet within two years after their sitting, if there appears to them an absolute necessity of amending any article of this constitution which may be defective - explaining such as may be thought not clearly expressed, and of adding such as are necessary for the preservation of the rights and happiness of the people; but the articles to be amended, and the amendments proposed, and such articles as are proposed to be added or abolished, shall be promulgated at least six months before the day appointed for the election of such convention, for the previous consideration of the people, that they may have an opportunity of instructing their delegates on the subject."

In an address of the Council of Censors to the Freemen of the State of Vermont by Increase Moseley, President, at Bennington on the 14th day of February, 1786, a number of interesting suggestions were made as follows: "Your Council of Censors, ..... have proposed certain alterations, here before offered to your consideration. In so doing, we principally had in view rendering government less expensive, and more wise and energetic objects in the opinion of the Council, more especially during the infancy of the Commonwealth, worthy of the attention of its Freemen. The taxes which have been collected some years past for the support of government, demonstrate the expediency of the former; and every man's observation will suggest to them the necessity, for - or political happiness and credit - of having government properly maintained and the judicial and executive officers therein, filled by persons of the greatest wisdom and virtue."

The Council of Censors called attention to many infractions of the Constitution by the Governor and Council and by the legislature and the Auditors.

The application of their censures should be read today by members of our legislature and the executive branch.

The second Council of Censors was held on November 30, 1792 with Samuel Knight as its President. One of their proposals was for the adoption of a Senate, the reason for which stated: "One inconvenience we conceive to be, the vesting of all legislative power in a single and cumberous body. Their numbers which are necessary, in order to comprehend all the national interests, passion, manners and sentiments to which law ought to be adapted, tend to encumber discussion and subject legislatures frequently to hasty and crude determinations. This we have apprehended to be a principal reason why so many amendments, explanations, and alterations have been constantly found necessary in our laws."

The Council of Censors further stated that, "for the first septenary, the senate should be composed of members from, and to be elected by, the several counties, as follows: Bennington and Orange Counties, each two; Windham and Windsor and Rutland, each three; Addison and Chittenden, each one; and every new county which might thereafter be organized, one; and that, after the first septenary, each county might elect one senator for every eight thousand souls in such county and that any county containing a less number, might elect one.

"The House of Representatives, it was proposed, should consist of one member for each town containing at the time of election, forty families; and that the Freemen of any two or more towns that might, together, contain forty families or upwards might meet and elect one representative."

Supreme executive power was vested in the Governor or Lieutenant Governor in his absence. An Advisory Council consisting of four, was to be annually elected by the Senate and House of Representatives and were to meet with the Governor at every session, "to advise with him in granting pardons, remitting fines, laying embargoes, revising bills."

See VHS 1894 Gov. Address.

## *NEW YORK CONCILIATES*

On July 15, 1789, the New York legislature passed an act which appointed commissioners with full power to acknowledge the independence of Vermont; and to settle all matters of controversy with Vermont. The legislature of Vermont on October 23, 1789 appointed a commission on their part to deal with New York, and with power to agree upon all matters of controversy with such state. On the same day, commissioners were again appointed to treat with New York, and to agree upon all subjects which would allow Vermont to join the Union. Two or three joint meetings were held before matters were peacefully and amically settled.

As a result of the powers granted to their commissioners by the New York legislature, they declared the consent of New York that the State of Vermont be admitted into the Union of the United States of America; and that immediately upon such admission, all claims of jurisdiction of the State of New York within the State of Vermont should cease; and thenceforth, the perpetual line between the State of New York and the State of Vermont shall be 'as was then holden and possessed by Vermont', namely the west lines of the most western towns which had been granted by New Hampshire, and the middle of Lake Champlain's deepest channel. Also they declared that on or before the first day of June, 1794, Vermont would pay to the State of New York the sum of thirty thousand dollars, which would immediately cancel all claims in Vermont by either the Colony of New York, or the State of New York.

## *VERMONT ACCEPTED INTO THE UNION*

"The difficulties with New York being then removed, the Assembly of Vermont proceeded to call a convention of the people of Vermont to consider joining the Union. After considerable discussion and a reluctance of some of those present, and due to the immediate need therefore, the affirmative vote was one hundred five to two."

The General Assembly of Vermont met at Bennington on June 10th, and on the 18th, of 1791, chose Nathaniel Chipman and Lewis Morris as commissioners to attend Congress and negotiate for the admission of the Vermont Commissioners to the Union. As a result of the request of the Vermont Commissioners to the President of the United States, on the 18th of February 1791, Congress - without any debate or a single dissenting vote - approved Vermont as the fourteenth State of the Union.

On the 28th of October, 1790, the Vermont legislature had passed the following: "An Act directing the payment of thirty thousand dollars to the State of New York, and declaring what the boundary between the State of Vermont and the State of New York shall be, and also declaring certain grants by New York therein mentioned";[16] thenceforth the perpetual boundary line between the State of New York and the State of Vermont shall be as follows, viz: beginning at the northwest corner of the State of Massachusetts, thence northward, along the south boundary of Pownall, to the southwest corner thereof, thence northerly, along the western boundaries of the townships of Pownall, Bennington, Shaftsbury, Arlington, Sandgate, Pawlet, Wells, Poultney as the said townships are now held, or possessed, to the river commonly called the Poultney River, thence down the same through the middle of the stream through the deepest channel thereof, to East Bay, thence through the middle of the deepest channel of East Bay, and the water thereof, to where the same communicates with Lake Champlain, then through the middle of the deepest channel of Lake Champlain to the eastward of the Island called the Four Brothers, and westward of the islands, called Grand Isle and Long Isle, or the two Heros to the westward of Isle La Motte to the forty-fifth degree of North Latitude."

## *EARLY HISTORY*
## *SELECTED BIBLIOGRAPHY*

Broadhead, John Romeyn, *Document Relating to the Colonial History of New York,* Albany, N.Y.: E. Mack, 1845.

Dunlap, William, *History of New Netherlands, Province of New York* and *State of New York to the Adoption of the Federal Constitution,* New York: Carter and Thorp, Vol. II, 1839-40.

16. John A. Williams, ed., *Public Papers of Governor Thomas Chittenden, 1778-1789 & 1790-1797,* Barre, Modern Printing Co., Vol. XVII, 1969, p. 724.

Nuquist, Andrew E., *Town Government in Vermont,* Government Research Center, University of Vermont, Burlington, 1964.
O'Callaghan, E. B., *Documentary History of the State of New York,* Albany, New York: Weed and Parsons, 4 Vols., 1849-51.
State of Vermont, *The Public Laws of Vermont, 1933,* Published by Authority, Montpelier: Capital City Press, 1934.
Stone, Mason, *History of Education, State of Vermont, 1777-1927,* Secretary of State, Middlebury, Vermont: J. W. Copeland, 1930.
Stillwell, Lewis D., *Migration from Vermont,* Montpelier: Vermont Historical Society, 1948.
Secretary of State, *Vermont Legislative Directory and State Manual.*
Secretary of State, *Vermont State Paper,* Compiled and Edited by William Slade, Jr., Middlebury: J. W. Copeland, 1823.
*Vermont Statutes Annotated,* 1958, Orford: New Hampshire, Equity Publishing Corporation, 9 Volumes, Titles 1-33, Index and Tables.

## *SELECTED BIBLIOGRAPHY*

Slade, William, Jr., Vermont State Papers, Middlebury, J. P. Copeland, 1823.
Wilbur, James Benjamin, Ira Allen Founder of Vermont, 1751-1814, Cambridge, Massachusetts, Riverside Press, 2 Vol., 1928.
Williams, John A., ed., The Public Papers of Governor Thomas Chittenden, 1778-1789 & 1790-1797, Barre, Modern Printing Co., Vol. XVII. 1969.

# Arts and Sciences

*PAINTERS, ENGRAVERS, AND SCULPTORS*

This article treats of those artists born in Vermont before 1900, together with those who came to Vermont in the early days, and some who came at a later date. It is very difficult to find any information about early artists, except that they were either landscape or portrait painters and quite often they were itinerants.

During the early days of settlement, art in Vermont was considered to be an unnecessary occupation when there were so many important tasks to perform - such as farming, operating a store or developing an industry. Even today there are some people who have little or no appreciation for the work of the artist. Some of the early artists were jeered and even had to leave home or work on their masterpiece silently and unknown by others.

Vermonters have studied art abroad and our citizens have read about and praised the work of foreign artists with small knowledge of those little-mentioned Vermonters who quietly developed their art at home.

In the town of Weathersfield there is a small settlement known as Greenbush which is three miles south of Felchville. Here in the early 1800's existed what was known as the "Greenbush School" of engravers. Issac Eddy, who was born in Weathersfield in 1777, is the first known Vermont artist. Eddy's copper engravings (which were first printed in a Vermont Bible in Windsor in 1812) were quite crude but true to life.

George White was born near Greenbush in 1797. His father, Thomas White, had migrated from Massachusetts to New Hampshire and then to Cavendish, Vermont where he died when George was only eight years old. In his teens George was apprenticed to Isaac Eddy, who must have greatly influenced his desire to follow up with printing and engraving. George White was about the same age as Isaac Eddy's son, Oliver Tarbell, who also learned the printing and engraving trade from his father. Oliver later became well known as a portrait painter. His first copper engraving *"Death of General Pike at York"* and George White's *"Kitty"* seemed to have some similarity in texture.

White in 1823 moved to Quebec where he worked in the printing establishment of Captain Ebenezer Huntington. Later White returned to Greenbush where he engraved and published twin maps of Vermont and New Hampshire. These maps were copperplate intaglio engravings, and are his best known works. White also produced engraved portraits of Millard Fillmore and James Buchanan. His printed campaign badges were widely distributed.

There was another artist from Weathersfield Zedekiah Belknap - who graduated from Dartmouth College in 1807. He showed much talent as a portrait painter. He spent much of his life in Weathersfield, where he was much concerned that Daguerreo-type, an early form of photography then in vogue, would replace painting.

William Morris Hunt, born in Brattleboro in 1824, later moved to Weathersfield. At the age of about twenty, he studied drawing and sculpturing in Rome, and a couple of years later at Dusseldorf, Germany. After viewing paintings in Paris where he studied, he decided to be a painter. From Paris he went to Holland where he copied the works of the old masters, especially Rembrandt. He painted portraits and landscapes, and was best known for his landscapes. He was noted for his paintings of Niagara Falls. Hunt is the only early Vermont artist whose name is enrolled in the Hall of Fame.

Another Vermonter from the town of Woodstock in Windsor County, Benjamin Franklin Mason, had a natural aptitude for painting which was against his parents' wishes. He was forced to leave home, where, as a result of his teacher's encouragement, he continued his portrait painting and received wide recognition. One of his paintings, that of Chief Justice Williams, hangs in the State House in Montpelier.

Hiram Powers, born in Woodstock in 1805, was one of Vermont's best known sculptors and inventors. While working fòr a merchant he used to open tubs of butter and make designs of frogs, snakes and other animals in the top layer of butter. He went to work in a wax museum where he learned to carve; there making many interesting carvings such as the *"Greek Slave"*, a well known piece of art located in the Corcoran Art Gallery. In Italy, he learned to carve in marble.

Charles Avery Aiken, born in Georgia in 1872, was a mural painter. He was a pupil of the Boston Museum of Fine Arts and exhibited his works in water colors at the Pennsylvania Academy of Fine arts.

Herbert Adams born in Concord in 1858 studied in Paris, and was a member of the National Academy of Arts. His excellent work was in portrait statues.

Truman Howe Bartlett of Dorset, 1835-1923, also studied in Paris. His works included "*Wells*" a bronze statue in Hartford, Connecticut and "*Benedict*", a cemetery monument in Waterbury, Connecticut.

Scott Clifton Carbee, born in Concord in 1830, studied at Providence, Rhode Island, Paris, and Florence, Italy. Among his oil portraits were those of Colonel Albert Clark and Major-General Grout.

Harry Chase of Woodstock, 1853-1889, studied at The Hague, Paris and New York. His principal work, "*The Harbor of New York*", hangs in Corcoran Art Gallery.

Edward Child, born in Governeur, New York, in 1869, at the age of eleven moved to Ludlow where his father was a Baptist preacher. He painted both landscapes and portraits, and did illustrations for some magazines.

Alban Jaspar Conant, 1821-1915, was born in Chelsea and moved with his family to New York when he was about 21 years of age. He was a portrait painter and a naturalist. His portrait of Lincoln known as the "*Smiling Lincoln*", is said to be the only painting of Abraham Lincoln with a smile. Others of his paintings include "*Fort Sumpter*" and "*Sherman*".

Richard B. Farley was born in Poultney in 1875; a pupil of Whistler, Chase and Cecilla Beaux. He was the recipient of an award from the Pennsylvania Academy of Fine Arts.

Margaret Foley of Dorset, 1820-1877, was a sculptress. She taught school for a time in Vergennes; and for a pastime she began carving from chalk, crayons and wood giving her statuettes to her pupils as prizes. She later opened a studio in Boston, where she carved cameos and portraits. She went to Rome at the encouragement of her friends, where she learned to carve from marble and had her own studio. Her principal sculptures include "*William Cullen Bryant*", "*Longfellow*" and "*The Young Trumpeteer*" which rests in the Vergennes Library.

Paul Bartlett, born in Dorset in 1867, went to Europe with his father where at the age of 14 he exhibited a bust of his grandmother in the Paris Salon. In 1880 he entered the Ecole des Beaux Arts. His work, "*The Bear Tamer*", is in the Metropolitan Museum of Art.

George C. Ellsworth of Berkshire, 1854-1870, painted a portrait of Governor Stephen Royce.

James Gilman was a crayon portrait painter. One of his works is that of General Perley Davis in oil.

James Guild, an itinerant painter of Tunbridge, traveled on foot from house to house painting portraits. Eventually he went to London where he became a renowned portrait painter.

The oldest son of Major Hardie, Robert Gordon, Jr., was born in Brattleboro in 1854. He studied at both Cooper Union and the Ecole des Beaux Arts in Paris. Some of his best known Vermont works are of Senator Redfield Proctor and Governor Levi K. Fuller.

Chester Harding, 1792-1816, was born in Conway, Massachusetts and was a portrait painter of Governor Charles Paine.

I. Hazen, 1754-1834, portrait of Governor Isaac Tichenor.

James Hope, born in 1811 in Scotland, moved to Canada at the age of nine with his father who died shortly thereafter. At the age of sixteen, this homeless, penniless boy decided to try something better, so he headed for the United States. Walking 150 miles he landed in Fair Haven where he apprenticed for five years to a wagon maker. By that time he had saved enough money to take an art course at Castleton Seminary. Due to an accident while chopping wood, he received a cut which made him house bound. He began with some common paints on a pine board and made a self portrait. Soon his paintings were bringing $100.00 each. With a limited field he moved on to Montreal for two years and returned to Castleton where he established a studio. Through a friend of the Hudson River School he learned landscape painting. In 1852, he opened a studio in New York City. Following his service in the Civil War, he went to explore Watkins Glen where he painted landscapes which brought him world renown. Many of his scenes brought him as much as $25,000.00.

H. Chester Ingham lived and worked in Vergennes from the 1880's to the 1930's. He led the life of a recluse; often adrift in a houseboat on Otter Creek, where he made landscape paintings. He received formal training at New York's National Academy of Design, traveled in Europe in 1914-15, and went to Florida in 1918 for a brief time. His works were of an impressionable style and a contrast with his still lifes and landscapes which are considered his most cherished works.

John N. Marble of Woodstock, 1855-1918, studied in France and Italy. His works include crayon portraits of Mary Baker Eddy and Brigadier-General Edward H. Ripley.

Larkin G. Mead was born in New Hampshire in 1835, and brought to Brattleboro by his folks when he was four years old. His early artistic abilities were depicted in the sculpture of a pig in marble. In 1858 he constructed in snow the *"Recording Angel"* which was admired by many. He was commissioned to make several likenesses of this image in marble. One of his interesting sculptures, the statue of *"Ethan Allen"*, is on the portico of the State House in Montpelier. In 1879 he was a professor of fine arts at the Academy of Fine Arts in Florence, Italy.

Abel Buel Moore was born in Doreset 1806, and was a high-spirited lad, full of pranks and with a love for beauty. With the use of materials at hand, while very young he painted landscapes on the walls of his father's house. He was sent to Boston and New York, where he entered the studio of one of the best portrait painters of the country. He later opened studios in Troy and Albany, New York, where his success as a portrait painter brought him great renown. In 1855-1878, he visited the great galleries in Europe.

William Picknell, born in Hinesburg in 1854, was the son of a minister. As a youth he studied in Italy and in Paris at the Ecole des Beaux Arts, where his works received honorable mention. His brother, George, was not an accomplished painter although he studied in Paris and exhibited there. He was chiefly an illustrator. William's work is in the Corcoran Art Gallery.

Theodore Robins, born in Irasburg in 1852, acquired the impressionist manner of painting from study under Claude Monet. He painted both indoors and outdoors scenes.

Rowland Robinson, born in Ferrisburg in 1833, was not only a writer but also a draughtsman and cartoonist, whose sketches were printed in *Harper's Weekly.*

Julian Rix, 1850-1900, Peacham, was a self-taught painter. He began as a sign painter and decorator at the age of 22. He later painted in San Francisco, and some of his paintings are in the Corcoran Art Gallery.

Julian Scott, 1846-1901, was born in Johnson and served as a drummer boy with the Union Army. He studied in Paris where his works were shown at the Paris exposition in 1904. One of his paintings of the Civil War, *"The Battle of Cedar Creek"*, is found in the reception room of the State House.

Julius Brutus Stearns, 1810-1885, of Arlington, was a painter of historical subjects. Five paintings were made of George Washington as farmer, solider, citizen, statesman and Christian.

Charles Sunderland of Brandon, born in 1838, was a portrait painter who studied in Paris and had a studio in Boston.

George Timothy, born 1864, Weybridge.

Elliot Bouton Torrey, born in 1867 in Hardwick, was a member of the Boston Art Club, and represented in the Art Institute in Chicago.

Abraham G. D. Tuthill was born about 1776 in Oyster Pond, Long Island, New York. He spent several years studying in London and had one year in Paris. There are some of his paintings in Montpelier, which include *"Colonel Langdon"* and *"General Walton"*.

Edward H. Walker, born in Fitchburg, Massachusetts in 1879, died in 1943, was a commercial artist for a New York City firm. He lived in Brandon.

J. Q. A. Ward, 1830-1910, born in Urbana, Ohio, was a sculptor, and carved a marble bust of Governor Erastus Fairbanks.

Thomas Waterman Wood, 1823-1903, was born in Montpelier. Mr. Wood is the immortal artist of Montpelier for whom its museum is named. For two years Mr. Wood traveled abroad, studying in London, Rome, Paris and Florence. He served as President of the National Academy of Design in New York City for eight years, where he had his studio. Wood became a foremost portrait painter, and a majority of his work is collected and shown in the Wood Art Gallery in Montpelier.

Edward Martin Taber, born in New York in 1863, came to Stowe for his health where he painted *"Mountain Canvasses"*.

Aaron Dean Fletcher, born 1817 in Springfield, Vermont, painted some portraits and some landscapes.

Benjamin Harris Kinney was born in Peru, Massachusetts in 1821. His childhood and youth was spent in Sunderland, Vermont. He sculptured a statue of Ethan Allen which was probably the first sculpture done in Vermont. The statue was made for the State of Vermont which offered him the sum of $3,000.00. He turned down the offer and soon left the state.

William Baxter Palmer Clossen, 1848-1926, was born in Thetford. He was a wood engraver as well as a painter in oils and pastels.

A man named Miller, born in Brattleboro in 1848, was an artist but about whom little is known.

Jonathan Fenton came to East Dorset in 1801 and established a small stoneware pottery a little east of the village. His son Christopher Weber Fenton born in 1806, became famous in the annals of the United States pottery. His oldest son was also a potter. Evidently for some reason or other the business was suspended in the 1830's.

Halls' *History of Eastern Vermont - History of Rockingham* describes the *Indian Sculpture* found in eastern Vermont in the following words: "The picture writing of the Indians is to be seen in two localities in eastern Vermont. At the foot of Bellows Falls and on the west side of the channel of the Connecticut River are two rocks, on which are inscribed figures. The larger rock presents a group of variously ornamental heads. The surface which these heads occupy is about six feet in height and fifteen feet in breadth.

"From a central figurehead, which is supplied by a neck and shoulders, six rays or feathers extend. Four of the other heads are adorned each with a piece of similar projection. On a separate rock, situated nearby, a single head is sculptured."

"The other place in eastern Vermont where similar pictures have been found is on the south bank of the West River in the town of Brattleboro, where the pictures are fewer in number, and only on one stone."

Helen Hartness Flanders began the collecting of folklore in 1930. In 1958 she ceased her collecting in Vermont, Maine, New Hampshire and the rest of New England and turned the amassed collection over to Middlebury College. It is considered to be the most extensive collection of folk songs of New England in the world.

In all she collected about 120 of such songs, of which only about nine can claim with any authority that they were of Vermont origin, and two of these are in doubt.

"Young Charlotte is a song of Vermont origin, sung during the wanderings of its blind composer, William Carter, who headed towards the Mormon settlements in Ohio and Utah after his father, a former Baptist clergyman of Benson, Vermont, adopted the faith."

The Green Mountain Songster dated April 8, 1823 contains the statement of the Unknown Soldier of Sandgate in his preface, "Most people are fond of singing".

The Vermont Sugar-Maker's Song is attributed to have been written by the Reverend Perrin B. Fiske, born in Waitsfield, Vermont in 1837. The West River Railroad, was written by Mr. and Mrs. Julian Johnson of South Londonderry for a home talent play.

## *MUSIC*

Some of the oldest music is the hymns which were played on the organ with the family or friends gathered round. Today many of these old hymns are as much alive as the day they were written centuries ago.

Many of the older people remember what was called the 'kitchen junket' or some other colloquially used term, where the music consisted of the fiddler. Many of the old dances were enjoyed to the music of a violin and a piano.

Much of the old time fiddling had nearly been forgotten until its recent resurrection. Let us hear the story of Clem Myers, who founded the Northeast Fiddlers Association. Clem who started violin lessons when he was ten years old has played with many groups beginning in 1938.

N.B. The information about the several artists on one page may be from several sources; The Dictionary of American Painters, Sculptors and Engravers; by Mantle Felding, 1945; The Hope Paintings, Larry Freeman, 1901; Vermont Historical Society, Vol. 42 #1, The Unknown Artist, Carl Taylor, Jr.; History of the Town of Brandon; V.H.S. Sept. 1943, Margaret T. Smalley; Enterprise and Vermonter, March 14, 1974.

After two fiddling contests arranged by Robert Clark of Goddard College did not seem to get off the ground, Robert made a call on Clem Myers to help. At a meeting in Hardwick in May 1966 a fiddling contest was held with 35 fiddlers and 450 fans attending. The organization which had been formed in 1965 has grown rapidly with fiddlers coming annually from all over the northeast region to the annual fiddling contests held in Montpelier.

Clem states that in the early days the fiddler was the most important person in the community. This was so because of the violin's light weight which was easy to carry when one had to walk through the wilderness from one settlement to another. Clem, though no longer president of the Association, still sprightly draws his bow.

### *Vermont State Symphony Orchestra*

The Vermont State Symphony Orchestra came into being in 1934 at a rural symphony group composed of dedicated musicians meeting for their first rehearsal in Rutland and Burlington. Founded by Dr. Alan Carter, chairman of the Music Department at Middlebury College, to meet the distinct cultural needs for a symphony orchestra to perform classical music in communities large and small. The Vermont State Symphony Orchestra was the first state symphony in the United States.

The Vermont legislature provided the historic distinction by adopting legislation in 1941 making the Vermont Symphony Orchestra a State Institution and giving it a yearly grant. The first appropriation was for $1,000.00 for each of the fiscal years 1942 and 1943. Because of the excellent performance made by the orchestra at the World's Fair in New York in 1959 the legislature made in 1959 another appropriation amounting to $5,000.00.

A highlight of each biennial session of the Vermont Legislature was the performance of the Governor's concert by the Vermont State Symphony Orchestra in the State House in Montpelier.

The Vermont State Symphony Orchestra is engaged in two major endeavors concerning music for young people. The Vermont Symphony Orchestra Association was incorporated in 1938 with Samuel R. Ogden as its President. A campaign was started in October 1938 to raise $18,000.00 for a maintenance fund to assure continuation of the operation of the orchestra for the first three years.

The Association initiated Vermont's first educational television program in 1957 with a 26 week series of half hour music programs for the grade schools on Monday mornings. The following year and each year thereafter music instruction for Vermont schools has been telecast under the auspices of the Association as part of "TV School", the daily instructional program presented over WCAX-TV with the cooperation of the Vermont Department of Education.

The Association's String Project, designed to meet the critical need in the state and nation for string players, utilizes a unique method for developing musicians by teaching children ranging from 6 to 12 years to play string instruments in their own music organizations, the Green Mountain Fiddlers. Each season the Green Mountain Fiddlers perform in a formal concert with the Vermont Symphony Orchestra not only to demonstrate their proficiency but more importantly to make music seriously with their skilled elders.

### *The Vermont Philharmonic*

John Borowicz as soon as he arrived in Northfield as the director of music at Norwich University began the formation of the Vermont Philharmonic Orchestra in 1958. Friends of the Vermont Philharmonic organized a supporting agency to aid in the raising of funds to finance the orchestra. The first concert was held at Norwich University with the program being, Handel's "Messiah". In 1960 the Philharmonic was chartered by the State of Vermont, as a cultural and educational institution with Morton Laird of Montpelier as its President.

The Orchestra has received statewide support since its inception. Today the orchestra is fully professional and all its members receive a modest remuneration.

## *INVENTORS*

Thaddeus Stevens platform scale, Frances Strong Howe scale, Electric motor Thomas Davenport, 1st U.S. patent Samuel Hopkins for potash, 1st successful time clock, James Sargent, 1st safety elevator, James Otis, Co-discoverer of Laughing water, Gardner Colton, Snowflake photography Wilson Bentley, Twine Binder, Hector Adams, Vermont Beehive John E. Weeks, Steel Square, Silas Hawes, 1st fireproof safe Silas C. Herring, Steel plow, John Deere, Gimlet screw Thomas Harvey, Marble saw Hiram Kimball, refrigerator Wm. B. Chandler, Automatic Railroad Brake J. Wheeler.

## *ARTS AND SCIENCES SELECTED BIBLIOGRAPHY*

Barrett, Richard C., *A Color Guide to Bennington Pottery,* Bennington Historical Museum, 1968.

Dana, Henry Swan, *History of Woodstock,* Boston and New York: Houghton Mifflin Co., 1889.

Fielding, Mantle, *Dictionary of American Painters, Sculptors, and Engravers,* New York: J. F. Carr, 1965.
Freeman, Larry, *The Hope Paintings,* New York: Anthony Howell, 1961.
Hayes, Lyman S., *History of Rockingham,* Town of Bellows Falls, 1907.
Hall, Benjamin Homer, *History of Eastern Vermont,* New York: D. Appleton & Co., 1858.
Huden, John C., Compiler, *Archaeology* in Vermont, Burlington: University of Vermont, 1960.
Humphrey, Zephine, *The Story of Dorset,* Rutland: Tuttle Company, 1924.
Kent, Dorman, B. E., *1,000 Men,* Montpelier: Vermont Historical Society, 1914.
McGrath, Robert, *Early Vermont Wall Paintings, 1790-1850,* Hanover, N.H.: University Press of New England, 1972.
Newton, Earl, *The Vermont Story, A History of the People of the Green Mountain State,* Vermont Historical Society, Burlington Free Press, 1949.
Selectmen of Brandon, *History of Brandon,* Town of Brandon, 1961.

*Hauling granite from Barre for Montpelier State House in 1837*

# Banks and Money

## *PAPER MONEY* [1]

Early in 1781 a general need was felt for a currency more reliable than that which was already in circulation, and an act "for the purpose" (as the preamble of the act states) "of carrying on the war and the enlargement of the paper currency", was passed after some debate authorizing the issue in April 1781 of Vermont's first paper currency.

The authorized issue was for 25,155 pounds in bills of the following denominations (and an equal number of each) 3 pounds; 40 shillings; 10 shillings; 5 shillings; 2 shillings and 6 pence; and 1 shilling. Three men, one of whom was the fiery Matthew Lyon of Fair Haven, comprised the committee which was empowered to make a design and forms and supervise the printing of the bills.

An early one-shilling bill had a vignette which read: *"Vermont Calls For Justice"*. There were thirteen joined chain links to depict the thirteen original colonies with Vermont still unlinked. The motto on the vignette represented Vermont's demand for recognition by the Continental Congress and her neighboring states.

Judah Spooner and Timothy Green, who had previously owned a printing shop, moved to Westminster where they printed the first currency. A committee, any two of whom could sign, was authorized by law to affix their signatures.

The notes were to remain in circulation until the first day of June 1782, at which time they were redeemed at the rate of six shillings to the Spanish Dollar; and to meet the anticipated expense, a tax of one shilling and three pence on the pound was laid on the grand list of the state. In addition a land tax of ten shillings was levied against every hundred acres in the state.

1. Terrence G. Harper, *Historical Account of Vermont Paper Currency and Bank.*

The committee reported that the amount of 21,300 pounds had been redeemed. On October 26, 1782 the Lyons committee was directed to burn the bills of credit which had been redeemed "in payment of taxes". The committee reported the burning of 10,000 pounds of Vermont Colonial currency. In February 1782 an act was passed directing the State Treasurer to burn all bills of credit. Shortly thereafter another act was passed which directed that after June 1, 1782, the bills of credit would no longer be legal tender for any payment except to the state treasury.

### *State Bank for Paper Money*[2]

A proposal in the legislature for the establishment of a bank for the issue of paper money on loan to people was defeated in 1786 by a vote of 2,197 to 456. On March 2, 1787, an act was passed making cattle, beef, wheat, corn, and rye legal tender at the value appraised by competent men under oath.

A distinction was made between scrip notes and fractional notes issued by a bank. Scrip notes (also known as *shinplasters*) were issued by anyone with a good credit rating, but usually by local governments or merchants to supply small change in periods of scarcity of coins.

Merchants' scrip notes were generally payable, usually in some aggregate of $1.00 or more, at a store and sometimes at a local bank. If at the latter, they were really checks on the bank. While most scrip notes were fractional, less-than-one-dollar denominations, they were sometimes issued for larger amounts - up to five dollars.

To finance the war, the United States government began the issuance of paper money in 1861. For a few years, the Government issues competed with or supplemented the notes of the state charter banks. In 1865, Congress passed a law imposing a ten percent tax on the circulation of paper money for purposes other than that of the obligations of the United States. This act had the effect of wiping out a primary source of banking profits, and of giving the United States a monopoly on paper money. Most local issues were redeemed, and the state bank era was at an end.

*Coins* are a specific form of money, the latter comprehending all media of exchange, of which there are many media. The Indians used wampums, which are shells that were worn on a string. Wampum was of two colors, black (or dark purple) and white: the black being twice the value of the white. From its convenience in the fur trade, it was largely used in the eastern colonies. In the early

2. Vermont Historical Society, Vol. 1, 1870.
Mayer Burns Coulter, *Vermont Obsolete Notes and Scrip,* 1972.
Rev. Edmund Slafter A.M., *The Vermont Coinage,* 1870.

days of the settlement the barter system was used before there were many coins or bills for sale.

Soon the precious metals came into use in most countries and their value was determined by their weight. Next the government for convenience placed a stamp on the coin to denote its face value, which was a great advantage over the tedious job of weighing.

The art of coinage had its origin about eight hundred years before Christ. The early coins were quite crude. The Massachusetts Bay Colony in 1652 issued silver coins having "New England" stamped upon them. These were soon followed by the *"Pine Tree"* money, which coinage was continued for more than thirty years. Other colonies - Maryland, North Carolina and Virginia - made attempts to establish mints but they had no success.

Between the Declaration of Independence of the American Colonies and the adoption of the United States Constitution in 1778, several colonies minted or authorized the manufacture and the issue of coins. Among these, Vermont was the leader - her first act authorizing the issuance of coins bore the date of June 1785. Next in order came Connecticut in the same year, while New Jersey and New York followed in 1786. These were the only states which issued coins during the period of the Confederation, and copper was the only type of coin struck. Massachusetts established a mint, but the other three contracted with private parties.

### *Vermont Coinage* [3]

At the General Assembly of Vermont held at Norwich on June 10, 1785, Reuben Harmon, Jr. of Rupert asked leave to coin a quantity of copper, which request was referred to a committee of four which reported the bill: "An act granting Reuben Harmon the right exclusively of coining copper for a term of two years; all copper to be one-third of an ounce Troy weight with such devices and mottoes as shall be agreed upon by a legislative committe." Harmon was required to furnish a bond of 5,000 pounds to the State Treasurer. By an act passed the following September, the coin weight was reduced to not less than four penny-weight, fifteen grains each.

*The mint* was established in the northeastern part of the town of Rupert on a small stream called Mill Brook, a tributary of the Mettawee River. The building is described as "about sixteen by eighteen feet wide, made of rough materials; simply clapboarded, unplaned and unpainted". Within the small area stood the furnace, the rolling machine, and those machines needed for cutting and stamping the planchettes. It is said that by means of a screw moved by hand from 30 to 60 coins per minute could be struck. The old mint building

3. Vermont HIstorical Society, Vol. I, 1870.

stands on the farm yard of Robert Graf, representative from Rupert, to which place it was moved from a point a short distance southerly.

The coins were described on the obverse side as "a sun rising, with mountains and trees in the foreground, and a plow in the field beneath". The legend in Latin read, *"Vermontisium, Res Publica 1785"*. On the reverse side was a radiated eye surrounded by thirteen stars with the legend, *"Decima Stella"*. The significance of the legend on the obverse side is the political attitude to which the population aspired. The reverse side alludes to the thirteen states as shown by the number of stars and the fourteenth star was in the nature of a prophesy that Vermont would become the fourteenth state.

In 1786 the legislature authorized an eight year extension of the coinage, making in all a ten-year term. Under the latter act, Harmon was to pay into the treasury for the use of the state, two and a half percentum of all copper he should coin during the last five years of the period.

During the year 1788 the operation of the mint came to an end, due to Vermont's ratification of the Constitution of the United States which gave Congress the exclusive right to coin money.

### *State Bank* [4]

In 1786 certain people were clamoring for a state bank, hoping that such an institution would relieve their sufferings. The legislature in October authorized a referendum for the people, a large number of whom were opposed to a state bank. No further attempts to create a state bank were made until 1803, when the General Assembly passed an act authorizing a bank at Windsor and one at Burlington by a vote of 93 to 83, which act was defeated by the Governor and Council. The clamor for a bank still continued and in 1805 haggling delayed action until the session in Middlebury in 1806. An act was then passed setting up two branches, one at Woodstock and the other at Middlebury, and at such other places as the legislature would from time to time establish. In 1807 additional branches were established, one at Burlington and the other at Westminster. All the stock in the bank and all the profits arising therefrom were to accrue to the state, and remain under the sole direction and disposal of the legislature forever.

The legislature annually in joint committee chose suitable persons for bank directors - thirteen in number - who were successful business men. No bank was allowed to put in circulation bills greater in amount than the actual sum of the deposits of silver, gold and copper coins in the vault of such branch bank. When the deposit

4. Governor and Council, Vol. IV, p. 388 & 408.

amounted to $25,000.00 they were allowed to circulate three times the amount of the deposit.

The first bills of the bank were issued on February 23, 1807. Trouble appeared when counterfeiting became rife in 1808, when many bills were found circulating in Canada, where they were said to be more numerous than those of the Vermont State Bank bills. Trouble was brewing: Massachusetts and other states by law would not accept our bills. Several private banks in the vicinity of this state had failed; and the policy of caprice by others was embarrassing.

To sustain the bank, laws were passed in 1809 and in 1812 "to make the bills of the bank receivable for land taxes"; however, the bank conditions continued to decline. The sum of the bills in circulation dropped from $548,000.00 to $95,000.00 in 1811. First the bank at Westminster was moved to Woodstock in 1812, and soon the branches at Burlington and Middlebury were also moved there.

In 1814 an act was passed directing the treasurer to burn all bills, "excepting such sums as may in the opinion of the treasurer be needed to meet the demands of the treasury, and it shall be the duty of the treasurer and directors who burn such bills, to keep an account of the sum of the bills issued from each branch bank, which they shall burn".

## *LOTTERIES*

From the very beginning of habitation in the New Hampshire Grants the need of funds for the common good was always a paramount issue. When we were having our problems for the control of the New Hampshire Grants, the citizens decided that they would fight if necessary to take possession of any land grant which the Province of New York had made in the grants.

A committee of Sequestration was established which took lands away from the New York grantees and sold the property to people of the New Hampshire Grants in order to raise money. This action caused a long series of discussions between the Province of New York and Thomas Chittenden, President of the Council of Safety.

It was soon thereafter that a lottery was thought to be an easy way to raise funds. Many examples of raising funds by lotteries may be found in the Acts of 1793 and 1794. Petitions were made to the General Assembly (The House) - (There was no Senate at the time.) If voted favorably, the petition then went to the Governor and Council for concurrence. Petitions for lotteries some of which were defeated in committee were in most cases for roads and bridges.

The first lottery of record was in 1793 to raise money for building a bridge over the Black River. Rutland was granted a lottery in 1793, amounting to 600 pounds to erect a court house.

A petition was submitted to raise the sum of 200 pounds by lottery for furnishing a malt house and brewery in the town of Weathersfield. It was brought before the House on October 24, 1794 and laid on the table until October 27, when the petition was accepted and later passed into law. Another petition by the town of Saltash (Plymouth) did not thrive so well. The petition requested the granting of a lottery to Asa Briggs so that he could build a gristmill in that town. The petition stated that without a mill in that town, people were obliged to travel eight to ten miles over poor roads to have their grist ground. An adverse report was given and the petition dismissed.

In August 1827 the papers carried a story of a lottery with 8,760 prizes with a total value of $72,080.00. The advertisement for the lottery stated; ''Gamboling in Vermont, via a state lottery, a popular pastime for sporting-minded residents''.

From about 1800 on there was a gradual change in public sentiment in regard to the propriety of raising money by lotteries. After 1804 the legislature made no further authorizations for lotteries. By 1826 the sale of foreign lottery tickets increased so much that a license fee up to $1,000.00 was enacted. From 1793 to 1804 the legislature authorized about 24 lotteries. Soon thereafter all lotteries were prohibited. Irish lottery tickets are sold in Vermont still today.[5]

Lotteries played an important part when the business of taxes and the act of carrying public burden was crude and ill-defined. People thought no more of buying a lottery ticket than buying a pound of tea. In a short time there was a lottery wheel in every city and town large enough to boast a court house or jail. Whether a bridge was to be thrown across a little stream, a public building enlarged, a school house built, a street paved, a church assisted or a college treasury replenished the legislature passed a lottery bill." A Lottery office was opened in Brattleboro in 1826.[6]

*BANKS AND MONEY*
*SELECTED BIBLIOGRAPHY*

Coulter, Mayre Burns, *Vermont Obsolete Notes and Scrip,* Iola, Wisconsin: France Publication, 1972.
Vermont, Governor and Council, *Laws of 1798,* Vol. IV.
Harper, Terrence G., *Historical Account of Vermont Paper Money and Bank Notes,* Reprint from the Numismatic Scrapbook Magazine), 1965.

5. J. Joslin, et. al., *A History of the Town of Poultney,* (Poultney: Journal Printing Office, 1875), p. 182.
6. Mary R. Cabot, *Annals of Brattleboro,* (Brattleboro: E. L. Hildreth & Co., 1921), p. 703.

Phillips, Henry Jr., A. M., *Historical Skethes of Paper Money in American Colonies,* Roxbury, Massachusetts: W. Elliott Woodward, 1865.
Slafter, Reverend Edmond, *The Vermont Coinage,* Vermont Historical Society, Vol. I, 1870.

*Primitive method of boiling sap*

# Communications

## *MAIL*

In 1691, a proper *postal service* was established in the colonies. In the early days a sheet of paper was folded instead of using an envelope. The letters were sealed with wax, and the postage was paid by the receiver on the basis of the mileage of the letter carried. Rates varied from 6 cents for a distance up to 10 miles, up to 25 cents for longer distances up to 50 miles. Mail was carried by post riders who traveled 30 to 40 miles a day and, by a change of horses, could travel fifty miles. Thus it was several days journey from Vermont to Boston.

The Governor and Council in session at Bennington on June 19, 1781, passed the following resolution: "Resolved: that Samuel Sherman be employed to ride post from his Excellency's in Arlington to Camp Headquarters in Castleton once a week for three months from date hereof; to go up one road by the way of Tinmouth and return by the way of Pawlet, that for his Encouragement he be allowed 14 shillings per week out of the State's Treasury, he to convey all Public Letters and Dispatches free of all other public expense."

On November 26, 1783: "Resovled: that Samuel Sherman be paid nine shillings per week out of the Public Treasury for riding post, carrying and bring intelligence to & from this place to Albany until the sitting of the General Assembly on February next."

On March 9, 1784 the General Assembly established a postal system within Vermont with Anthony Haswell as Postmaster General to carry mail to the following post offices: Bennington, Brattleboro, Rutland, Windsor and Newbury. On the 3rd of March 1791, Congress gave the U. S. Postmaster General authority to extend the Federal mail service from Albany to Bennington.[1]

1. Julia C. Kellogg, *Vermont Post Roads and Canals* (Vermont: Montpelier Historical Society, Vol. XVI., No. 4, 1948) pp. 135-148.

As Vermont roads by 1791 were widened to accommodate ox-drawn carts, and public highways were built to connect Vermont settlements with one another and adjoining states, stage coaches came into use. In 1798 mail was carried once a week each way between Windsor and Burlington by the way of Woodstock, Randolph and Montpelier.

## *POSTAL HISTORY*

Postage stamps were not in use officially until an Act of Congress was passed on March 3, 1845, fixing the rate of postage at 5 cents on a single letter for distances up to 300 miles. In 1846 the Brattleboro Provisional Stamp, valued at 5 cents, was issued by postmaster Frederick Palmer; however, the issuance of such stamps was rendered illegal to use by the federal act of July 1, 1847.

Mail was carried on Lake Champlain steamers as early as 1831. The captain took charge of letters which were delivered from port to port, for which he received the sum of 2 cents for each letter. It was not until the 1825 Postal Act of Congress that the class of steamboard letters was recognized for the first time in the postal laws and regulations.[2]

## *EARLY NEWSPAPERS AND PRINTING*

When the Vermont legislature began to hold meetings in 1778, a need was felt to have their records, proceedings and laws printed. Previous to that time there was no printer in Vermont, so the printing was done in Hartford, Connecticut, and in Exeter and Portsmouth, New Hampshire.

Two brothers, Judah Paddock Spooner and Alden Spooner, printers, had come to Dresden - one of the towns east of Connecticut - which was then a part of Vermont. It was at Dresden that the first printing for the State of Vermont was made. The legislature made overtures to the Spooners to establish their plant in Westminster, but to no avail. A legislative committee contacted Timothy Green, son of the Connecticut state printer, and Judah Paddock Spooner, who moved to Westminster in the fall of 1780, where they started their duties as state printers. Much public printing was needed to make a printing office profitable. They published in December 1780 a newspaper called the *Vermont Gazette* and the *Green Mountain Post Boy*.

It is interesting to note that the first press used for printing in Vermont (known as the Stephen Daye press) rests in the Pavilion

2. George C. Slawson, et. al., *The Postal History of Vermont* (New York: The Collectors Club, 1969) p. 308.

office building under the watchful care of the Vermont Historical Society.

Anthony Haskell and David Russell, printers, moved from Springfield, Massachusetts to Bennington in May of 1783. Here they published in 1784 the Vermont newspaper called the *Vermont Gazette* or *Freeman's Depository.*

Before the arrival of Haskell, the legislature had appointed another committee to locate a printer, due to the fact that Judah Spooner and Timothy Green were having difficulties. Alden Spooner, still in Dresden, and George Hough of Connecticut were contacted by the committee and agreed to become state printers. They established their plant in Windsor in 1783. a third newspaper, *The Vermont Journal* and the *Universal Advertiser* was established and operated until 1792.

Under the Acts of October 1790, the printing of the state laws was divided alternately between Alden Spooner and Haskell and Russell, since the legislature met alternately on one side of the Green Mountains and then on the other. Haskell was appointed Postmaster General of Vermont in 1784. He ran into financial difficulties with his printing business and sold his newspaper to Orsamus C. Merrill and Robert Langdon, who changed the paper's name to *Tablet of the Times.* They operated barely a year when Haskell again took over the newspaper. He set up an office in Rutland in 1792, and started another newspaper, *The Herald of Vermont* or *Rutland Courier,* but again ran into financial difficulties.

Another paper was started in Rutland by James Lyon in 1793 and the next year sold to Judge Samuel Williams and the Reverend James Williams. The paper's name was changed to the *Rutland Herald,* which name has been retained until today.

In the next few years many newspapers were started. Printing offices were opened in Brattleboro, Burlington, Peacham, Putney and Vergennes, where a newspaper was established soon after opening of the office.

Along with the newspaper business, the printers branched out into publication of broadsides, almanacs, sermons and religious treatises, hymns and poems on religious subjects.

*Vermont Imprints 1778-1820,* compiled by Marcus McCorison, shows only eight items printed in 1778 by J. P. Spooner at the Dresden press. In 1780, three items were printed at Westminster by Spooner and Green in addition to the *Westminster Gazette.* Not until 1783 is there listed any printing in Bennington by Haswell and Russell. During 1778 the printing was chiefly for the State of Vermont. Some work in 1779 was printed for Dartmouth College. Printing of a religious nature appeared in 1782. In the following year, Haswell developed the idea of printing an almanac which was calculated for the meridian of Rutland and in the next year he used the Bennington meridian.

The *Rutland Herald* was established in 1791 and the *Burlington Free Press* began operations in 1828. The legislature in 1801 directed that all advertisements for warning of proprietor's meetings and land sales or for notifying land owners to work out their road tax must be published in the *Middlebury Mercury* in addition to the *Rutland Herald* and the *Vermont Journal.* Lands for sale in Chittenden and Franklin counties were to be advertised in the *Vermont Sentinel* of Burlington. In 1810, in order that there be no preference shown, all advertisements carried in the *Vermont Journal* of Windsor were also carried in the *Vermont Republican,* also of Windsor.[3]

## *TELEPHONE AND TELEGRAPH*[4]

The first telegraph line in Vermont began operation in 1848 along the Central Vermont Railway right of way between Bethel and White River Junction.

The Vermont International Telephone Company (chartered on December 16, 1869) had 12 stockholders with Arthur Stone of St. Johnsbury as president. Its lines extended along the St. Johnsbury and Lake Champlain Railway line. The New England Telephone and Telegraph Company was organized under New York laws on October 19, 1883. The Postal Telegraph Cable Company was organized under Connecticut laws on the 20th of March 1884. It had 185 miles of pole line in Vermont.

The Canadian Pacific Corporation, a Canadian firm, was incorporated in Canada on February 17, 1881 and in 1910 maintained 21 and a half miles of pole line in Vermont.

The Western Union Telegraph Company originally known as the New York and Mississippi Printing Telegraph Company operated under a New York charter granted in April 1851.

George W. Benedict, formerly a science teacher at the University of Vermont, established the Vermont and Boston Telegraphy Company which received and sent the first telegraph message from Burlington on February 2, 1848.

Local *telephone* companies have headquarters in Cornwall, Ludlow, Shoreham, Topsham, Waitsfield, Marshfield and Fayston; also the Franklin Telephone Company and the Continental Telephone Company. The Telephone Data System acquired the Northfield and Perkinsville telephone companies.

3. Marcus McCorison, *Vermont Imprints,* 1778-1920 (Worcester, Massachusetts: The Printing Trade 1963) p. 441.

4. Information furnished by the companies concerned and Vermont Laws.

The switch to dial phones in Burlington occurred in September 1951, which did away with the old wall phone with its crank. Theodore N. Vail of Lyndonville was for a time the organizing genius of the telephone business. He served at times as president of both the American Telephone and Telegraph Company and the Western Union Company.

## *RADIO AND TELEVISION* [5]

Radio broadcasting in Vermont began with Station WSYB in Rutland in 1930, followed by WDEV in Waterbury on July 16, 1933. The Waterbury system was started by Harry Whitehall who many times financed the enterprise by trading air time for materials to construct his station. Mr. Whitehall (along with Lloyd Squire and William Ricker) developed the radio station in St. Albans with the Call Letter WWSR, after the first initial of the names of these three promoters.

Radio stations now (1974) operating on a regular daily schedule are located as follows: Bennington - WBTN; Brattleboro - WTSA, WKVT; Barre - WSNO; Burlington - WDOT, WETK, WJOY, WVMY; Newport - WIKE; Montpelier - WSKI; Randolph - WCVR; St. Albans - WWSR; St. Johnsbury - WTWN; Rutland - WSYB, WHWB; and Waterbury - WDEV.

The first television station to operate in Vermont was Station WCAX in Burlington established on September 26, 1954. Other television broadcasts heard over considerable portions of Vermont are brought by Burlington WETK, Plattsburg WPTZ, Poland Springs, Maine WMTW, Schenectady WRGB, Montreal CBMT, CFCF, CBFT (French).

Vermont Educational Television went on the air on October 16, 1967 and was placed under the management of the University of Vermont. The State of Vermont appropriated for the fiscal year 1975 the sum of $611,257.00 to operate this station which is located at Fort Ethan Allen, Vermont. The public Service Board in 1970 was given authority for general supervision over any cable television company within the state owning, operating or providing a cable television system. The companies are licensed annually under the regulations of the board.

There were 34 cable television companies incorporated in Vermont in 1972.

5. From information furnished by companies and personal knowledge.

*COMMUNICATIONS*
*SELECTED BIBLIOGRAPHY*

Fairbanks, E. H., *The Town of St. Johnsbury,* St. Johnsbury: The Cowles Press, 1914.

Kellogg, Julia C., *Vermont Post Roads and Canals,* Montpelier: Vermont Historical Society, Vol. VI, No. 4, 1948.

McCorison, Marcus, *Vermont Imprints, 1778, 1820,* Worcester, Massachusetts: The Printing Trade, American Antiquarian Society, 1963.

Slawson, George C., et. al., *The Postal History of Vermont,* New York: The Collectors Club, 1969.

Vermont, *Public Laws of Vermont*

Williams, John A. ed., *Public Papers of Governor Thomas Chittenden,* Barre: The Modern Printing Company, 1969.

*Old Stone schoolhouse in Plymouth attended by President Coolidge*

# Education

The development of our educational system, starting from the first constitution and continuing through the period of our 1974 legislature, has been a constant battle between people of pioneer spirit who wished to keep education under local control, and those who favor centralized state direction. Through the years, legislation has been passed which retreated to more local control. The battle rages around the power of the State Board of Education to regulate the content, direction and construction of buildings.

Under the Constitution as hereafter quoted, Vermont was the first state in the Union to provide a complete and plainly expressed system of education, which covered the educational needs of her citizens from the ABC's of the primary grades to the university grade of B.A. or Bachelor of Arts.

*SCHOOL DISTRICTS*

The first school law stated that: ''A school or schools shall be established in each town by the legislature for the convenient instruction of Youth, with such salaries to the Masters, paid by each town, making proper use of school lands in each town, thereby to enable them to instruct Youth at low Prices: - ought to be established by the Direction of the General Assembly''. And there was: ''An act for appointing and supporting schools. For the due encouragement of learning and the better regulating and ordering schools''. Under this act, the town had authority to vote at town meeting to divide a town into as many school districts as they thought convenient. Each town appointed one or more persons who together with the selectmen shall be trustees of the schools in the town, and they shall have broad powers.

In 1782 the district was established as the unit of school administration in towns. With a heavy rural population, towns had many school districts usually with a school in each district. As an example, in the town of Waterbury there were 16 school districts. Control over education in the district was held by a committeeman who exerted considerable power over which teacher should be hired, what books should be used and how the school should be operated. A school district could be established, abolished or united with another district. The town also had the power to set a citizen of one district into another, which occurred quite frequently. Fractional districts were sometimes established. In 1795 these powers were transferred to the district school committee.

The laws of 1797 prescribed the subjects to be taught in the common schools as "English, reading, writing and arithmetic". From 1782 to 1827, the unit of school administration was the town district with a district administrator. By 1840, there developed a great decrease in the rural population with people leaving the hilly farms, so many districts had to close. One district was joined with another until there existed a single district in the whole town. Thus by 1870 the need for a township school system became unnecessary, though it was permissive and passed as a palliative for something better than the district system.

### *UNION DISTRICTS*

In 1841, Union Districts were first authorized "for the purpose of maintaining a school, to be kept for the benefit of the older children of such associated districts". The foundation of the state's present extensive school system was developed in 1844 when power was granted to these union districts to provide for the teaching of the "sciences or higher branches of a thorough education, which may not by existing law, have been authorized".

### *INCORPORATED SCHOOL DISTRICTS*

Graded school districts evolved from the creation of the union districts; incorporated graded schools came into the picture by the evolution of the graded schools, being also known as incorporated school districts. Montpelier was the first incorporated school district granted by the General Assembly, and which was abolished in 1894 when the Village of Montpelier became a city. In 1914 there were twenty-eight incorporated school districts.

### *UNION SCHOOL DISTRICTS*

By 1970 if a union school district was organized to operate for grades kindergarten (or one) to twelve, it was known as a unified school district. Earlier contiguous districts were given power to form a union district for the benefit of the older children of the district. In

1935 the State Board of Education was given the authority to combine several school districts into a supervisory union of about fifty teachers. Any two or more towns of not less than thirty nor more than seventy schools could form a union and elect a superintendent.

### *DEMONSTRATION SCHOOL DISTRICT*

In 1971, the Commissioner of Education was given authority to operate a demonstration school district in a town which had voted approval. The town was required to pay the state a specified agreed-upon amount according to a formula. Agreement was made with the town of Middlesex but was finally repealed by the laws of 1973 due to dissatisfaction of the majority of the people of the town.

### *SCHOOL COMPACTS*

The New Hampshire-Vermont Interstate School Compact was authorized in 1967 so that towns on opposite sides of the Connecticut River could form a junior school district. This compact (which comprises about thirty pages) incorporates the laws of New Hampshire and Vermont.

The Interstate Compact of 1967 was conceived to maintain a closer cooperation and understanding among executives, legislators, professional educators and lay leadership on a nationwide basis at the state and local level. The Education Commission of the States (which comprises seven members of each party, one of whom shall be the governor, two from the state legislature, four appointed by the governor; and not to exceed ten non-voting members) may be selected by the steering committee.

### *TOWN SUPERVISORS OR SUPERINTENDENTS*

Early legislation directed that each town should elect at an annual meeting a town superintendent of common schools who was to visit each school at least once a year. He was to advise the teachers on the subjects to be taught, and on the management of the school.

In 1888, the position of town superintendent was repealed. A supervisor of schools was authorized, with power to issue permits (not to exceed three) to teach for a single term, with right of renewal for three more terms.

In 1906 by vote of the school districts concerned, a superintendent was authorized for two or more towns having as a total of not more than seventy nor less than thirty schools. By 1923, the town superintendent, the supervising principal, and the union superintendent were selected by the town school directors.

## *STATE SUPERINTENDENTS*

In 1880, a state superintendent of schools was elected biennially by the General Assembly; in 1888, this title was changed to Superintendent of Education.

A Commissioner of Education was appointed in 1917 by the State Board of Education, who could also appoint for an indefinite period as many state supervisors as might be found necessary to insure reasonable supervision of all public schools. In 1933, the Commissioner was appointed for an indefinite term, and his duties were to advise the supervising principals and the town and union superintendents. He could appoint a deputy commissioner and as many helping teachers as were needed; also he could employ teachers for one or two teacher training classes and for the School of Agriculture. These powers were broadened in 1947.

Each supervisory union board and each district school board was authorized in 1970 to elect a superintendent of schools with the advice of the Commissioner of Education.

## *STATE BOARD OF EDUCATION*

The General Assembly in 1827 established a Board of Commissioners for Common Schools which consisted of five members. Their duties were very limited and supervisory in nature, with the right to make a list of textbooks to be used in the schools. Previous to this act, the towns had full authority over schools, and when the Board began to exercise its powers over textbooks they soon reacted through the legislature by the repeal in 1833 of this act. By 1845 there seemed to be enough interest to enact a law which authorized a state superintendent, with very limited powers to inspect schools and make recommendations. These powers were somewhat broadened in 1849 when it was suggested that the state superintendent should awaken a broader and deeper interest in the subject of popular education.

By 1856 educational interest on a statewide basis had increased to the stage where a new board of education (comprising the governor, lieutenant governor and three others) was authorized. This sytem weathered the increased opposition until 1874, when the legislature abolished the board and set up a state superintendent of education which seemed to work well without political interference until 1915. In 1912 a new state board of education (comprising the governor, the superintendent of education, both ex-officio, and three appointed members) was authorized.

The entire board of education resigned in 1923, due to a new law which allowed the appointment of a board consisting of three persons appointed by the governor with the advice and consent of the senate. Their staggered terms were for six years each.

In 1947 the legislature had a new turn of mind and authorized a seven-person board, two of whom were to be women. Their term was for six years, and they were not eligible for reappointment. From this date up to the 1970's, feeling toward the progress of education has been directed to the superintendent or commissioner of education. During this period there have been six commissioners of education.

## *TRANSPORTATION*

Since the first census was taken in 1790 towns have lost population in the rural areas. As a result many town school districts were abandoned and eventually a single school district prevailed. The first transportation law was passed in 1882 which permitted the town school directors to provide for conveying pupils to and from the public schools at the expense of their respective towns. In 1888 the law was broadened whereby payment could be made for transportation of pupils who went to school in an adjoining town. The law was again extended in 1898 whereby - upon written application of ten resident taxpayers of the town - a sum (not to exceed twenty-five percent of school funds) could be used to pay for transportation of pupils whose residence was one and one-half miles or more from the school.

The payment of a reasonable sum for board in lieu of transportation was incorporated into the 1900 school laws. In 1915 the law prescribed that the State must pay one dollar per week per child transported.

The first provision for transportation of high school pupils was permitted in 1908 - if transportation was furnished to elementary pupils over the same route. In 1915 the law allowed transportation of pupils of the first two years of high school if they lived one and one-half miles or more from school, and in 1917 was extended to any high school pupil.

In 1955 an appropriation of $20,000.00 was distributed among the towns to help pay for pupil transportation. (In 1912 the law authorized up to twenty-five percent of the cost of transportation and board under certain exceptions; the 1915 legislature made an appropriation of $100,000.00 for this purpose). By 1973 the state funds available for such reimbursement amounted to $32,000,000.

The legislature in 1971 voted that each pupil be furnished in whole or in part transportation or board as the local board determined the need.

*SCHOOL FINANCING*

Funds for financing local school districts were in the early days raised by taxation, and were equally divided among the districts according to the number of children between the ages of four and twenty in each district. This age was later increased to 5 and reduced to 18. The districts were empowered to raise by taxation one-half of the money needed to operate the schools, and the other half could be raised by a tax on the ratable polls and real estate or by subscription in proportion to the number of children each person sent to the school district. Later, subscription was made obligatory.

A town tax of one percent on each person's grand list was increased to 12 percent in the period 1810 to 1884. In 1886 one-third of the tax money assessed by the selectmen was divided equally by them among the common and district schools in the town, without regard to the number of schools in the district, and the remainder was divided between the districts in proportion to the aggregate attendance of scholars of each district between the ages of four and twenty. Today in sate funding we use a quite similar method which we call ADM, avergage daily membership. Over the years different percentages in the distribution of funds have been made to towns instead of to districts.

Money to operate the schools could be raised in 1880 as usual except that expenses for fuel and teacher's board could be apportioned by the school board among the families of those attending school. Families also had to pay for textbooks. In 1890 a state tax of five cents on the dollar of the grand list was assessed, and the state reapportioned these funds to the towns based upon the number of legal pupils attending. The rate was increased gradually to ten cents in 1912.

To equalize educational opportunity, towns were required in 1906 to vote not less than one-fifth of the town's grand list (which sum increased to two-fifths by 1917 and three-fourths in 1947) for education. The 1963 act required the Commissioner of Taxes to establish fair market value of all taxable property in each town, so as to determine an equitable formula for the distribution of state aid to towns.

"The average daily membership for a school operated within a town or incorporated school district shall be calculated by dividing, (1) the aggregate number of days of membership of all pupils in the school during the school year by, (2) the number of days on which the school was officially in session during the school year."

Distribution of the state school tax was directed to the town or incorporated school district in the following manner:

(1) Town school district with a grand list under $10,000.00 shall

be entitled to an amount obtained by multiplying the number of equated pupils in such school by $15.00 diminished by the sum obtained by multiplying the grand list of such school district by 17 cents.

(2) If the grand list as above was between $10,000.00 and $15,000.00, the town was entitled to only 80 percent of the amount and method of (1).

(3) With a grand list of $15,000.00 to $20,000.00, a factor of 60 percent is used.

(4) With a grand list of $20,000.00 to $25,000.00, a factor of 40 percent is used.

(5) Above a grand list of $25,000.00, a factor of 20 percent is used.

(6) An equated pupil as used in this 1935 act is a term used to define a theoretical number of pupils determined by Mort's table, which equalizes the variations in size of schools and the differences in costs between elementary and secondary schools.

In 1967 the Commissioner of Education was authorized to determine the aggregate fair market value of all property in a town, including that which had been exempted. In 1969 the Miller Formula for the distribution of state aid was adopted. This formula required the determination of a district multiplier, which was defined as the district's equalized grand list per pupil in ADM divided by that for the entire state. The state aid per district was computed annually by the Commissioner for each district:

(1) As state aid for the next school year, each district shall be entitled to a percentage of its current expense of the school year preceding according to the following formula: State aid percent of the district's current expenditure equals 100 - 60 times the district multiplier. Beginning with the distribution of state aid funds by December 1, 1969, if the state aid to which a school district is entitled under subdivision (1) of this section is less than the amount payable under the 1963 limitation, the difference shall be reduced until such time as a school district shall receive that amount to which it is entitled under subdivision (1) of this section:

In 1969 districts shall receive up to 75 percent of 1963 allotments;

In 1970 districts shall receive up to 50 percent of 1963 allotments;

In 1971 districts shall receive up to 25 percent of 1963 allotments.

As of 1972 and thereafter, all districts shall receive the allotment due under subdivision (1) of this act." (Miller Formula, 1969)

In 1971 the definition of the ADM was changed to read: "The ADM of a district means the average enrollment of resident pupils of the district attending schools for the first 30 days of the school year in which the school was actually in session; it is the quotient obtained by dividing by 30 the aggregate membership of resident pupils in the school district during the first 30 days in which the school was actually in session but excluding pupils whose education was paid for by the department of social welfare." State aid was limited to the payment of the following items: transportation, advanced instruction, supervision and teachers' salaries.

Effective March 1, 1971 any school district could vote a special school tax of $8.00 (which would be a poll tax in addition to any other taxes) which was to be used to pay interest and indebtedness for school improvement bonds.

During the 1968 session of the legislature there appeared to be a considerable amount of dislike of being told by the State Board what type of school building should be built. In 1971 the legislature directed that the fiscal year should be from June 30 to July 1 of the following year, effective by July, 1979. Laws were passed from time to time limiting the amount of tuition which could be charged.

In 1825 a school fund was established from the amount of the funds accrued to the state from the late Vermont State Bank upon its closure. The funds were sequestered and granted to the towns for the benefit of the common schools (and no other use) to be managed as a school fund. Section 2 of the Law reads: "The amount of this state's funds accruing from the six percent on the net profits of the respective banks chartered by the state X X X is hereby sequestered for the benefit of the common schools. The State Treasurer is in charge of school funds which shall be accumulative. The accumulated school fund shall not be diminished, improved or appropriated to the use of the schools until the principal of said fund shall increase to a sum sufficient to yield an annual profit, and interest, adequate to defray the current expense of keeping a good, free school in each district in the respective towns".

## *HUNTINGTON FUND*

Arunah Huntington, a native of Roxbury, Vermont, when he died in 1877 left in his will $211,131.46 which he recommended be left in a bank until the earnings should amount to $100,000.00 per county; that the revenue arising from the aggregate capital then be divided equally among the several counties; that no one whose property valuation was less than one thousand dollars be assesed for school purposes; and that the usury laws of the state be repealed. Mr. Huntington changed his residence to Canada; some believed this was due to Vermont's usury laws.

## *WAR CLAIMS FUND*

The United States Government in 1904 reimbursed Vermont in the amount of $240,000.00 as Civil War Indemnity. This money was sequestered by the General Assembly and placed on deposit as a nucleus for a permanent school fund, though efforts were made to divert it.

## *SCHOLARSHIPS*

### *Senatorial*

By the Acts of 1892 a senator could nominate one student each to the University of Vermont and Middlebury College. An appropriation of $6,000.00 to the University of Vermont and $2,400.00 to Middlebury College was available in 1906. This act along with one to Norwich University which was recognized then as a military college, has been repealed.

By the Acts of 1953 senatorial scholarships were established which allotted the sum of $3,000.00 to each senator, from which he could grant scholarships of not more than $300.00 or less than $100.00 each to qualified, worthy and needy applicants. Unused grant money is turned over to the student assistance corporation.

### *National Guard*

A Vermont National Guard scholarship entitles its holder to free tuition at a Vermont university, college or technical institute supported in whole or in part by public funds appropriated from the State Treasury. By this 1967 Act, scholarships beyond high school were granted to sons and daughters of deceased members of the Vermont National Guard who since 1955 have been killed while on active or inactive duty.

### *Student Assistance Corporation*

This corporation, established by the Acts of 1965, consists of five members appointed by the governor with staggered terms of six years. The corporation has charge of the grants of scholarships made by the legislature to Vermonters. It also assists in the administration of the National Vocational Student Loan Insurance Act to provide low interest loans to students.

### *Incentive Grants*

Each qualified student whose family taxable income is less than $10,000.00 may apply for an incentive grant. There are cases of extreme need where this amount of taxable income may be exceeded if the board so votes. A loan not to exceed $1,000.00 per school year is available.

### *Honor Scholarships*

Up to 100 honor scholarships valued at $100.00 each awarded annually to high school seniors are based upon their scholastic excellence established by such examinations as the board may prescribe.

### *Town Scholarships*

A town may vote up to $80.00 for a scholarship to an institution of higher learning.

## *SCHOOL OPERATIONS AND CUSTOMS*

A teacher or principal (on request and in the presence of another teacher) may resort to any reasonable form of punishment including corporal punishment. (1912)

Secret societies in schools were forbidden in 1904. A teacher's institute was established in 1827. In 1906, teachers were allowed time not to exceed four days to be spent at teachers' institutes or conventions, for which an appropriation of $200.00 was authorized. A summer school was authorized for teachers.

## *HEALTH AND SAFETY*

In 1935, three percent of a school budget was designated to be used to improve the physical efficiency of children of indigent parents. This action included the purchase of milk, hot lunches for the indigent, glasses and dental services and tonsil removal. The school board had the job of determining which family should be classified as indigent.

In 1921 the State Board of Education was authorized to reimburse towns an amount not to exceed 50 percent of the cost of installing equipment and facilities for providing school lunches. The State

Board of Education was required in 1971 to adopt regulations governing grants from the federal government for school lunch programs as defined by federal law.

Books selected by the State Board of Education in 1856 included grammar, geography, arithmetic, and spelling. Later, textbooks of georgraphy and history were added. *Hall's Geography* and *History of Vermont* were intended to be used for ten years. By 1906 more liberal instruction was allowed, since subjects included English language, literature, higher mathematics, natural science, ancient and modern history, modern languages; also political science, commercial subjects, music, physical education, fine and mechanical arts.

Beginning in 1886, school directors were allowed to establish kindergartens for children under five years of age; and this age was raised to six years in the 1933 statutes.

## *SCHOOL DAY-TERM-AGE*

The school day was established in 1872 as having a minimum of three hours in the morning and three hours in the afternoon. Five days made a school week and four weeks a school month. At least twenty weeks of school were required. School districts had power to designate at their annual meeting the number of weeks for which schools should be maintained during the winter and summer. The school year was set as April first to the last of the following March. No child under five years was allowed to enroll. Every healthy child between 8 and 14 years was required to attend at least three months of school each year.

In 1906, the legal school age was from 5 to 18 years and children of these ages wer required to attend school. In 1894 a legal pupil was defined as a child between the ages of 5 and 21 years. In the same year, children under 16 who had not finished the 8th grade (unless excused) could not be employed on railroads, mining, manufacturing or in the delivery of messages by a corporation except during a vacation or outside of school hours. In 1935 the fiscal year was established as July 1 to June 30. The school year for secondary schools was set at 36 weeks. In 1971 all towns were required to have the same fiscal year (July 1 to June 30) by 1977. The laws of 1972 - due to the constitutional amendment defining a minor - established the school age of a legal pupil as from 6 years to 18 years. Also every school must operate at least 175 days each school year. The State Board of Education now sets the number of hours which constitute a school day.

## *RELIGION*

In 1872 the law stated that no money raised on the grand list shall hereafter be apportioned for the maintenance of strictly secular or religious schools. The school directors at a legal meeting may vote to grant the use of the school house for religious workshop, lectures or similar purposes when not needed for school purposes. After considerable argument over the use of public funds for secular schools, it was voted in 1970 to give pupils released time to attend religious services not on school property.

## *SCHOOL LUNCHES*

In 1947 the State Board of Education was authorized to reimburse towns a sum not to exceed fifty percent of the cost of installing facilities for providing school lunches. In 1969 the law was changed so that the State Board of Education may, from funds appropriated for the purpose to the Department of Education, award grants to school boards which establish and operate or supervise nonprofit food programs, provided the amount of any grant shall not be more than the annual amount necessary, in addition to the charge made for the meal and reimbursement from federal funds, to pay the actual cost of the meal.

Also at the same time they authorized the State Board of Education to adopt regulations which may provide that grants under state funds be allocated to all or to specifically designated food programs as defined under federal law, and shall provide for the grants to be made at a uniform rate per meal within an eligible food program.

In 1948 the attorney general ruled the matter of legality to disburse funds for school lunch programs is not conditioned on whether the child who is benefited is in attendance in public or nonprofit private school.

A bill in the 1974 legislature requiring all towns to provide a school lunch program was defeated.

## *SCHOOL CLASSIFICATION*

### *Graded Schools*

Schools maintained by a town for not less than 30 weeks, of four or more departments with four or more teachers, and under the control of one principal teacher, shall be a graded school. - 1876 law.

### *District High School*

District High School may direct the science or higher branches of study to be taught in such school.

### *Union School*

Contiguous school districts may form a Union School for the benefit of the older children of the district.

### *Town High School or Central School*

Town may establish one or more.

### *Elementary School*

Elementary School - described in 1906 as one performing the work prescribed in a nine year course of study.

### *High Schools or Academies*

High Schools or Academies were graded as follows:
First Class - 4 year course;
Second Class - 3 year course;
Third Class - 2 year course;
Fourth Class - 1 year course.

In 1933 a six to twelve year school was known as a rural school. A six to fourteen year school was an elementary school and a nine year school was known as an elementary school.

In 1935 secondary schools of the state were divided as follows:

Junior High School - having 3 courses, grades 7, 8, 9.
Junior-Senior High School - having six year course, 7th through the twelth grade.
Four-Year High School - grades 9 through twelve.
High School having two or more years.

## *ADVANCED EDUCATION*

### *County Grammar Schools*

Under the original town and county grants, grammar school lands were set aside in each county except Chittenden and Bennington and Windsor for the purpose of providing revenues for a County Grammar School. Beginning with the legislation for the establishment of a county grammar school in Norwich in 1785, schools were authorized up to 1836 in all counties except Grand Isle and Windham. These two counties did not have sufficient acreage set aside to finance such grammar schools.

At the present time the old Washington County Grammar School income is received by the Montpelier City School. In 1805 the Orange County Grammar School was established at Randolph Center. Other grammar schools were established as follows:

Peacham, Middlebury, St. Albans, Waterbury, Randolph, Guildhall, Montpelier, Johnson, Castleton, Richmond (the last in 1836).

## *TEACHER TRAINING CLASSES*

Sporadic teacher training classes were held by interested school superintendents from 1840 for many years. From 1894 to 1908 two-year certificates were given to graduates of teacher training courses at high schools and academies. Due to the shortages of qualified teachers, the legislature of 1910 authorized the establishment of teacher training courses in academies and high schools with a grant of $800.00 per teacher, with the proviso that the academies or schools matched this sum with $200.00.

In accordance with a special act of the General Assembly in 1876, a graded school, situated in a county with no normal school, may establish in connection with such school a teacher's training school. A 1917 act directed that a teacher's training class be established at high schools, seminaries and academies to train teachers for elementary schools. The State Board of Education was later allowed to employ teachers for one and two-year teacher training classes and at the State School of Agriculture.

The State empowered the State Board to employ a specialist. By the Acts of 1920 not less than three nor more than five two-year training classes were allowed, which resulted in courses at the University of Vermont, Castleton, Johnson and Lyndon. Up to forty teacher training classes were held throughout the state in private academies and high schools in one ten-year period.

## *NORMAL SCHOOLS*

The need for more trained teachers was realized in 1868 when the Orange County Grammar School at Randolph Center was established as a Normal School. At about the same time the Lamoille County Grammar School at Johnson became a Normal School, followed the next year by the Rutland County Grammar School at Castleton.

A Board of Normal School Examiners, Supervisors and a Commissioner was created in 1896 consisting of the Superintendent of Education, ex officio, and two persons appointed by the Governor. During the 1908 legislature, the bureaucrats got their foot in the door and supplanted the Board with the State Board of Education.

The Randolph Normal School in 1911 became the State Agricultural School. The Theodore N. Vail Agricultural School in Lyndon was established by the legislature with an appropriation of $20,000.

## *VERMONT STATE COLLEGES*

In 1961 the legislature established a public corporation known as "Vermont State Colleges, which shall plan, supervise, administer and operate the facilities for education above the high school level supported in whole or in substantial part with state funds; however, while the corporation shall maintain cooperative relations with the University of Vermont and State Agricultural College, nothing in this act shall give the corporation any responsibility for the planning, supervision, administration or operation of the University. The corporation shall own the real estate and personal property of the Castleton, Johnson and Lyndon Teachers' Colleges and the Vermont Agricultural and Technical Institute and of any other state operated institutions of higher learning which may be established.

The corporation is governed by a board of nine trustees appointed by the governor, with staggered terms of six years. The governor is an ex-officio non-voting member as well as the presiding officer of the corporation.

It should be noted here that the Randolph Agricultural and Technical Institute at Randolph Center had an interesting development. In 1805 it was established as the Orange County Grammar School; in 1867 it became the Randolph Normal School; and in 1911 it became the State Agricultural School.

## *OTHER TRAINING CLASSES*

Reverend Samuel Reed Hall started an institution for the training of teachers in Concord in 1823, which was later chartered by the state and became a county grammar school.

During the period 1785 to 1788 a Quaker Town Clerk in the town of Danby conducted a class to aid young men who desired to teach.

In 1814 Emma Hart Willard started a school in Middlebury which afforded instruction to young ladies, giving them a knowledge of subject matter rather than a professional knowledge of teaching.

In 1835 the Board of Trustees of Hinesburg Academy was granted the authority to confer degrees "on all such pupils as shall have acquired a thorough knowledge of such elementary studies as such board shall prescribe, preparatory to their becoming thorough and efficient teachers of common schools".

In 1840 the Reverend Samuel R. Hall organized another teacher training class this time at Craftsbury Academy.

In Brattleboro in 1847, Reverend Addison Brown, a County Superintendent of Schools, conducted a teachers' institute for two years.

A teacher training class was organized at Royalton Academy in 1856. The principal of St. Johnsbury Academy maintained a teacher

training course in 1858. A teacher training class was operated in connection with the Orange County Grammar School at Randolph Center. In connection with the Bennington graded school a teacher training department was organized in 1871.

## *TEACHER CERTIFICATION, PAY AND RETIREMENT*

The first act providing for the examination and certification of teachers was passed 1827. The duties of the superintendent committee were to require full and satisfactory evidence of the good moral character of all instructors...to satisfy themselves, by personal examination, of the literary qualifications for teaching, and the capacity of granting schools to issue certificates to qualified teachers, none of whom was entitled to compensation unless he possessed a valid certificate.

This examining power was imposed in 1845 upon the town superintendent or the county superintendent, who could grant certificates valid for one year. A State Teachers Association was formed in 1850 which probably had some influence upon the certification of teachers. Authority for giving examinations changed several times in the next thirty years. In the early days teachers boarded around the neighborhood at meager pay.

A county examining board of three persons, the county superintendent and two practical teachers, was authorized in 1876. Incidentally, discrimination was shown, since men had to be twenty years of age to take an examination, whereas women could get by at the age of eighteen. Such licenses were then good for five years.

In 1880 the town superintendent was required to hold two public examinations annually, in order for teachers to teach in town schools. A certificate of graduation from the lower course of a normal school or of a training school department of a graded school was deemed acceptable for a license to teach in the common school for a period of five years. Graduation from higher courses entitled the teacher to a certificate to teach for ten years. Life certificates were first granted under the laws of 1888. Until 1906, only those who had held two five-year certificates were eligible; after that year, the range of life certification was considerably extended.

By the laws of 1971, the State Board of Education could regulate and define teacher's certificates as follows: "A professionally certified teacher is the holder of a professional three-year certificate, a professional probationary certificate, a professional standard certificate, or a professional continuing certificate."

In 1933, the Teachers Retirement Board was established; a 1972 law authorized retirement if:

(1) A teacher had reached the age of sixty or completed thirty years of creditable service;
(2) A teacher must become a member of the retirement system within one year.

## *COLLEGES*

As stated elsewhere, Vermont was the first state to authorize under her constitution a complete education for her citizens from the primary grades through the university.

On the sixteenth of August, 1774 a mandamus order of George the Third, by the Grace of God, of Great Britain, France and Ireland and Defender of the Faith, granted to the Governor of King's College a tract of land in Cambridge and Johnson, County of Gloucester. The condition of the grant was an annual rental of six shillings and eight pence in lieu of quit rent. The term of the lease to the premises was for three lives or any term not exceeding ninety-nine years. Another grant was made to King's College (now Columbia University) founded in 1754. This grant made in March 1770 was for the township of Kingsland, now Washington. All the patents declared that the grants should be null and void, "if the grantees do not within three years settle one family to every 1,000 acres and within three years plant and effectually cultivate at least three acres for every fifty of such, as is susceptible to cultivation". If Columbia ever had possession, she had lost it, since records do not appear to substantiate the grant conditions.

All towns chartered in Vermont after 1777 contained a grant for a university or college. On the founding of the University of Vermont in 1791, these grants were transferred to the University of Vermont. In addition, the University of Vermont has received gifts of land in several townships. Today the University has an aggregate of about 30,000 acres of land, which is gradually being sold (1974).

Eleazar Wheelock, the first President of Dartmouth College, wrote a letter to the General Assembly of the State of Vermont for consideration at their June, 1778 meeting held in Bennington. He requested that the state take the University under its friendly patronage and that the glebe lands of the Propagation of the Gospel in Foreign Parts be sequestered for the benefit, use and support of the college. The legislature voted to take the college under its patronage.

Wheelock was evidently quite interested in having a state capital near the college. The Capital of New Hampshire at the time was at Exeter, some distance away, where state representation was by population rather than by towns as prevailed in Vermont. The sixteen towns of New Hampshire had split off at the time and joined Vermont, so he felt that the Vermont Capital could be in a town near the college. Not long afterwards the sixteen towns rejoined the State of New Hampshire, so Eleazar Wheelock's dream was not fulfilled. However he was successful in receiving a grant embracing 23,000 acres for Dartmouth in the town of Wheelock.

On October 17, 1785, the Honorable Elijah Paine proposed that a college or university be established at Williams Town which action was turned down by legislature. If the University idea had been given more serious consideration earlier, the grant of land to Dartmouth would probably never have been voted and the proposition for a university in the State of Vermont would not have been dropped as a subject from its later constitution.

### *STATE AGRICULTURAL COLLEGE*

Vermont's great senator, Justin S. Morrill, was the author of the Act named after him which established the agricultural colleges throughout the nation. By the Morrill Act, Vermont received 30,000 acres of public land for each of the two senators and each of the three representatives to which it was entitled. The state sold this western land for about ninety cents per acre. An attempt was made in 1863 to join Vermont's three colleges into a single institution, which would be joined by a college of agriculture supported by the income from the $135,500.00 derived from the sale of the federal land grant. Since the attempt to unite the colleges failed, in 1864 the legislature asked for a subscription of $100,000.00 to supplement the federal land grant funds in the formation of a Vermont Agricultural College. The subscription funds did not materialize, and the legislature did not appear ready to appropriate the funds for agricultural education, so the alternative measure taken in 1865 was to form a new corporation known as the University of Vermont and the State Agricultural College. The income from the Morrill Act was given to this corporation, as well as the annual grants from the United States government authorized by subsequent legislation.

In 1867 Congress passed the Hatch Act which provided funds to establish in the Morrill Land-grant Colleges a department known as the Agricultural Experiment Station. The object of this act was to carry on researches into and experiments upon agricultural subjects. Vermont had in the previous year appropriated $3,500.00 in support of an experiment station, which sum was increased by an annual appropriation of $35,000.00 of federal funds.

### *VOCATIONAL EDUCATION*

The State Board of Education was authorized in 1917 to direct vocational courses for agriculture, manual arts, commercial subjects and domestic science and to accept federal aid for vocational education.

"High Schools shall include within the course of study, as the Commissioner may prescribe, one or more of the following subjects: manual training, domestic economy or agriculture". (1933)

The State in 1963 appropriated $40,000.00 to the Education Department to purchase rehabilitation services. The Department of Labor and Industry was approved as the agency for business engaged in apprentice training. Vocational courses in high school may be in the areas of agriculture, industrial arts, trade and industrial business or homemaking. (1970)

A school district not having a vocational course desired by a pupil must since 1971 pay full tuition to the school which the pupil attends.

## *EDUCATION OF HANDICAPPED CHILDREN*

The state recognized early in 1872 the need for special education of the handicapped by appropriating a sum of $2,000.00 for the instruction of idiots and feeble-minded children of indigent parents at a school in Boston. Eight years later schools at Hartford and Northhampton were added to the list for such instruction. Previously, the Governor in 1840 was designated as a chairman of a committee for the deaf, dumb, blind, feebleminded from indigent families. Suitable equipment for such education was started in the school in 1904 by a small appropriation of $600.00.

Realizing the need of a nearby institution for such instruction the state school for feebleminded was established in 1912 with the governor as chairman ex-officio of a committee of five who served without pay. The next step occurred in 1953 when the sum of $100.00 per child was allowed for transportation per school year. An advisory council of the directors of agencies dealing with children including the Commissioner of Education was established in the same year and is now known as the Advisory Council on Special Education. A Director of Special Education was also authorized.

In 1953 a handicapped child was defined as follows, "any educable child inhabitant of the state under 21 years of age, whose educational needs cannot be adequately provided for through the usual facilities and services of the public schools, school districts or state institutions because of physical or mental deviations of such child".

The State Board of Education was authorized to enter into reciprocal agreements with other states in this area.

### *EDUCATIONAL TELEVISION*

A resolution was adopted by the legislature in 1953 authorizing a committee to make a study of educational television. Several joint resolutions were presented each session until a bill was finally passed. Much of the delay can perhaps be ascribed to the fact that there was some question whether this should be undertaken by a private corporation, by the University of Vermont or directly as a separate state entity.

The 1967 Act gave authority to the University of Vermont and State Agricultural College to proceed with the construction of a television station, for which the state authorized a bond issue of $2,334,329.00 to be reduced by any amount that the University shall receive from pending grants from the federal government in excess of $450,000.00. The station was established at Fort Ethan Allen with transmitter stations on prominent mountain peaks. The appropriation for the operation of the station for the fiscal year 1974 was $560,628.00 and $137,500.00 was authorized to convert to colored television.

### *DRIVER EDUCATION AND TRAINING*

A driver education and training course was authorized by the 1966 legislature and approved by the departments of education and motor vehicles. It consisted of at least thirty hours of classroom instruction and six hours behind the wheel. The instruction is made available to those pupils whose parents or guardians are residents of the state. The pupil must have reached his fifteenth birthday and be enrolled in a public or private school approved by the state board of education.

The state will pay to each school for this purpose the reasonable cost thereof. The appropriation for driver training in 1968 was $117,760.00 was increased to $660,269.00 for fiscal year 1974.

### *PRIVATE SCHOOLS*

Burr and Burton Seminary, Manchester - 1820
First Co-ed school in Vermont.
Bishop Hopkins Hall, Burlington - 1888
A diocesan boarding and day school.
Goddard Seminary, Barre - 1863
Lyndon Institute, Lyndon Center - 1867
Montpelier Seminary, Montpelier - 1865
The legislature gave a charter for the new school to take the place of the one in Newbury and called it the Vermont Conference Seminary and Female College
The Putney School

South Royalton
Peacham Academy - 1795
St. Johnsbury Academy - 1843
Stowe Preparatory School - 1961
Troy Conference Academy - 1834 (by Methodists)
Vermont Academy, Saxtons River - 1876 (by Baptists)
College of St. Joseph the Provider
Community College of Vermont, Montpelier - 1970
St. Michaels College, Winooski - 1903
Trinity College, Burlington
Marlboro College, Marlboro
Bennington College, Old Bennington
Windham College, Putney
Goddard College, Plainfield
Vermont College, Montpelier
Royalton College
Middlesex College
  Operated only a short time.
Castleton Medical School
Norwich University, Norwich - 1819
  Moved to Northfield - 1866
Middlebury College, Middlebury - 1800
Castleton College
Johnson College, Johnson - 1828
Lyndon College
Randolph
Champlain College, Burlington
  A two year college
Concord School of Business
Green Mt. College, Poultney
St. Joseph College, Bennington

## *COMMUNITY COLLEGE*

The Community College had its beginning in Vermont in December 1968 as a result of the Vermont Technical Education Feasibility study. In May 1970 the New Career Conference urged the U.S. Office of Economic Opportunity to fund a community college demonstration project. In August 1970 Governor Deane C. Davis issued an executive order, No. 27, creating the Vermont Regional Community College Commission.

Three regional offices were established; Northeast, Central and Southeastern with the present headquarters located in the Town of Berlin.

The Carnegie Corporation of New York City made an award of

$98,000.00 for the Community College. In September 1972 the College was merged with the Vermont State College system.

In March the Community College received an award of $75,000.00 from the Jessie Smith Noyes Foundation. This gift was followed in April, when the legislature made an appropriation of $50,000.00 for the fiscal year 1974. The Community College received in July 1973 the sum of $110,000.00 from the U.S. Office of Education as financial aid. The Office of Health, Education and Welfare made a grant for a study of the improvement of Postsecondary Education for the years 1974-75. The legislature in 1974 appropriated the sum of $175,000.00 for the fiscal year 1975.

The Community College owns no buildings and brings its classes to the student using local schools, offices, churches, factories and other community buildings for classroom space. This system of education also avoids the high cost of campus construction.

This type of college is well adapted to aid those who have never had an opportunity to go to college and to those who for one reason or another dropped out.

The subjects taught vary from home heating and plumbing, welding and automotive repair to psychology, data processing and principles of management. Not all students seek degrees. For those who do, the College offers the Associate degree of study: Human Services, Administrative Services, and general studies. Each candidate desiring a degree receives personal consultation with trained site staff to outline what the student will accomplish in order to receive a degree. When a student has completed a program of study, a degree or certificate is granted based upon the skills and abilities a student has acquired rather than on the number of courses taken.

When a student needs credits to transfer to another institution, a formula based on the broad guide lines of the Carnegie Unit and recommended by the Vermont State College System is used.

Tuition is $30.00 per course to help instructional costs only. Financial aid grants and work/study opportunities are available to help students to meet the expense of attending the College.

From the Publications of the Vermont Community College, 1974.

### *SUPERINTENDENTS OF SCHOOLS*

1845 Horace Eaton, Superintendent of Common Schools
1850 Charles G. Burnham, Superintendent of Common Schools
1851 Vacant
1856 J. Sullivan Adams, Secretary, State Board of Education
1867 A. E. Rankin, Secretary, State Board of Education
1870 John H. French, Secretary, State Board of Education
1874 Edward Conant, State Superintendent of Education

1880 Justus Dartt, State Superintendent of Education
1892 Mason S. Stone, State Superintendent of Education
1900 Walter E. Ranger, State Superintendent of Education
1905 Mason S. Stone, State Superintendent of Education
1915 Mason S. Stone, Commissioner of Education*
1916 Milo B. Hillegas
1921 Clarence Dempsey
1931 Francis Bailey
1940 Ralph Noble
1949 A. John Holden
1965 Richard A. Gibboney
1967 Daniel O'Connor, Acting
1968 Harvey B. Scribner
1970 Daniel O'Connor, Acting
1971 Joseph Oakey
1972 Robert A. Withey

### *EDUCATION SELECTED BIBLIOGRAPHY*

Andrews, Edward D., *The County Grammar Schools and Academies of Vermont*, Montpelier: Vermont Historical Society, Vol. IV, #3, 1936.
Brown, Addison, *Elgin Garden, Columbia College, New Hampshire Grants*, Lancaster, Pennsylvania: New Era Printing Company, 1968.
Stillwell, Lewis Dayton, *Migration from Vermont, 1776-1860*, Vermont Historical Society, Vol. V, #2, 1937.
Stone, Mason Serino, *History of Education, State of Vermont*, Montpelier: Capital City Press, 1933.
Swift, Thomas, *History of the Town of Middlebury*, Rutland: Charles E. Tuttle, reprint, 1971.
Williams, J. C., *History and Map of Danby*, Rutland: McLean & Robbins, 1869.
Vermont, *Laws of State of Vermont, 1779 to 1975.*
Vermont, *Department of Education Reports.*
Childs, Hamilton, ed., *Washington County Gazetteer*, New York, Syracuse: The Syracuse Journal Company, 1889.

*From this date on the same title was kept.

# Government

*FRENCH SEIGNIORIES ON LAKE CHAMPLAIN*

The French colony in Quebec made some early settlements which never endured. Samuel de Champlain first discovered the Lake to which he gave his name in 1609, just one year after Hendrick Hudson sailed into New York Harbour. In the spring of 1666 Sieur de la Motte completed a fort on Isle La Motte and on July 26 dedicated it to Saint Anne. This settlement was given up however when the English defeated the French in Canada.

Peter Kalm, a Swedish professor and naturalist, came down Lake Champlain in 1749 and landed at what is now known as Chimney Point. He stated that he found "quite a settlement, a stone windmill and a fort with five or six small cannon mounted, the whole enclosed by an embankment".

"Within the enclosure was a neat church and throughout the settlement, well kept gardens, with some good fruit, apples, plums and currants. During the next ten years this settlement was extended north on the Lake some four miles; the remains of old cellar holes, and gardens still to be seen, indicate a more thickly settled street than occupies it now". Within four miles of Chimney Point, there are still some cellar holes in the Daughters of the American Revolution State Park which undoubtedly are some of those mentioned by Kalm.

Under the French feudal system the seigniories owned homage to the Crown and the tenants rendered fealty to the seignor.

The Seigniories in Vermont were laid off, beginning with the oldest one "to Sieur Contrecour, fils on July 7, 1734, beginning at the mouth of the Riviere aux Loutres (Otter Creek) one league and a half above; and one league and a half below, making two leagues in front by three leagues in depth together with so much of said Riviere aux Loutres as is included therein with three Islands or Islets which are in front of said concession and depend thereon".

"To Sieur de la Periere on the banks of Lake Champlain beginning at the mouth of the Ouynouski (Winooski) one league above and one league below making three leagues in depth with the extent of said river which will be found comprehended therein together with the Islands and Buttresses adjacent.

"To Sieur Beaubois, Jr. on July 1734, two leagues in front by three leagues in depth together with the peninsula which is found in front of said lands." (Now known as Hog Island, Swanton.)

North of the la Periere grant, "to Lieutenant General Pierre Rambault on east side containing four leagues deep, the said four leagues commencing as descending the lake, from the bounds of the seigniory of granted Sieur de la Pierre, on the 6th of July 1734 in which is included the river called La Moille (LaMoille) with the Isles, Islets and Buttresses adjacent". The price was ninety thousand pounds (livres) half in gold and silver specie and one half in merchandise. In 1739 a French order in Council stated that if land was not settled and cultivated that it would be forfeited by the seignor. The seignors could not get families to settle these seigniories because there were no French guns to protect them. Captain de La Pierre sold his grant to residents of the Colony of New York for 90,000 livres. (About $18,000.00.)

"A grant was made to Sieur Douville (which lay north of Sieur Rembaults) on October 8, 1736 which was described as two leagues in front by three leagues deep on the east shore of Lake Champlain".

"In 1743 the King being at Versailles *** his majesty has granted to M. Hocquart a tract about one league in front by five leagues in depth, situated in said colony on Lake Champlain opposite Fort St. Frederic, bounded on the west by the said Lake, east by uncontested lands, north by a line drawn east and west, and south by a line parallel to this, which two lines form the division of lands to be conceded at a quit rent. The requirements were that he was to preserve timber of all description for his Majesty's ships, to inform His Majesty of all mines and minerals; to allow roads for public convenience, to allow beaches free to all fishermen and to make any land available for forts, garrisons, arsenals."

"In 1745 the King again favored his Intendant with an additional grant this time to the north of Chimney Point, bringing the total acreage to 115,000. Monsieur Hocquart was replaced by Francois Begot in January 1748 and recalled to France." In 1763 these lands were sold to Michale de Lothbinere and were described as the lands now embracing the towns of Panton, Addison and Bridport.

## *STATE GOVERNMENT - Then and Now.*

The young state got along with a treasurer, secretary of state, an auditor and someone in charge of military affairs and someone to collect taxes. Since then especially over the past twenty years the number of departments and special boards have multiplied rapidly. The reasons for some of the changes may be ascribed to the desire of the governor or the legislature to get rid of a department head or a member of a board. Boards were changed in number and the name of the department was given a new face though the duties remained the same as previously.

One of the first extensive changes in government occurred in 1923 under the governorship of Redfield Proctor. The Little Hoover Commission in 1959 made many recommendations into structure changes in government. The greatest change came in 1970 and 1971 when the departments of: Agency of Development and Community Affairs, the Agency of Human Services and the Agencies of Environmental Conservation and the Agency of Administration were authorized by the legislature as a result of requests by Governor Deane C. Davis.

*Agency of Development and Community Affairs - 1970*

Secretary and Advisory Board of Five persons.
- Planning Division
- Administrative Division
- Department of Housing and Community Affairs
- Department of Development
  - Division of Historic Sites
- Information and Travel Division
  - Joined to the Agency for administration; Boards of Architects, Land Surveyors and Real Estate Commision.

*Agency of Human Services - 1970*

Secretary
- Administrative Services Division
- Planning Division
  - Human Services Board (5)
- Department of Corrections
  - Director of Research and Program Planning
  - Director of Probation and Parole
  - Supervisor of Windsor State Prison
  - Director of Community Correctional Centers
  - Director of Drug and Alcohol Treatment Program
  - Superintendent of St. Albans Correctional Center
  - Superintendent of Weeks School
  - Board of Parole
- Department of Health
  - State Health Board (8)

Commissioner of Health and Indigent Tuberculosis Persons
Chief Medical Examiner
Hospital Advisory Council (10)
Plumbers Examining Board
Department of Mental Health
Superintendent of Brandon Training School
Superintendent of Vermont State Hospital
Director of Mental Health Programs
Department of Rehabilitation
Division of Alcohol and Drug Abuse
Alcohol Rehabilitation Board (5)
Drug Rehabilitation Board (5)
Division for the Blind and Visually Handicapped
Division of Vocational Rehabilitation
Department of Social Welfare
Director of Income Maintenance
Director of Medical Services
Director of Quality Control
Office on Aging
Advisory Board (15)
Office of Child Development
Office of Economic Opportunity
Advisory Board (8)

*Agency of Administration*
Department of Budget and Management
Advisory Committee on Administration Coordination (9)
Department of Finance
Department of Personnel
Department of Taxes
Public Records Division
Advisory Board (5)
Purchasing Division
State Buildings Division
Board (5)
For administration purposes; Connecticut River Valley Flood Control Commission, State Employees Compensation Review Board, Supervisor of Unorganized Towns and Gores.

*Agency of Environmental Conservation - 1971*
Administrative Services Division

*Planning Division*
Environmental Board (9)
Air Quality Variance Board (5)

Division of Environmental Protection
  Mobile Court Advisory Commission (5)
Department of Fish and Game
  Board (7)
Department of Forests and Parks
  Board (3)
  Director of Forests
  Director of Parks
  Camels Hump Advisory commission (17)
    Forest Festival Week Committee (9)
    Northeastern Forest Fire Protection Commission (3)
    Board on National Forests. (Department Heads)
    Pesticides Advisory Board (9)
  Interagency Committee on Natural Resources
Division of Recreation
  Board (3)
State Natural Resources Council (11)
Department of Water Resources
  Board (3)
  Water Supply and Pollution Control
  Management and Engineering
  State Geologist
  Vermont Whey Pollution Abatement Authority (5)
  River Classification Authority (7)

*Departments with dates of establishment.*

*Agriculture*

1870 - State Board of Agriculture, Manufacturing and Mining
1878 - Separate department under a State Superintendent of Agricultural Affairs
1880 - Vermont Board of Agriculture
1892 - Absorbed the Board of Cattle commissioners, named to Board of Agriculture for Vermont
1908 - Board of Agriculture and Forestry. Commisioner of Agriculture appointed by the board.
1910 - Commissioner of Agriculture made ex-officio Inspector of Nurseries, Apiaries and State ornithologist
1917 - Livestock Commissioner added, name changed to Office of the *Commissioner of Agriculture*
1923 - Department of Agriculture which included Agriculture and Forestry with Commissioner of Agriculture ex-officio Creamery Inspector.
1935 - State Ornithologist position transferred to Fish and Game Service

1937 - Commissioner of Weights and Measure transferred from Public Service and Division of Standards established.

*Aeronautics*

1945 - Vermont Aeronautics Board (3) created

*Adjutant General*

1789 - Office created

1821 - Name change to Office of Adjutant and Inspector General

1900 - Absorbed the office of Quartermaster General and Inspector General

*Banking and Insurance*

Banking

1896 - Commission to Inspect Banks

1831 - Name changed to Bank Commissioner

1839 - State Banking Commissioner office created

1906 - Bank Commissioner took over duties of Inspector of Finance

1923 - Banking and Insurance consolidated into a department

Insurance

1852 - Board of Insurance comprised, Secretary of State, Treasurer, Auditor

1862 - Auditor dropped from Board

1904 - Name changed to Insurance Commissioner

1917 - Created the Office of Insurance Commission

1923 - Transferred to Department of Banking and Insurance.

*Education*

1845 - State Superintendent of Common Schools created

1856 - Abolished State Superintendent and created Board of Education

1874 - Board Abolished. State Superintendent elected by legislature

1908 - State Board of Education created

1912 - State Board abolished. Board of Education created with power to appoint a Superintendent of Education

1915 - Name change to State Board of Education

1923 - Department of Education created, administered by a State Board that appoints the Commissioner of Education

The education department has several advisory councils. Alcohol and Drug Abuse (8), Special Education (38) Vocational and Technical Education (31), Arts and Crafts Council (5), Vermont State Educational Advisory Council (17)

*Employment Security*

Created in 1936, Operates an Employment Service and Unemployment Service, an Employment Security Advisory Board of ten persons. In 1935 the legislature passed an act No. 164 accepting the provisions of Congress to establish a Vermont State Employment Service, which was placed under the aegis of the Commissioner of Finance. All but about ten percent of the cost of operating the department comes from federal funds.

*Finance Inspector*

1860 - Created to help State Auditor and Treasurer

*Finances*

1923 - Created-Administered by the Commission of Finance-included Tax, Purchasing Agent and Banking and Insurance.
1927 - Governor became ex-officio Commissioner of Finance.
1939 - Abolished, duties given to State Treasurer and Auditor Accounts

*Fire Marshal*

1917 - Established with Commissioner of Insurance ex-officio in charge
1967 - Transferred to Public Safety. Now Department of Fire Prevention

*Highways*

1898 - State Highway Commissioner created
1921 - State Highway Board replaced the above position
1923 - Department of Highways created with a State Highway Board.

*Historic Sites Commission*

1937 - Hubbardton Battlefield Commission
1947 - Vermont Historic Sites Commission
1961 - Name changed to Board of Historic Sites
1970 - Absorbed in the Agency of Development and Community Affairs.

*Labor and Industry*

1912 - Office of Factory Inspector
1915 - Industrial Accident Board
1917 - Office of Commissioner of Industries
1923 - Under Public Service with the Weights and Measures

1925 - Separate Department of Industrial Relations - Renamed Department of Labor and Industry.
1967 - Department of Labor and Industry
State Apprenticeship Council (10)
Board to Award Compensation to State Employees (3)
Electrician's licensing Board (5)
Occupational Safety and Health Review Board (3)
Passenger Tramway Board (5)
Arbitration Board (4)
Industrial Safety Advisory Council (as many as deemed necessary)
Labor Emergency Board (as many as deemed necessary)
Wage Board (6)

*Libraries*

1894 - Board of Library Commissioners
1908 - Authority of Commissioners repealed
1912 - Name changed to Free Public Library commission
1923 - commission abolished, placed under State Board of Education
1937 - The Free Public Library Commission restored
1960 - Name changed to Free Public Library Service
1970 - The Free Public Library Service joined with the Vermont State Library to form the Department of Libraries.
Library Board (3)
State Librarian
Director of Extension Service
Law and Document Librarian

*Liquor*

1934 - Liquor Control Board (3)
1959 - Department of Liquor Control with a Commissioner.

*Livestock commission*

1912 - Commission established
1917 - Placed in Department of Agriculture.

*Military*

1789 - Office of Adjutant General Created.

*Motor Vehicle*

1904 - Secretary of State served as Register of Motor Vehicles.
1925 - Motor Vehicle Bureau established under Secretary of State

1927 - Motor Vehicle Department established
Dealers' Advisory Registration Board (3)

*Personnel Department*

1941 - Personnel Board (3)
1947 - Department of Personnel
1971 - Department placed in the Agency of Administration

*Public Safety*

1925 - State Police
1947 - Department of Public Safety
State Police
Civil Defense Division
State Fire Marshal
Boxing Control Board (3)
Vermont Law Enforcement Training Council

*Department of Public Service*

1856 - Vermont Railroad Commission
1908 - Public Service Commission established
1960 - name change to Public Service Board (3)
Advisory Rate Setting Committee (5)
Natural Gas and Oil Resources Board. (5)

*Planning*

1935 - State Planning Board (7)
1945 - Placed in the Development Commission

*Publicity*

1910 - Publicity Bureau
1930 - Name changed to Publicity Service
1935 - Became part of Department of Conservation and Development
1945 - Became part of Development Commission

*Taxes*

1820 - State Equalization Board
1882 - Name change to Office of Commissioner of State of Taxes
1923 - Placed in the Department of Finance
1933 - Department of Finance which included the Commissioner of Taxes, Commissioner of Banking and Insurance and the Purchasing Agent
1939 - Abolished Department of Finance
1960 - Department of Taxes created.

*Water Resources*

1935 - State Planning Board
1947 - Water Resources Board
1960 - Department of Water Resources
1970 - Placed in Agency of Environmental Conservation.

*Weights and Measures*

1910 - Department of Weights and Measures
1923 - Combined with Public Service Commission
1933 - Moved to Department of Industries
1937 - Transferred to Agricultural Department as Division of Standards.

## *COURTS*

The organization and structure of Vermont Courts has undergone many changes since their original establishment in the Vermont Constitution of 1777. The Constitution stated that Courts of Justice should be maintained in every county of the state; and the judges of the Supreme Court shall be Justices of the Peace throughout the State; and they shall be the several judges of the County Courts in their respective counties by virtue of their office.

The Acts of 1793 read in part: "elect judges of the Supreme Court and several County and Probate Courts, Sheriffs and Justices of the Peace." This section was later amended to read:"The assistant judges of the County Court shall be elected by the Freemen of their respective counties as were the sheriffs and the High Bailiffs. The judges shall be elected by the Freemen of their respective Probate Districts." Each town was allocated a number of justices of the peace from one to 15, depending upon its population.

The number of the Supreme Court Judges and the County Court Judges under our present Constitution are ex officio Justices of the Peace, and are elected by the legislature.

The number of the Supreme Court Judges has varied as follows: 1778-1786 - 5; 1786-1825 - 3; 1825-1827 - 4; 1827-1846 - 5; 1846-1849 - 6. Under the Acts of 1849 the number of justices of the Supreme Court was reduced to three because of the institution of Circuit Courts, which lasted until 1857. Four judicial circuits were authorized in 1949 and each year the General Assembly elected a Circuit Judge for each of the four judicial districts.

In 1857, all the judicial powers and duties, both in law and in equity, which appertained to circuit judges, were thereafter vested in and incumbent upon the Supreme Court, which again was comprised of one chief judge and five assistant judges. Before 1906, except during the brief period from 1850 to 1857, the justices of the

Supreme Court had performed the dual role in the court system, not only in the Supreme Court, but also they presided over the county courts.

The first chief judge of the Supreme Court was Moses Robinson, an office which he held until 1781. In that year not having been elected as the chief judge, he refused to accept the position of second judge, in which action he was joined by others. However, in the 1782 election he was elected a chief judge after reconsideration.

Superior Judges were established in 1906 to preside over county courts. These judges rotate in the counties. Formerly under the prevailing custom, a superior judge might become a chief justice if he lived long enough. It was also the general custom that judges would pass on in line of seniority. In 1913 Governor Fletcher broke the usual tradition and designated Judge George M. Powers as chief justice over three judges with greater seniority. This action stirred quite a controversy in the press; however, it gradually subsided. The tradition was again shattered by him in 1914. A more recent case was when Governor Philip H. Hoff appointed F. Ray Keyser, Sr. to the Supreme Court, thus by-passing Superior Judge Natt L. Divoll.

### *Municipal Courts*

Municipal Courts grew out of a law passed in 1788, which established the charter of the City of Burlington. Section 20 of that charter read as follows: "There shall be chosen annually from the legal voters of the city, a recorder and so many justices of the peace.....and a representative to the General Assembly. The recorder shall have all the powers and jurisdiction that a justice of the peace has within the County of Chittenden." The title recorder, which means a magistrate, comes from its use in English courts.

The first city charter of Vergennes, voted by the General Assembly in 1788, established a city court. The mayor and first two aldermen were elected at the annual meeting to be judges of the court.

From 1852 to 1915 there were fourteen municipal courts established by special acts. They included the villages of Rutland, Bellows Falls, Bennington, Newport, Brattleboro; the cities of Barre and Montpelier; the counties of Addison, Orleans, Caledonia; the town of Brighton, and the Probate Districts of Hartford, Fair Haven and Windsor. By checking the statutes one may learn the date when all these individual courts became Municipal Courts under the General Statutes.

### *District Courts*

In 1965 the act establishing municipal courts was repealed and the district courts were established. A district court system was created which established a district court named for, located in, and having jurisdiction throughout each county except three joint districts: Caledonia-Essex, Orleans-Essex and Franklin-Grand Isle. During the succeeding biennial session, the 1965 act was repealed and in its place a new statewide district court was established. For administrative purposes, the Supreme Court from time to time is authorized to organize the district court into territorial units, designating the town within the unit and may organize territorial units of two or more circuits. The district court was given civil jurisdiction over civil actions when the debt is not over $5,000.00 and title to real estate is not involved. A district court has all the powers of a county court except as specifically limited by law. There are in 1973 ten district judges.

### *Judicial Selection Board*

In 1966 a judicial selection board of eleven members was created to make an initial selection of justices of the supreme and superior courts. The selection board consists of : the governor, who appoints two members who are not attorneys-at-law; three members elected by the senate, at least one from the minority party and only one of whom may be an attorney-at-law; in the same manner, the house elects three members, and the attorneys-at-law elect three of their members.

Prior to the submission of three names to the legislature, the board submits six names to the Supreme Court for their approval or disapproval. The legislature then from the list of names furnished the selection board elects three persons to be supreme court members and in like manner, three superior judges are elected if there is a vacancy.

The legislature of 1967 established the position of *Court Administrator*, the first incumbent being Lawrence J. Turgeon.

The Court of Chancery was established by the Constitution, the powers of which are vested in the Chancellor. Each Judge of the Supreme Court is a Chancellor.

*Justices of the Peace* as established in the constitution were allowed to try cases of a criminal nature where the fine did not exceed ten dollars. They had jurisdiction in civil cases where the debt was under $2,000.00, and in acts of trespass where the fine was not over $30.00. The legislature in 1974 by No. 249, sections 122 and 123, took away from the justices of the peace the power to hold court.

There have been times when it appeared that if you were a lawyer with qualifications and probably with attorney-at-law friends, you would have a better chance of being elected to the Superior Court if first you had become a member of the House of Representatives.

### *Public Defender*

The position of *Public Defender* of the state is not new. In 1819, the legislature allowed the appointment of a person at state expense to defend a suit in favor of the Society for the Propogation of the Gospel in Foreign Parts, against the town of New Haven and one William Wheeler for the recovery of one of the rights originally granted by the the Government of Great Britain to said Society.

In 1972 the state established the office of Public Defender.

### *Probate Court*

The probate court looks after the personal estates of citizens. As established in the constitution which reads in Part II. Section 35. Judges of Probate and Justices of the Peace shall be elected on the first Tuesday after the first Monday of November.

Section 46 of Article II. states; Juges of Probate shall be elected by the freemen of their respective probate districts. The general jurisdiction of the probate court is described as having ''Jurisdiction of the probate of will, the settlement of estates, the appointment of guardians, and of the powers, duties and rights of guardians and wards.

### *Urban Renewal*

The Agency of Urban Renewal was created by the legislature by No. 264 of the Acts of 1959. The mayor of a municipality has the power to appoint a board consisting of five commissioners for a one year term. No one in any public capacity in the municipality may be a commissioner. The Commission has very broad powers to acquire by any means, including eminent domain and dispose of any real or personal property in the municipality and rebuild the area through private or public funds. Each project must first have the approval of the voters of the municipality at a meeting duly warned.

The resolution to be voted on shall be for the purpose that:
(1) One or more slum or blighted areas exist in the municipality; and
(2) The rehabilitation, conservation and redevelopment of the area is necessary in the public interest.

## *COUNTIES*

County lines in Vermont are perhaps not as sacred as some persons seem to feel since from the initial settlement of this state many changes in the name and area of the counties have occurred.

### *New York Counties*

In 1765 when the Province of New York claimed sway over Vermont, a petition was introduced into the provincial legislature to designate five counties in Vermont. The following names were suggested:

1. Colden County (named after a New York Governor) on the east side of the New Hampshire grants and west of the Connecticut River, bordering on Massachusetts Bay Colony - with New Flamstead as the county town.
2. Sterling County - north of Colden, the rest of the east side of the grant to the Canadian line.
3. Stillwater County on the west side.
4. Kingsbury County with Kingsbury as the county town.
5. Pitt County - with the county town on the east side of Lake Champlain near Crown Point.

It is assumed that Kingsbury County included a part of New York, since there was a town by the name of Kingbury there.

At about the same time, another petition was submitted to the New York Provincial Legislature requesting that all the land east of the mountains and west of the Connecticut River from Massachusetts Bay to the Province of Canada be called Colden County with New Flamstead as the county town. Evidently the legislature did not enact these petitions since later another petition was acted upon favorably.

### *Cumberland County*

Cumberland County was designated as that area which now encompasses Windham and Windsor Counties. Chester was designated as the county town, now called the county seat. The act, passed on the 24th of March, 1772, stated that the said County of Cumberland shall forever hereafter be bounded and limited as follows, to wit: Beginning on the west bank of the Connecticut river, opposite to the point where the partition line between the colonies of Massachusetts Bay and New Hampshire touches the east side of the said river, and extending from thence north eighty degrees west until such line shall meet with and be intersected by another line proceeding on a course south ten degrees west from the northwest corner of a tract of land granted under the Great Seal of this colony on the fourth day of December, on thousand seven hundred and seventy, to James Abeel and nine other persons; extending from said point of intersection north ten degrees east until such line shall meet with and be intersected by another line to be drawn on a course north fifty degrees west, from the southwest corner of a tract of land granted under the Great Seal of this Colony on the thirteenth day of November in the year of our Lord, one thousand seven hundred and fifty-nine and erected into a township by the name of Royalton; and running from the last named point of intersection south fifty degrees east to west bank of the Connecticut River, and down along the west bank of said river, as the same river winds and turns to the place of beginning.

The south line of the present towns of Randolph, Tunbridge, Strafford and Thetford was established as the boundary line between Cumberland and Gloucester Counties.

A vote was taken to change the name of Cumberland County to Unity which vote was repealed in the same year.

On February 28, 1770, Gloucester County was established:

*Gloucester County*

"The County of Gloucester shall, forever hereafter, be bounded and limited as follows, to wit: On the south by the north bounds of the County of Cumberland, on the east by the east bounds of this colony, on the north by the north bounds thereof, on the west, partly by a line to be drawn from the northwest corner of the County of Cumberland on a course north ten degrees east until such line shall meet and be intersected by another line proceeding on an east course from the south bank of Otter Creek, and partly by another line to be drawn and continued from the said last-mentioned point of intersection, on a course north fifty degrees east, until it meets with and terminates at the said north bounds of the colony; all and singular which lands included and compressed within the limits and description last aforesaid shall be and forever remain a district and separate county to be called, known and distinguished by the name of Gloucester."

In 1770 when Gloucester County was established the town of Kingsland (now Washington), which had no population at all was established as the county town.

*Albany County*

Originally the County of Albany encompassed all of western Vermont as well as northeastern New York. On March 12, 1772 New York passed an act which divided Albany County into three counties, described as follows:

"***Thence east (until it intersects a north line drawn from the high falls on the Hudsons River, which lays next above Fort Edward, thence south to said falls, thence along the east bank of the Hudsons River) to a certain creek called Stoney Creek, thence east five hundred and ten chains, thence south to the norht bank of Batten

Creek (Battenkill), thence up along the north bank of said creek until the said creek intersects the southern boundary of Princetown, thence along the same to the southeast corner thereof, thence east to the west bounds of the County of Cumberland, thence south and easterly along the west and south bounds thereof to the Connecticut River, thence along said river to the north bounds of the Colony of Connecticut, thence along the north and west bounds of the same to the County of Dutchess."

You will note that at this time New York claimed that part of Massachusetts Bay.

### *Tryon County*

Lands westward of Albany County and of a north line drawn from the Mohawk River, continued to the north Bounds of the province, erected into a separate county by the name of TRYON.

### *Charlotte County*

The lands northward of Albany County in Vermont and east of Tryon County and westward of Cumberland and Gloucester Counties to be a separate county by the name of CHARLOTTE.

### *New York Persists*

The New York Legislature of 1788 passed an act defining the boundaries of all its counties. Even though the State of Vermont on July 8, 1777 at Windsor had adopted a new Constitution, New York still persisted in establishing counties in Vermont. The counties of Gloucester and Cumberland were continued on the east side and Albany County on the west side. Charlotte County was divided into two counties, namely; Washington County bounded on the south by Albany County, on the east by Cumberland and Gloucester Counties, and on the north by a line running due east from the northerly point of Rogers Rock on the west side of Lake George and thence due east to the west bounds of Gloucester County, bounded southerly by Washington County, easterly by Gloucester County and on the north by Canada.

### *Vermont Counties*

Under the original Vermont Constitution the Vermont General Assembly was allowed to create counties in the same manner as towns. Their status was to remain as long as the General Assembly wished to retain them. The General Assembly had the power to consolidate, divide or create counties as they desired. Section 6 of our present constitution gives the General Assembly the power to "Constitute Counties".

The General Assembly of 1779 divided Vermont into two counties: Cumberland (on the east side) and Bennington (on the west side).

By the Acts of February 16, 1781 two counties, Bennington and Rutland, were divided out of Bennington, and three counties, Windham, Windsor and Orange north to the Canadian line, were formed out of Cumberland County.

On April 11, 1781 the General Assembly voted that the New Hampshire towns opposite Orange County be annexed thereto, and the towns opposite Windsor County be annexed thereto. The towns which became a part of Vermont for a time were: Cornish, Lebanon, Dresden, Lyme, Orford, Piermont, Haverhill, Bath, Lyman, Apthorp, Enfield, Canaan, Cardigan, Landaff, Gunthwaite and Morristown.

In June 1781, it was voted to annex the following New York towns to Vermont: Hoosack, Cambridge, White Creek (alias New Perth), Black Creek, Skenesborough (Whitehall), Kingsbury, Patent (Argyle) and Fort Edward.

The Acts of October 18, 1785 established Addison County as all the original Bennington County north of Rutland County to the Canadian line and east to Orange County.

A new county, Chittenden, was established on October 22, 1787 from what is now the north line of Addison County to the Canadian line and east to Orange County.

### *Present Counties Formed*

An Act of November 5, 1792 stated: "Whereas from the extensive limits and increased population of the counties of Orange and Chittenden, it hath become convenient and necessary to divide Orange and Chittenden Counties into six separate and distinct counties." Orange County included lands north of the present Windsor County and the towns of Roxbury, Northfield, Berlin, and Barre. Caledonia County included lands north of Orange County and included the present towns of Calais, Montpelier, St. Andrews (now Plainfield), Cabot and Marshfield. Essex County included the present Essex County and the towns of Newark and Westmore. Chittenden County included the towns of Worcester, Middlesex, Moretown, Waitsfield, Faystown, Duxbury and Waterbury and the towns of Stowe, South Hero and Grand Isle and its present towns. Franklin County, as now comprised, together with the towns of Cambridge, Johnson, Waterville, Belvidere and Old Sterling, plus the towns of North Hero, Alburg and Isle La Motte.

Orleans County included all lands between Franklin and Essex

Counties and the towns of Hyde Park, Morristown, Wolcott and Elmore (now in Lamoille County).

On November 1, 1810, the General Assembly established the County of Jefferson which included the towns of Duxbury, Fayston, Waterbury, Stowe, Worcester, Middlesex, Moretown and Waitsfield (previously in Chittenden County), Plainfield (from Caledonia County) and Barre, Berlin and Northfield (from Orange County). In 1814, Jefferson County was renamed Washington County. The Acts of 1835 established a new county - Lamoille, to include Eden, Hyde Park, Wolcott, Morristown, Cambridge, Belvidere, Waterville, Johnson, Sterling, Stowe, Elmore and Old Mansfield.

It was not until 1820 that the town of Roxbury was transferred from Orange to Washington County. For several years the citizens of Roxbury had petitioned to have this change made.

In 1794, a petition was entered to make the Islands in Lake Champlain (including Alburg) a county; however the petition was withdrawn the next year.

The County of Grand Isle as now constituted was legislatively established in 1805.

In 1785 Addision and Colchester were established as half-shire towns. Earlier Bennington and Manchester were likewise established.

## *NEW YORK GRANTS*

"The land patents issued by New York Governors covering lands now within Vermont, with four early and one late exception, were granted between the years 1765-1776. During the period Sir Henry Moore, the Earl of Dunmore and William Tryon were regularly commissioned governors of the colony or province; the interims between their actual terms of service were filled by Cadwallader Colden, who had been commissioned as Lieutenant Governor on April 14, 1761; and served continuously in that office during the entire time covered by the issue of the New York patents covering Vermont; and until he died in September, 1776.

There follows a list of the grants made by each chief executive in order of their issue:

By Lieutenant Governor Colden: Nov. 1761-Nov. 1765, the Schneyder patent of Mapleton, Princeton and the Napier and Embury tracts.

By Sir Henry Moore: Nov. 1765 till his death in September 1769: Chester, Brattleborough, Hertford, Putney, Adair Tract, Beekman and Grand Island.

By Lieutenant Governor, acting: 1768-1770, Warrens Town, Camden, Royalton, Kempton, Middlesex, Kent, Whitingham,

Kingsland, Besborough, Charlotte, Readsborough, Moore Town, Gageborough, Kelso, Newbrook, Kingsborough, Wallace Tract, Holton, Leyden, Dunmore, Virgin Hall, Hillsborough, Abeel Tract, Farquhar Tract and Kersborough.

By Governor Dunmore from October 1770 to July 1771: St. Catherines, Benzel's two tracts, Cole's Tract, Munro's Tract, Chimney Point to Benzel, Socialborough, St. Clair's Tract, Reid's Tract, Fincastle, Halesburgh, Montressor's Tract, Deerfield, Morrisfield, Newry, Mecklenburg, Richmond, Metcalfe's Tract, Kelby, Leinster, Skenesborough, Prattsburgh, and McLure's Tract.

By Governor Tryon, from July 1771 to April 1774: Col. Howard's Tract, Durham, Eugene, Corinth, Nicholl's Tract, Truro, Penryn, Newbury, Windham, Westminster, Windsor, Norbury, Weathersfield, New Fane, Reading, Springfield, Nicoll's Tract, Woodstock, Townshend, Cavendish, Saltash, Minto, Van Vleck's Tract, Lawrence's Tract.

By Lieutenant Governor Colden, during Governor Tryon's Absence in England, April 1774 to June 1775. Kellybrook, The Governor of King's College, Samuel Avery's Tract, Captain Harry Gordon's Tract, Humphrey Avery's Tract, New Rutland, Sidney, Wickham, St. George, Peter Gordon's Tract, Bamf, Meath, Thirming, Thompson's Tract, Ryegate, Smithfield.

By Governor Tryon from June 1775 to the Revolution July 4, 1776. Stratton, Whippleborough, Topsham and Underhill.

Thus it will be seen that forty-five patents were issued by Lt. Governor Colden; seveny by Governor Moore, twenty-three by Governor Dunmore, and twenty-eight by Governor Tryon.

Of the ninety-two townships under New Hampshire charter, which had asked for a confirmation of title by New York, only eighteen had passed "the beech seals" when the colonial government of New York ceased to issue land patents at some time in 1776.

The grant to the Governor of King's College Tract in the towns of Cambridge and Johnson, County of Gloucester was a mandamus order by George the Third on the 16th of August 1774. The condition of the grant was an annual rent of six shillings and eight pence in lieu of quit rent. The term of the lease was for three lives or any term not exceeding ninety-nine years. King's College, now Columbia University was founded in 1759.

Another grant to King's College was made on the 14th of March, 1770 in the town of Kingsland now Washington.

### *Grant Reservations*

From all grants there was reserved forever all mines of gold and silver.

All white pine or other sorts of pine trees fit for masts of the growth of twenty-four inches diameter and upward at twelve inches from the earth were reserved for masts for the Royal Navy.

Each town grant was divided into the number of equal parts comparable to the number of persons to whom the grant was made. The annual rent was two shillings and six pence, sterling, for each and every hundred acres.

Another grant condition was that in each township there should be two assessors, one treasurer, two overseers of highways, two overseers of the poor, one collector and four constables, elected yearly.

Within three years from the grant there shall be settled so many families as shall amount to one family for every one thousand acres. Further within the three year period at least three acres for every fifty acres of the grant land, as are capable, shall be cultivated.

### *Glebe or Lease Lands*

Every township whether laid out by a grant of New Hampshire or New York reserved 500 acres as a glebe for a protestant minister and not over 250 acres for a school master.

It was later proposed to pay the Society for the Propogation of the Gospel in Foreign parts for land granted by the Governor of New Hampshire. The sum to be paid to the Society was 30 pounds for each township granted.

### *NEW YORK GRANTS*

| | |
|---|---|
| Abeel, James | West part of Jamaica, Wardsboro |
| Adair, John | Athens |
| Alexander, Hough, and McGill Wallace | Orwell |
| Avery, Humphrey | Lincoln and Warren |
| Avery Samuel | Ripton, Hancock |
| Bamf. | Sutton, Sheffield, Wheelock |
| Beekman | No. Hero |
| Benzel, Adolph | 2 tracts - Chimney Point and New Haven, Weybridge |
| Besborough | Lyndon, St. Johnsbury |
| Camden | Dover, Jamaica, Wardsboro |
| Charlotte | Charlotte |
| Cole, Ebenezer | Shaftsbury |
| Chimney Point | Addison |
| Corinth | Reported to be called Conway |
| Deerfield | So. Burlington, Essex, Williston, Jericho, Richmond |

| | |
|---|---|
| Dunmore | Concord, St. Johnsbury, Waterford |
| Durham | Clarendon, Wallingford |
| Eugene | Pawlet, Rupert |
| Farquhar, Wm. | Benson |
| Fincastle | Sherburne, Stockbridge |
| Great Island or Grand Isle | So. Hero, Grand Isle |
| Gageborough | Vershire |
| Gordon, Harry | Fairfax, Fletcher |
| Halesborough | Brandon, Sudbury |
| Hillsborough | Danville, Walden |
| Hilton | Mt. Holly, Shrewsbury |
| Hoosick | Bennington, Pownal |
| Howard, Col. Thomas | East part of Vernon |
| Kelso | Ira, W. Rutland, Clarendon, Middletown Spgs |
| Kempton | Orange |
| Kersborough | Concord |
| Kilby | Middlesex, Montpelier, Berlin, Moretown |
| Kingsborough | Montpelier, E. Montpelier, Plainfield, Marshfield, Calais |
| Kings College | Cambridge, Johnson |
| Kingsland | Washington |
| Lawrence, John | Whiting, Leicester |
| Leinster | Glastonbury, Somerset, Woodford |
| Leyden | Northfield, Roxbury |
| McClure, Alexander | Cornwall, Leicester, Middlebury, Salisbury, Whiting |
| Mecklenburg | Ferrisburg, Monkton, New Haven, Waltham |
| Middlesex | Bethel, Randolph |
| Minto | Richmond, Bolton |
| Medcalfe, Simon | Highgate |
| Moores Town | Bradford |
| Monckton | Whiting |
| Montressor, James | Panton |
| Morrisfield | Cornwall, Middlebury |
| Munro, John | Arlington |
| Napier & Philip of Embury | Arlington |
| Newbrook | Barre City, Town, Berlin, Williamstown |
| Newry | Brandon, Chittenden, Goshen, Leicester, Mendon, Shrewsbury |
| Nichols, William | Hubbardton, Shoreham |

| | |
|---|---|
| Norbury | Calais, Worcester |
| Penryn | Orange, Groton, Plainfield |
| Prattsburgh | Highgate, Swanton |
| Princetown | Arlington, Manchester, Sunderland |
| Readsborough | Readsborough |
| Reed, John | New Haven, Weybridge |
| Richmond | Poultney, Wells, Middletown Spgs |
| Royalton | Royalton |
| St. George | Coventry, Newport |
| Schneyder, Hendrick | Bennington |
| St. Catherines | Poultney, Wells |
| St. Clair, John | Addison, Bridport, Panton |
| Sidney | Cabot, Marshfield |
| Skenesburgh | Fair Haven |
| Socialborough | Pittsford, Rutland |
| Thirming | Canaan |
| Thompson, John | Pawlet, Rupert |
| Townshend | Fairfax, Fairfield |
| Truro | Calais |
| Van Vleck, Henry | Ira, Castleton |
| Virgin Hall | Andover, Landgrove, Mt. Holly, Weston |
| Wallomschack | Bennington |
| Warren Town | Athens, Townshend |
| Wickham | Brookfield, Braintree, Randolph, Roxbury |
| Whitingham | Whitingham |
| Windham | Bethel, Northfield, Roxbury |

## *NEW YORK GRANTS BY TOWNS*

| | |
|---|---|
| Addison | Chimney Point, St. Clair |
| Andover | Virgin Hall |
| Arlington | Princetown, Philip Embury, Munro |
| Athens | Adair, John, Warren's Town |
| Barre City | Newbrook |
| Barre Town | Newbrook |
| Bennington | Hoosick, Wallumschack, Schneyder |
| Benson | Farquhar |
| Berlin | Newbrook, Kilby, Windham |
| Bethel | Middlesex |

| | |
|---|---|
| Bolton | Minto |
| Bradford | Moore's Town |
| Braintree | Wickham |
| Brandon | Halesborough, Newry |
| Bridport | St. Clair |
| Brookfield | Wickham |
| Cabot | Sidney |
| Calais | Kingsborough, Truro, Norbury |
| Cambridge | Kings College |
| Canaan | Thirming |
| Castleton | Van Vleck |
| Charlotte | Charlotte |
| Chittenden | Newry |
| Clarendon | Kelso, Durham |
| Concord | Dunmore, Kersborough |
| Corinth | Corinth |
| Cornwall | Morrisfield, Cornwall |
| Coventry | St. George |
| Danville | Hillsborough |
| Dorset | Princetown |
| Dover | Camden |
| E. Montpelier | Kingsborough |
| Essex | Deerfield |
| Fairfax | Townshend |
| Fairfield | Townshend, Gordon |
| Fairhaven | Skenesborough |
| Fletcher | Gordon |
| Ferrisburg | Mecklenburgh |
| Glastonbury | Napier, Leinster |
| Goshen | Newry |
| Grand Isle | Grand Isle |
| Groton | Penryn |
| Hancock | Samuel Avery |
| Highgate | Prattsburgh |
| Hubbardton | Nichol's |
| Ira | Van Vleck |
| Jamaica | Abeel, Camden |
| Jericho | Deerfield |
| Johnson | King's College |
| Landgrove | Virgin Hall |
| Leicester | Newry, McClure's |
| Lincoln | Humphrey Avery |
| Lyndon | Besborough |
| Marshfield | Sidney, Kingsborough |
| Manchester | Princetown |

| | |
|---|---|
| Mendon | Newry |
| Middlebury | Morrisfield, McClure's |
| Middlesex | Kilby |
| Middletown Spgs | Richmond, Kelso |
| Monkton | Mecklenburgh |
| Montpelier | Kilby, Kingsborough |
| Mt. Holly | Hilton, Virgin Hall |
| Moretown | Kilby |
| New Haven | Mecklenburgh, Adolph Benzel, Reed's |
| Newport | St. George |
| Northfield | Windham, Leyden |
| North Hero | Beekman |
| Orange | Penryn, Kempton |
| Orwell | Alexander |
| Panton | St. Clair, Montressors |
| Pawlet | Eugene, John Thompson |
| Pittsfield | Pittsfield |
| Pittsford | Socialborough |
| Plainfield | Penryn, Kingsborough |
| Poultney | St. Catherines |
| Pownal | Hoosick |
| Randolph | Wickham, Middlesex |
| Readsboro | Readsboro |
| Richmond | Deerfield, Minto |
| Ripton | Samuel Avery |
| Roxbury | Leyden, Windham, Wickham |
| Royalton | Royalton |
| Rupert | John Thompson |
| Rutland | Socialborough |
| Salisbury | Alex McClure |
| Shaftsbury | Napier, Ebenezer Cole |
| Sheffield | Bamf |
| Sheldon | New Rutland |
| Sherburne | Fincastle |
| Shoreham | Wm.Nichols |
| Shrewsbury | Hilton, Newry |
| Somerset | Leinster |
| So. Burlington | Deerfield |
| So. Hero | Grand Isle or Great Island |
| Starksboro | Starksboro |
| St. Johnsbury | Besborough, Dunmore |
| Sudbury | Halesborough |
| Sunderland | Princetown |
| Sutton | Bamf |

| | |
|---|---|
| Swanton | Prattsburgh, New Rutland |
| Stockbridge | Fincastle |
| Townshend | Warrens Town |
| Vernon | Thomas Howard |
| Vershire | Gageborough |
| Walden | Hillsborough |
| Wallingford | Durham |
| Waltham | Mecklenburg |
| Wardsboro | Camden, James Abeel |
| Warren | Humphrey Avery |
| Washington | Kingsland |
| Waterford | Dunmore |
| Wells | St. Catherines |
| Weston | Virgin Hall |
| W. Rutland | Kelso |
| Weybridge | Adolph Benzel, John Reed |
| Wheelock | Bamf |
| Whitingham | Whitingham |
| Whiting | Monckton, Alex McClure, John Lawrence |
| Williamstown | Newbrook |
| Woodford | Leinster |
| Worcester | Norbury |
| Williston | Deerfield |

## *TOWN OFFICERS*

Among the early town officers there were several which do not exist today. *DEERRIFTS* were elected officers, whose duty it was to enforce the deer laws. *THE HAYWARDS* as appointed officers, were to keep cattle from breaking through fence from the commons or roadways into enclosed fields. They also had the duty to impound such stray cattle.

*TYTHINGMEN* were among the officials chosen by the town for many years. They were from one to seven in number, who were to act as a sort of local police. They were empowered with many duties which now fall into other offices. One of the duties was to preserve order in gatherings, especially at public worship on the Sabbath, and to arrest travelers on that day. By the laws of 1797, no person was allowed to visit from house to house unless for the purpose of religious or moral conversation, edification or instruction therein.

There were inspectors of potash and pearlash, inspectors of hops, inspectors of flour, measurers of salt, weighers of wool and shire reeves, which was the former name for sheriffs. The early official term for a sheriff was a shrievalty. The position of hearse warden was created to prevent local undertakers from having a monoply at the time of sorrow. When everything was shipped in barrels there was a culler of hoops, poles, staves and headers.

In 1779, an Act regulating the choice of town officers and petit jurymen read as follows: Town meetings were called for some day in the month of March, annually, at ten o'clock in the morning. The meeting was to choose a moderator and town clerk or register, then they shall choose a number, not exceeding five, to be selectmen or townsmen to take care of the prudential affairs of such town; also a town treasurer, one or two constables, listers not exceeding five, collector of rates, leather sealers, one or more grand jurors, one or more tythingmen, haywards, branders of horses, sealers of weights and measures, and every other town officer that the law of the state shall direct.

In 1808 the law allowed the election of a moderator, town clerk and town treasurer, selectmen, overseer of the poor, listers, constables, collector of town rates, grand juror, surveyor of highways, fence viewer, pound keeper, sealers of weights and measures and leather, tythingmen, haywards, and auditors. These differences show the changes taking place in town authority during only ten years time. Many changes have been made since.

## *UNORGANIZED TOWNS AND GORES*

Vermont's unorganized towns are those which have never had sufficient population to justify town government. Those towns now include Averill, Ferdinand and Lewis in Essex County, Glastenbury in Bennington County and Somerset in Windham County.

Gores are unincorporated wedge shaped pieces of land of a few thousand acres. They include Warren's Gore and Warner's Grant in Essex County. Avery's Gore in Franklin County was divided by legislative act in 1961 and made a part of the towns of Bakersfield and Montgomery. Avery's Gore in Chittenden County lies just south of Huntington.

These towns are supervised by a supervisor who has the same powers as a selectman and many other town officials. (No. 58 of the Acts of 1973). The supervision of the Essex County unorganized towns and gores was transferred in 1973 to the county clerk. The governor appoints the supervisors for the unorganized towns and gores in Chittenden, Bennington and Windham Counties.

The Legislature (by numbers 269 and 292 of the Acts of 1937) designated Glastenbury and Somerset as unorganized towns. Glastenbury in 1930 had a population of seven persons. The town was represented in the Legislature from 1927 through 1937 by Ira Mattison. Mr. Mattison had at times held the following offices:

Town Clerk, Selectman, Lister, Justice of the Peace, Road Commissioner and Grand Juror. There are about ten miles of road in the town. Most of the land which is forested is owned by the McCullough family.

A commentary about Somerset should be of interest. In 1925 the town had a population of eight men and two women, which included John Taylor and his wife Katie. Katie was born on Prince Edward Island in 1887 and came to Somerset in 1920. Most of the important town offices were held by the Taylors. They cared for about a half-dozen state wards, for whom Katie taught school in addition to here duties as first selectman, lister and clerk of the school board. During the summer, Katie was occasionally seen driving a large dump truck with a load of gravel to be used for maintenance of the six miles of town highway leading north from Vermont Route No. 9. Another position which Katie held from 1925 through 1937 was the town's representative to Montpelier. Soon after the Legislature made Somerset an unorganized town the Taylors moved away. A large portion of this town is owned by the New England Power Co., which has a large power dam there.

### *GOVERNMENT*

### *SELECTED BIBLIOGRAPHY*

Allen, Ira, *History of Vermont,* Montpelier: Vermont Historical Society, Vol. I, 1870.

Allen, Ethan, *A Vindication of the Opposition of the Inhabitants of Vermont to the Government of New York,* 1779.

Cabot, Mary R., *Annals of Brattleboro,* Brattleboro: E. L. Hildreth, 2, V., 1921.

Broadhead, John Romeyn, *History of the State of New York,* Albany, N.Y.: Weed and Parsons and Company, 2 Vol. 1858-1860.

Crockett, Walter Hill, *Vermont the Green Mountain State,* Burlington: Vermont Farm Bureau, 4 Vol. 1938.

Hall, Hiland, *History of Vermont from its Discovery to Its Admission into Union,* Albany, N.Y.: J. Munsell, 1868.

Hill, William C., *Vermont Judiciary and Tradition,* UVM Thesis, 1968.

Lovejoy, Evelyn Mary Wood, *History of Royalton, 1769-1811,* Burlington: Free Press Association, 1911.

Ludlum, David M., *Social Ferment in Vermont, 1791-1850,* New York: Columbia University Press, 1939.

National Society of Colonia Dames, *Survey of Court Houses.*

Newton, Earl Williams, *The Vermont Story,* Montpelier: Vermont Historical Society, 1949.

New York, *Documents Relating to the Colonial History of the State of New York* by John Romeyn Broadhead, Albany, N.Y.: Weed and Parsons, in 14 Volumes, 1850-1855.

Nuquist, Andrew E., *Town Government in Vermont,* Burlington: Government Research Center of University of Vermont, 1964.

Nuquist, Andrew E. and Nuquist, Edith, *Vermont State Government and Administration,* Burlington: Government Research Center of University of Vermont, 1966.

O'Callaghan, E. B., ed, *The Documentary History of the State of New York,* Albany: Weed and Parsons, 4 volumes 1850-1851.

Ibid, *Documents Relating to the Colonial History of the State of New York,* Albany, N.Y.: Weed and Parsons, 12 Volumes, 1853.

Swift, Thomas, *History of the Town of Middlebury,* Rutland: Charles E. Tuttle Company, reprint 1971.

Van DeWater, Frederic, *Lake Champlain and Lake George,* New York: Bobbs Merrill Co., 1946.

Vermont, *Legislative Directory,* 1972.

Vermont, *Statues from 1779-1975.*

Wilbur, Benjamin James, *Ira Allen Founder of Vermont,* Boston and New York: Houghton Mifflin Company, 2 Vol.

Williams, Samuel, *Natural and Civil History of Vermont,* Walpole, N.H.: I. Thomas and D. Carlisle, Jr., 2 Vol., 1794.

## *GOVERNMENT COURTS SELECTED BIBLIOGRAPHY*

City of Burlington, *charter of City of Burlington,* Vermont Statutes, 1853.

Hill, William, Judge, *Vermont Judiciary and the Tradition,* Mimeographed Copy, pp. 97-101.

National Society of Colonial Dames, *Survey of Court Houses,* 1966.

Thurber, Harris E., *The Vermont Judiciary, A Study in Cultural Adaptation,* Monograph, 1955.

Vermont, *Laws of the State, 1797 to date.*

Vermont, *Legislative Directory and State Manual,* Published by Authority, Secretary of State, ed. 1970-1974.

# Health and Welfare

Early settlers were not only pioneers but they also realized the need of the preservation of health. In 1779 a law was passed which prohibited the importation of feathers, since it was assumed that the people in New York, Philadelphia and other places were afflicted with the putrid yellow fever.

As early as 1789 the selectmen of the towns were ordered by the legislature to observe the prevalence of smallpox and provide medical services for those who could not personally afford it. The selectmen were made the Boards of Health of their towns and for over 100 years they were the only boards of health in the state, until the State Board of Health was established in 1866. A little later the State Board of Health was authorized to appoint a health officer in each municipality. This board consisted of the local health officer, selectmen or aldermen, village trustees and bailiffs of incorporated villages.

Previous to 1784, physicians were scattered about the state without any organization, but in that year the doctors of Bennington and Rutland Counties applied to the legislature for a charter for a medical society. In 1813, the formation of the State Medical Society was approved by the legislature.

The Medical Department at the University of Vermont was organized in 1807. In 1809, an honorary degree (Doctor of Medicine) was given by the University. A professor was employed to give medical lectures and teaching; attendance at which would make a person eligible for the degree of Bachelor of Physics. The Medical College had its ups and downs; however, it survived its troubles and finally received a Class A rating which it has today.

In 1818 the Castleton Medical Academy was established. The name was changed to Vermont Academy of Medicine in 1822, and in 1841 the name of Castleton Medical College was adopted. The college operated until the outbreak of the Civil War. Lectures were given in 1827 at Woodstock, which resulted in the incorporation of the Vermont Medical College in 1835, (which closed down operations in 1836). Many doctors were graduated from those three medical colleges.[1]

Many early graduates from these medical colleges were real practitioners who in the dead of night hitched the old grey mare to the sleigh and wended their way often several miles to the bedside of an ailing patient. Oftener, they travelled by horseback over roads and byways impassable to wagons or sleighs, due to high water or deep snow drifts. Occasionally they were forced to travel on foot with their medicine cases filled with health-giving drugs and medicines.

Most drugs were extracted from plants which grew wild in the fields and forests. Many families knew which plants furnished the relief or cure for each ailment, and home remedies for minor ailments were prescribed by a member of the family.

In the early 1800's, dysentery reached such an epidemic proportion, that it occasionally wiped out entire families as is evidenced upon the several tombstones of such families. In Abby Hemingway's "Vermont Historical Gazeteer" a description for treatment of this fatal disease reads: "The chief remedy was the prompt use of a hot bath made of a hasty concoction of hemlock boughs, and the pineboard bathing vessel made in the shape of a coffin was daily seen in the streets of Montpelier during the heighth of the disease, borne on the shoulders of men rapidly moving from house to house to serve the multiplying victims."[2]

During the year 1811 and particularly in the winter of 1812-13 the state passed through a most severe epidemic known as "spotted fever", which was probably the disease known as Cerebrospinal Meningitis. It was believed to have originated with the soldiers quartered at Fort Ethan Allen. The disease spread rapidly and over 6,000 deaths were estimated to have occurred during those winter months.[3]

The first registration law in the country (of births, marriages and deaths) was passed in Vermont by the Legislature in 1856. The State Homeopathic Society was chartered in 1858, followed by the Vermont Eclectic Medical Society in 1866. In 1879 the practice of law was restricted by law to licensed physicians.

To go back 85 years, there were about 700 licensed physicians, most of whom were located in small communities, while today they

1. Zadock Thompson, *Natural and Civil History of Vermont*, 1842, p. 161.

2. Abby Maria Hemenway, *Vermont Historical Gazetteer*, (Montpelier: Vermont Watchman and State Journal), p. 264.

3. Ernest W. Butterfield, *The Early History of Weathersfield*, (Address at First Congregational Church, Weathersfield, 1921), p. 26.

are in the larger towns and cities. Medical centers in rural area (where two or more doctors and perhaps a dentist have their practices) have been developed in recent years. In 1974, few doctors in the Montpelier area go outside their offices for house calls, day or night, to treat their patients.

## *HOSPITALS*

Previous to 1876, Vermont had no hospitals. The dates and locations of the early Vermont hospitals are as follows: Mary Fletcher in Burlington - 1876; Fanny Allen in Winooski - 1894; St. Albans - 1888; St. Johnsbury - 1895; Rutland - 1892; Proctor - 1896; Heaton in Montpelier - 1895; Brightlook in St. Johnsbury - 1899; Brattleboro Memorial - 1904; Barre City - 1904; Rockingham in Bellows Falls - 1910; Springfield - 1914; Putnam Memorial in Bennington - 1912.

Hospitals in some localities have merged due to economic conditions, need for more modern or larger facilities, and other reasons. Heaton Hospital and Barre City merged to form the Central Vermont Medical Center in Berlin in 1968. The Mary Fletcher and Bishop De Goesbriand in Burlington became a unit known as the Medical Center Hospital of Vermont in 1967. The St. Johnsbury and Brightlook hospitals in St. Johnsbury were merged and are known as the Northeastern Vermont Regional Hospital. A new hospital was opened in Newport in 1972 under the name of North Country Hospital and Health Center. Other Vermont hospitals include those in Hardwick, Middlebury, Morrisville, Townshend, Windsor, and the Kerbs Memorial in St. Albans. The public hospitals include Brattleboro Retreat, Vermont State Hospital in Waterbury, The U.S. Veterans' Hospital in White River Jct. and the Soldiers Home in Bennington.

In 1948 a report of the Vermont Hospital Survey and Construction Commission was made in accordance with federal law 725 of the 79th Congress. This very detailed report suggested that the state be divided into five public health centers and twelve public health auxiliary facilities and a public health mobile unit in Northern Essex County. The report furnished statistics on births, number of hospital beds, percentages of use and projected future needs.

## *PROPRIETARY MEDICINES*

Perhaps you have heard your grandmother say that when she was a girl there were few doctors and people had to depend upon home remedies. Each one of the older citizens knew the plants of the wild which would produce the desired effect upon certain ailments. They used the roots, leaves and berries of the plants to make the needed medicine. A hundred years ago much advice was given for individual remedies such as: "To dissolve stones in the bladder, take goldenrod tea by simmering, not boiling. Simmer 12 honey bees in the tea for a man and nine for a woman."

Later many concerns developed in Vermont and elsewhere which advertised to the wide world the cures obtainable from their particular concoction. Everyone had heard of or used the well-advertised Lydia Pinkham's Vegetable Compound, a cure-all for almost any affliction. Everybody learned the ditty about "Lydia Pinkham and her love for the human race."

Some of the Vermont trade names are of interest. Dr. B. J. Kimball (whose business was in Enosburg Falls) advertised Blachery Balsam, which was supposed to be good for quick relief for internal and external use, cures at once for sore throats, prevents diptheria, cure colic and is good for man or beast. In Bradford we learn that Dr. Doty's Mandrake Bitters will cure home complaints, jaundices, piles and loss of appetite; is not an alcoholic beverage, but a medicine for the sick. In Vergennes there were ads for Dr. Ingram's Nervine Pain Extractor; good for croup, congestion of the lungs and pleurisy; good for speakers with a husky voice, and used successfully for obstinate rheumatism and sick headaches. He also advertised Eureka Headache Cure and Grip Syrup which would stop a cold in the beginning.

In Burlington, the Wells and Richardson Co. (which made Diamond Dyes) advertised their Paine's Celery Compound "which makes people well". Lester H. Greene of Montpelier produced a Syrup of Tar which was "guaranteed to cure a cough or the money would be refunded." Dr. Amos Robinson of St. Albans in 1884 advertised "New Cancer Remedy. I extract cancer root and branch in less time and with less pain than can be done by any other method without the use of arsenic, the knife and drawing blood, and if applied in time is a certain death to cancer".

L. H. Farrand of Essex manufactured several remedies. The most interesting one: Farrand's Anodyne Liniment for colics, colds, sore throat, measles and all pains; epizootic in the horse, garget in the milk and black leg in cows. He also had Blood and Liver Bitters good for jaundice and all liver complaints, and Dyspepsia Powders for dizziness and dyspepsia.

In Bennington, H. Koon & Sons manufactured Wilcox Balsam and Koon's Toothache Powder. Other Vermont manufactured or Vermont-advertised remedies included: Smith's Green Mountain

The information on this page was found as scattered advertisements in several old newspapers.

Renovator of St. Albans; Thorn's Extract of Sarsparilla; Dana Carpenter of Middletown Springs (which was a Spa in the early days) naturally had Dana's Grip Remedies. Hinesburg advertised Lithia Water from "The Old Sweet Spring"; the Brown Drops Medical Company was in Richford; Dr. Storr's Pulmonary Balsam, the great pain killer, was advertised in Winooski. In Rutland, Higgins' Tar and Cherry Compound was stated to be good for coughs, colds, throat and lung complaint. There were many more manufacturers and retail outlets which were advertised in Walton's Vermont Register.

There were advertisements of medicines for animals which included Kendall's Spavin Cure of Lyndonville, and T. Harvey Hall's Cow Medicine from the same town. In Eart Barnet Barron W. Brown manufactured a horse medicine. The Equine Remedy was located in Brandon. Other advertisements included Buckingham's Dye for whiskers; Hoe's Oil for Gladness; Ayer's Cherry Pectoral; and Bancrofts Liniment. One may note that many of the drug companies were held in the name of one of the early doctors.

## *NURSING HOMES*

For many years invalids were cared for in their homes or by a nurse in other homes. Today there are 56 nursing homes licensed by the State Board of Health, which furnish care for the aged and infirm. For some years a district nurse was employed by some communities to give free service where applicable to persons in the area. This system was carried on through the assistance of private organizations with municipal support. A state law now allows a municipality to appropriate funds for a nurse or doctor. In some localities nursing homes are operated by hospitals. Heaton Hospital and Barre City hospital are now aftercare hospitals for patients from the Medical Center as well as nursing homes for the aged and infirm. Some hospitals for a number of years had nurses' training courses. More recently such institutions as Castleton State College, the University of Vermont, and Vermont College, Montpelier have furnished such instruction for nurses.

The legislature established a board for the registration of nurses in 1910 and defined the education and training necessary to become a registered nurse. Due to the shortage of the number of nurses and other reasons the title of practical nurse was adopted for those with lesser education and training. Miss Ada M. Stewart of West Rutland, a graduate nurse from Massachusetts, began nursing in Proctor in 1894, thus becoming the first district nurse in the United States.

## *HEALTH BOARDS AND PROFESSIONS*

The following health board and professions were authorized by the legislature on the following dates: Board of Dental Examiners 1882; State Board of Pharmacy 1894; State Board of Osteopaths 1904; State Board of Examiners of Optometry 1908; Board of Examiners of Embalmers 1910; Board of Chiropractic Examination and Registration 1919; Dental Hygienists 1921; Board of Cosmetology 1937; Funeral Directors 1941; and Board of Physical Therapy 1957.

## *AMBULANCE SERVICES*

Ambulance services were cared for chiefly by funeral directors previous to the enactment of 1969 law. The State Board of Health was given authority to divide the state into ambulance districts. The function of such districts is to foster and coordinate ambulance services within the district to insure adequate overall services. The agencies operating ambulance services vary, some being performed by a fire department as in Montpelier.

There are a number of allied agencies which care for our health. The home health agencies number 17; the area agencies on the aging 9; community health agencies 11; and district office of the social welfare department 11.

For years invalids were cared for in their own homes or by a nurse in her home. Today there are 56 nursing homes, licensed by the State Board of Health, which furnish care for the aged and infirm. For some years past a district nurse was hired by some communities to give free service to persons in the area wherever applicable. This system was carried on through the assistance of private organizations together with municipal support. Under state law, a municipality is allowed to appropriate funds for a nurse or doctor. There are three levels of nursing homes: 1) those like Heaton Hospital which gives continued nursing care and is eligible for medicare payment; 2) those like McFarland House in Barre where less care is needed; and 3) which are chiefly rest homes for aged and infirm with lesser amounts of care needed. Some of the hospitals for a number of years provided training courses for nurses. More recently some of the colleges have given such instruction, e.g., Castleton State College, University of Vermont and Vermont College in Montpelier.

In 1910, the legislature established a board for the registration of nurses and defined the education and training necessary to become a registered nurse. Due to the shortage of registered nurses and for other reasons, the position of practicial nurse was adopted for those with lesser education and training. In 1894 Miss Ada M. Stewart of West Rutland, a graduate nurse from Massachusetts, began nursing in Proctor, thus becoming the first district nurse in the United States.

## *OTHER HEALTH BOARDS AND PROFESSIONS*

The following boards and professions were authorized by the legislature on the dates as shown: Board of Dental Examiners - 1882; State Board of Pharmacy - 1894; State Board of Osteopaths - 1904; State Board of Optometry - 1908; Board of Embalmers - 1910; Board of Chiropractic - 1919; Dental Hygienists, Board of Cosmetology - 1937; Funeral Directors - 1941; and Board of Physical Therapy - 1957.

## *OVERSEER OF THE POOR*

From the beginning of statehood, the state recognized its debt to the poor or needy by authorizing the selectmen or the Overseer of the Poor to disburse up to ten pounds to a needy person. Transient persons who came to reside in the state could at the direction of the selectmen be notified that they depart. Such persons so warned did not gain residence. Any person who had been removed from a town was subject to whipping, not to exceed ten stripes at the direction of the justice of the peace, should he return. Today any person is allowed to vote if he has been here 30 days and has fulfilled all voting requirements.

Another act required that those persons who were without either close relative or real estate (which could be sold to provide for them) were to be taken care of by the town to which they belonged. The state granted recompense to the town of Dummerston in such a case.

The strife for more equality in the distribution of the almighty dollar was prevalent in the 1830's. The rights of the underprivileged classes were expressed in the formation of workmen's organizations among the artisans, farmers and mechanics. Many workmen's organizations were formed throughout Vermont; a few of these were in Burlington, Calais, St. Albans, Middlebury and Woodstock. One of the objects of the organization was to do away with imprisonment for debt, and another was for a more general and liberalized educational system. According to the sixth annual report of the Prison Discipline Society in Middlebury for the year 1831, there were 94 men and women incarcerated; 25 of them were for sums less than $5.00. According to the report it was estimated that over 4,000 citizens were annually imprisoned for debt.

Finally the legislature recognized the need for assistance to the poor. A law was passed which allowed a town to build, purchase or hire a house of correction (or work house) in which to confine (or set to work) such persons. Each town was to appoint a superintendent of the poor. Towns could jointly establish a poor farm. One of the last such joint actions was the Sheldon Poor House Association. All poor houses were discontinued by later legislation. Later the law was changed to read, "a town may provide housing for the aged and poor who are entitled to receive aid and assistance."

Under the acts of 1967 the Overseer of the Poor was continued in office (by vote of the selectman after October 1, 1968) solely for the purpose of closing out affairs of his office. The act also repealed the law which the towns were required by contract to pay for the support, clothing and transportation or other aid assistance to an inmate of a state institution.

In 1972, the legislature abolished the office of Overseer of the Poor and placed general assistance to the poor and transients within the Department of Social Welfare. A town service officer was established who acted under the direction of the Commissioner of Social Welfare. He could make investigations for general assistance and administered the grant of funds advanced to him for emergency general assistance. This legislation took away any local control of this program.

The Social Welfar Department was given broad powers to take over the administration of all laws which affect the aged, blind and disabled; all services and aid to needy families and children; general and medical services to the needy; and services and their rehabilitation to the blind.

Working-Man's Gazette, Woodstock, September 23, 1830.

## *MINERAL SPRINGS*

"Few of the springs in the state have gained great celerity abroad and visitors to them are not so numerous as those resorting to the acidulous or carbonated springs at Saratoga, but the number of those sojourning at the watering places in Vermont is annually increasing. Clarendon, Highgate, Alburg, Williamstown and Newbury are just becoming the resort of those in quest of health or pleasure during the warm weather of summer."

Sulphurous or sulphurated springs seemed to be the most numerous in Vermont. The springs in Newbury Village, though not broadly publicized gained in attendance due to the efficacy of the water, which closely resembled the water of the famous Blue Lick Water of Kentucky.

Alburg Springs were a place of resort beginning in 1816 and were reputed as being very efficacious for the curing of all forms of cutaceous and scrofulous diseases. With the building of a hotel, the

"Mansion House", the springs gained great popularity for many years.

Highgate Springs was developed in 1840 and a hotel the "Franklin House" was built to accommodate visitors.

The Brunswick Mineral Springs located about a mile and a half south of Brunswick Village contain several springs. The area was developed with hotels in the past which for some unknown reason each time burned. There are about six or seven separate springs which pour forth waters each of which is said to contain a different mineral content, but all contain salts of iron.

The Claredon Springs were first discovered in 1776 and were doubtless among the first ever visited in Vermont for their medicinal virtues. The springs were considered for many years highly efficacious in the cure of bilious complaints, dyspepsia and all cutaneous disorders. From fifteen to twenty-five hundred persons annually visited them before 1860. Spacious hotels were constructed there.

The Williamstown Gulf Spring was noted for its medicinal qualities and a hotel was erected nearby in the Gulf to accommodate visitors.

There are many other springs to which people came to carry away the water in jugs, demijohns and barrels. From others the water was shipped to Boston or New York. One such place was in Sharon owned by Charles Downer and given by him as a State Forest. Some of the springs were reported to give rapid cures to scrupulous afflictions.

E. H. Hitchcock, et. al., Geology of Vermont

### *HEALTH AND WELFARE SELECTED BIBLIOGRAPHY*

Butterfield, Ernest W., *The Early History of Weathersfield,* Address First Congregational Church, Weathersfield, n.p., 1921.
Crockett, Walter H., *Vermont, the Green Mountain State,* Burlington: The Vermont Farm Bureau, 1921.
Hall, Hiland, *History of Wells,* Rutland: The Tuttle Company, 1869.
Ludlum, David M., *Social Ferment in Vermont, 1791-1850,* New York: Columbia University Press, #3, 1939.
Miller, Edward & Wells, Frederic, *History of Ryegate,* St. Johnsbury: The Cowles Press, 1913.
Town Committee & Broad Brook Grange, *Official History of Guilford, 1678-1961,* Town of Guilford, Brattleboro: Vermont Printing Company, 1961.
Wood, Grace Esther Pember, *Wells 200 Years,* Published by Author, 1953.

# Immigration and Emigration

A study of immigrants to Vermont, their nationalities, when and why they came, furnishes us with some interesting facts.

Generally it is thought that the early settlers of Vermont were offspring from those who came over on the Mayflower. A mixture of the races has toiled in our fields and factories since then, and has brought to this state and country a great harvest of knowledge and experience.

As a first example, let us consider the setlement of Ryegate and surrounding towns which began in 1773 when James Whitelaw and David Allen came into possession of the south half of the town of Ryegate in behalf of the Scotch American Company. They immediately wrote to the backing company in glowing terms about the countryside, and in particular said: "There is a road begun to be cut from the Connecticut River to Lake Champlain which goes through the middle of our purchase." Whitelaw followed General Allen as surveyor general for Vermont. He was also manager of the Scotch-American Company, to which he reported that about 121 lots were sold to new emigrés from the Scottish hills and dales.

Sometimes one wonders why they came. The following statement is of interest: "A journey through those portions of Scotland from whence our colonists came would take us among some of the most interesting scenes of a land where, upon every hill and valley, glows the light of history and song. There is no more attractive section in Great Britain and we may wonder how people could bring themselves to leave it for the wilderness of North America."[1] Many of the new immigrants came to those localities where there was employment in the same industries in which they had previously been employed in their native land.

1. Edward Milles and Frederic P. Wells, *History of Ryegate*, 1913.

In the early twenties, the YMCA activities in Proctor included classes for foreign-born men in a new building, where in the beginning there was a class of 40 Hungarians studying English. The classes increased quite rapidly to an average attendance of 61. Due to the generosity of the Proctor family, this nice building helped cement ties with the new citizens. "There are in St. Dominic's Parish about twelve hundred similar native Americans of Irish and French stock predominately, but there is also in the congregation a considerable number of Italians, Hungarians and Poles."

"The Greek Catholic Church was erected in 1906. At the time of its erection the congregation consisted mostly of Austro-Hungarians. The Swedish Evangelical Lutheran St. Paul Society dates back to 1889. The so-called St. Paul Society was formed at that time. The Swedish Evangelical Mission Congregation Church was organized in 1888."[2]

Occasionally immigrants were interested in departing from their mother country so that they would not have to serve in the military.

In Springfield "a new ethnic faction, which started in the 1890's came into more local prominence as the twentieth century began. This was the coming to Springfield of the Russians and Poles to work in the machine shops. Nearly all this group came from an area between Minsk, Russia and Vilna, Poland (as the boundaries were then). They spoke about the same language, called White Russian. The Poles were Roman Catholics; the Russians, Greek Orthodox."

"The first one to arrive in Springfield was probably Peter Kisler, who came about 1892. Mr. Kisler, himself a Russian, married a Polish girl here, with (among her other luggage) 17 petticoats. Alexander Loweul (Lovell) arrived about 1895, and then returned to Russia, but in view of the prospect of military service in the Russian-Japanese War (1904-1905) he returned. Polish and Russian immigration to Springfield continued from then on until 1913. Many of them came after friends already here had written them of the high living standards and the giddy wages (at least relatively) they enjoyed, plus the absence of military training". The only Russian Church in Vermont is located in Springfield with naturally a smaller number of parishioners.[3]

There were some early all English settlements in Vermont such as the one in Newbury. "Our forefathers in Coos, when they applied for a charter to this town, gave it the name of Newbury whence most of them originated, as their ancestors had given the name of that English town to the New England settlement in Massachusetts."[4]

In 1852, John Humphrey and some other Welchmen who had

2. David C. Gale, *The Story of a Marble Town*, 1922.
3. Keith Richard Barney, *The History of Springfield*, 1885-1961, 1972.
4. Frederic P. Wells, *History of Newbury*, 1902.

been drawn hither (Poultney) by recent slate discoveries, while out prospecting found the slate deposit now known as the Eagle Quarry. There was another "industrious Welchman by the name of Griffith Hughes, well acquainted with slate working, with which he had become familiar in his native Wales." In the slate belt are many families now living (such as the Jones and the Williams, to name a few) whose forebearers came from Wales.

The first settlement of Jews in Vermont dates back to 1873. On the 25th of May 1875 a conregation was established in Burlington and built a synagogue there. Many of the early Jews traveled from house to house selling their wares. Today the descendants of those hard-working God-fearing citizens are in the forefront in our mercantile business and legal professions.

Barre and Montpelier were the destination points for many Spaniards in the 1890's and early 1900's. Many of them who came from farms in northern Spain went to work in the granite industry. Some of them emigrated due to their dislike to fight the Riffs in Morocco. The older citizens here together with their children are successful merchants and lawyers, such as (to mention a few names) Joseph Canales in Montpelier, Manuel Villa and Jose Monte in Barre. Many of their number have left Vermont for other parts of the country like California and Florida.

The Italians came from southern as well as northern Italy and Sicily. Probably most of these from Sicily went to work on the railroads at the main railroad centers in Vermont. Another group of workmen flocked to the granite and marble centers. It is quite interesting that a small group settled in Readsboro to work in the wood using plant there.

John Jacob Rettig, a German who wished to avoid drafting into the German Army, came to America with his wife. When the new State House was built in Montpelier in 1857, he worked on Larkin Mead's statue of Ethan Allen and fashioned from wood the Goddess of Agriculture, *Ceres*, which surmounts the State Capitol. The statue, which had deteriorated, was taken down by the late sergeant at-arms, Dwight Dwinell, who constructed the present one out of two-inch pine planks in 1950's in the carpentry shop in the rear of the State House. The statue was designed by Larkin G. Mead, the noted sculptor.

## *SEARCH FOR NEW LANDS*

The early settlers of Vermont came from Connecticut, Massachusetts and New Hampshire. It is thus quite natural that three quarters of the state's population in 1790 was found in the four southern counties, Windham, Windsor, Bennington and Rutland.

These settlers migrating urge was first to the wilderness areas in the northern counties.

A time arrived when the speculators had taken up all of the grants in the state. Settlers then looked to the lands across the border in Quebec, for which newspapers carried glowing accounts of rich lands open for settlement. By 1840 hundreds of Vermonters had migrated to Canada to take up lands in a new country.

Vermonters also crossed Lake Champlain, some on winter's ice, to establish homesteads in Northern New York in such places as Vermontville in Franklin County and Rutland in Jefferson County. Beginning in 1800 and continuing through the 1820's many Vermonters pulled up stakes and sought new lands. As early as 1808 many had headed into central and western New York in some towns of which the population consisted of nearly 75 percent Vermont stock.

As the migration stream pushed further westward into Ohio and other nearby states, glowing letters were sent back telling about the rich farm lands to be found there.

There were many reasons for migrating. After the hilly farms had been cleared and farmed for a generation their thin friable soils were not producing good crops. Vermont had a good trade with Quebec and her citizens prospered until President Thomas Jefferson placed an embargo on all trade with Canada. In the year 1811 there were severe floods particularly in Rutland and Windsor counties. Many saw and grist mills were washed away and the farm lands were covered with gravel and sand or seriously eroded. Following upon the heels of the flood was the closing of the Vermont State Bank in 1812 which probably caused many citizens to suffer losses. The War of 1812 seemed to have had the same effect upon trade with Canada as the previous embargo. However smuggling proceeded with increased momentum. The British army was fed chiefly by Vermont beef and the trade in "ardent spirits" prospered.

As the British Army made its way south up Lake Champlain, many citizens in the northern part of the state left their homes and moved southward and perhaps swelled the westward tide. At about the same time there was a serious outbreak of "spotted fever", which was probably what we now know as cerebro-spinal meningitis. To add to all their problems the winter of 1816 known as the 'cold season' furnished frosts and snow in June, so all crops had to be replanted. Does anyone now wonder why so many tried a new life in a new land?

Population of Vermont: Earliest Census to 1970

| | *The Date* | *Population* | *Number* | *Percent* |
|---|---|---|---|---|
| 1790 | (August 2) | 85,425 | | |
| 1800 | (August 4) | 154,465 | 69,040 | 80.8 |
| 1810 | (August 6) | 217,895 | 63,430 | 41.1 |
| 1820 | (August 7) | 235,981 | 18,086 | 8.3 |
| 1830 | (June 1) | 280,652 | 44,671 | 18.9 |
| 1840 | (June 1) | 219,948 | 11,296 | 4.0 |
| 1850 | (June 1) | 314,120 | 22,172 | 7.6 |
| 1860 | (June 1) | 315,098 | 978 | 0.3 |
| 1870 | (June 1) | 330,551 | 15,453 | 4.9 |
| 1880 | (June 1) | 332,286 | 1,735 | 0.5 |
| 1890 | (June 1) | 332,422 | 136 | |
| 1900 | (June 1) | 342,641 | 11,219 | 3.4 |
| 1910 | (April 15) | 355,956 | 12,315 | 3.6 |
| 1920 | (January 1) | 352,428 | -3,528 | 1.0 |
| 1930 | (April 1) | 359,611 | 7,183 | 2.0 |
| 1940 | (April 1) | 359,231 | -390 | -0.1 |
| 1950 | (April 1) | 377,747 | 18,516 | 5.2 |
| 1960 | (April 1) | 389,981 | 12,134 | 3.2 |
| 1970 | (April 1) | 444,732 | 54,851 | 14.1 |

Up to 1890 Rutland had exceeded Burlington in population. In 1900 6 counties, Addison, Essex, Lamoille, Orange, Orleans and Rutland lost in population. The counties with the chief gain during the past decade were Chittenden and Washington.

William L. Wheaton, ed., Vermont Facts and Figures, 1972, n. p. 4

*IMMIGRATION AND EMIGRATION*

*SELECTED BIBLIOGRAPHY*

Barney, Keith Richard, *The History of Springfield,* Springfield: William L. Bryant Foundation, 1972.
Brigham, Lorimer, *Calendar of Manuscripts, MS-133,* Catalogued in 1970.
Cabot, Mary R., *Annals of Brattleboro, 1681-1895,* Brattleboro: E. L. Hildreth and Company, 2 Vol., 1921.
Haskins, Harold, W., *History of Bradford,* Littleton, N.H.: Courier Printing Company, 1966.
Ludlum, David M., *Social Ferment in Vermont, 1791-1850,* New York: Columbia University Press, 1848.
Smith, Martha Votey, *Remedies of 100 Years Ago.*
Thompson, Zadock, *Natural, Civil Statistical History of Vermont,* Burlington: C. Goodrich, 1842.
Walker, Mabel Gregory, *The Fenian Movement,* Colorado Springs, Colorado: R. Myles, 1969.
Miller, Edmund, and Wells, Frederic P., *History of Ryegate,* St. Johnsbury: The Caledonian, 1913.
Gale, David C., *Proctor: The Story of Marble Town,* Brattleboro: Vermont Printing Company, 1922.

# Indians

John C. Huden[1] writing in the Vermont Quarterly in 1958, summarizes very well the history of the Indian occupation in Vermont through its various periods.

"(I) The Pre-Algonquian ?? B.C. - 2,000 B.C. ??. Evidences of this culture and the Eskimo culture in the form of fish lures and sinkers have been unearthed in Hubbardton. Polished slate knives were located in Swanton, whale-tail ceremonial objects in the Otter Creek region.

(II) The Old Algonquian - 2,000 B.C. ?? - 1,300 A.D. ??. Some artifacts of this age were found at Swanton in the 1870's and near Orwell in 1933-34.

(III) Recent Algonquian 1300 A.D. - 6100 A.D. These tribes included several: the Abanakis who lived along Lake Champlain from Mississquoi Bay to possibly Chimney Point, around Lake Bomoseen, Lake Memphremagog and along the Connecticut River; the Ammonoosuki around Wells River and Barnet; other tribes (all of whom spoke Algonquian dialects) could understand one another and lived in some parts of Vermont. They hated the Iroquois which in Algonquian term means "real adder snake".

(IV) The Iroquois - 1300 A.D. - 1700 A.D. The Iroquois, "People of the Extended Lodge", were in Central New York and the St. Lawrence estuary as early as 1550. They included the Five Nations: Swanees, Cayugas, Oneidas, Onondagas and Mohawks. They controlled Eastern New York north of the Mohawk River plus all of Lake Champlain and the Richelieu River, which on the old maps was called "The Sea of the Iroquois". Thus it is no surprise that Mohawk pottery has been found in the Champlain Valley in Vermont."

When Coos country was first visited by whites, large clearings

1. John C. Huden, *Indian Groups in Vermont,* (Vermont Historical Society, 1958), p. 112.

were found on the intervales and overgrown with a kind of coarse grass. On the high ground east of the mouth of Cow-Meadow Brook in Newbury, domestic implements of various kinds of Indian manufacture were found in considerable number. On the meadow was located the burying ground where the Indians were buried in a sitting posture.

Prior to the settlement of Canada by the French, the Iroquois in numbers occupied all the country south of the St. Lawrence River and resided around Montreal and in the Champlain Valley. They were driven off by the Adirondacks, who lived near Three Rivers. Later the Adirondacks were driven to a safer situation near Quebec City. The Algonquins, a warlike nation were always moving about on the chase instead of cultivating the soil.

When Samuel De champlain arrived in Quebec he found that the Abenakis, a branch of the Algonquins, were actively fighting with the Mohawks of the Five Nations. He left Quebec with only two Indians and on July 4, 1609 he approached Lake Champlain, which bears his name. They were followed by a party of Frenchmen and a few hundred Algonquins, which number was reduced to about sixty.

Champlain proceeded up the Lake where they encountered some Iroquois. A hail of arrows were sped toward his canoe, but to no harm; though on a signal by the Abenaki leader, Champlain discharged his aquebus and instantly killed three Indian chiefs. Champlain was very disgusted with the Algonquin behavior toward the Iroquois.

All the country southward of the St. Lawrence River (which originally was claimed by the Iroquois) was called on ancient maps as "Mere du Iroquois" for Lake Champlain; "Riviere des Iroquois" for the St. Lawrence and the tract of land on the east side of the lake (now Vermont) "Iroquoisia".

As early as 1683 the Five Nations by treaty with the Governor of New York submitted to the sovereignty and protection of Great Britain; and have ever since considered themselves as subject to, and their country as part of Dominion of the Crown.

The routes which the Indians took in going from Canada to Fort Dummer and other places on the Connecticut River were by the way of Lake Champlain, Otter Creek and then down the Black or West River to the Connecticut; also from Lake Champlain they traversed by canoe and portage up the Winooski and over to the White or Wells Rivers to the Connecticut.

Previous to white settlement, the Massachusetts Indians had carried on a war with the Mohawks of Central New York. As the English settlements advanced their boundaries, the enmity by the Indians toward one another lessened and was directed at those whom they considered as their joint enemies. King Philip's War which raged most fiercely during the latter part of 1675 was characterized by the savageness and determination with which the red men hunted the white and the white men, in turn, attacked the red.

The attack and slaughter of persons at Deerfield which occurred in 1765 resulted in the Indians being driven up the Connecticut River by the combined forces of Massachusetts and Connecticut. From the year 1689 when the French began to spread their doctrines among the Indians in Canada and until the year 1763, the Indians attached the border settlements along the Connecticut and Merrimack Rivers.

The peace of Ryswick in 1697 - though ending the war between England and France - did not stop the Indian attacks on the English colonies.

On the death of William III, of England in 1702, war was again declared between the French and English with the result that the French and English colonies in America were at each other's throats again.

The original block houses and forts like Dummer were built to ward off the attack of the Indians. A number of Indians were employed in the building of Fort Dummer where they (the Maquas) were given special treatment, as is evidenced by the following statement of a committee: "That none of ye Indians are stinted as to allowance of provisions, that they have use of their arms gratis, and that their guns be mended at free cost; a supply of knives, pipe, tobacco, lead, shot, flints be given free to them and that one gill of rum a day be given to each Indian. Though the Indians received two shillings a day and the aforesaid provisions, they could not be induced to remain at the Fort for more than a year". The combined attacks from the Abanaki Indians abetted by the French occurred in the 1720's, first at Fort Dummer, then on the upper Connecticut and into New Hampshire.[2]

On August 9, 1780 a party of 21 Indians attacked Barnard and captured three prisoners. Each time that some trouble occurred, the Board of War authorized the recruitment of men to serve with the ranger units and provide for their food and care.

The *Royalton Raid* as described by Zadock Thompson[3] is as follows: "On the morning of the 16th of October 1780 before dawn of day the inhabitants of this town were surprised by the approach of about three hundred Indians of various tribes. They were led by the

2.Benjamin H. Hall, *History of Eastern Vermont,* (New York: D. Appleton & Company, 1858), p. 21.

3.Zadock Thompson, *History of Vermont Natural Civil and Statistical,* (Burlington: C. Goodrich, 1842), p. 69.

Caughnewaga tribe, and left Canada intending to destroy Newbury, a town in the eastern part of Vermont on the Connecticut River. A British lieutenant by the name of Norton was their commander, and one LeMott, a Frenchman, was his second.

"Their pilot or leader was a despicable villain by the name of Hamilton who had been made a prisoner by the Americans at the taking of Burgoyne in 1777. He had been at Newbury and Royalton the preceding summer, on parole of honor; left the latter place with several others under the pretense of going to secret lands in the northern parts of the state; and went to the enemy directly.

"On this day they came across several men from Newbury who were engaged in hunting near the place, where the village of Montpelier now stands, and made them prisoners. They asked whether there was any armed force at Newbury and were told that an armed garrison was kept at New Bury. They then turned toward Royalton, reaching as far as Tunbridge, where they rested over the Sabbath. At the first house near town they took John Hutchins and his brother, Abijah; plundered the house. They threw a spear through the body of Thomas Pember, whom they had pursued. They overtook another youth whom they scalped. An aged woman was saved by having a string of gold beads, which they took instead of murdering her. Zadock Steele was taken as a prisoner to Canada. Twenty-six other persons were taken and delivered to the British in Canada; with them they took thirty horses. They laid waste to 21 houses and 16 new barns filled with hay. They killed about 150 head of cattle, all the sheep and swine found. All household furnishings were also destroyed.

"James M. Hotchkiss, who was appointed by the Governor to examine the claims of the Iroquois Indians made a report on November 3, 1865. I recommend the claims of the unfortunate people to the favorable consideration of the legislature. The habit and customs of the Indian Tribes of the country at an early date were such that the occupation of any territory for the purpose of hunting and fishing rendered the possession of the territory as really theirs; as though they had cultivated the fields, built homes, etc.".[4]

The chiefs of the Caughnewagas, a branch of the Iroquois, met with Mr. Hotchkiss. A tribe of the Iroquois at the Lake of the Two Mountains was not represented. Since they had traveled from place to place in Vermont and no claim of ownership was set up for nearly a century and a quarter, it seems that they had parted with their title in some manner. In their treaty with New York they accepted the sum of about $20,000.00 and extinguished their claim to a tract

4. James Hotchkiss, *Report of the Commissioner Appoined by the Governor on the Claims of the Iroquois Indians,* 1855.

much larger than the State of Vermont for which they asked $89,000. Several appropriations as gratuities were made and rejected.

Colonel John Lydius born in Albany, New York 1694, the son of a Dutch minister, purported to have a deed from the Mohawk Indians to a tract of 60 miles south from Otter Creek and 24 miles wide. It covered nearly all of Addison County and a large part of Rutland County. His deed dated 1st February 1732 is about the only evidence that the Mohawk Indians, themselves, counted the land as their own.

Kalm in 1748 on his visit to Chimney Point stated that the country does not contain such extensive forests of fir, black, white and red as formerly due to the great fires set by the Indians when they were hunting.

Hemingway in the History of Addison County states: "On the morning previous to the taking of Crown Point by Burgoyne, Mrs. John Strong was sitting at her breakfast table. Her two sons, Asa and Samuel, had started at daybreak to hunt for young cattle that had strayed into the woods. Mr. Strong had gone to Rutland to procure supplies of Beef for the American forces at Ticonderoga and Crown Point. A Mrs. Markham came to her cabin and rushed in with the statement, 'The Indians are coming, we are all flying. There are bateau at the Point to take us off, and you must hurry!'.

"Mrs. Strong though in feeble health with a baby six months old who was placed in a sack with head and shoulders showing; and with the babe fastened to an older sister's back, directed them to go to the Point, which she eventually reached just as the boat with her children was about to leave. They arrived safely that night in Whitehall. At dusk the boys returned and found their house in a blazing ruin." [5]

*INDIANS*
*SELECTED BIBLIOGRAPHY*

Bailey, John H., *Archaeology in Vermont*, pp. 4, 1938.
Daniels, Thomas, *Vermont Indians*, 1963.
Crockett, Walter, *History of Vermont*, Vol. I.
Grout, William, *Indian History of Northern Vermont*, 1870.
Hall, Hiland, *Early History of Vermont*, 1868.
Hayes, Lyman, S., *History of Rockingham*, 1902.
Hotchkiss, James, *Commissioner's Report on the Claims of Iroquois Indians*, 1855.
Juden, James C., *Archaeology in Vermont*, Monograph, 1957.
Ibid, *Indian Place Names in Vermont*, Monograph, 1957.
Lovejoy, Evelyn W., *History of Royalton*, 1911.

5 Abby Maria Hemenway, *Vermont Historical Gazetteer*, (Montpelier: Watchman and State Journal, 1882), p. 104.

Perkins, George Henry, *Aboringinal Remains in the Champlain Valley*, Reprint from *American Anthropologist*, Vol. 14, #I., 1912.
Swift, Samuel, *History of Middlebury*, 1859.
Thompson, Zadock, *Thompson's Vermont*, 1842.
Vermont Historical Society, *Prehistoric Vermont - Evidences of Early Occupation of Indian Tribes*, Proceedings of 1905-6.
Vermont Archaeological Society, *VAS Newsletter*, 1974.
Wright, Ruth, *From Icecap to Interstate*, (*A History of Colchester*), 1963.

*A marble quarry of Vermont Marble Co. of Proctor, Vermont*

*Rock of Ages granite quarry, Barre, Vermont*

# Industry

Vermont industry began in the home in a modest way to meet the needs of the early settlers. Since they had no great amount of ready money, much of the trade was carried on by barter. The first industry was the burning of the wood made from clearings to produce potash and pearlash.

Lye leached from the wood ashes was boiled down in iron kettles to a solid mass known as "black salts". The black salts were burned in a brick kiln at a high temperature, resulting in a salable product known as pearlash, which found use as a baking powder and many other uses.

The first gristmills and sawmills[1] were driven by water impounded behind small dams. Corn was ground between two massive stones driven by water power, one stone a rotating one known as the runner which revolved over the fixed one known as the "bedder". The upper stone had to be sharpened quite frequently by a heavy hammer and chisel.

The village blacksmith was an important person, who procured iron from the numerous Vermont iron works and made the necessities for farm and factory. Such tools included spuds, axes and adzes for the loggers and carpenters, scythes for the hand mowers, crozers for the coopers and numerous other small tools.

There were many home industries such as the hatter who made fur hats from muskrat, beaver and rabbit skins, which were brought to him by the trappers.

In a large stump at the top of a log of wood, a hole was chipped or charred out with fire so it could hold a few quarts of corn. A spring pole was attached by one end to the side of the house or some other weight sufficient to hold it down so the other end would be directly over the charred bowl or mortar. To the upper end of the pole there

1. Perry and Barney, *History of Swanton,* 1882.

was attached a heavy piece of wood called a "plunger or plumper" which served as a pestle. By moving the spring pole up and down and guiding the direction of the plumper enough corn for a meal was speedily ground.[2]

The making of starch was an interesting process. Loads of potatoes were dumped into capacious troughs where they were washed; put through a grinding machine, strained and then put into vats to settle. After the water had been drawn off, the pulpy starch was spread on drying racks. When it was sufficiently dried it was broken up into lumps ready for use.

Prior to 1830, the Fairbanks Brothers in St. Johnsbury made forks and hoes which were hammered out by hand. This type of manufacturing business was taken over in 1848 by George W. Ely and was known as the Moose River Works. Another plant in Wallingford known as the Batchelder Works together with the Ely Plant in St. Johnsbury are now owned by the True Temper Corporation. The metal working division was later transferred outside Vermont so that these plants now manufacture wooden handles for such tools.[3]

Silas Howe of Shaftsbury invented in 1817 the steel square out of two old saw blades. These are still being made in the Town of Shaftsbury. Later other types of carpenter tools were made there but have since been discontinued. The lumber for tool handles is processed at a plant in Gaysville. These enterprises are now owned by the Stanley Works, a Connecticut firm which purchased the old Eagle Square Manufacturing Company.

## *WOOLEN INDUSTRY*

An increased number of sheep were raised as a result of the introduction of Merino sheep. The Legislature was kept busy with the approval of woolen manufacturing companies to make use of the wool produced. Some of the corporations included both wool and cotton in their operations. The Farmers Cotton and Woolen Manufacturing Co. was incorporated in 1811 for operation in Hubbardton. In 1834, a woolen mill was built in Proctorsville which burned in 1844. Eighteen cotton and woolen manufacturing companies were chartered from 1828 to 1834 for operation in the following municipalities: Barnet, Bellows Falls, Bennington (2), Bridgewater*, Ludlow*, Middlebury, Montpelier, Norwich, Perkinsville, Rutland (2), Springfield (2), Weathersfield (2), Windsor, and Woodstock. Of these mills only those marked with an asterisk are in operation today. Mills chartered at other dates include those at Burlington (2), Cavendish*, Danby, Highgate, Ludlow, North Montpelier,

2. Edward T. Fairbanks, *The Town of St. Johnsbury, Vermont,* 1914.
3. Henry S. Wardner, *The Birthplace of Vermont,* 1927.

Rockingham, Sheldon, Stockbridge, Swanton, Vergennes, Manchester, Northfield and Winooski. In 1834 there were four fulling mills which operated in Cavendish to cleanse, scour and press woolen goods, and there were such mills in other communities.[4]

Woolen fabric mills were a major state industry for a hundred years until the plants were gradually moved to the south to get cheaper labor. So there are left only three such mills in the state. Notable among the old mills were the Dewey Mills in Quechee built in 1836, Gay Brothers in Cavendish, and the large mills of the American Woolen Company in Winooski.

In recent years mills manufacturing woolen ski wear and employing about 200-250 persons each have operated successfully in Johnson, Newport and Bennington.

There are several plants, employing about the same number of persons, which are located in the towns of Randolph, Bennington, Bradford, Poultney, and the cities of Burlington and Rutland which manufacture dress goods.

There are about thirty other plants classified as textiles which make men's and boys' clothing, women and childrens' underwear and knited fabrics.

*Mills operating in 1974

## *TANNERIES*

Tanneries were also one of the first Vermont industries, due to the need for good leather for boots and shoes. Tanneries were established in the early 1800's in many towns throughout the state. To name a few: Cavendish (2), Middlebury, Ripton and many others. In 1810 in Cabot, a distillery was converted into a tannery and hemlock bark was ground very fine between stones by horse power (later by water power).

In early times after the hair had been removed from the hides, they were washed and then soaked in a solution of salt, hen manure and water. The hides were then laid out in layers in huge vats, into which ground hemlock or chestnut bark (this was before the chestnut trees in Vermont were killed by the chestnut bark disease) in the right amount was placed, and the vat filled with water.

It required about six months for the hide to be properly tanned. The hair was sold to plasterers who used it to hold mortar together, as one may observe in many of our older homes.

In order to outfit our soliders with a sufficient amount of leather for shoes and other necessities, an early law was enacted which

4. Childs, *History of Addison County.*

prohibited the transport or sale of raw or untanned hides out of the state, unless they were exchanged for leather.[5]

## *IRON*

With the development of the iron industry, a large amount of timber was burned to produce charcoal. In the Vermont hills there were many varieties of minerals and rocks from which new industries developed. The discovery of iron ore in many towns was the beginning of the iron industry. Bog iron or hematite was found scattered throughout the western side of the state and in some places on the eastern side. Many of the forefathers were very foresighted, as is evidenced by a vote taken in the town of Brandon in February 1787. "The five acre pitch which is the school falls is to be let to build iron works on, if there be found iron ore sufficient to supply the same." Iron ore was mined or excavated near Forestdale, where a forge made shovels which were sold in 1810 in Boston.

In 1820, the first blast furnace - probably located on the aforementioned site - produced from this hematite a soft, superior grey iron, not liable to crack on exposure to heat, and yielding, thus treated, fifty percent pure iron.

Charcoal, the heat producer, was brought from Goshen, where there was a settlement of charcoal burners who mingled little with their townsmen. The old "Conant Stove", the first cook stove to be made in Vermont was cast at this first blast furnace. Previously, stoves had come from a factory in Troy, New York. "It was the inauguration of a new era in the culinary kingdom; the pleasant old fireplace with swinging crane of well-filled pots and kettles, hearth spiders with legs, and bake kettles and tin bakers to stand before the blazing fire.logs and bake custard pies in, all went down at once and disappeared before that first stove, without so much as a passing struggle."

By 1845, the iron industry in Brandon produced some 1200 tons of iron and employed 200 men. The Iron and Car Wheel Company there employed 50 men. A variety of kettles, tools, wagon equipment, fireplace furnishings and stoves made there were sold in New York, Ohio and New England. Heavy transportation costs caused the end of this industry.[6]

"Iron ore is found in the south part of Monkton in large quantities. This ore makes excellent iron and it has been extensively manufactured at Vergennes and Bristol. But it is said that it is not rich, and is usually mixed with ore from Crown Point, New York,

5. J. C. Williams, *The History and Map of Danby* (Rutland: Mclean Robbins, 1869) p. 389.
6. Committee of Six, *History of Brandon,* N.P. 1962, p. 46.

and other palces west of the Lake."[7] The writer's father in winter drew the high grade ores from the Town of Moriah, N. Y. across Lake Champlain, when ice bound, to Vergennes. In 1801-2, there was an iron forge in Woodford Hollow which made bar iron and anchors for United States gunboats. The Vergennes forge made chainshot and armaments for the War of 1812. It was here that McDonough's boats were outfitted. Other locations which had iron forges included: Fair Haven, Bennington, Elmore, Bristol, Troy, Lincoln, Salisbury, East Middlebury and others.

There are two large scale companies which have operated for years in Vermont - the E. T. and H. K. Fairbanks Company, now known as the Fairbanks Morse Company, and the Howe Scale Company of Rutland now known as the Howe-Richardson Company. The Howe Scale Company was started in Brandon in 1857.

In 1828, Ashael Hubbard was successful in the manufacture of a hydraulic engine, and founded the National Hydraulic Company in Windsor in 1830.

## *COPPER INDUSTRY*

"There appears to be two divisions or lines of copper deposits in Vermont; one on the eastern side and one in the middle portion of the state. The eastern portion is represented by the Corinth, Vershire and Strafford mines, which were prosecuted for years with great vigor and success. The Vermont Copper Manufacturing Company, founded by local people, was incorporated in 1831 to dig ore and minerals and sell them. Excavations were made on the vein, but in consequence of the inexperience of those having the business in charge, little or no copper was ever obtained from the ore smelted. In 1854 a new charter was granted under the name of Vermont Copper Mining Company, which was owned by Boston and Maryland interests. The operation was quite successful, having sold up to 1860 about 2,500 tons of copper."

Nearly three-quarters of the recorded production of the Elizabeth Mine was achieved since its reopening in 1943 by the Vermont Copper Company under the active leadership of George Ellis of Bennington, and Stanley C. Wilson, former governor of Vermont, and others. From 1943 to the end of 1952, the company reported a production of copper ore amounting to 1,568,000 tons.

This mine was discovered in 1793 and for several years operated for copper as ore. The operation which lasted for several years was not very profitable so it was discontinued in 1839. Under a new company there was produced monthly about five tons of pig copper, which had a ready market in Boston. Production at all places

7. Leon Bushey, *History of Monkton* (N.P., 1962)

continued until the drop in prices after World War I. Only the Elizabeth Mine was active at any time since then.[8]

## *KAOLIN*

Commercial quantities of Kaolin were extensively manufactured from the foundries in Bennington, Brandon and Monkton. The Kaolin has been used in the manufacture of paper, fire bricks, white earthen ware, procelain, vulcanized India rubber, ironstone, china and other minor products. Pure Kaolin is white in color.

"The Monkton Kaolin Works was under the management of B. F. Goss since 1894. The production of 1500 tons yearly gave employment to 13 men."[9] The product there was used chiefly as a filler in the manufacture of paper. The Brandon Iron and Car Wheel Company sold their product from the mine in Forestdale by the name of paper clay.

## *SLATE*

Roofing slate in Vermont is found to exist in three distinct areas, occupying the eastern, middle and western portions of the state. The argillaceous or clay slate extends from Guilford in the south until it meets the granite outcrops in Essex County. In 1855 slate was quarried by the Waterford Slate Company about four miles east of St. Johnsbury. Some of the slate was used for tombstones and has weathered for over a hundred years. Slate companies operated in the Fairlee and Thetford areas in the 1850's. The New England Slate Company, the oldest in the state, began operations in Guilford in 1812. This slate was hard to split and necessitated heavy timbers to support the thicknesses, and further, it tarnished with iron oxide. The importation of Welsh slate and the factors mentioned above curtailed these regional businesses.

The middle range extends from Lake Memphremagog to Barnard. It includes the Northfield slate belt, which runs in a continuous area in the western part of the town just east of Dog River. The belt was approximately one mile wide and became narrower as it approached the southern part of the town. The slate which varied from a bluish gray to black in color, was fissle and could be trimmed. It had a fine texture and the cleavage surface was smooth. Several quarries were operated in the 1860's and 1870's, and the Black Slate Company was the largest operator, suspending operations in 1917 due to financial problems. The state geologist report of 1919 stated that the slate

8. H. E. McKinstry and Aimo Mikkola, *Elizabeth Copper Mine*, (Vermont Reprint from Economic Geology, Vol. 9, No. I, 1954)

9. Leon Bushey, *History of Monkton* (Monkton, N.P. 1962), p. 157.

was of excellent quality, and that the quarries could be operated with good financial returns on the money invested.[10]

The principal zone in the eastern belt extends from Lake Bomoseen and Glen Lakes area south 25 miles to the Villages of Pawlet and West Pawlet. The slate in this belt resembles the Welsh slate and is remarkably free from silex and othe foreign impurities. Green and purple are the predominating colors, with some on the reddish tinge.

In 1845, Alanson Allen of Fair Haven first commenced working the slate quarries in the region, limiting his business to the manufacture of school slates and pencils. The West Castleton Railroad and Slate Company in 1853 commenced sawing slate for black boards, billiard beds, and two years later successfully enameled slate, which was used for mantle pieces, table and bureau tops. During the year 1866 there were many slate companies incorporated by the legislature. About 1847, the manufacture of school slates was abandoned for roofing slate.

"In 1852, John Humphrey and some other Welchmen had been drawn to Poultney by the recent slate discoveries. There was another industrious Welchman by the name of Griffith Hughes, well acquainted with slate working, with which he had become familiar in his native Wales."[11]

## *MARBLE*

The only scientifically-called true marble is metamorphosed limestone, which is found in a belt extending from Manchester to Middlebury. Marble as its name implies, includes those varieties of carbonate of lime, or lime and magnesium. The Champlain marbles which are not metamorphic are just as they were originally deposited. They extend south from the Canadian border in a narrow belt along Lake Champlain. They belong to an older period than the true white marbles to the south. Their colors are white with various shades of red, and from dark red-brown to delicate flesh color. Sometimes the colors of olive and green are found.

The Chazy black limestone is a trade black marble, the quarries of which are located on Isle La Motte, and are owned by the Vermont Marble Company. The Isle La Motte quarries, some of which were opened prior to the revolution, make excellent tiling. This marble contains many trilobites as may be seen on the floor of the State Capitol Building in Montpelier. Marble from Isle La Motte was used for the fortifications of Isle aux Noix, locks on the Chambly canal,

10. John Gregory, *History of the Town of Northfield* (Montpelier: Argus and Patriot, 1878) pp. 209-245.

11. Joseph Joslin, et. al., *History of Poultney* (Poultney: Journal Press, 1875).

and as abutments and piers for the bridge over the Richelieu River at Chambly, Quebec.

There are four classes of marble - Vermont (aeolian) white marble, the Winooski, the variegated of Plymouth, and the Isle La Motte. The serpentine of Roxbury and Plymouth is known as Verd-antique. Green bands are found in the marble about West Rutland.[12]

In 1795, Jeremiah Sheldon opened up the first marble quarry in Pittsford. In 1804 Eben Judd of Middlebury adopted the plan and sawed the first marble in a mill, built by Ephraim Jones in 1806 on Stevens Brook. The True Marble Company started quarrying in Whipple Hollow in 1807. Following this operation, many marble companies sprang up in Clarendon, Brandon, Pittsford and Rutland. The variety of marble which is most used is the granular white.[13]

The Verd-antique quarry in Cavendish was opened about 1835 before the Rutland Railroad was conceived, and operations were suspended in 1858.

The legislature in 1866 incorporated the following companies: the American Marble Co., Eureka Marble Co., Excelsior Marble Co., Fair Haven Marble and Marbelized Slate Company, Leicester Marble Company, Munger Street Marble Company, Neshobe Marble Co., Powers Marble Co., West Rutland Steam Marble Company (formerly the Sheldon and A. Slason Marble Company); in 1856, the St. Albans Marble Company, and the Sudbury Marble Company.

The marble factory in Middlebury was built in 1802 and enlarged in 1808.[14]

## *GOLD*

Gold in small quantities has been found in several localities of the state. Traces of gold have been found in Plymouth, Wolcott, and Bridgewater. William Hankerson discovered gold and secured a claim at Plymouth Five Corners, where from a small space not over five feet deept, he extracted $400.00 worth of gold. It has been stated that between seven and eight thousand dollars worth of gold was mined during 1859. Dry diggings have been made, but no bonanza has ever been reached. Gold is today panned in the stream leading into Five Corners, but only a few flakes are obtained.

Several companies - the Plymouth Gold Mining Company, the Warren Gold Mining Company, and the Boston and Vermont Gold Mining Company - were established for the purpose of mining gold, silver, lead, iron and all manner of minerals.

12. E. H. Hitchcock, et. al., *Geology of Vermont* (Claremont, N.H.: Claremont Mfg. Co., 1861) p. 860.

13. H. P. Smith and W. S. Rann, *Childs History of Addison County.*

*14.* Childs History of Rutland County.

## *LEAD*

Lead veins were early described by geologists as being located one-half mile northeast of Thetford Hill. Other small veins were located in Morristown and Norwich. As a result of these reports, the Vermont Lead Refining and Manufacturing Company was incorporated in 1825, and the Sunderland Mining and Manufacturing Company in 1836.[15]

## *SALT*

As a result of finding of salt wells near Syracuse, N.Y., interest developed toward its exploration in Vermont. The legislature in 1828 incorporated the Vermont Salt Company in Montpelier. The state treasurer was authorized to pay the company $500.00 as a premium for the first 500 bushels of salt produced from water obtained by boring. In Montpelier a well was drilled on the banks of the Winooski River near the present Red Arch Bridge; however, their search was fruitless, although they drilled to some considerable depth.

## *GLASS*

A glass factory in Salisbury flourished during the War of 1812, but soon folded up. The legislature incorporated several companies to manufacture glass: The Vermont Glass Company in 1810, the Otter Creek Glass Company of Vergennes, which operated during 1834-9, the Manchester Glass Company of 1835, the Pittsford Glass Company, 1840, and the Champlain Glass Company of Burlington, 1827, which manufactured window glass for several years.

## *GRANITE*

Granite is found on the eastern side of the state from Canada southward. It varies in texture and color from white to darker colors, depending upon the admixture of other materials.

The best quality granite is found in the Barre belt. There are two areas, Millstone Hill and Cobble Hill to the north of Barre. When John Wheaton acquired property on Cobble Hill, he probably little realized how great an amount of granite would be taken later from Cobble and Millstone Hills. Robert Parker was probably the first quarry operator on the land which Wheaton acquired.

From 1833-37, the State of Vermont paid Mr. Wheaton $100.00 per year for the stone needed in building the capitol building. Joseph Glidden and his son, Mark, drew granite from the Cobble

15. E. H. Hitchcock, et. al., *Geology of Vermont,* Vol. II. (Claremont, N.H.: Claremont Mfg. Co., 1861), p. 838.

Hill quarries to the Montpelier Capitol site. They left home at four o'clock in the morning with a four-horse team and a yoke of oxen for the quarry. With their load they traveled to Montpelier, unloaded and returned home at ten o'clock that night. For eighteen hours work and twenty-five miles journey, they received the sum of $4.00. The Wheaton quarry, the oldest in the town, was later sold to the E. L. Smith Granite Company, which later removed their operations to Millstone Hill.

There were, in 1903, not less than about 100 quarries in and about Millstone Hill, which were operated by about 35 companies, the principal ones which were the E. L. Smith Company, Wells and Lamson Company, Marr and Gordon, Barclay and Gazely. About 3,000 men were employed at this time in mining and manufacturing monuments and building stones in the Barre area (which includes Montpelier and other surrounding towns.) The oldest of the present operators on Millstone Hill is the Wells and Lamson Quarry, which was organized in 1883 by S. O. Wells, George Lamson, and J. K. Pirie.

By 1950, only two firms, the Rock of Ages Corporation and the Wells and Lamson Quarry Company have survived in the quarry phase of the industry. There are a hundred fabricating plants and several industries which service the granite industry.

Some granite was drilled at Blue Mountain in Ryegate as early as 1783. This granite lies in thin sheets ranging from a few inches thick to twenty feet. It varies from fine to medium to coarse in texture; has both light and dark colors, and lacks any iron or other blemishes. Granite was cut here by 1808, for lintels and stone steps. The first monuments were cut here in 1854. The National Granite Cutters Association branch was organized here in 1885.

The granite quarry in *Dummerston* had both light and dark stones. It was operated in 1898 by the C. E. Lyon Granite Company of Brattleboro. When the West River Railroad was washed out by the 1927 flood, the operations of this quarry soon ceased.

The Woodbury granite quarries were opened about 1888 and operations were begun in six quarries in 1898. A railroad was built by the St. Johnsbury and Lake Champlain railroad to the quarries and Hardwick where there were several finishing plants. The railroad was abandoned and quarry operations ended several years ago.

The granite in the quarry at *Bethel* goes by the trade name of Bethel White Granite. A spur track was built from Bethel station of the Central Vermont Railroad to the quarry, which is now owned by the Rock of Ages Corporation.[16]

16. E. H. Hitchcock, et. al., *Geology of Vermont*, Vol. II. (Claremont, N.H.: Claremont Mfg. Co., 1861), p. 736.

An interesting episode occurred a few years ago. The federal government advertised for bids for Bethel White granite for a new building to be constructed on Constitution Avenue, in Washington, D.C. A Massachusetts concern received the bid, and they were unable to arrange a suitable price with the Rock of Ages Company. One day the owner of the Massachusetts concern while traveling from Rutland to White River Junction, observed the granite in the church at Sherburne. From inquiries he learned that this granite had come from a quarry in *Plymouth,* now a part of the Calvin Coolidge State Forest. A sample rock from this quarry was sent to the architect of the capitol, who pronounced it acceptable. A purchase agreement was entered into with the state for the needed granite. Over $10,000.00 was realized up to 1970 by the state from this quarry, all from the particular area which was purchased in 1925 for $3.00.

On the east side of *Ascutney* Mountain there is a quarry which furnished what was called Windsor granite. However, it is really a handsome dark green syenite. Columns about 3½ feet in diameter and about 28 feet long were quarried for pillars which were used in the library of Columbia University. Such columns were also used in a bank in Montreal. The quarry has been inoperative for some time.[17]

## *SOAPSTONE*

Steatite is known by various names the most common of which is soapstone. Other names include potstone it having been used for culinary vessels by the aborigines, and chalkstone, due to its leaving a trace like chalk. Soapstone has been used for numerous purposes, such as architectural, and its ability to withstand heat makes it very valuable for lining furnaces, lime kilns, stoves, fireplaces and arches.[18]

The quarries in Grafton and Athens were worked for soapstone longer and with more profit (up to 1861, at least) than any other such quarry in Vermont, having been successfully worked beginning about 1820. In the environs of Amsden, a genissoid rock was found in 1860 that covered and encased a bed of soapstone. Stoves were made here in 1861.

The Windsor County Soapstone Company owned quarries located on the quarry road which were opened by J. M. Billings about 1850. At that time they were said to be about the best in the county, and turned out about a thousand tons of soapstone each year. The business was later developed by the Hicks family, with a mill beside

17. Vermont State *Geologist Report,* Vol. II. 1903-1940.

18. E. H. Hitchcock, *Geology of Vermont,* Vol. II. (Claremont, N.H.: Claremont Mfg. Co., 1861), p. 783.

the Black River in Perkinsville which was demolished when the North Springfield Dam was constructed by the Army Engineers in 1960.[19]

## *URANIUM*

In the 1960's after determining from the air of the existence of Uranium on Okemo Mountain, Ludlow in the Okemo State Forest a Texas Company was given the authority by the state to explore the area further by drilling. After considerable drilling to some depth, it was determined that the lode was not of sufficient depth to make it economically feasible to mine the area.

## *MACHINE TOOLS*

The Jones and Lamson Company was founded in 1829 as the National Hydraulic Co. of Windsor, which had there a conglomerate business of machine tools and textiles. The Jones and Lamson Co. split off in 1876 and established itself in Springfield solely as a machine tool industry. Three new manufacturing firms appeared on the scene. William L. Bryant who worked as chief draughtsman for Jones and Lamson received a patent on a new chuck grinding machine and formed the Bryand Chuck Grinding Co. He had the support of Mr. Hartman and W. D. Woolson in the new company which began manufacturing in 1910.

Edwin R. Fellows came to Springfield in 1889 as an associate of James Hartness in the Jones and Lamson Co. In 1896 Fellows obtained a patent on his gear shaper machine and formed the Fellows Gear Shaper Co. James Hartness arrived in Springfield on Jan. 1, 1889 and at once took over the management of the Jones and Lamson Company. Since his boyhood days he had demonstrated an unusual aptitude which reached fruition in Vermont. With his invention of the flat turret lathe, he pursuaded the officers of the company to give up the manufacture of many different products and concentrate upon his invention, which pulled the company out of its poor financial situation into a thriving firm. In 1919 he was elected governor of Vermont.[20]

## *VERMONT PAPER MAKING*

The first paper mill in Vermont was built in Bennington in 1784. The first paper mills used only rags. A legislative commission reported in 1809 that there were 7 mills in the state, which number had

19. Thelma P. Hoisington, *Glimpses of Weathersfield*, 1761-1961.

20. Keith Richard Barney, *The History of Springfield*, 1885-1961 (Springfield: William L. Bryant Foundation, 1972), p. 72.

increased to 15 by 1820 and gave employment to 69 men, 38 women, 33 boys and 5 girls. Anthony Haskell and David Russell, printers, petitioned the Vermont legislature in 1783 to conduct a lottery of 200 pounds to build a paper mill in Bennington Falls, which petition was granted, and the mill was built the next year, using 15 tons of rags.

The second paper mill in the state was built on the banks of the Castleton River in Fair Haven in 1794. Colonel Matthew Lyon stated, 'When it was known three quarters of a pound of rags saved from worn out linens and cotton clothes of every soul in the county annually, would be ample to supply a mill Lyon offered storekeepers writing paper and wrapping paper in exchange for rags. A method of making paper from a combination of basswood and rags was developed at the mill as announced by Matthew's son, James, in the local paper in 1794. In 1799 Mr. Lyon disposed of his mill, and all other interests in business enterprises due to his removal to Kentucky two years later.

The third mill in Vermont was built on Otter Creek at Middlebury Falls about 1800. Many paper mills were built in succeeding years. Abijah Burbank of a paper making family from Sutton, Mass. built a mill in Sharon in 1801. A mill built in 1802 at Bellows Falls by Elisha Kingsberry and William Blake of Alstead, N.H. in 90 years grew to be one of the largest mills in the country. Silas Burbank, a brother of Abijah erected a paper mill in Montpelier in 1806 on the banks of the Onion river at the falls. The mill was sold and burned in 1818 and rebuilt. Across the river from this mill in the town of Berlin, Samuel Gove built a mill in 1810 which was sold to E. P. Walton. Other mills were located in Milton 1810; Bradford, 1810; Guilford, 1810; Wells River 1819; Brattleboro, 1811; Bennington, 1812; Burlington, 1820, and the last mill built in Vermont prior to 1821 was built in Putney and is still operating.[21]

In 1906 the Ryegate Paper Company was incorporated under the laws of New Hampshire and makes a tissue paper.

## *SILVERSMITHS*

Roswell and Bradbury Smith became the greatest silversmith craftsmen in Vermont, both for quantity and quality of work. Roswell was born in Unity, N.H. in 1804 and came to Woodstock in 1839 after apprenticing to his brother in the art of working silver. He went into business for himself and soon had the largest establishment in the state, employing a dozen journeymen in addition to the

21. Marcus Allen McCorison, *Paper Making and Trade, Vermont* 1784-1820 (Vermont Historical Society Vol. XXI.) p. 209.

apprentices and traveling salesmen, who sold his wares from door to door. His specialty was silver cream spoons.[22]

## *ELECTRICAL ENERGY*

### *Green Mountain Power Corporation*

''Electricity was very much in the news during the 1800's. Michael Faraday demonstrated the first dynamo in 1831, by which electricity could be produced mechanically. Arc lighting systems were invented and replaced gas lights in commerical installations during the 1870's in some large cities. Thomas A. Edison invented the first practical light bulb in 1879 and soon after designed an efficient electrical generating and distribution (direct current) system.

A bookbinder in Montpelier, M. W. Wheelock, followed the headlines with imaginative interest and finally persuaded the Edison Company to send a representative to Montpelier to demonstrate an electric dynamo. The dynamo was attached to a water motor and the combination was set up in the Cross Baking Company building, where it provided demonstration lighting for several weeks. Later in 1886, the Thompson Houston Electric Company sent a small engine, boiler and six-light generator to Montpelier on a flat car. Six street lights were set up and wired on Main Street for demonstration purposes. During the same year the Standard Light and Power Manufacturing Company was organized for this purpose in the area now served by the Green Mountain Power. The Brush Swan Electric Light and Power Company of Burlington was organized the year previous. They constructed a hydro-generation plant at Winooski Falls and extended lighting power to Burlington by a two-mile circuit.

The Standard Light and Power Company of Montpelier established their plant at a site behind the buildings on State and Main Street in back of the French Block. For energy to turn their generators, the Company depended upon the water pressure in a ten-inch pipe from the city water system. The following equipment was installed: six water motors, two incandescent light dynamos and one arc light machine. The dynamos had the capacity to operate 300 incandescent lights and the arc light machine could serve 45 arc lights. The plant operated from nightfall to ten o'clock every evening except Saturday, when it operated until midnight because the stores remained open longer.

The Green Mountain Power Company was actually born in 1891 when the Vergennes Electric Company was organized in Vergennes

22. Henry Swan Dana, *History of Woodstock* (New York: Houghton and Mifflin Co., 1887) p. 520.

with a hydro plant below the waterfall on Otter Creek. Many changes have taken place in the Green Mountain Power Company's holdings by the consolidation of forty or more separate roots.

In 1931 all the common stock of the Green Mountain was acquired by the New England Electric System and in 1951 all the previously-owned distribution facilities were reacquired.

The contract of 1956 between the State of Vermont and the New York State Power Authority provided 100,000 kilowatts of low cost St. Lawrence power. Later, more power was contracted with New York for Niagara. The Green Mountain Power Company, the Central Vermont Public Service Corporation and the Citizens Utilities Company joined to incorporate the Vermont Electric Power Company known as Velco for financing and developing the ten million dollar transmission grid required to bring the energy into Vermont and distribute it to the desiring agencies. The system was completed in 1958. The 1951 legislature gave authority to the Public Service Commission as the agent of the State to have full power in any negotiation for the procurement of electrical energy from outside the state. It also has the right to contract for the purchase and resale of such power to electrical distribution agencies within the state.

In 1931, the legislature imposed an excise tax of five-tenths of one mil upon each kilowatt hour of electricity produced within the state. In order to aid and encourage the development of an energy plant in the state, the above excise tax was repealed by the Acts of 1967 and the following legislation was enacted in its stead: "As of March 1968 there is assessed upon any electric generating plant constructed in the State subsequent to July 1965 and having a generating capacity of 200,000 kilowatts or more, a state tax of 1.9 percent of the appraised value thereof. From this tax there is deducted all real estate and personal property taxes paid to any municipality."

In the fall of 1966, Green Mountain Power Corporation and the Central Vermont Public Service Corporation agreed to sponsor a 540,000 kilowatt nuclear power plant to be constructed at Vernon, Vermont on the Connecticut River. A total of ten electric utility companies (including the two previously mentioned) purchased stock in the new entity, Vermont Yankee Nuclear Power Corporation, which - though started in 1967 - was not able to begin operation until 1972. The delay has been partly due to legal actions of environmental groups and to technical reasons.

The first general rate increase requested by the Green Mountain Power Company in its entire history was made in 1971. During 1974 high rate increases have been made by the companies.

Early Electric Power Companies were incorporated as follows: 1884 - The Consolidated Lighting Company of Montpelier; 1894 - the

Village of Barton was granted authority to build a municipal plant; 1900 - the Peoples Lighting, Heating and Power Company of Barre; 1902 - the Essex Power Company with an office in Burlington, J. J. Flynn, President; 1902 - the City of Burlington. In the beginning this plant used coal. In May 1971 when the gas line from Canada had entered Burlington, it turned to the use of gas for generating purposes."

### *Central Vermont Public Service Corporation* (*CVPSC*)

The Central Vermont Public Service Corporation was organized on August 20, 1929 by the consolidation of eight operating utilities then under the common control of the New England Public Service Company, an Augusta, Maine holding company. These companies included, Public Service Corporation of Vermont, Pittsford Power Company, Windsor Electric Light Company, Rutland Railway, Light and Power Company, Middlebury Electric Company, Vermont Hydro Electric Corporation, Bradford Electric Light Company and the Black River Power Company, Inc. Four of these larger companies were built up from the purchase of smaller companies which were first organized in 1902.

These original component firms were doing business for the most part in Vermont, as well as in part of the Connecticut River Valley section in New Hampshire, in addition to a manufactured gas business in Rutland.

Subsequently the company during the period through 1945 acquired the Twin State Gas and Electric Company, Vermont, Inc., the Public Electric Light Company of St. Albans which added 6,600 new customers, and four small electric distribution systems. With the purchase of the Public Electric Light Company it was found necessary to construct a 66,000 volt transmission line to connect those properties with its main system.

The company's New Hampshire intrastate business facilities were transferred at the end of 1949 to a wholly-owned subsidiary corporation, Connecticut Valley Electric Co., Inc. of New Hampshire.

Currently CVPSC serves an area comprising a major portion of eight counties, Addison, Bennington, Caledonia, Franklin, Orange, Rutland, Windham and Windsor and parts of Chittenden, Essex, Lamoille and Washington counties with about 95,000 customers.

Over the years CVPSC has disposed of some of its business such as gas companies, which were acquired with the electric utilities. The companies revenue comes from the following sources, 48% residential, 13% commercial, 27% industrial and 12% other. Its power sources are, 42% nuclear, 40% hydro, 8% oil, 5% coal, and 5% from NEPOOL, purchased power.

NEPOOL is an agreement to which the major investor-owned utilites in New England, including CVPSC and Velco and certain municipal cooperative utilities belong. The agreement provides for joint planning and operation and transmission facilities to insure that the entire region will not be without electric generated power.

Velco, Vermont Electric Power Company, was organized in 1958 to transmit in Vermont St. Lawrence and Niagara power for sale to Vermont utilities. CVPSC owns 86.5% of Velco's Class A common stock with 9% held by Green Mountain Power Company and 4.5% by Citizens Utilities Co. of Newport.

The Vermont Yankee Nuclear Power Corporation constructed a nuclear plant in Vernon, which began power production in 1972. CVPSC owns 31.3% of the common stock of Vermont Yankee, while the Green Mountain Power Corporation holds 17.9%, as leading Vermont sponsors. Together with other Vermont utilities 55% of Vermont Yankee common stock is held by Vermont companies and entitles them to 55% of the output of the unit. CVPSC holds stock in the Yankee Atomic Electric Company in Rowe, Mass., Connecticut Yankee Atomic Power Co. in Haddam Neck, Connecticut, Maine Yankee Atomic Company of Wiscasset, Maine as well as Vermont Yankee Nuclear Power Corporation in Vernon, Vermont.

The CVPSC like all Vermont corporations is regulated by the Vermont Public Service Commission.

From information furnished by Central Vermont Power Co.

### *Municipal Plants*

Early Electric Power Companies were incorporated as follows: 1884 - The Consolidated Lighting Company of Montpelier; 1894 - the Village of Barton was granted authority to build a municipal plant; 1900 - the Peoples Lighting, Heating and Power Company of Barre; 1902 - The Essex Power Company with an office in Burlington, J. J. Flynn, President; 1902 - The City of Burlington. In the beginning this plant used coal. In May 1971 when the gas line from Canada had entered Burlington it turned to the use of gas for generating purposes.

The Connecticut River Power Company was authorized by the Legislature to build a dam on the Connecticut River south of the mouth of the West River in the Town of Brattleboro.

In 1972 there were municipal electric plants in the following communities: Barton, Burlington, Enosburg Falls, Hardwick, Hyde Park, Jacksonville, Johnson, Ludlow, Lyndonville, Morrisville, Orleans, Readsboro, Stowe and Swanton.

### *Gas Heat*

On November 15, 1852 the Burlington Gas Light Company was incorporated. The St. Albans Gas Light Company was incorporated on the 16th of November 1859. As a coal gas plant, the Brattleboro Gas Company was incorporated in 1858. The Capital City Gas Company was incorporated in 1902. The Peoples Gas Light Company of Rutland was incorporated in 1902. Vermont Gas Systems Inc. was authorized to do business in 1971. They purchased gas from Trans-Canada on a long-term contract extending to 1991. Their supply of gas came from Canada by pipeline which also furnished the municipalities of Swanton, St. Albans, Essex, Winooski, South Burlington and Burlington. Some New England companies are importing liquified natural gas from Algeria. The gas companies in Barre, Montpelier, St. Johnsbury, Rutland and Bennington began using propane gas in 1972.

### *Rural Electric Cooperatives*

When Congress established the Rural Electrification Administration in 1935, there were only ten percent of the farm families in the Country who had electricity. The REA was authorized by Congress to loan money to the electric cooperatives at an interest rate of two percent. This low rate was due to the fact that the cooperatives were required to serve all customers along their lines.

Electric cooperatives sell appliances and furnish technical assistance to their members. They also make loans at 3 to 4 percent to their members for the purpose of installation of wiring, electrical machinery and equipment and the purchase of the same including appliances. The names of the three original Vermont cooperatives are Halifax, Washington of East Montpelier and Vermont Electric of Johnson. The incorporation dates of these cooperatives were: Halifax 1952, Washington Electric 1939 and Vermont Electric 1938. The Halifax Electric Cooperative, which was acquired in 1969 by the Vermont Electric Cooperatives serves approximately 1400 members in 16 towns in the counties of Bennington and Windham. The Vermont Electric Cooperative serves 5600 members in 49 towns in the counties of Chittenden, Franklin, Lamoille and Orleans. The Washington Electric Cooperatives serves 5168 members in 41 towns in Caledonia, Orange and Washington Counties. Figures are as of July 1, 1974.

Information furnished by companies.

CHRISTMAS TREES For many years the cutting and sale of Christmas trees has been a considerable business. Trees have been shipped as far away as the sunny south and into the mid-west until competition arose a few years ago by the marketing of Christmas trees from the west coast. All Christmas trees were cut from natural stands until a few years ago. The two species, which were in demand were the balsam fir and the red spruce.

For many years it was easy to find out how many trees were shipped because they were sent by railroads. The trees were shipped on flat cars. The number of trees shipped, the kind and destination was obtained from the railroad companies. Methods of shipment and the species of trees shipped have changed radically during the past few years. White spruce, known to some as "skunk spruce" and black spruce have been added to the list. A tree must have the ability to retain its needles from the cutting in October until Christmas day.

Many plantations are made today for Christmas trees rather than for timber production. Among the Christmas tree species now planted is the Scotch pine, which retains its needles well. In some localities red cedar and white pine are grown.

Not all trees have a symmetrical form, so in recent years the young trees are shaped annually by a sharp long bladed knife or machete. In common with today's practises most all of the Christmas trees are shipped by trucks.

## *WOOD INDUSTRY*

At the time of the construction of Fort Dummer in 1724 Vermont was a wilderness except for a few glades and openings caused by fires. By 1840 the early settlers had cleared about 4,000,000 acres for agricultural use. From that time down to the present the forest area has increased as farm lands were abandoned so now we find that there are about 4,000,000 acres of forest land in the state. There is today an apparent tendency of an increase in the area of forested lands since there are still many high and rough acres upon which modern agricultural machinery cannot be used.

Sawmills and grist mills were first established along streams in nearly every township since mills were driven by waterpower. The timber cut was chiefly softwoods such as pine, hemlock and spruce with a sprinkling of other softwoods. The timber cut and sawn was chiefly for home consumption. All timber suitable for His Majesty's Navy was marked and saved for that purpose in early times. At the foot of the Winooski falls timber was tied into rafts and floated down the Lake and Richelieu River to Quebec, where it was taken by steamers to England.

With the opening of the Champlain Canal the market changed and in the 1840's with the coming of the railroads the markets for lumber took another change. With the advent of the automobile and especially in the past twenty-five years trucks are carrying lumber directly from the mills to factories in Vermont and the northeastern states, principally Massachusetts.

After cutting enough timber for settlers' log homes the market for logs to make clearings for agriculture was for charcoal to use in the growing iron industry. With the construction of pulpmills (see section on paper making) logs were floated as well as pulpwood down feeder streams to the mills on the Connecticut River and to other locations.

Today pulpwood is trucked up to 100 miles to pulpmills in Vermont, New York and New Hampshire. Pulp wood in the Northeast Kingdom is transported today by rail to mills in northern New York. Formerly only spruce was used for pulpwood, however during the past 50 years the pulping processes have been developed to also use hardwood and all softwood species of trees.

Logging was carried on successively by the use of oxen, horses, tractors and trucks which in many cases take the logs from stump to the sawmill. The portable sawmill which was set up on or near the woodlot to be harvested numbered about 100 forty years ago. Today with motor transportation there are very few portable mills operating within the state.

The volume of lumber and wood processed shipped to factories outside the state has increased to 105,761,000 board feet out of a total amount sawn in 1973 of 182,286,000 board feet. The total volume of logs, pulp wood, bolts, posts and poles cut in 1973 amounted in board feet to 258,417,000.

In 1909 there were 593 plants producing lumber and lumber products compared with 221 active mills in 1973.

The power used to operate mills has progressed from water to steam from waste wood, gasoline and diesel fuel to electricity. Due to environmental regulations some mills have now been stopped from burning waste wood to operate their boilers.

The products made from wood have changed greatly over the last fifty years. In 1909 there were 29 cooperage plants which made butter tubs, sap buckets, gathering tanks, and barrels. We had several bobbin plants, the largest manufacturer in the country making golf tees, shoe lasts, ice refrigerators, and a number of other such industries. Today technology and the use of metals and plastics and electricity have closed those earlier industries. Vermont has a number of large furniture plants making high quality furniture, which has been aided by the use of resins, glues and new finishes. There are a number of small plants making furniture. The manufacture of toys has changed to meet today's needs.

In the woods the logging methods have changed during the past fifty years from the use of horses and oxen to tractors to haul and skid logs by means of winches and arches. Modern machinery has been developed to dry lumber and process it.

Today selective cutting of our forests instead of the old clear cutting methods are universally used. Open lands which have been abandoned are being reforested by small seedlings grown at the state nursery at Essex Junction.[1]

## *OTHER INDUSTRIES*

There are over 800 industrial plants as listed by the Agency of Development and Community Affairs, which are operating in Vermont. They include in addition to those mentioned: Food Products, Textile and Apparel Products, Printing and Publishing, Chemical and Allied Products including Plastics, Metals Products including Machinery, Electrical Equipment and Supplies, Transportation Equipment, Instruments and related products.

## *INSURANCE*

A fire insurance company was established in Vermont about twenty-five years previous to a life insurance company. The Ascutney Fire Insurance Company was chartered to operate in Windsor in 1825. In the following year the Vermont Fire Insurance Company began operations in Middlebury with Ira Stewart as its first president. The Vermont Mutual Fire Insurance Company of Montpelier was open for business in March 1828 with John Spalding as president. The Union Mutual Fire Insurance Company of Montpelier was charted on March 24, 1874.

The New England Fire Insurance Company of Rutland was organized in March 1881 with J. M. Havens as president.

The history of life insurance companies in this country goes back to 1812 when a company was formed known as the "Pennsylvania Company for the Insurance of Lives." Insurance companies had existed many years earlier on the continent. The Vermont Life Insurance Company of Burlington was organized on January 1, 1869 with Russell S. Taft as President.

The National Life Insurance Company of Montpelier began business in 1850. Its formation was largely due to the untiring efforts of Dr. Julius Y. Dewey who early became its president and guided its destiny until his death in 1877.

1. Vermont, Reports of the Department of Forests and Parks of several dates.

## *INDUSTRY*
## *SELECTED BIBLIOGRAPHY*


Barney, Keith Richard, *The History of Springfield, 1885-1961* (Springfield: William L. Bryant Foundation, 1872).

Bushey, Leon, *History of Monkton* (NP. Town of Monkton, 1962) p. 6, 157

Butterfield, Ernest W., *Early History of Weathersfield*

Town of Brandon, *History of Brandon,* (Town of Brandon, Brandon, 1962) p. 45.

Dana, Henry Swan, *History of Woodstock* (New York: Houghton, Mifflin & Co. 1887) p. 520.

Fairbanks, Edward T., *The Town of St. Johnsbury, Vermont* (St. Johnsbury: The Cowles Press, p. 592, 1914) p. 148 et seq.

Gregory, John, *History of the Town of Northfield* (Montpelier: Argus and Patriot, 1878) pp. 45, 69.

Hitchcock, E. H., et. al., *Geology of Vermont,* Vol. II.

Hoisington, Thelma P., *Glimpses of Weathersfield,* 1761-1961.

Joslin, Joseph, *History of Poultney* (Poultney: Journal Press, 1875).

McCorson, Marcus Allen, *Paper Making and Trade, Vermont, 1784-1820,* (Vermont Historical Society, Vol. XXXI, #4), p. 209, 245.

McKinstry, H. E. & Mikkola Aimo, *Elizabeth Copper Mine,* Vermont (reprint from Economic Geology, Vol. 9, No. I, 1954).

Perry and Barney, *History of Swanton*

Smith, H. P. & Rann, W. S., *Child's History of Addison County* (Syracuse: D. Mason & Co., 1886).

Ibid, *Child's History of Rutland County.* Ibid.

Thompson, D. P., *History of Montpelier,* (Montpelier: E. P. Walton, 1860).

Vermont, *State Geologists Reports,* Vol. II, 1903-1940.

Wardner, Henry Steele, *The Birthplace of Vermont* (New York: Charles Scribner and Sons, 1927).

Williams, J. C., *The History and Map of Danby* (Rutland: McLean Robbins, 1869), p. 389.

*Main Street Montpelier, City Hall on left, 1927 flood.*

# Labor

Every railroad company in the state according to the laws of 1849 was required to obtain from contractors "sufficient security" for the payment of all labor performed in constructing the road of such company by persons in their employ and such company shall be liable to the day labourers employed by the contractor for labor actually performed on the road.

### *CHILDREN AND WOMEN*

The first child labor laws were passed in Vermont in 1849. The law required that no child between the ages of 8 and 14 could be employed in a mill or factory unless he had attended a public school three or more months within the preceding school year. By 1888 the pupil was required to present to the place of employment a statement from the school to show such attendance. In 1894 the employment of a child under 15 years was required to have had 26 weeks of school together with the certificate.

Now children under sixteen are not permitted to work in any plant on such jobs as working around machines, including oiling, tightening belts or operating saws, jointers and other woodworking machinery.

The 1910 laws prohibited women from working in plants where they would be continually standing. The hours of labor for women and children over 16 and under 18 were then set at not more than ten and a half or 56 hours during a week. Pregnant women were denied employment two weeks before and four weeks after childbirth. There were restrictions that no child may work in certain prohibited industry such as railroading, mining or quarrying if under 16 years of age unless he had completed the 9th grade and then only during vacation, after school and not later than 8 p.m. The law was later extended to those in the two year junior high school. They could not work more than six days a week or before six in the morning or after

7 p.m. in such added locations as pool rooms, bowling alleys, hotels or delivering messages.

*WORKMEN'S COMPENSATION ACT in 1915* was elective between the employee and the employer unless prior to injury it was expressed or implied by the worker that he wished to come under the act. The applications of the act specified what injuries were not covered; liability of third party; contracts, death benefits, periods of compensation, rights of dependents, medical examinations and accident reports. Since 1915 many amendments have been made to strengthen the act, up to 1973. Municipal employees, national guardsmen, and certain highway employees now come under the act.

Compensation has been extended to cover occupational diseases such as silicosis and dermatosis et.al.

## *MEDIATION AND ARBITRATION*

The Commissioner of Labor in 1939 was given authority to confer with the parties in a labor dispute and make a report to the governor. The governor selected a person, unattached from either party to the conflict to try to obtain an amicable settlement of the differences. Should mediation fail the next step was to get the disagreeing parties to submit their differences to a board of arbitration, appointed by the governor. The findings and awards of the board of arbitration were to be binding upon both parties for a period of one year.

The law was later amended stating that the parties should be persuaded to submit their difference to a board of arbitration of three members. The final award of the board of arbitration can be extended for more than a year by agreement of both parties.

## *MINIMUM WAGES*

After the federal government established minimum wages for labor in interstate commerce, Vermont adopted the practice by setting up minimum wages for Vermont. Vermont's first law in 1957 set up a minimum wage of $1.00 per hour. Exceptions and exemptions to the law have been made at nearly every biennial session of the legislature since then. The minimum wage was increased by steps, $1.25; $1.40; $1.60; to $2.00 in 1974.

# Morals and Ethics

## *EARLY LIFE AND CUSTOMS*

The early Vermont settlers had received a grant of land or pitch, or had purchased a tract from some original grantee. His first task was to cut a swath through the forest. When the settler had arrived at his property, he set about cutting the virgin maples, beech, birch, spruce and pines. The trees were felled in long rows where they could be easily burned for potash which is described elsewhere. A further clearing gave him some space for agriculture. His primary interest was housing for his wife and family.

Many of the logs from the clearing were used for the construction of a log house, which could be put together without any metal by using wooden pegs. The cracks between the logs were chinked in with local mosses to keep out the winter cold and rain. The floors were made of split logs hewn on one side and worn smooth by constant use. The door hinges were of wood, as were also the latches. A string or piece of leather passed through a hole to the outside was the means of lifting the inside latch. By pulling the string inside, the door was made fast from the outside. Thus there arose the saying (as an emblem of hospitality): "The latch string always hangs out".[1]

A few sheep, a cow and a pair of oxen together with Shep, the faithful dog, were the first animals on the new farmstead. For many years these people had to depend upon what they raised for food and what they could make for themselves. Since the supply of milk and butter was more desired, few cattle were butchered until a good sized herd was obtained. In the forest were plenty of wild animals (such as deer, bear, squirrels and partridge) plus a bountiful supply

1. Edmund Miller and Frederic P. Wells, *History of Ryegate,* (St. Johnsbury: The Caledonian, 1913), p. 97.

of fish in the streams and lakes, so the food supply of meat was well provided. A wooden plow made from a crooked stick and a sharp point was used in the little clearing to stir up the rich soil so that common vegetables could be raised for the table. Buckwheat and rye were the first crops which were planted in the virgin soil, followed in a couple years by wheat.

The sheep gave from their backs the wool to clothe the family. With considerable handiwork, aided by the nimble hands of the women and children, the sheep were shorn and the wool was washed and carded and spun. It was then woven into cloth for the wife to make the clothes for the entire family.

The juices of sumach, butternut and smart weed were used to dye the cloth. Later hemlock and chestnut bark was also used. As soon as wool and flax could be raised, spinning wheels and looms were set in motion. The charge for a week's spinning was four shillings. One person could card the wool as fast as another could spin it.

Root cellars which were dug into banks of earth served to keep the vegetables from freezing during the winter months.

Oxen to be shod were forced to the ground and their legs were tied together. It was not until about 1800 that the ox sling was introduced to make shoeing easier, by raising him off the ground. The oxcart and sledge were the original vehicles found on the farms, the latter being used both in winter and summer for hauling. Shoulder yokes were built for the oxen. In the early days horses were used chiefly for riding until carriages and wagons were introduced at a later date.[2]

Water was carried from a stream or spring by means of a hand-hewn neckyoke until pump logs were developed for the purpose. Later dug wells were lined with flat stones from which the water was raised with a bucket and rope or with a sweep. With the advent of slate for roofs (see under industry) a cistern was placed in a cellar to catch the water from the roof. Later development of a handpump placed in the kitchen made life much easier for the housewife.

When a new barn or house was to be built, all the neighbors joined in at the raising. Farmers exchanged work with one another at harvest time.

Before the building of tanneries, the cattle were killed, skinned and properly treated on the farm to form leather. The traveling cobbler visited from farm to farm to make the family's yearly supply of boots. In addition to the booter, there were other artisans who traveled about plying their trade. Many industries started up in Vermont from these people who carried their tools and wares first on

2. Ibid, p. 186.

their backs, then later by wagons, followed by the automobile in the late 1890's. The tinkling of a bell announced to the housewife that she should haul out those dull scissors and shears which needed to be sharpened. The next visitor might be the umbrella mender, who would put in a new rib or mend a tear in the umbrella. The rag man knocked at the door with an offer of shiny tin dishes for a supply of old rags. Of a later date traveling salesmen entered the state from Massachusetts with wagons loaded with whips with which the farmers could goad their trusty steeds. Due to the excessive freight rates charged, these same salesmen later added dynamite and powder to their wares.

The old farm houses had the barn attached to the house with a shed attached between as may still be seen today. There was a passageway from the house to the dry toilet in the barn from whence the human refuse was carted by sled in winter and placed on the fields along with the animal excrement. For the country school a small privy was built in the rear of the school. Pupils did not long linger there in winter.

The old houses had large fireplaces for heating and cooking. Some more pretentious homes had a fireplace in several rooms as well as on the second floor and in the cellar. Many of these fireplaces had small ovens for baking and cooking, as well as a crane in the fireplace from which a kettle or skillet could be hung and swung over the hot coals. At no time and in no other occupation were all the members of the family so closely associated as in farming, in the way that it was carried on beginning in the 1830's. The young women and girls spread and raked the hay, drove the teams; were skillful reapers, husked the corn and did the milking by hand.

Children from very poor families were bound out by the authorities until their majority, when they received a certain sum in cash and a few valuables with which to start life.[3]

Before the days of radio, television and movies, entertainment was provided at home by the individuals of each family. During the long winter evenings there were whist parties for the men and quilting parties for the women; soap shows, so called, where a traveling company put on a short skit or play and then spent the rest of the evening praising the type of soap which they had for sale, were quite common.

Quilting was distinctly a feminine affair and often betokened an approaching wedding. It gave the women of the neighborhood a chance to discuss the merits of the coming bride and listen to the latest neighborhood news. Later in the evening a young man might show up, taking a considerable interest in what was being done, but

3. Edward Miller and Frederick Wells, *History of Ryegate*, (St. Johnsbury: The Caledonian, 1913), p. 207.

probably more especially interested in, "Seeing Nellie Home From Aunt Dinah's Quilting Party".

Huskings and apple parings partook of the play-work motive. In both of these common tasks jest was added by having mixed company. An ample supply of corn in shocks was placed on the barn floor and nearby the lads and lassies were busy stripping the husks and throwing the ears of corn into the middle of the floor. The red ear was sure to be found and after much laughter the forfeit of a kiss to a maiden was paid. When the required amount of corn had been husked, the floor was cleared and an enjoyable evening of dancing, squares and quadrilles and playing games ensued.

Apple parings were reserved for late winter evenings and were held in the kitchen before the fireplace or old iron cookstove with the hot water reservoir attached. One or more paring machines fastened on boards were brought in and placed on chairs. The apple was fastened on to the fork of the parer, the crank turned the apple against the knife deftly held so as to take the parings in long curls. When the apple was removed from the fork, quick hands quartered it, while others strung the quarters on long strings to be hung from across the kitchen ceiling to dry. Considerable work was accomplished and much merriment was enjoyed. When the stint had been reached, refreshments (with a full glass of sweet cider) were brought on and games and dancing were enjoyed by all.

Another evening's entertainment might include a large wash tub filled with water into which large rosy red apples were placed. The boys and girls took turns bobbing for apples with great glee.[4]

In the 1830's, full beards were the usual facial adornment which are again now sported by a few of the younger generation, though usually not as well barbered as those of their ancestors.

A method of punishment was the whipping post, which was usually about eight inches square and seven feet high, set in the village green or before the town hall. Here the culprit received the number of lashes on the bare back with a beech seal as proclaimed for the offence. An altercation between two parties was occasionally settled at the whipping post. Early Vermont laws required that each town should have a stock with keys where people were punished. In 1816, the justice of peace was prohibited by law from inflicting punishment by whipping.[5]

The settlers used pitch and candles for light; however, after a strenuous day's work they usually retired early thus not needing lights for the evening. The first street lights of many communities

4. William M. Newton, *History of Barnard, 1761-1927,* (Montpelier: Vermont Historical Society, 1928), p. 39.

5. Abby Maria Hemenway, *Vermont Historical Gazetteer,* (Montpelier: Watchman and State Journal, 1882), p. 1193.

were kerosene lights, later followed by gas lights, which were tended by the lamp lighter.

## *EARLY SETTLERS*

Over the years since the settlement of Vermont the way of doing things and the types of equipment used have undergone great changes due to technology and economic conditions. We have progressed from the pioneer methods of handmade and handused tools to the giant machines and equipment of today. Much of this change can be ascribed to Thomas Davenport of Williamstown who invented the electric motor in 1802, followed by other patents.

Let us examine the tools used on the farm of yesterday as compared with those used today. Changes have been brought about by new methods of producing, marketing and packaging of goods by the use of machinery. Cows were formerly milked by hand; cream was skimmed from the milk with a small hand skimmer after the milk had been placed in a long iced cooler. Butter was produced by an up-and-down churn, operated by hand. Ice was cut by hand saws on the frozen ponds, lakes and streams, stored in icehouses and insulated by sawdust. Later power saws were developed for ice cutting. Scattered about Vermont there were a number of small plants which made wooden butter molds, tubs, and boxes, now collectors items.

In former years most families had one cow which provided them with their needed milk, or had a neighbor from whom they bought their milk. The creamery was for the purpose of separating the cream from the skim milk (which was then returned to the farmer for feed for calves and swine) while the cream was made into butter.

The cream separator was invented in the earliest part of the twentieth century. This made it possible for the farmer to separate his cream at home, a time-saving convenience made necessary by the increasing number of milch cows. At first, these gravity separators required a man to take two or three steps up to reach the receptacle into which the milk was poured, the cream coming out one faucet, and the skim milk out another. Later, pulleys were used to drive the separators by means of power. Before gas engines came into use, early sheep-treadmills were often used as motive power. Today, most butter comes from the Lake States, and the old cooperative creameries have passed into other usage.

Changes in the handling of milk soon did away with cream separators on the farm. Changing lifestyles and increasing population were gradually eliminating the family cow, and a market was opening up for the sale of fluid milk. To properly cool large quantities of milk, the Baldwin Ice Refrigerator (made in Burlington) came onto the market; it was later phased out by the development of the electric refrigerator of today.

Based upon demand for more sanitary methods, and also for economic reasons, processing and handling of milk from the farm to the market has undergone revolutionary changes. On today's modern farm, most farmers who have herds of 60 or more cows have built what is known as a milking parlor. Here the cows are led into the elevated milking stall where their bags are thoroughly washed before the cups of the milking machines are attached. From the cow to the consumer, milk now has little chance of coming into contact with the atmosphere. It goes directly from the milking machine through glass or other sanitary tubes to an insulated cooling tank. From there it is daily pumped into a refrigerated tank truck and transported to a creamery where it is blended with the milk of other producers. Under refrigeration, it is now trucked to the cities and towns of New England and New York where it is bottled for consumer use.

After the early settlers had cut the trees to make room for planting they placed the trees in windrows and burned them. The ashes were then used for potash and pearl ash.[6] To prepare the area for planting, a plow was made out of a sharp pointed curved stick. Later John Deere of Middlebury revolutionized farming by the invention of the steel plow. Before the period of the drag and harrow, small saplings and later a wooden stone boat were used to smooth the fields to be planted.

Manure from the stable was first cast outside or drawn on a wheel barrow to a manure heap. In the early spring before the ground thawed, it was drawn by a pung or sled to the field where planting would be done. With the development of the metal carrier and the barn cleaner (which operates by means of a series of paddles in a trough behind the animals) the manure is moved up an elevator and dumped into a manure spreader which is now drawn by a tractor to the fields. In some states the manure is dumped into a pit and liquified. From this location it is then pumped into the fields and woods. This method is now used in our state parks for distribution of human waste. Eventually it will be used by progressive communities instead of the sewage treatment plant which disposes of treated waste into our streams.

The development of the tractor has caused most farm work to be done without the use of oxen or horses. The use of the hand scythe for cutting grass, and the cradle for cutting grain, together with the hand bull rake have surrendered to the automotive method of mowing machines, reapers and binders. Instead of a pitchfork to

6. Mary R. Cabot, *Annals of Brattleboro, 1681-1895,* (Brattleboro: E. L. Hildreth Company, 2 Vol., 1921), p. 115.

turn over the hay the power drawn hay tedder does this drying work. After the hay is dried sufficiently, the farmer now uses his modern equipment. He sits on his tractor which pulls a modern wagon. He is able to load his wagon with baled hay tossed from the baler. To beat the rainy weather, some farmers have installed large fans in their barns to dry the hay. The latest method is to cut the hay and - without drying it - have it blown into the silo after shredding.

For corn planting, a homemade implement made with two pointed sticks fastened to an upright crossbar was formerly used to mark off squares. By traversing the area at right angles, hills were placed so that the field could be cultivated by a horse drawn cultivator. In the beginning corn was dropped by hand into a hole made by a hoe at each square. The next development was a hand drill which sowed just the right amount of seed in each hill when pressed down into the soil at the designated spot. This toilsome task was superceded by the invention of a drilling machine. With adaptations it would also sow grain, which was once done by broadcast hand seeding.

At harvest time in the fall the corn was cut by a sickle and placed upright against a horse which consisted of a twelve foot pole raised on one end by the attachment of two legs. A dowel was placed through a drill hole at the leg end so it would hold the stalks upright. When sufficient corn had been placed on the horse, the stalks were tied by binding twine to form a shock. Sometimes the corn was husked from the shocks in the field. The shocks also were drawn to the large barn floor where the corn could be husked at leisure and stored in corn cribs.

Oats and other grains were drawn to the barn to await threshing - which in earliest times was done with a hand flail. The flail was made of two sticks fastened by the ends with rawhide. The grain was then passed through a fanning machine which removed dirt, chaff and poor seed. In the course of time, this job was accomplished by a horse treadmill and later by gasoline motor power. Ears of corn were passed through a hand-operated machine which shelled the kernels off the cob.

As the dairy business increased, necessary changes took place in farming methods. Corn is now sown by machine in rows, and harvested when in the "milk" by machines. It is then drawn to the silo where the chopper cuts it into pieces, and it is blown into the silo for winter feeding use. The correct amount of molasses is also added to enrich the ensilage.

Our forefathers sheared their sheep with hand clippers. They cleaned, carded, spun and wove the wool into cloth on home looms for family use. Around 1820, with the great increase in number of sheep, there were many requests made to the legislature for the incorporation of woolen factories in the state. With the increased exportation of sheep to the midwest and later to Australia and New Zealand, together with the importation of wool, a steady decline occurred in Vermont's woolen industry until today there are only three woolen mills operating in Vermont - at Bridgewater, Ludlow and Northfield.

## *ANTI-MASONRY*[7]

The institution of Freemasonry was imported from England and during the Revolutionary period expanded rapidly, with the first Vermont lodge being located in Springfield in 1781. As a result of a disgruntled Mason, William Morgan of New York, putting out a publication supposedly disclosing the secrets of Freemasonry, an Anti-Masonic Society developed in Vermont. There were many in Vermont who were opposed to any secret organizations, and among the churches the Baptists were very energetic in opposing all form of secrecy.

Stories about Morgan of Batavia, New York being murdered, and other gruesome stories made good reading. Propaganda, as it still does today, inflamed many Vermonters. A Mason of Springfield resigned from the lodge there and made public protests, calling it treason against the government. A few other prominent Vermonters followed suit which helped to inflame the populace further.

The subject of Masonry erupted in Vermont churches, and the Baptists were in the forefront of those denouncing Freemasonry. Many a preacher spoke out against Masonry. A preacher who withdrew from the order stated that: "I believe it is a moral evil in that its specious ceremonies are a combination of Christianity, Judaism and Heathenism. Its oaths are licentious and profane, and so far as there is weight in them, they rob its votaries of the inalienable rights of man. In its titles and degress it is highly profane and blasphemous."

The Baptist Church of Bristol dismissed its pastor who had already withdrawn from the Masonic lodge because he would not divulge its secrets. The Methodists were less receptive to Anti-Masonry than the Baptists.

In Montpelier, a Congregational pastor took an active part in condemning Masonry and in 1830 he preached a sermon in which he condemned Masonry and Judaism.

In 1833 the Democrats and National Republicans had agreed upon a "Union Ticket" over which Palmer had gained a clear majority.

As a result of the victories of the Anti-Masons, the local lodges throughout Vermont turned their charters in to the Grand Lodge, in

7. David M. Ludlum, *Social Ferment in Vermont, 1791-1850,* (Vermont Historical Society, 1948), pp. 86-133.

the hopes that peace would be restored in every community. From 1834 to 1845, the Grand Master of the Lodge and a faithful few met at two-year intervals and transacted what business was necessary. This action deprived the Anti-Masonic Party of its issue, so the party joined with the Whigs in 1936, signalling the demise of the Anti-Masonic Party in that year.

## *SLAVERY*

Vermont was the first state to ban slavery in its constitution, which was done in 1793. The first article in this constitution read in part as follows: 'No male person born in this country or brought from overseas, ought to be holden by law, to serve any person as a servant, slave, or apprentice after he arrives to the age of twenty-one years, nor female in like manner after she arrives at the age of eighteen years; unless they are bound by their own consent after they arrive at such age, or bound by law for the payment of debts, damages, fines, costs or the like."

Should there have been any question of the meaning of this statement in the constitution, the 1786 legislature announced to the world that: "The idea of slavery is totally exploded from our free government, that all former slaves have been liberated by the constitution, and that any attempts to transport Negroes out of the state are in open violation of the laws of the land."[8]

In 1777 Capt. Ebenezer Allen freed Dinah, the slave of a British officer.

In 1819 a group of men founded the first *State Colonization Society* in America at the State House in Montpelier. The objects of the colonization movement were to remove all negroes, free and enslaved, from America to Liberia; introduce civilization into Africa and to eradicate the slave trade. In the list of society members were three Vermont governors: Van Ness, Butler and Galusha, and three senators together with clergymen. For the next thirty years the society's membership was comprised of ministers. Up to 1857 the Vermont Society had contributed $31,000.00 to the National Society; paid the expense of 600 emigrants to Liberia; and shipped several hundred volumes to the schools and public libraries of Monrovia. As late as 1868 the society continued to issue reports.

In *1819* a Vermont resolution approved the Colonization Society's action to colonize the free people of colour of the United States on the west coast of Africa. Another resolution of a later date requested our representatives in congress to use their influence in getting efficient aid to the American Colonization Society.

8. David M. Ludlum, *Social Ferment in Vermont, 1791-1850* (Montpelier: Vermont Historical Society, 1948), Numerous page citations.

"Resolved that slavery is an end to be deprecated by a free and enlightened people, and that this General Assembly will accord in any measures which may be adopted by the general government for the abolition in the United States, that are consistent with the rights of the people and the general harmony of the state."[9]

As the Panic of 1837 was enveloping the country, there was a marked turning point in the anti-slavery crusade. The subject of slavery was now brought into the Vermont political campaigns. George C. Beckwith of Middlebury, a pacifist, began the issue of a small quarterly, *The Herald of Peace,* in January 1837. This action was followed by a Peace Convention at Middlebury in August which brought together many Vermonters prominent in reform. The Vermont Peace Society lasted only one year.

The Liberty Party (or Third Party as it was called) had its origin in New York state. Though the Liberty Party candidates were soundly beaten in Vermont in 1840 by the Whigs and Democrats, they gained enough votes in 1841, 1843 and 1845 to throw the vote into the legislature. The original idea of the Anti-Slavery Party had become so embroiled in politics that it became apparent in 1845 that the party had outlived its usefulness.

For the next ten years from this date, the legislature at every session passed a resolution expressing its sentiment in regard to slavery. Many of these resolutions were directed to Congress and read as follows: "We do protest against the admission to the Union of any state whose constitution tolerates domestic slavery, or the annexation of Texas or any other territory in which slavery exists." One act passed forbid any court officer, magistrate or judge to do any act contrary to an act of Congress passed in 1793 known as the Fugitive Slave Act. No person claiming to be a fugitive slave could be seized or detained. Vermont considered the abolition of slavery in the District of Columbia and the Territory of Florida as within the province and constitutional powers of Congress. Another resolution stated that "Vermont will not give its countenance, aid or assent to the admission into the federal union of any new state whose constitution tolerates slavery, and does hereby appeal to each of her sister states to concur, in its own name, in this declaration."

Recognition was given to the Kansas-Nebraska troubles by an act passed in 1856 which appropriated $20,000.00 to aid those who were deprived of many needs due to their feeling against slavery. Committees of the Vermont legislature passed a number of resolutions in regard to slavery. In 1820 they voted their sentiments with alarm at the attempt of Missouri trying to join the Union under a constitution which approved slavery. In 1855 they directed their

9. Vermont Colonization Society Reports, 1833 and 1841.

representatives in Congress to use their efforts to repeal the Fugitive Slave Law of 1850 since it was an insult to Vermont and an outrage to man.

*The Underground Railroad* system as it develped in Vermont between 1820 and the Civil War is well described in a book by Wilbur H. Siebert. Fugitive slaves entered Vermont at five main points, namely: 1( from its southeast corner up the Connecticut Valley, 2) a few miles west of Bennington, 3) where the Battenkill crosses our western boundry, 4) from Lyme, N.H. into southern Orange County, and 5) from Littleton, N.H. into Lunenburg. Their routes traversed the length of the state and criss-crossed within. Hundreds of Vermonters provided escape places from the southern slave hunters. Many interesting places were made or used to hide the slaves, such as a horse stall filled with straw or a secret compartment built near a chimney, as was done at the Strong Mansion in Addison. Hundreds of slaves passed through Vermont to Canada.[10]

## *CHURCHES AND RELIGION*

When the ravages of war were over, there usually appeared a religious revival. This action was increased by the appearance of missionaries, crusaders, reformers and enthusiasts of all kinds who trooped through Vermont, urging Vermonters to follow them.

The Connecticut Missionary Society of the Congregational Churches about 1800 began a religious invasion in Vermont. Other religious groups appeared, including the Free Will Baptists, the Universalists, and a real split-off from the Baptists calling itself simply "Christian". Also there were the Methodists. Though a certain amount of time between 1800 and 1810, was spent in denouncing one another, Vermont was thoroughly "converted."

With increased pitch in religious fervor, many traveling preachers held wild revival meetings. One preacher was the famous Lorenzo Dow, a traveling Methodist preacher who had preached in many of the North Atlantic States. In Vermont, he was known as "Crazy Dow" as he flashed on his steed from meeting to meeting always promising to return on a specific date, which he did. The more sober, steady clergy were not too happy with these itinerant preachers who stirred up the people with such religious fervor.

## *SABBATH LAWS*

The early laws of the state were quite explicit as to how one should act on the Sabbath. A 1797 law read: "The first day of the week shall be kept and observed by the good people of the state, as a sabbath,

10. Wilbur R. Siebert, *Vermont's Anti-Slavery and Underground Railroad Record.*

holy day of rest from secular law and employment. .... nor shall they use or exercise any games, sports or plays.... Nor shall any person visit from house to house, unless for the purpose of religion or moral conservation, edification or instruction.''

## *EARLY RELIGIOUS SECTS*

During the early days of the nineteenth century there were numerous sects which were preaching doom and the end of the world. One of these sects was known as the Millerites after its founder William Miller who lived at Low Hampton in Poultney in 1831. He predicted that the second coming of Christ would occur between March 1842 and March 1843. About 1839 Miller preached at Waterbury, where he stated that as a result of his studies of David and Revelations he felt that the end of the world would be in 1843. Many people flocked to his creed and cause. Some in their excitement sold all of their worldly goods and watched and waited for the second coming of Christ. The 1842 date arrived and though nothing happened as predicted his followers were only slightly dismayed, and eagerly awaited the March 1843 date. March 1843 arrived and passed. With much chagrin, and with undismayed belief, Miller stated that the error of the date must have occurred due to miscalculations of time.

There was a man by the name of Chandler who lived in the town of Jamaica. He was a follower of Millerism who also preached in regard to the second coming of Christ. He was an eloquent speaker and drew excited audiences. In their religious fervor, farmers left their fields untilled since they believed that the world would end before they would have an opportunity to harvest their crops, while others became insane and committed suicide.[11]

A man by the name of Davidson called on the Congregational preacher in Fairfax and offered to preach in September 1829. He preached to larger and larger groups when on one occasion he announced in a loud voice that he was a prophet sent by God. He opened a mission and announced that God, the Father, was on earth; that God, the son, who was coequal with the father, came in person to introduce the last Gospel dispensation, and with it wind up affairs on earth. He stated that the world would end in 1832, which was believed by a few. Shortly thereafter he hung himself.[12]

John Humphrey Noyes founded a movement in Putney in 1838 which he called Perfectionism. It was a Christian communism, assuming that all things should be held in common - even husband

11. Abby Maria Hemenway, *Vermont Historical Gazetteer*, (Montpelier: Vermont Watchman and State Journal, 1882), Vol. IV, p. 846 and Vol. V, pp. 416, 426.
12. Ibid, Vol. V, p. 237.

and wife. Due to so much pressure by his conservative neighbors, he was forced to leave the state. He settled at Oneida, New York, where his teachings flourished for a while. The great silver plate industry there was begun by the Perfectionists.[13]

A sect by the name of Dorrilites, very limited in number, appeared in the town of Guilford in 1798. A refugee from Burgoyne's army by the name of Dorril was the founder. Mr. Dorril assumed to possess supernatural powers by which he was protected from injury and the evils of human life. All persons who accepted his teachings were supposed to have eternal life. Every one lived on milk and vegetables. By mutual agreement, much of one's property was placed in common stock. Proselytes soon gained admittance to the sect. At one of the meetings when Dorril was expostulating on his doctrine with a statement that no harm could hurt his flesh, a member of the audience knocked Dorril down until he cried for mercy and finally admitted that he was an imposter.[14]

In 1837 a small band of families calling themselves, New Lights, commenced a brief career in Hardwick. Their leader, a professed Universalist who apparently became somewhat discouraged, was not long, however, in getting some followers. They began by interrupting other religious meetings. They finally came together in the South Meeting House in Hardwick, where they drew large crowds from the surrounding towns. Their exercises consisted of the most ludicrous and foolish performances, such as frightful yellings, imitating dogs, foxes and cuckoos, jumping, swinging the arms and rolling on the floor. They thus became known as the "Holy Rollers". They believed that their leader had had it revealed to him that man should not shave. A later revelation by another member was that they *should* shave and so it came to pass. In 1838 Rev. Charles Wright of Hardwick pronounced such a discourse about the New Lights that some of their number were imprisoned for the disturbance of religious worship, and so ended this type of fanaticism.[15]

A vagabond sect under the leadership of Isaac Bullard from Lower Canada began his Vermont pilgrimage in 1817. Due to a long sickness which rendered him into a visionary, he assumed the character of a prophet. With a few adherents he entered Vermont and reached Woodstock with his small following. He was able to proselyte two families by the name of Ball, one of whom was a Christian minister, and increased his following to about forty persons, among whom

13. Ibid, Vol. V, p. 236

14. Zadock Thompson, *History of Vermont Natural Civil and Statistical,* (Burlington: C. Goodrich, 1842), p. 202.

15. Ibid, p. 204.

was a Methodist minister. He proclaimed himself as a Prophet and directed that all who joined his company should place all their property into the common stock. It was used and distributed according to his will.

After exhausting their means of livelihood in Woodstock, they traveled to Bennington where they increased their membership. They then proceeded into New York state, Ohio, and down the Ohio River to near Cincinnati, where they augmented their membership by 200 to 300 persons. Their final stopping place was New Madrid, Ohio, where the last words of their efforts were written.[16]

## *FREEDOM OF WORSHIP*

The Constitution of the State of Vermont reads as follows: That all men have a natural and unalienated right to worship God, according to the dictates of their own consciences and understandings, as in their opinion shall be regulated by the word of God: and that no man ought to, or of right can be compelled to attend any religious worship, or erect or support any place of worship, or maintain any minister, contrary to the dictates of his conscience, nor can any man be justly deprived or abridged of any civil right as a citizen, on account of his religious sentiments, or peculiar mode of religious worship; and that no authority can, or ought to be vested in, or assumed by, any power whatever, that shall in any case interfere with, or in any manner control the rights of conscience, in the free exercise of religious worship. Nevertheless, every sect or denomination ought to observe the Sabbath or Lord's day, and keep up some sort of religious worship, which to them shall seem more agreeable to the revealed will of God''.

The institutions of Religion are more or less regarded in every town. The Sabbath, it is true, is deplorably profaned by many persons, yet the laws are strict in enjoying its observance, and most of the people respect and observe it.

The Vermont Bible Society has existed for a number of years and has done much towards assisting the poor and destitute to obtain and read the word of God. In early years the Vermont Juvenile Society did much toward the supplying the destitute churches with preaching of the gospel. The Colonization Society was active in providing for the emancipation of slaves and sending them to Africa, to form a colony there.

Lemuel Hayes, the first Black in America to serve as a pastor to a white congregation was the first Black to be ordained. His white

16. Zadock Thompson, *History of Vermont, Natural, Civil, Statistical,* (Burlington: C. Goodrich, 1842), p. 203.

mother is thought to have been of a family prominent for three centuries in Hartford. His father was a full-blooded Black. The five months old baby was indentured until his twenty-first birthday to a family in Massachusetts. In 1775 he enlisted in the minutemen and served 24 days and was discharged. He marched with Benedict Arnold north to Castleton to join with Ethan Allen.

When he was 23 he was frequently called upon to preach. He studied Latin and Greek with members of the clergy and after a few months study he accepted a Connecticut post as a school teacher. After examination by several ministers he was licensed in 1780 to preach. He was married in 1783 to a 20-year-old lady who taught in Granville, Massachusetts, and ten children were born to them. After his ordination he became a circuit preacher in frontier settlements in Vermont. At the age of 34 he was invited to become the pastor of the West Parish Congregation of Rutland, where he served successfully for the next 30 years; he also served at several other parishes thereafter. He died in 1836 in his 80th year. Lemuel Hayes was awarded an honorary degree at Middlebury's second commencement in 1804, being the first Black to be awarded a degree by a college or university in North America.[17]

### *CONGREGATIONALISTS*

The early Vermont settlers (coming almost entirely from Connecticut, Massachusetts and New Hampshire) were of Puritan stock, and were Congregationalists by inheritance. The first church was built in Bennington in 1762 and the next in Newbury in 1764. The beginning of a church was coincidental with the settlement of a town. Growth of Congregationalism was aided by two ministers from Connecticut who acted as missionaries in Vermont. The Congregational Conference in Vermont was organized in 1795.

### *PROTESTANT EPISCOPAL CHURCH*

The first clergyman was the Reverend Samuel Andrews of Connecticut who in 1767 visited Arlington, where in a private residence the first Episcopal services were held. During the Revolution the church members were under suspicion as to their loyalty, but after the end of hostilities the parish took on new life with the building of St. James Church in Arlington in 1786. Under the New Hampshire grants, reserved land was set aside in each township: a glebe right for the Church of England and a right for the Society for the Propogation of the Gospel in Foreign Parts. The

17. Lemuel Hayes in Alumni News Letter of Middlebury College, 1973.
Rev. John M. Comstock, *Congregationalists*, (White River Jct.: The Vermonter, 1902), p. 155.

Episcopal Church of Vermont tried to claim both of these rights. After a recourse to the courts, which was finally decided by the United States Supreme Court, it was decreed that the glebe should revert to the state and the other to the church, which still collects rentals on such church lands.

## *VERMONT BAPTISTS*

The first Baptist church in Vermont was organized in 1768 in Shaftsbury, and arose from Separatists New Lights, who came from Massachusetts and settled in the town of Bennington seven years earlier. These Separates were the Evangelical Congregationalists of that day. The oldest Baptist church standing in the state since that time is located at Wallingford, being organized on February 10, 1780. The first state convention was organized in Brandon in 1824.

An interesting commentary states that when persons came to Bennington to purchase land, that Samuel Robinson (who was one of the original settlers with an eye to the peace and tranquility of the church) inquired of the person's denominational preference. If they were Congregationalists they were offered tempting tracts in the vicinity of Bennington; if Baptists, they were sent to Shaftsbury; and Episcopalians were sent to Arlington or Pownal, which was pictured as a land flowing with milk and honey.

## *QUAKERS*

The Quakers appeared in Vermont about 1784. In 1785, they held meetings in a log house built in Danby, which was used until 1806. They prospered until in 1827 a substantial brick building was erected. At that time, due to the preachings of Elias Hicks, there appeared a breach in the society called the Hicksite Division. A half acre was purchased for $12.50 in Starksborough Creek in 1826, for a meeting house and burial ground. This church was for the use of members living on the Creek, or living nearby. A church was erected in 1830, and torn down about 1840, due to reduction of members and financial troubles. Meetings were often held in a log house, and in a school house. Meetings as follows were allowed by this sect: Sharon-1795; Peru-1798; Lincoln-1797; Monkton-1799; Strafford-1799; Montpelier-1799; and at the home of David Morrison in South Lincoln-1815.

J. C. Williams, *History and Map of Danby,* (Rutland: McLean and Robbins, 1869), p. 97.

Rev. Allen D. Brown, *Protestant Episcopal* (White River Jct: The Vermonter, 1903), p. 215.

Rev. S. H. Archibald, *Vermont Baptists,* (White River Jct.: The Vermonter, 1903), p. 187.

### *UNIVERSALISTS*

There were scattered Universalists in different parts of America before 1770. The movement which added the Universalist Church to the list of American churches began in 1770 with the arrival of Reverend John Murray from England. Few records are available which have been left by the pioneer Universalists in Vermont.

In 1795 the General Convention of the Universalist Church met in Bennington. Among the early preachers, the name of Hosea Ballou who came from Dane, Massachusets to Barnard, stands high among the great names in the history of Universalists in America. The State Convention, now the "Convention of Vermont and the Province of Quebec", was organized in 1835 at Montpelier. This convention was divided into five missionary districts.

### *METHODISTS*

Methodism as a religious movement had its beginning in England in 1739. It was organized under the guiding hand of John Wesley. In the early 1770's a class was organized at Hampton, New York, which served Poultney in Vermont. From other societies in eastern New York and northern Massachusetts the work was first extended into southwestern Vermont from 1788 to 1798, when the first appointment was made in western Vermont, circuits were included in several towns. The first Methodist appointment was made in 1796 at Vershire, Vermont. The first church erected in Vermont by the Methodists was at Danby early in 1793.

Occasionally a Methodist preacher riding from town to town on horseback with his library in his saddlebag, preached in some school house or private dwelling. Among these was Lorenzo Dow, who is described elsewhere in this treatise. On October 23, 1823, an organizational meeting of the Methodist Society of Burlington was held. The numerical increase was greater in 1843 when the Millerite excitement was at its crisis than at any other time.

### *PRESBYTERIAN*

The Reverend David Goodwillie, sent by the Presbytery of England, settled in Barnet in 1788 and Reverend William Gibson settled in Ryegate as pastor of the society in 1797, serving afterwards as town minister in 1800. There was friction between the Covenanters and the Sessists, though in the middle of February 1817 they met and drew up a constitution which was unanimously adopted. On August 27, 1785 a meeting of delegates from the several bodies of ministers

Rev. J. F. Simmons, *Universalists*, (White River Jct.: The Vermonter, 1903), p. 221.
Rev. A. L. Cooper, *Methodists*, (White River Jct.: The Vermonter, 1902), p. 161.

of Vermont was held at the home of the President, John Wheelock. The first regular meeting was held at the home of Mr. Whiting in Rockingham on June 21, 1796.

Meetings of the Presbyterian and Congregational ministers were held jointly until about 1823. At the 1840 convention held in Burlington, it was voted to amend the constitution by striking out the words "and Presbyterian" and substitute the word "churches" for "delegates" in the first article.

The Vermont Missionary Society was organized at Middlebury in 1807. The Vermont Domestic Missionary Society was organized in Montpelier in 1816.

## *THE CHRISTIANS*

The Christians in New England first rose in Vermont about 1792 when Abner Jones, M.D. of Lyndon, a member of the Baptist Church, denied the name Baptist. Calling himself by the name CHRISTIAN he began preaching at Lyndon in 1801 and organized the first church there. As early as 1812 a general conference meeting of the Christians was held at Woodstock. In 1840 the State of Vermont was divided into the Eastern and Western Christian Conferences. Later in 1893 at Lincoln, the churches of both conferences were merged into the Vermont State Christian Conference.

## *UNITARIANS IN VERMONT*

"Unitarianism in this country was at first a doctrinal development in the churches of Massachusetts; organized by the early colonists it was the liberal way of the great Congregational body which founded the first colonies in New England".

Organized Unitarianism in Vermont dates back to 1810, the year of the separation between the Calvinists and the liberal portions of the one religious society in Burlington. Services had been held in the courthouse for some ten years and the division came about in the attempt to settle a minister and resulted in the settlement not only of one, but of two; and in the building (within six years) of two fine churches costing over $20,000.00 each. The liberal members established the First Congregational Society of Burlington. The Unitarian church in Brattleboro was founded in 1831.

## *CATHOLIC CHURCH*

The history of Catholicism in Vermont really goes back to 1609,

James Mulligan, *Narrative of a Controversy Between the Associated Reformed Presbyterians of Ryegate and Barnet.*

Rev. M. T. Morrill, *The Christians,* (White River Jct.: The Vermonter, 1903), p. 228.

Rev. J. Edward Wright, *Unitarianism,* (White River Jct.: The Vermonter, 1903), p. 194.

when Samuel de Champlain explored Lake Champlain. Somewhat later a fort was built on Isle La Motte and called St. Anne, where a battalion of French soldiers was stationed in 1664. The chapel within the fort was the first sacred edifice in the state. A permanent chapel was built at the present village of Swanton which was still in existence in 1777. For many years during the 18th century, visiting priests came from Montreal and New Hampshire and attended to the spiritual needs of the Catholics in Vermont. The first residential priest in Vermont (coming in 1830) was Reverend Jeremiah O'Callaghan. His headquarters was in Burlington, where he caused to be built in 1831 the first Catholic church. In 1853 the state was set aside as a territory for a new diocese and the See located in Burlington with the Very Reverend Louis DeGoesbriand, Vicar General of the diocese of Cleveland, Ohio, as the first Catholic Bishop of Vermont.

## *ADVENT CHRISTIAN*

The body of people known in Vermont and elsewhere as "Advent Christians" has had existence as a denomination with a specified district since 1860 when first organized at Salem, Massachusetts. There are several classes of people who call themselves "Adventists", who adopt such names as Evangelical Adventists, Seventh-day Adventists, The Life and Advent Union and the Age-to-Come Adventists. In the State of Vermont, the Advent Christians are identified with three different conferences: one which includes western Vermont; one, the Northern District; and the third includes the rest of the state.

## *THE SEVENTH-DAY ADVENTISTS*

The Seventh-day Adventists date their origin to the year 1845, when believers began to band themselves together under this name; the first church being organized at Washington, New Hampshire. Soon thereafter preachers came to Vermont, where the first houses of worship were erected at Sutton and Wolcott. A new church and denominational school was built at North Wolcott, with later schools at Rutland and Taftsville.

The Vermont Conference of Seventh-day Adventists held its first meeting at Wolcott in October 1862. Two important departments of the conference are the Tract and Missionary Society and the Sabbath School Associates. The former, with an office in Burlington, deals in books, tracts and other literature. Temperance is one of the

Right Rev. John S. Michaud, *The Catholic Church,* (White River Jct.: The Vermonter, 1903), p. 189.

Mrs. M. McKinstry, *Advent Christian,* (White River Jct.: The Vermonter, 1903), p. 225.

strong points of the Seventh-day Adventists. The smallness of the membership compared with other denominations may perhaps be explained in part by the fact that the Seventh-day Adventists observe their sabbath on the last day of the week, Saturday, and not as is done by other denominations. They believe in the second coming of Christ on earth but do not set any exact date therefor.

## *JUDAISM*

The first settlement of Jews in Vermont dates back to 1873. On the 25th of May 1875, a congregation was established in Burlington; they later built a synagogue there. Today there are a number of synagogues located in the larger Vermont communities.

## *THE UNION CHURCH OF PROCTOR*

Previous to 1880 the people of Sutherland Falls (now known as Proctor) held their meetings in a stone school house, but had no regular or settled minister. A chapel was built and used by two Protestant Societies; the Swedish and the American. The chapel was later destroyed by fire and the two societies separated into two sects; the Congregationalists and the Lutherans, each of whom built their own church. Among the American portion of the population, the spirit of unity prevailed and on June 18, 1880 the organization known as the Union Church was effected.

## *MORMONISM - THE CHURCH OF THE LATTER DAY SAINTS*

Joseph Smith was born in Sharon, Vermont on the 27th of December, 1805. With continued sickness pursuing the family, and after crop failure for three successive years, his father decided to move the family to Palmyra, New York, which was considered to have a milder climate. Later the family removed to nearby Manchester, where Joseph Jr., in 1823 had a vision of Moroni who supposedly told him about the Golden Plates which were necessary for the translation of the Book of Mormon. He visited the site, the hill of Cumorah, as directed, and there he found the Plates. With the power transmitted to him by Moroni, Joseph was able to translate the Plates. Sworn statements to this were made by three witnesses who first accompanied him to the hill. On a later visit with eight

Charles K. Drury, *Seventh-Day Adventists,* (White River Jct.: The Vermonter, 1903), p. 295.

Rabbi H. W. Sachs, *Judaism in Vermont,* (White River Jct.: The Vermonter, 1903), p. 227.

George W. C. Hill, *Union Church of Proctor,* (White River Jct.: The Vermonter, 1903), p. 231.

witnesses (including his father, Joseph Sr., and a brother), they viewed the Plates which revealed the history of a people who left Jerusalem up to 600 B.C. built a boat and journeyed to South America and from thence to North America where the Plates were deposited. The site in Sharon where Joseph Smith Jr. was born is now a well-developed Mormon shrine.

## *PERIODIC RELEASED TIME*

The legislature desired to meet the demand for religious education in schools, so they came up with the following policy statement. "It is the policy of the State of Vermont to cooperate with religious groups by adjusting the schedule of public schools to provide periodic released time for religious instruction, provided that such adjustments do not interfere with the conduct of secular educational programs in the schools.

Unless otherwise expressly provided the words and phrases mean:

(1) Periodic released time is a program whereby public school students are released from school at least once a week to attend religious education courses sponsored by and given under the authority of a religious group.

(2) Religious group is any association of persons for religious purposes, including any organization of religious denominations, communions, or traditions. (Chapter 24, paragraphs 1051 and 1052 of Vermont statutes, annotated).

No person shall conduct a periodic released time religious education course on public school property."

## *TEMPERANCE*

The subject of Temperance dates back to the founding of the state. In the early history of the state the merchant's trade in many towns was to a large extent based on credit to be paid in potatoes, cattle, or grain the following fall or winter. It was the custom of merchants to go to market and bring back a good supply of rum and molasses. There were people, known as drovers, who drove cattle to the Boston and other markets, and brough back goods in trade which included rum and other liquors. There were many people in those days who drank intoxicating liquor. Under the laws the selectmen were empowered to grant licenses to maintain public inns.

It was the condition of poverty among people in the hilly backwood settlements of most states that flared into the Whiskey

Book of Mormon, and Appendices, (Utah: Church of the Latter-Day Saints).

Abby Maria Hemenway, *Vermont Historical Gazetteer*, (Montpelier: Watchman and State Journal, 1882), V. , P. 89.

Rebellion (1781, 1792) when the new Constitutional Government tried to raise money for frontier protection against Indian outrages by laying an excise tax on one of the most salable and easily transported products, whiskey, made from their patches of corn, rye or potatoes.

In 1810 a distillery was erected on Cabot Plains to use potatoes. So many potatoes were thereafter soon raised that another distillery was bult in 1816 to take care of the surplus potatoes for which a good price was paid. Up to this time the spirits were consumed locally. A new market had to be developed, which was found when the product was carried by teams to Boston. During the War of 1812 a lucrative market for whiskey was found in Canada, only about fifty miles distant. The good orthodox citizens of Cabot seemed quite content on obeying the divine injunction, "if thine enemy hunger feed him, if he thirst give him a drink." Eventually there were 12 distilleries in Cabot.

"Until quite recently there were thousands of bushels of "cider apples", ungrafted fruit and culls from the better grades of grafted fruit. It was unusual to find a farm place without one to 40 barrels of cider in the cellar, which was somehow prevented from going to vinegar."

"No occasion seemed ever to be perfect without it. If a neighbor came for a friendly visit; or to join a couple in the holy bonds of matrimony, or to perform the last rites of burying the dead, and especially when a child was born into the world, the whiskey and flip went around merrily; and when the ladies had a quilting party, every time that they rolled the quilt all must take a little toddy, and when they had rolled about four times, they were ready to drop work, tell stories and have a jolly time."

Two brothers leased a school right and planted potatoes which they had bought from a place several miles away. After they had planted their potatoes they ran out of food, so they dug up some of the seed potatoes. They shot a deer and from then on they seemed to fare better. Augustus Walker made potato whiskey for years, and it is said that was how he paid for his farm. In 1813 his brother-in-law wrote him that if the war with England continued, he should hold the sales for a time since the price would be better. He also said that "if the war lasts, the maple sugar will bring one shilling if not 20 cents per pound, therefore look out and make the best of it."

When the *temperance movement* began to stir up sentiment against liquor, Augustus was at first offended at being asked to sign the pledge, though he was a pillar of the Methodist Church and a little later he gave up his still.

The Council of Censors expressed the situation in regard to imtemperance in the following words: "No crime is perhaps attended with more evil consequences to society and individuals than that of drunkenness. In proportion as this vice prevails, the morals of old and young appear to be affected. If there be any reformation on this head, we rejoice and are glad; for we are sure that the glory of our state must consist of the virtues of her sons."

## *LIQUOR LEGISLATION*

During the early years of occupation - and later in the organized State of Vermont - the use of spirituous liquors was quite prevalent, as was expressed in legislation which was passed. The Governor and Council took notice of the sale of small quantities of spirituous liquors at exorbitant prices, causing drunkenness, idleness and quarrels. The Council resolved that, until a General Assembly was established to act, the local officers be authorized to issue licenses at six shillings each. On February 12, 1770 the General Assembly passed a law to punish drunkenness: "A fine of eight shillings and, for the want of goods whereof to make payment, the offender shall sit in stocks not less than one hour or more than three." Every town was required to have a good pair of stocks with a lock and key.

A tavern keeper, alehouse keeper or a victualer was forbidden to have in their place of business any cards, dice, bowls, shuffle boards or billiards. The fine was twenty pounds for each offense. It was the duty of the selectmen to post at every tavern and every store and in at least three places, the names of each town resident who shall become in their opinion a common tippler. Everyone was forbidden to sell spirituous liquors to a posted tippler.

Many early settlers planted apple orchards, and apples became plentiful and cheap giving rise to large quantities of cider. In 1806, cider was worth $3.00 per barrel and three years later it had dropped to $1.00. About 1830 with the beginning of the temperance reform, a large number of the apple trees were destroyed.

A committee of the legislature with Governor Galusha as chairman, together with members of the House and Senate, at a meeting held in Montpelier on October 15, 1817 listened to an address on the ardent spirits. A motion was made to appoint a committee to enquire into the expediency of adopting some measure for discontinuing the too free use of ardent spirits and make a report the following evening.

An interesting commentary of the times is the law of 1821 which exempted those engaged in the harvest work from observation of the statutes to curb drunkenness.

## *TEMPERANCE SOCIETIES*

With the beginning of the temperance crusade preachers were

careful about too strongly combatting the use of liquor because to them it was a monster of unknown power. Temperance societies sprang up and in 1826 in Boston, the American Society for the Promotion of Temperance was formed, and in Vermont a Society Auxiliary was formed. Many leading citizens together with preachers joined the Society and they carried forth a campaign of sobriety.

A sect known as the Millerites (from William Miller, the exponent) received a warning from him that they should not drink "another draught, lest He come and find you drunken."

The Vermont Temperance Society (as it was called) for a quarter of a century after its formation held a central position in the fight against the use of Alcohol. It changed its viewpoint from education to the prohibition of the use of alcohol, which was accomplished by a law passed in the legislature of 1852. At a special election in February 1853, at the end of a temperance revival which swept the state, the prohibition act was approved by a majority vote of 1,171 out of a total vote of 43,259 cast.

The moral inquisition reached into the everyday affairs of the people. Habits of a lifetime were given up, and the customs of long standing discarded. As is the case today the farmers want to stow away potent cider for the long winter evenings and for threshing time.

The efforts of reformers were also extended to tobacco. At an early convention of the Society a motion was passed which declared "that the use of tobacco by chewing, snuffing, or smoking is not only injurious to the individuals themselves, but it is an invasion of the rights of their fellow citizens."

There were many people who felt that the Temperance Society was driving them too far away from sobriety. William Slade, who later became Governor, suggested local option. The legislature of 1845 passed a resolution which was suggested by him and signed by him, putting local option up to each town. Of 30,000 votes cast, the local option partisans won by 83 votes.

Under the prohibitory act of 1852 the town was permitted to appoint an agent whose business was to carry and disperse for mechanical, chemical and medicinal purposes the liquors thereby obtained. The agent's stock in trade was furnished by the town, which give a small profit to the town.

Before the organization of the Vermont Temperance Society, the use of intoxicating liquors was condoned and even encouraged; however, a quarter of a century of agitation by reformers resulted in the enactment of a prohibition law. The enforcement of this law was quite lax for some years.

The Vermont Home Crusade (a temperance magazine) in the year 1899 carried an advertisement from a lady in Lower Cabot which read, "I will give a high grade bicycle, lady's or men's, for selling 250 packages of flavoring powder."

## *ELECTIONS*

The efforts of the Women's Christian Union gradually bore fruit. In 1902 the legislature passed a local option law. The election of a Governor in the primaries hinged on the prohibition question. Percival Clement of Rutland stumped the state during six weeks in favor of local option.

In addition to Mr. Clement, there were two other candidates, General John McCullough, and Senator Redfield Proctor who withdrew from the race. Senator McCullough received the nomination. Upon the failure of the people to elect a governor, the legislature in joint assembly on October 1, 1902 selected John J. McCullough over Mr. Clement, who had run on a Local Option ticket as well as on both the democratic and prohibition tickets.

In 1919 Vermont ratified the prohibition amendment to the constitution, the so-called Shepard amendment, which had been passed by Congress. This amendment prohibited the manufacture, transportation, or sale of intoxicating liquors, the importation into or exportation thereof from the United States and all territory subject to the jurisdiction thereof.

In 1918 Governor Clement won the primary and the election. After the passage of the prohibition amendment a new era of smuggling began. A large number of prohibition agents were employed by the federal government at the Vermont and other borders of Canada and Mexico; also within the States, and the ports of entry. There are many interesting methods which were used to evade the prohibition laws. Funerals with a hearse loaded with liquor instead of a corpse crossed the line from Canada several times before they were caught.

Some enterprising citizens collected a train of pack horses, which were led by a trusty steed. A trail from the Canadian line across northern Essex county to a rendezvous near the present road leading from Vermont 102 to Maidstone State Park was a favorable spot at which to pick up the contraband liquor which had been brought in by the pack train unaccompanied by any individual. Eventually, the pack train was intercepted at the rendezvous in Maidstone by the internal revenue officers; the pack horses were sold at auction and the contraband confiscated. The horses were bid in by a representative of the owner and the smuggling continued.

A member of the legislature who voted for the bill which enabled the construction of the farm at the Windsor State prison was caught with too great a supply of hard cider on hand, sentenced to the hour of correction at Windsor, and placed on the prison farm. His statement after arriving at the farm was, "If I had known that I would ever be sent here, I would never have voted for the prison farm bill".

## *REPEAL OF PROHIBITION*

However, the anti-prohibitionists kept up a strong campaign against the prohibition amendment until its repeal by Congress in 1934. At a special session of the Vermont legislature in 1934, the sale of liquor in Vermont went back to local option. At each March meeting a vote is now taken on two questions: "Shall licenses for the sale of malt and vinous beverages be granted in this town? Shall spirituous liquors be sold in this town?" The number of towns voting wet has increased almost every year since 1934.

The 1934 legislature established the Department of Liquor Control, with a board and a secretary acting as liquor commissioner. The board of three members is not allowed to have more than two members of the same party. All sales of spirits are made through state liquor stores. Malt and vinous beverages are sold through local stores in those towns which have voted local option.

## *VERMONT PROHIBITION PARTY*

The Vermont Prohibition Party held its first convention in 1874. On the state ticket for Governor in 1888, the Party listed Henry M. Seeley. Except for one year, the party filed a ticket for governor each year until 1918, when it joined with the Democratic party. In 1920 and 1922, the party joined with the Republicans, after which it filed its own ticket for two years, that being the last time the name Prohibition Party appeared on the Governor's ticket.

### *CHURCHES AND RELIGION*
### *SELECTED BIBLIOGRAPHY*

The following religions have been described in the Vermonter published by Charles R. Cummings, White River Junction in the publications of the years 1902 and 1903 as listed here below.

Archibald, S. H., Rev., *Baptists*
Brown, Allen D. Rev., *Protestant Episcopal*
Cooper, A. L. Rev., *Methodists*
Comstock, John M., Rev., *Congregationalists*
Drury, Charles K., *Seventh-Day Adventists*
Hill, George W. C., *Union Church of Proctor*
McKinstry, Mrs. M., *Advent Christian*
Michaud, John S. Rt. Rev., *The Catholic Church*
Morrill, M. T., Rev., *The Christians*
Sacks, H. W. Rabbi, *Judaism in Vermont*
Simmons, J. F. Rev., *Universalists*
Wright, J. Edward, Rev., *Unitarianism*

Other Publications

Crockett, Walter H., *Vermont, The Green Mountain State,* Burlington: Vermont Farm Bureau, 1921.
Fuller, Edmund, *A History of the Green Mountain State,* Perfectionism, Montpelier: Vermont State Board of Education, 1952.
Hall, Samuel R., *The Child's Assistant to a Knowledge of the Geography History of Vermont,* Montpelier: C. W. Willard, 1871.
Hemingway, Abby Maria, *Vermont Historical Gazeteer,* Montpelier: Vermont Watchman and State Journal, Chandlerism, Davidism, and Millerism, 1867.
Mulligan, James, *Nattative of a Controversy between the Associated Reformed Presbyterians of Ryegate and Barnet,* 1819.
Lemuel Hayes, *Middlebury College Alumni News,* 1973.
Mormon, Book of, and Appendices, Utah: Church of the Latter-Day Saints.

*Dedication ceremony at Hyde Log Cabin, Grand Isle, Vermont*

# Natural Resources

## *AGRICULTURE*

The early settlers cut their way through the forests until they came to a likely place on high ground which they selected and cleared for their farm. Eventually, many found that they needed to move to the valleys due to early as well as late frosts. After farming the shallow friable soil, the crops became poorer. Those who first came into the Connecticut River and Champlain valleys found a longer growing season with much more fertile soils. In the Champlain valley they found areas, once cleared by the Indians, which now supported medium growth trees surrounded by virgin forest. In the Coos section of the Connecticut River valley were rich open fields earlier occupied by Indians.

The first settlers in the Champlain Valley raised wheat and other grain crops, such as barley, corn and buckwheat. Without roads, the farmer had to travel on foot several miles over trails to get his seed grain and grist, which he toted on his back. Not only was the trip a tedious one, but also dangerous because the forests were the homes of many wild animals, such as bear, moose, and deer, which were also a danger to the farm animals.

The Champlain valley (and especially Addison and Rutland Counties) were celebrated for the raising of wheat, rye, buckwheat, barley and corn. The intense cold and drought of 1816 diminished the yields; however, in 1817, the yields were luxuriant. Wheat sold for $2.00 to $2.50 a bushel. Corn, potatoes, beets, carrots and other roots for livestock also produced well.

The cause for the reduction of wheat growing was damage from insects which attacked many of the fields in the area. There followed many years of wheat crop failure so that the farmers turned to the growing of hay, which was more encouraging. The change from wheat to use of hay, and the grazing of stock including sheep required larger acreages, which gradually crowded out smaller land owners.

Vermont climate and soil were admirably adapted to sheep growing. The history of the sheep industry in Vermont dates back to the earliest settlement of the state. Many families raised a few sheep from which the wool was sheared, carded, spun, woven and sewn right at home, providing clothing for the family. Occasionally, more wool was produced than was needed and was sold, leading to the production of wool as a primary source of income.

This industry increased rapidly, and early attention was given to the quality and quantity of wool produced by each animal.

William Jarvis of Weathersfield, Vermont, the American Consul in Lisbon, imported about twenty thousand Spanish Merino sheep, and placed many of them on his home farm during the period of 1810-11. These sheep produced a much higher quality wool than our inferior American breed.

These new imports thrived in Vermont, and placed the state in the forefront of the wool industry. Soon flocks of sheep dotted all farms. During the War of 1812, the price of wool advanced to $1.50 per pound, and at its close, dropped to $.40. Favored by a high tariff, the ten-year period ending in 1840 saw the number of sheep on Vermont farms quadrupled. At that time, Addison County produced more wool than any other area in the United States in proportion either to area or population. The number of sheep per square mile then averaged 373. Large sales of sheep were made from Vermont to the middle and north Atlantic states. However, with the loss of tariff in 1841 and 1846, prices fell to $.25, with a steady decline after 1850. This was the year in which French Merino sheep were introduced on some farms, although they were not as profitable as those from Spain.

Early laws were passed by the Vermont legislature to aid the sheep industry. Acts were passed to restrain dogs, and to pay for damage to sheep caused by dogs.

Another act intended to promote distinctive breeds of sheep and to preserve the purity of breed, required that all rams be restrained from running at large during the breeding season, subject to a $5.00 penalty. Further, the owner was required to have his initials marked on his rams' horns in a durable and legible manner.

To further this industry, the Maidstone Merino Sheep Company was incorporated, and in 1825, the Vermont Agricultural Society was incorporated. In late years, there has been some increase in the raising of sheep.

### *Dairying*

At an early date there were numbers of imported cattle breeds which were both full-bloods and cross-breeds of Ayrshires, Herefords and Durhams. At the time the raising of sheep was waning, there appeared a growing interest in the raising of livestock, since the farmer desired a year round income. The opening of the Champlain canal in 1822 provided a market for butter and cheese in New York. In 1840, the construction of the railroads was a great incentive to increased production of dairy products. Dairy cattle were replacing beef cattle on the farms by 1847 and the year of 1850 began the great butter era with significant increase in the production of butter and cheese.

The interest in the dairy industry was expressed in 1872 by the organization of the Vermont Dairy Makers Association. Manufacturing of butter in the creamery rather than in homes began about 1880. St. Albans was the "Butter Center" of the country and "Butter Trains" began their runs to Boston. In 1888 the legislature passed an act to promote the dairy industry, and gave $1,000.00 to the Dairymen's Association with the stipulation that the association should hold annual meetings. Soon after 1900 there was a transition from butter and cheese to fluid milk sales.

In 1870 there were 33,827 Vermont farms which supported 180,285 milch cows and 112,740 other kine, 27,809 oxen and 65,015 horses. By 1900 the cheese production amounted to 5,119,764 pounds. The number of farms decreased by over a thousand in 1910 although according to the census there were over a half million more acres of improved acreage.

The number of farms today (1974) is slightly under 4,000, having decreased from a high of 33,000. Many small farms have been purchased by adjoining landowners. Other farmers have given up farming due to age, shortage of labor, inability to use modern machinery on steep slopes, wage costs and perhaps the most typical reason, that their sons have left the farms for more attractive employment.

With the use of fertilizer and lime and modern farm practices milk production per cow has increased. The recent figures of the Vermont Department of Agriculture show the animal population of Vermont as follows: Milk producing cattle from calves to milch cows - 289,750; Beef cattle - 9,399; Steers and bulls - 3,889; Swine - 2,194; Poultry - 366,834. About 65 percent of all milk used in the Boston area comes from Vermont. Large quantities are shipped to the New York market and also to southern New England.

### *Development of Department*

Interest in agriculture was increasing, as was evidenced by the establishment in 1856 of the Vermont Agricultural Society, which (probably due to the wool interests) was incorporated in 1866 as the Vermont State Agricultural Society and Wool Growers Association.

Evidently, there was as much interest in industry as there was in agriculture when in 1870 the Department of Agriculture, Manufacturing and Mining was established by the legislature. A board was authorized, consisting of the Governor, President of the State Agricultural College and six others appointed by the Governor and confirmed by the Senate. The appropriation to the board was $2,500 per year. In the next legislature, a secretary to the board was established. In 1878 the board was abolished and a state superintendent of agricultural affairs was established. In 1880 the Vermont Board of Agriculture (with the same composition of membership as in 1878) was established upon repeal of the Act of 1878. A bill to abolish the State Board of Agriculture and set up a Commissioner of Agriculture in each county was defeated in 1884. In 1888 the Governor was authorized to appoint a committee to investigate the agricultural and mining interests of the state and devise a means for their development. This act the legislature repealed during the next session.

In 1904, the legislature authorized the Governor to appoint one member of the Board of Agriculture as Forest Commissioner. Ernest Hitchcock of Pittsford became the first forest commissioner and an officer in the Vermont Forestry Association. He was succeeded in 1906 by Arthur Vaughan of Randolph. During 1906 to 1908 a movement was on foot to have a Commissioner of Agriculture instead of a board. A bill was written and rewritten during the 1908 session and finally the legislature authorized the establishment of a Department of Agriculture and Forestry. This consisted of the Director of the Agricultural Experiment Station, Dean J. L. Hills and two others. From 1908 to 1917 Dean Hills acted as secretary to the board.

Governor Fletcher Proctor had much to do in promoting legislation to establish the position of state forester. In the legislature were two former members of the board, Arthur Vaughan and C. F. Smith of Morristown, who were very helpful in getting the legislature (which was somewhat opposed to change) to ac. The main duties of the board were the appointment of a Commissioner of Agriculture and a State Forester, professionally trained, with salaries of $2,500 each per annum. The appropriation of $25,000 to the department was equally divided between the divisions of agriculture and forestry. The board meetings, held once a year, lasted for a very short time. Mason Stone, then Superintnendent of Education, suggested to Governor Prouty the name of Orlando L. Martin of Plainfield as Commissioner of Agriculture, and Professor L. R. Jones of the University of Vermont Botany Department recommended Austin F. Hawes, then state forester of Connecticut, as state forester - both appointments being approved by the Governor.

The legislature of 1917 abolished the Board of Agriculture and Forestry and set up the state forester's duties in the office of the Commissioner of Agriculture, who appointed a chief forester. The legislature in 1923 enacted a law which created a separate forest service headed by a Commissioner of Forestry.

In 1902 the Board of Cattle Commissioners was established, changed in 1906 to a single commissioner, and in 1912 to a Livestock Commissioner, whose duties were transferred to the Commissioner of Agriculture in 1917.

## *MAPLE INDUSTRY*

The Indians first discovered the making of maple syrup. To get the sap they used a tomahawk to cut a long slanting gash through the bark of the tree; below the lower end of this gash a notch was cut to hold a chip along which the sap could flow into a birch bark receptacle. It was then boiled in a kettle to make syrup.

The entire maple sugar production of the country in 1889 was only 50,000,000 pounds, in the production of which Vermont lead. In the early days an axe or tapping iron was used; the sap being caught in a trough cut out of basswood logs and boiled in a kettle hung from a pole. Wooden troughs were replaced by wooden buckets or pails and later by tin and now by galvanized ones. In some orchards today

*An old Maple Sap House*

pipe lines lead from each tree to a collection tank at the sugar house. The original sap spouts were wooden ones, many being made out of sumach which has a hollow pith. Later metal spouts of different designs were developed. Metal covers were made to keep rain and leaves and other extraneous matter out of the buckets. Sap was carried in spring on snowshoes with a shoulder neckyoke to the sugar house to be boiled into syrup. Next came the bobsled with gathering tank thereon, drawn by oxen or horses. The change from the method of boiling the sap for syrup production has proceeeded from the iron kettle to the large tin vat to the modern evaporator. Today instead of the use of wood some of the most modern outfits use oil for fuel. Today Vermont produces about 327,000 gallons of syrup annually.

## *APPLE GROWING*

Grand Isle county in 1896 featured by the Vermont Agricultural Experiment Station as increasingly devoted to commercial apple growing. They reported a crop of marketable apples of 40,424 barrels from 34, 885 bearing trees with young unproductive trees to the number of 17,229. The varieties of trees listed were Northern spy, Rhode Island Greening, baldwin, fameue, Tallman sweet, pound sweet, Golden russet, Ben Davis and Yellow Belleflower.

At that time there were 192 growers and their sales of apples from the Islands went by boat in barrels to New York points. Greenings sold for $3.00 per barrel and fameuse for $1.90 per barrel.

## *BIRDSFOOT TREFOIL*

Birdsfoot trefoil was recognized in Europe over 300 years ago. It was brought into this country and spread, probably either from ballast dumps along the Atlantic Coast line and Hudson River or through forage and hayloft sweepings, and other materials, accompanying the importation of livestock from Europe, both of which appear logical.

Over fifty years before its cultivation in this country, it was tested by some agricultural experiment stations. However it was given only a limited amount of attention until about 1934 when it was found in several New York counties, during a pasture survey there.

Through the efforts of the Vermont Agricultural Experiment Station at the University of Vermont and the Vermont Industrial and Agricultural Products Commission led by Joseph Winterbottom, an agricultural philanthropist of Burlington, the growth of trefoil was started in a few Vermont pastures.

A. R. Midgley, K. E. Varney and Earl Stone of the U.V.M. Agronomy Department formed a corporate farm business in 1950 and acquired 175 acres of farm land in West Addison upon which test plots were laid out. It was here that the first certified trefoil seed was grown and marketed through the Champlain Valley Cooperative at Westport, N.Y. In 1961, a top year, 154,500 pounds of Vermont Certified trefoil seed were produced on 1650 acres by about 40 growers.

Birdsfoot trefoil (Lotus corniculatus), a three leaved plant, which shape of the seed head and pods resembles a birds foot, is grown for hay, pasturage and silage, chiefly in Vermont's Champlain Valley. It is tolerant of clay soils, which are wet in the spring and dry in the summer.

After a considerable selection of the wild plants the variety EMPIRE was assigned to one of the promising types by Cornell University. In the meantime a professor at the U.V.M. Botany Department achieved success in breeding a type with higher yields, which stood more erect, for which he named MANSFIELD. A similar development occurred at Cornell, for which a quite similar variety was named VIKING.

## *POTATO GROWING*

Potato growing in Vermont is a minor farm enterprise with more potatoes brought in than are shipped out. There are some farmers with lands which are reasonably level and of large acreages, where potatoes can be profitably raised by the use of modern machinery. For a number of years Vermont farmers have specialized in disease free seed potatoes which are sold to buyers in Long Island and New Jersey.

Poultry growing in Vermont is today a separate business which is not connected to a main farm enterprise. Modern poultry houses have been developed so that the poultry can be fed and the eggs collected in one spot by the use of endless belts, which reduce the amount of labor necessary. A few operators produce cracked eggs and dried egg powder.

## *COOPERATIVES*

Several cooperatives promote the interest of certain phases of the farming industry. These most helpful groups include - State Dairyman's Association, State Breeders Association for the four dairy breeds, several county dairy breed associations, several dairy herd improvement associations, state poultry breeders association, state beekeepers association, county fair association, state and local certified potato growers association.

About 80% of Vermont milk is sold through some type of cooperative organization. The New England Milk Producer's Organization with about 7500 members is a cooperative bargaining organization which negotiates for its members the sale of their product with the large Boston milk dealers. The Dairyman's League, which operates in the New York City milk shed and the Sheffield produce association, an organization fostered by the Sheffield farmers organization handle milk in the New York City area.

The New England Dairies Inc. has as its objective the closer cooperation of the various dairy marketing groups.

## *AGRICULTURAL EDUCATION*

Senator Justin Morrill, the father of the Land Grant College Act, passed by congress in 1862, made it possible to receive federal grants in agricultural education. In 1865 Vermont accepted the legislation which united the land grant college with the University of Vermont. The first four year students under this act received their diplomas in 1892.

The University of Vermont's Agricultural Experiment Station was authorized by the legislature in 1886. The legislature of 1913 established the Vermont Agricultural Extension Service. The State School of Agriculture was founded by the legislature at Randolph Center in 1910.

## *ANIMAL DISEASES*

As with humans there are many diseases which affect farm animals, though only the more important ones will be treated here.

### *Bovine Tuberculosis*

Bovine Tuberculosis was discovered in the Vermont Agricultural Experiment Station herd in 1893. Tuberculosis in both the human and bovine form had been known and described by Hippocrates four hundred years before Christ. In the middle ages the bovine type was considered to be contagious to persons and the flesh was discarded.

In Vermont in 1917 action was started in earnest to control bovine tuberculosis in cattle when the owner was required to pay the costs of tests. He was entitled to be indemnified if the test was made by a state approved verterinarian, and if the reacting cattle were a slaughtered. In cooperation with the U.S. Bureau of Animal Industry in 1917 the entire salary and expenses were paid for an inspector-at-large and seven testers; the state paying the cost of a stenographer and two clerks. Under an accredited herd plan a herd of cattle had to pass two or more tuberculin tests without reactors. The indemnity appraisal in 1932 was reduced somewhat and the owner received the net salvage value of the animals which went to the rendering plant.

Public interest in getting the number of tuberculin free cattle increased, so in 1925 testing by township was adopted. If a petition of the owners of 90 percent or more of the cattle in any town was received by the commissioner, he could require that all the cattle in that town should receive the test. Should any owner refuse, his herd was quarantined and he was prohibited from shipment of any dairy products from his farm. Testing continued under the accredited herd plan and the area town plan with interest. On November 2, 1936 Vermont was declared by the U.S. Bureau of Animal Industry as a bovine modified tuberculosis free accredited area, which meant that the infectuous disease had been reduced to ½ of one percent of the dairy cattle. As of June 30, 1938 the number of accredited cattle was 409,904.

### *Rabies*

In the spring of 1927 there was a serious outbreak of rabies in Vermont. The disease which has been known from the beginning of the Christian Era, is a fatal, acute and infectious disease, which is transmitted to all warm blooded animals and from animals to humans. Rabies can be spread by dogs, foxes or other wild animals. In 1927 Rabies first appeared in the town of Richmond when a dog after examination at the State Laboratory was killed and showed positive evidence of the disease. Within sixty days of that outbreak the disease was discovered in Barre.

In 1927 with the spread of the disease 36 people had been bitten by dogs and only 18 took treatment though no deaths resulted. A quarantine was enacted which covered the entire state. It required that no dog license should be issued by a town or city clerk until a certificate signed by an authorized authority was presented, showing that the dog had been vaccinated within six months. All dogs were required to have a muzzle and leash when out-of-doors. In 1967, 1968 and 1969 there were about 70 cases which appeared chiefly in foxes and about eight in cows.

Cattle may be infected by cats, foxes, skunks, dogs, bats and racoons. In the fiscal year 1967 there were only 2 rabid cattle detected. The spread rate is directly related to the number of foxes per square mile.

### *Brucellosis*

Brucellosis or Bangs disease causes cattle to abort. A law authorized the Commissioner of Agriculture in 1949 to establish a test plan for cattle and make rules and regulations therefor. All owners of cattle were soon required to come under a testing plan when the owners of 70% or more of the cattle in a given area had signed up under the vaccination test plan.

Owners were first given the privileges of requesting the Commissioner to place their herd under state supervision. Under the plan owners were indemnified for the cattle which had to be slaughtered.

### *Hoof and Mouth Disease*

Legislation enacted in 1951 gave the commissioner the authority to make rules and regulations to control this disease which affects cattle and horses. All animals after test, which show symptoms of the disease have to be killed and the owner is indemnified for this loss.

### *Anthrax*

Anthrax, an infectious disease, fatal to animals and in some instances to man, had an outbreak in 1919 resulting in the death of several cattle.

### *Mastitis*

Mastitis carried through milk causes epidemics of sore throats. In 1932 Vermont began the control of mastitis and is probably the first state to exercise its control on an official state basis. A systematic examination of milk samples is made regularly for all milk delivered to patrons.

### *Hog Cholera and Pullorum-Typhoid*

Hog Cholera in swine and pullorum-typhoid in poultry need to be prevented to insure the health of the animals.

## *ECONOMICS OF AGRICULTURE*

Agriculture provides jobs for about one fifth of the state's labor force, including both farmers and those working in businesses dependent upon the demands of the farmers. The rural landscape maintained by farmers plays an important part in the beauty of our landscape and lends a decided inducement to our tourist business. About one third of the state's land area is connected with farms of which about 40% is in woodland. To maintain a good economy and the other public values inherent in farm land, Vermont is striving to retain as much land as possible in farms, though the number of farms have dropped from the high of about 33,000 to a little over 4,000. Small farms uneconomical under today's economy have been added to adjacent larger farms. The high taxes laid against many of the farms of small size have accelerated this movement. The age of the farmers and their inability to hire and pay for labor is another factor. Today dairying furnishes about 85% of Vermont's total farm income. The increased demand for farms for residence of non-residents has increased the value of Vermont farms and also the taxes to be paid.

Vermont State Planning Report, 1973, ed. Benjamin Hoffman

## *SOIL CONSERVATION DISTRICTS*

The U.S. Soil Conservation Service was established in 1935. In 1936 a Winooski Soil Demonstration District was established to inform the public about soil conservation, establishing soil conservation farms and research problems of soil erosion. In 1936 the legislature passed Act No. 246 providing for Soil Conservation Districts. Under a later Act in 1938 it was stated: "the district shall constitute a governmental subdivision of the State of Vermont and a public body corporate."

As an agency of the state to perform the functions conferred upon it a state committee of five persons was established. They consist of the director of the state extension service, the director of the agricultural experiment station, the chairman of the state planning board and one person appointed by the governor for a term of two years. The Secretary of Agriculture was granted authority to name a person to the board.

Fourteen Soil Conservation Districts were formed, some of which followed county lines. Each district committee comprises five persons; two persons appointed by the state committee and three elected by the land owners of each district.

The supervisors have the following duties:

a) to conduct surveys, investigation and research relating to the character of soil erosion and the prevention and control measures needed.
b) to conduct demonstration projects.
c) to carry out measures for the prevention and control of soil and stream bank erosion.
d) to cooperate or enter into contracts with, to furnish financial or other aid to any agency, governmental or otherwise or any land owner in the control of soil erosion.
e) to acquire property, real or personal.
f) to make available machinery, equipment, fertilizer, seeds, and seedlings.
g) to construct, maintain or improve any authorized structures.
h) to develop comprehensive soil conservation plans.
i) may regulate contributions to any operator who receives benefits.

In 1968 the name of the organization was changed to the Natural Resource Conservation Council and the power of the Council and supervisors broadened.

## *FISH AND GAME*

Early in the history of the state it was found necessary to pass laws against taking certain kinds and quantities of fish and game at certain specified times. Down through the years much legislation has been passed, which has not always been best for the continuation of game, but rather because some of the members of the Legislature thought that they knew more about the subject than the biologists. At times, however, they did. In the early years of farming when sheep were the chief farm income, wild animals were very numerous, so a bounty was placed on them in 1779. Wolves and bears roamed the hillside. In the same year a bounty was placed on foxes due to their great numbers.

A law was passed in 1819 which prohibited the use of scoop nets in the waters of the Town of Bennington. At the same time another law prohibited the taking of pickerel in Fairlee Pond for a period of two years. Reports show that salmon, shad, trout, pickerel and suckers jammed the various Vermont streams in shoals so that they were caught in nets and packed in barrels with salt for winter use and export. On the Upper Connecticut salmon were reported to have reached a weight of forty pounds.

### *Fish*

The first legislation noted in regard to fish depletion was taken in 1857 when Governor Ryland Fletcher appointed George Marsh to investigate the artificial propogation of fish, which resulted in the appointment of a Board of Fish Commissioners in November 1866. Meetings were held with the commissioners of other states in regard to pollution of streams, dams impeding the passage of fish to upper spawning areas, use of seines, and overfishing at spawning seasons.

Citizens throughout the state were asked to give their assistance in restocking streams with salmon, shad, herring, alewife, trout, black bass and lamprey eel. Individuals, notably a Mr. Hagar, hatched thirty to forty thousand salmon fry and distributed them in the West and Winooski Rivers. California salmon were stocked in the Connecticut River, while many thousands of shad were planted in Lake Champlain.

As interest in fish conservation developed it was possible to get legislation passed to prohibit fishing during the spawning season. Town officials were authorized to stock streams and to appoint fish wardens to enforce the closed season law. Natural ponds were considered as state property with free public access. Landowners were permitted to post their lands against fishing by others.

Black bass were stocked in some ponds, where they prospered. Walleye pike were successfully grown in some bodies of water as were landlocked salmon.

In 1836 ten thousand California trout, evidently rainbow, were first introduced and successfully planted in Lunenburg waters. Eggs were later taken from these fish and rainbows have been reared successfully in Vermont since that date.

### *Hatcheries*

The first state fish hatchery aided by federal funds was constructed in Roxbury in 1891, where over 553,000 fish were raised. The species included brook, lake and rainbow trout, and landlocked salmon. The construction of more hatcheries followed to meet the needs and wishes of politicians. A rearing station was built in Arlington in 1919 and soon moved to Bennington because of an insufficient water supply. A hatchery was built in Vernon in the same year but has been discontinued. The Canaan Hatchery was built in 1916, as was the Morgan Rearing Station. Salisbury Hatchery was built in 1932 and the one at Bald Hill in Newark in 1940.

A federal hatchery, which raised and distributed only brook trout, was built in 1893. A federal hatchery in Swanton, built in 1900, functioned on occasion and was partly financed by the states adjoining Lake Champlain where walleyes were planted. There is a federal hatchery at Holden and one at York Pond in New Hampshire, a part, of which trout production, is planted in Vermont. In recent years airplanes have been used to plant fish in ponds which are inaccesible to trucks.

### *Operations*

In 1892 the department was supervised by fish commissioners until 1904 when the Legislature decided that a single commissioner was sufficient. By 1900 most of the fish and game wardens were appointed by the commission. Joint meetings were held with Canada to eliminate seining in Lake Champlain, which efforts were successful seventy years later when most of Canada's seining right expired.

The first resident fishing and hunting license fee enacted in 1908 was for .50 cents, which was increased to .60 cents in 1915 and today, 1974, it is $8.00. The nonresident hunting and fishing license now is $40.50. If an applicant is 65 years of age or older, and not blind, he may apply for a fishing, hunting or combination license by paying the sum of $1.75 for a life-time license.

It was not until 1923 that the department established test streams to determine whether the waters were suitable to support fish. In 1953 the department began the acquisition of access right to lakes, ponds and rivers, and the construction of parking areas thereat. Up to now, over a hundred such areas have been built.

## *Game*

DEER When Vermont was first settled deer were numerous. Over the years due to slaughter and natural causes the number decreased rapidly. To build up the herd the department in 1878 imported fourteen deer from the state of New York. The deer herd from then gradually increased until 1961 when there developed excessive damage to crops by them. So the Legislature permitted a licensed hunter, who had not taken one by legal means, under his license to take one wild deer without antlers or with antlers less than three inches long in five stated Vermont counties.

This law resulted in much discussion both before and after the passage of the act as to whether it was good for the deer herd. In 1968 the previous act was repealed and for a period of time as designated by the fish and game board, both does and bucks with horns less than three inches long could be taken. The act was repealed in 1972.

BEARS Prior to 1831 and up to about 1941 there was a bounty on bears varying from $5.00 to $10.00 each. In 1950 the Legislature realized the the number of bears was becoming scarce and placed a closed season on them.

The bear was finally declared a sport animal and a report was required on the number of bear shot, which has averaged three hundred shot annually since 1960.

PORCUPINES For many years Vermont law allowed the town clerks to pay a bounty of .40 cents for a pair of porcupine ears. This system did not show any reduction in the number of animals and the damage to property seemed to increase. Many thousands of dollars were spent on bounties.

FISHER CAT The fisher cat, a member of the martin family, is the only known predator of the porcupine. For a number of years the number of fishers in the state was reduced to a minimum by the demand for their fur. The number of porcupines and their damage increased. Arrangements were made by the Department of Forests and Parks in 1957 with the Maine Fish and Game Service to procure fishers to restock our forests. By 1966 it was determined that a sufficient number of fishers had been released in Vermont to obtain natural control of the porcupines.

The seasons and the number of fish and game allowed to be caught has varied over the years depending upon the population of the animals and the whims of the Legislature.

OTHER ANIMALS There are closed seasons for mink and other similar animals. The transmission of *Rabies* to cattle by the red fox is treated under the section, Agriculture.

GAME BIRDS The seasons and the number of ducks and geese which may be shot is determined by federal regulations. The season for woodcock, grouse and other birds is fixed by the state depending upon the population of these birds.

### *Green Mountain Conservation Camps*

"In keeping with the Vermont Fish and Game Department's belief that every boy and girl has a right as well as a responsibility to become acquainted with our natural resources, the idea of a Conservation Camp, which was originated by Commissioner Kehoe, came into being in 1966 in June. Arrangements were made for using the facilities at Fair Haven Community Camp located at Lake Bomoseen in Castleton, which could accommodate 50 to 60 youngsters.

During that first year 108 boys were enrolled at camp. All phases of conservation and outdoor safety were covered by courses taught by personnel from the Fish and Game Department, U. S. Forest Service, Dept. of Water Resources, Public Safety, and Forests and Parks. A thirty dollar fee was charged per boy-per week. Half of this sum was paid by parents and half by sponsors such as Rotary, Lions and Fish and Game Department to balance actual costs. Resident camp counselor positions were filled by game wardens.

In 1967 Conservation Camp was held again after the encouraging results of the previous first year. An additional course in canoe and boat handling instruction was given by a Castleton resident on a voluntary basis. Resident counselors were hired outside of the department, leaving more wardens free to do routine work. A day nurse was hired. More time for fishing and hunting and other recreation was made available, as a balance for the time spent in classes. The accent was still, however, on LEARNING. Two hundred eighty two boys graduated from camp in 1967. They received a camp certificate showing successful completion of all courses as well as a NRS Hunter Safety Certificate and a Red Cross First Aid Certificate.

On August 26, 1967, the Fish and Game Board approved the camp as a permanent program.

The 1968 Legislature earmarked $44,500 from the raise in 1969 license fees to enlarge and staff the camp so that it could handle 500 boys and girls for 10 weeks in the 1969 program.

Also in 1968 a similar camp was begun at Lake Salem in Derby, Vermont, on a lease agreement similar to the one at Bomoseen. We were able to run two camps, and began to include two weeks for girls in the schedules of the camps. Approximately 900 boys and girls were graduated each year from these conservation camps. The fees were increased to the present rate of $20, which is paid by either the sponsor or the parent, $5.00 of which goes towards the purchase of a windbreaker type jacket with insignia, for the student. It costs the department around $50 per student per week, so we are picking up a cost of around $30 per student.

Each year we have added additional pertinent courses, and feel that this is the most important program we have today. Last year we were able to go into an advanced camp, which was held at Salem, during the last three weeks of the camp season. This was for students who had participated in previous camp sessions, and evinced a further interest in the project.

Our camp sessions begin at the end of June and run for 9 weeks at both camps.

Because of increased pressure from the lessee at Lake Salem, we have decided this year to open our own camp at Buck Lake in Woodbury. Plans are proceeding well, and we hope to have this camp operational for this coming season."

Letter from Commissioner Edward Kehoe.

*Land Acquisition Department*

"From the time of its establishment to shortly after World War II, the ownership of land for its purposes was not a primary concern of the Vermont Fish and Game Department.

There were few demands upon the land, hunting pressure was light, and generally well-dispersed. Little posting of land was experienced; in most instances there was an access to most bodies of water.

Hatchery land and the nucleus of the Sandbar Waterfowl Refuge in Milton were the major State ownerships managed by the Department—some 1400 acres.

The late 1940's and the 50's saw the start of an increase in ownerships by non-residents and as the more desirable water front parcels were purchased, it became apparent that steps should be taken to purchase sites which would insure public access to lakes, ponds and streams.

Meanwhile, a country-wide movement was afoot to meet the needs of restoring and protecting waterfowl habitat and acquiring public access to critical areas. This was financed by excise tax monies from the Dingell-Johnson fund for fisheries-related efforts and Pittman-Robertson monies for hunting-related efforts. This Federal funding was provided through the U.S. Fish and Wildlife Service.

The intervening years have seen the inclusion of a total of 84,916 acres of land in Fish and Game administered State ownership and managed primarily with wildlife in mind. Upland game management is practiced on 55 management areas throughout the State and 12 Waterfowl Management areas located mainly along Lake Champlain which provide nesting and rearing habitat for waterfowl and other non-game species of birds.

Some major upland game management areas are: the 7841 acre Arthur Davis W.M.A., in Plymouth and Reading; the 2,183 acre Hawk Mountain W.M.A. in Cavendish; the 9,130 acre Hurricane Brook W.M.A. in Holland, Norton, Warner's Grant and Warren's Gore; the 6668 acre Les Newell W.M.A. in Barnard and Stockbridge; the 2110 acre Pond Woods W.M.A. in Benson and Orwell; the 5,157 acre Stamford Meadows W.M.A. in Stamford, the 7,675 acre Steam Mill Brook W.M.A. in Walden, Stannard and Danville, and the 4,492 acre Victory Basin W.M.A. in the Town of Victory. Additionally 13 of the remaining upland game management areas run in excess of 1,000 acres each.

The major waterfowl management areas are: the 2,223 acre Dead Creek WMA in Addison and Panton; the 1,115 acre Fairfield Swamp WMA in Fairfield, Swanton and St. Albans; the 1,022 acre Mud Creek WMA in Alburg; and the 1,668 acre Sand Bar WMA in Milton. A late addition is the 1,266 acre South Bay WMA in Coventry and Newport at the southern end of Lake Memphremagog.

These wildlife management areas compliment the extensive acreages controlled by The Vermont Department of Forests and Parks and the U.S. National Forest Service, and serve to permit a management effort directed totally towards fish and wildlife habitat improvement.

Concurrently, acquisition efforts have resulted in the purchase of 207 access sites on Vermont's ponds, lakes and streams. Twenty-six of these are on Lake Champlain alone. To date 142 of these areas are developed to provide the fishermen access to the water. Purchases have been made against future need and development may be some years away on some sites although most are usable as-is. Insuring future access to trout streams commenced in the mid-1960's by the purchase of over 100 miles of streambank utilizing Bureau of Outdoor Recreation Funds. An additional 250 miles of streambank have been acquired under all other Department programs.''

Written by Richard E. Sears, Fish and Game Department of State of Vermont.

## *FORESTRY*

### *Development and Growth of Forestry*

Every public movement needs to have some leading spirit. There were many people who assisted Professor L. R. Jones of the Botany Department of the University of Vermont (1890 to 1910) in realizing the need for the care and development of Vermont's forests. George Aitken, a native of Scotland, and superintendent of the Billings' estate in Woodstock and a member of the State Board of Agriculture, was also an active co-sponsor of farreaching legislation. The third person of note was Dean L. J. Hills, formerly secretary of the State Board of Agriculture and later director of the Vermont Agricultural Experiment Station. Dean Hills played a very important role in the development of forestry in Vermont.

The first legislative step in regard to forestry was taken in 1882 when Colonel Joseph Battell of Middlebury introduced a resolution in the Vermont House to appoint a committee to investigate and make a report to the House in regard to the forestry situation in this state. Governor John J. Barstow appointed Senator Redfield Proctor as chairman of the investigative committee. Both the Senate and the House in 1884 established adjoint committee on forestry. In 1888 Governor Samuel E. Pingree proclaimed the First Arbor Day in Vermont.

The 1904 legislature authorized the Governor to designate one member of the Board of Agriculture as Forest Commissioner. In June, 1908 Forest Commissioner Arthur M. Vaughan recommended the employment of a technical forester and the purchase of waste land for forest planting. The serious forest fires of 1903 and 1908 probably had much to do about the establishment of such a position. The appointment of a commissioner of agriculture, and a professionally trained state forester was authorized by the 1908 legislature. Each of these two positions was granted a salary of $2,500.00 per year out of the $25,000.00 legislative appropriation which was divided equally between the two agencies.

Due to politics, the legislature in 1917 abolished the board of agriculture and forestry and established a new one, which imposed the duties of the state forester, Wilmot G. Hastings, upon the commissioner of agriculture. A new title for the state forester was that of chief forester. The 1923 legislature took away from the Commissioner of Agriculture these powers and created a separate forest service under the direction of a commissioner of forestry. Perry H. Merrill, then assistant state forester, was promoted to Commissioner on December 1, 1929, following the resignation of the former Commissioner, Robert M. Ross.

Once more in 1935, the politicians decided to establish a new Department of Conservation and Development, the policy of which was to be directed by a board of three persons designated by the governor. The departments in the new organization consisted of fish and game, forests and parks, the publicity service and the state geologist. Under the act, the state forester by virtue of his office was state geologist (this section repealed in 1937) and state nursery inspector. Another group of politicians not satisfied with the way things were going were able to convince the legislature to abolish the department of conservation and development and create a new department of natural resources with a five-man board. There was still dissatisfaction with the large department - chiefly by the fish and game clubs and some of the hotel interests, so in 1945 the publicity service was removed from the departmental organization, followed by the fish and game service 1947. This action left each of the agencies separate with three-man boards.

DUTIES OF STATE FORESTER Such powers and duties, as the state forester now has, have been built up by new laws and amendments nearly a dozen times since 1908. The chief duties of state forester are: control and suppression of forest fires, the raising of forest seedlings for the reforestation of idle and waste lands, the acquisition and management of state forests, assistance to private forest landowners in regard to the reforestation and management of their forest lands and assistance to sawmill and lumber industries.

COMBINED AGENCY The legislature of 1955 created the Department of Forests and Parks, directed by a commissioner who administers the actions of a forest service and a state park service. After about 75 years of education, the general public throughout the country learned the words ecology and environment, which are the basis of the forester's education. Feeling for a bigger superorganization swept the country, and Vermont joined it in 1970 by the establishment of the Agency of Environmental Conservation. The agency consists of the major resource departments: fish and game, forests and parks, and water resources. The natural resources conservation council and the division of recreation were attached to the agency, which is directed by a secretary. In this action all policy powers were taken from the boards and given to the secretary, thus leaving the boards in an advisory capacity only.

### *Interagency Committee on Natural Resources*

The Interagency Committee on Natural Resources was created by the legislature in 1964 and placed in the office of the governor. The committee comprises the governor as chairman ex officio, and the commissioners of the departments of agriculture development, fish and game, forsts and parks, health, highways, public service and water resources. The duties of the committee include coordination of activities of the member agencies for the proper development, management and preservation of Vermont's natural resources; to develop policies for the proper and beneficial development of resources in harmony with the state's comprehensive planning program, and to promote the effective application of these policies by the departments affected. Appropriations which previously had been made to enable the department of forests and parks and other departments to take advantage of grants of the federal bureau of outdoor recreation, were appropriated to this committee for management and distribution. This committee was transfered in 1970 to the Environmental Conservation Agency. There were many in the legislature then - and still are now - who felt that the protection of Vermont's natural resources could be better cared for by giving further strength to this committee rather than establishing a large superagency with centralized powers.

### *Natural Areas*

The 1963 legislature granted powers to the state board of forests and parks to acquire, by gift or purchase, land to be held, developed and administered as "natural areas". In the following year the act extended such action to public lands. Natural areas are described as limited areas of land which have retained their wilderness character, although not completely natural and undisturbed, or have rare or vanishing species of plant or animal life or similar features of interest which are worthy of preservation for the use of the present and future residents of the state, and may include unique ecological, scenic and contemplative areas on state lands.

Natural areas include and are designated by one of three classes or types:

(1) Semi-wilderness areas which by their size or location are in effect untouched by urban civilization and can therefore offer the experience of solitude and self-reliance. Lands at higher elevations which are important for watershed protection are considered ecologically vulnerable if unwisely altered by human interference.

(2) Units of importance for all the natural sciences and especially, ecology and notwithstanding value for education and research for the appreciation of natural processes. Visitation should be regulated so as to preserve the desired natural condition.

(3) Areas which are not of ecological or semi-wilderness stature, but which have the appearance of being in an untouched natural state. These shall normally contain at least a hundred acres.

Practices on all these areas shall be subject to regulations of the administering department to carry out the purposes of the law.

GREEN MOUNTAIN NATIONAL FOREST An enabling act allowing the Federal Government to acquire National Forests in Vermont was passed in 1925. The act defined the boundaries of the national forest by designating the towns in which purchases could be made. The United States government was given jurisdiction over the national forest lands to make and enforce such laws, rules and regulations as the United States shall deem necessary for the administration, protection and management of such forests. In all other respects, the jurisdiction over persons and property within such territory shall not be affected nor changed by reason of such acquisition by the United States.

Amendments to the original act by subsequent laws of 1935 and 1937 gave the United States the right to purchase such lands in the area defined as shall be approved by a board consisting of the lieutenant governor, speaker of the house, auditor of accounts and the attorney general, and approved in writing by the governor. The permission to purchase in any town so defined must first have the approval of the town selectmen.

The counties in which purchases were authorized are Addison, Bennington, Rutland, Washington, Windham and Windsor. The first purchase was made in January 1932. The federal government pays no taxes to the towns. In lieu thereof, twenty-five percent from the gross sales from the national forests goes back to the towns. The income to towns has increased in relation to the increase in the volume of timber cut. The amount paid in lieu of taxes in 1974 was $100,000.00. In addition to this sum, ten percent of the gross income is expended on the maintenance and construction of highways in such towns.

Several public recreation areas have been developed in the Green Mountain National Forest. The gross area which has been approved for purchase is 580,000 acres, of which 243,383 acreas were acquired up to July 1, 1974.

STATE FORESTS In the fall of 1909 the state board of Agriculture and Forestry approved the purchase of a tract of 450 acres in the town of Plainfield at an average price of $4.50 per acre. This tract was named the L. R. Jones State Forest in honor of Professor L. R. Jones of the University of Vermont, because of his deep interest and zeal in the development of forestry in Vermont. The first gift of land for a state forest was made by Charles Downer of Sharon, a tract of 340 acres. This gift was followed by another in 1911 by Colonel Joseph Battell of Middlebury, which included an area of 1,000 acres encompassing the summit of Camel's Hump. Many other substantial gifts have been received and are recorded in the reports of the state forester.

The first large purchase of land for the Groton State Forest was made in 1919 and includes lands in Marshfield and Peacham which were acquired at an average price of $2.00 per acre. This tract includes either partially or wholly the following bodies of water: Groton Pond, Osmore Pond, Kettle Pond, Peacham Pond, Seyon Pond and Ricker's Pond. The last acquisition made in 1974 in the towns of Orange and Groton was a tract of 3,100 acres for which the sum of $392,450.00 was paid. As of July 1974 the total area of state forests was approximately 110,000 acres.

Over the years as timber reached maturity, cuttings have been selectively made. The amount cut in the fiscal year 1974 amounted to 1,303,000 board feet and 6,134 cords of pulp and fuel wood.

Under the Norris-Doxey Farm Forest Act, the federal government furnished to the forest service upon a match basis the sum of $1,750.00 to employ a service or county forester to aid farmer and other woodlot owners in the proper management of their woodlots. This project has been very worthwhile since it has not only insured a supply of good quality of timber but in many ways has been an aid to our environment.

This situation today is quite different from that of 1914 as stated by State Forester Hawes: "In a few sections of the state, however, destructive lumbering is progressing on a scale hitherto unknown, and unless prompt steps are taken, considerable areas of Vermont will be turned from productive forests to worthless barrens. The reactionary policy of these large concerns, which pay no heed to the future, force one of two alternatives upon the public. Either the state must assert its right to regulate the cutting of these mountain forests, or it must embark more extensively upon the policy of state ownership."

MUNICIPAL FORESTS Municipal forests were established by the legislature in 1915. Under the act any town or city having 40 acres or more of forest land may have the property examined by the state forester and classified as a municipal forest. Such forests have been acquired by gift and purchase and in some places lands acquired for other purposes have been included under this category. Through the efforts of Governor Lee E. Emerson in 1951, a bill was passed which requires each municipality to have an article in its warning yearly until the town votes for a municipal forest. As of July 1, 1974, there were 105 municipal forests which had a combined acreage of 38,691 acres. Timber is usually cut annually from these forests. Many forests have been acquired for the protection of their watersheds.

REFORESTATION An appropriation of $500.00 annually for a period of five years was made by the legislature in 1906 to the Vermont Agricultural Experiment Station to establish and maintain a forest tree nursery. Upon the creation of the Vermont Forest Service, the administration of the nursery (which was located at what is now Centennial Field in Burlington, was turned over to the Vermont Forest Service. The first trees were imported from Germany in 1909, which included 150,000 white pine seedlings which were infected with the white pine blister rust, the source of this disease in Vermont. A small nursery was operated for a few years on The Downer State Forest.

In 1932, the tree nursery, to make room for the University's athletic field, was transferred from Burlington to Pearl Street, Essex Junction. Under the Federal Soil Bank Act, the state was granted in 1957 the sum of $122,215.00 to enlarge its nursery capacity at a new site in Essex, where about 8,000,000 tree seedlings were raised. Beginning in 1936 under the federal agricultural program, landowners were paid a subsidy for reforestation and improvement cuttings in their timber stands.

FORESTRY ASSOCIATIONS The Vermont Forestry Association held its first meeting on January 5, 1904, in Burlington with George Aitken of Woodstock as its temporary chairman. An address by the Honourable Gifford Pinchot, Forester of the United States, was the highlight of the meeting. Subsequent meetings were addressed by other noted people in the field of forest conservation. Professor Henry S. Graves, Director of the Yale Forest School and later Chief Forester of the United States, and Bernard E. Fernow, Chief of the old Division of Forestry of the United States, came to Vermont at later dates to assist in Vermont's new conservation role. A bill drafted by the association to make a member of the state Board of Agriculture as Forest Commissioner was passed by the legislature. The appointment of Ernest Hitchcock of Pittsford as the first Forest Commissioner was made.

RECREATION AND PARKS In 1925, the Vermont Forest Service

developed two small picnic areas; one on the Townshend State Forest and the other on the Mt. Mansfield State Forest in Smugglers' Notch. As time went on, people began to bring their tents and camp on these areas. The legislature in 1929 recognized the public demands and authorized the State Forester to accept gifts of land and to purchase land to be held, developed and administered as state forest parks. The first gift for the park purposes was made by Mrs. Frances Humphreys of Charlotte, who gave Mt. Philo to the state on the condition that it should always be open to the public.

Beginning with a small appropriation of $2,000.00 for the purchase and maintenance of state parks, the sum of over one million dollars had been expended yearly by 1974.

THE CIVILIAN CONSERVATION CORPS In October 1929 the stock market nosedived and there followed ever-widening waves of depression. In 1933, banks throughout the country closed. Some banks were closed for months while others like the Montpelier National Bank reopened within a few days, probably due to their good financial management. March 1933 was known as the bank holiday month. Unemployment increased throughout the state and nation. President Franklin D. Roosevelt under Congressional authorization on April 5, 1933 established the Civilian Conservation Corps (C.C.C.). The Emergency Relief Act (ERA) and the Works Progress Administration (WPA) of that May placed many people in jobs. Many Vermonters were given work under these relief programs during the severely cold winter of January and February 1933. At this time, the Public Works Administation (PWA) was established to aid business. The National Recovery Act (NRA) of 1933 spurred business by means of price and wage agreements which took the form of fair practices and which set a floor under wages and a ceiling over hours. The Blue Eagle flags floated over many Vermont industries which subscribed to their business codes.

Few people in Vermont today who are under fifty years old are unable to realize the serious situation of the thirties and the possibility of its repetition. Department heads receiving a salary of $3,000.00 had it reduced to $2,500.00 and the other state employees received a similar reduction in pay. People were taken care of by the municipalities who furnished food and shelter until the federal programs came into operation.

The object of the C.C.C. program was to utilize profitably and more efficiently the historic and natural resources which had been so obviously wasted during the depression years and to provide employment. Very soon after the passage of the C.C.C. Act, the heads of Forest and Parks and other conservation agencies were summoned to Washington to meet with President Roosevelt and learn of his new program.

Vermont was initially allotted 550 youths between the ages of 17-25. The task of enrolling them for the first six months was first under the direction of your author and thereafter by William Dyer, Commissioner of Social Welfare. It is hard to realize today how emaciated and underfed many of these youths were. They had never worked so this was an entirely new experience for them.

The supervision of camp construction for 200 enrollees and their care provisioning and pay ($1.00 per day) was under the direction of the army commander. The enrollees worked under the supervision of a representative and his assistants of the Department of Forestry.

Vermont had made no sizable appropriation for state park development previous to the advent of the C.C.C. period.

*The U.S. Army* was charged with payment of all camp costs and all personal expenses of the enrollees. The conservation agencies were granted federal funds to pay for technical assistance in the camps and in the forestry offices, and for payment of all tools, equipment and heavy equipment used by the enrollees in the field. The state forester hired the technicians and assigned them to each camp. Positions were so scarce that any technician to whom a position was offered seemed to arrive before his letter of acceptance.

Small picnic areas had been built at the Townshend State Forest and at the Mt. Mansfield State Forest in Smuggler's Notch area. Since the federal government provided funds to buy the necessary tools and materials for the work projects, Vermont was quite fortunate to be blessed with manpower and funds for state forest and park development. The acquisition of lands was a task for the State.

By June 19, 1933, negotiations were consummated to accept a gift of land - Burke Mountain - from L. A. and Henry Darling. Here a 200-man-camp was soon established from which a road was built to, near the mountain summit and a parking area there. Other recreational facilities were constructed to make this area a fine State Park. On July 19, 1933, negotiations were completed to acquire lands on Ascutney Mountain in Windsor for a state park. Camp buildings for 200 youths were soon occupied and work started on the constuction of the mountain parkway, and camping and picnic facilities.

Another major project was the building of ten miles of highway through the unbroken forest area within the Groton State Forest in the towns of Marshfield and Groton. This road (later taken over as a state highway) connected U.S. Route 302 in Groton with U. S. Route 2 in Marshfield, a distance of fourteen miles. Several camping areas, a picnic area, bathing beach, caretaker's quarters and another 10 miles of forest road were built within the forest from 1933 to 1940.

Probably the main incentive to skiing in Vermont, which is described in another chapter, was the ski trails, parking area and warming shelter built in the Mt. Mansfield State Forest in the Smuggler's Notch area. Several miles of down-hill ski trails were built on both sides of the mountain under the direction of Charles D. Lord and Albert W. Gottlieb now a retired State Forester.

Altogether about 100 miles of forest and park roads were built within the state areas, and much improvement was made to town roads leading to the areas. The development of facilities within the state areas included facilities for camping, picnicking, bathing, hiking, skiing, forest fire towers, timberstand improvement projects, and insect and disease control programs. Vermont received more camps per population than any other state because plans were ready for such developments, and the state owned or acquired the needed land. Vermont had twenty-nine C.C.C. camp locations during the period from June 1933 to 1941. Over twenty State recreational areas were developed during this period, as well as other cultural and control work which was accomplished in these areas and ten others.

BONDING Twenty-five state parks had been acquired up to 1958. However, little development work had occurred since the CCC days. In 1957 the legislature authorized the first bond issue of $200,000.00 to be used for the development of state recreational areas. Construction of access and camp roads was then accomplished by the State Highway Department. Governor Robert Stafford in 1958 recommended a bond issue of $1,000,000.00 yearly for four years. The bond money was used for the purchase of land and the development of recreational facilities. The income from the use of the recreational facilities is placed in a revolving fund which is used to amortize the bonds as they become due. Seventy-five to eighty percent of the use of the state parks is by nonresidents, who have paid the major share for the purchase and development of Vermont's recreational facilities instead of taking funds from the general fund. In other words the dancers have paid the fiddlers.

## *SKIING AND WINTER SPORTS*

In the early days travel over snow was chiefly on snowshoes, which were adapted from the ones used by the Indians. According to a St. Johnsbury report, snowshoes were not used extensively before 1900. In 1886 the town was struck by a toboggan craze from Canada.

*Dr. S. T. Law, Veterinarian, Forerunner of skimobile*

Hand-drawn sleds were first made at home and later made commercially. This step was followed by two sleds attached by a long plank known to some as a double runner. In the early 1900's such a sled was made at the Lane shop in Montpelier, which would seat 15 to 20 persons, and was used on Main Street hill in Montpelier. Without the worry of meeting automobile traffic, the occupants could coast downhill almost to State Street.

Many farm boys made what were termed jumpers. They were built by using oak barrel staves to which were nailed upright blocks two or three inches in diameter. At right angles to a stave, a piece of hardwood board four inches wide and a foot long was nailed to the top of the block. This jumper was used for sliding down a grade in back of the barn, and probably got its name from a small hill of snow over which the rider made a jump.

Skating is an old pleasure and sport, and every farm boy kept an ice-covered pond free of snow for the sport of skating until the snow depth made the task of snow removal too arduous. The types of skates have varied greatly from the early wooden base to which curved up steel runners were attached, to the modern racing skates.

Snowshoes were of two types, the bear paws with no extended tail, which was an advantage in traveling through brush country, and the long snowshoe with a tail.

A modern development, the ''skidoo'' hit the country in a great rage during the past twenty years. It was probably first built as an adaptation of the tractor. Some of the first ones were extensively used in Canada. There are over 30,000 such vehicles registered in Vermont as of 1974.

The pleasurable use of skis to any great extent is a development of the past 35 years. Farm boys of the late 19th century made their own skis out of barrel staves. They raided their father's harnesses and cut out short pieces from the reins to be used as toe straps.

### *Mt. Mansfield*

The first development of commercial skiing in Vermont occurred in Stowe, Vermont. Craig O. Burt, late of Stowe, related that in the winter of 1906 after a day's difficult trip on snowshoes while looking over his timber holdings, he became tired and worn out. One day after a hard day's trip of inspecting a lumber operation, he noticed an advertisement of the Northland Ski Company of St. Paul, Minnesota. He ordered a pair of flat skis about eight feet long, with two grooves, which he thought would be about right. The skis with leather bindings and bamboo poles appeared to be a relief in his pursuits.

Around 1912 three Swedish families came to Stowe and bought farms. They made their own skis and left their tracks as they traveled cross country to visit one another.

Beginning in 1921, winter carnivals were held in Stowe, which were financed by minstrel shows. The funds were used to build

*Original State Ski Shelter, Mt. Mansfield*

toboggan slides and ski jumps, skating rinks and other kindred projects. From this carnival until the first ski trails were cut on Mt. Mansfield ten years later, the youth of the village cut their own ski trails and packed their jumps. Competitive events were held in Stowe and Jeffersonville. The interest in winter sports resulted in the formation of the Stowe Ski Club, which functioned successfully until the increased popularity of the sport extended beyond Stowe's bounds. It was then that the Mt. Mansfield Ski Club was formed.

The first known ascent of Mt. Mansfield on skis was made on the last day of January, 1914. Nathaniel Goodrich, a librarian at Dartmouth College and his friend, Charles Blood of Boston, made the ascent without trouble. The next known ascent on skis to the mountain top was made on February 22, 1926, by Craig O. Burt, Sr. and his son Craig, Jr. and Robert Wells. On February 6, 1927, Robert Cate, then of Montpelier, and Dr. Edwin Steele of Waterbury made the first known ascent to the Chin by a route other than by the Toll Road. This trip was the first overnight ski expedition to the mountain top. In those days the town road was plowed only to the foot of the old Harlow Hill. It took them nine hours to reach the hotel on top.

The early climbs up the mountain were chiefly via the old carriage road, now a toll road, which was constructed about 1850 to allow a man on horseback to reach the top. It was not until 1857 that William Henry Bingham induced the town of Stowe to build a road as far as the site of the old halfway house, from whence a trip was made on horseback. The carriage road to the summit at the old hotel was completed in 1870.

In 1914 Vermont's first State Forester, Austin F. Hawes, acquired for the state over 5,000 acres which included the land to the summit of Mt. Mansfield and land lying southerly of the Smugglers' Notch road. It was little realized then that the site of this state forest would afford the development of Vermont's first commercial ski development about twenty years later.

### *No Ski Trails Until 1933-34*

The climb up the mountain was by the Toll Road and the trip down was by the same windy route at times. Tours could also take you over some of the old log roads, or if you desired you could climb up the unplowed road to the top of Smugglers' Notch and ski back down.

During the summer encampment of Squadron A., Cavalry of the New York National Guard unit in training at Fort Ethan Allen several years previous to 1932, one of its members, Roland Palmedo, climbed the western slope of Mt. Mansfield. He had been an enthusiastic skier while at Williams College. When he reached the summit, he observed the Toll Road on the east side of the mountain, which he thought would be a fine downhill ski run. In 1931 he organized the Amateur Ski Club of New York City and the next winter decided to investigate the skiing possibilities of Mt. Mansfield.

After a trip to the mountain with a friend he made a report which was printed in the Mt. Mansfield Ski Bulletin. It told of the ways to get to Stowe by the Montrealer which left Pennsylvania Station, New York, at 9 p.m. and arrived in Waterbury at 6:30 a.m., from whence an electric trolley connected with Stowe. He stated that it was painfully slow and often late in starting so he advised hiring a taxi for the trip. He gave an excellent description of the Stowe environs for ski jumping and downhill skiing, available lodging facilities, the large amount of snow and the hospitality of the Stowe people.

Your author, having spent the college year 1920-21 as an American-Scandinavian fellow at the Royal College of Forestry in Stockholm, Sweden, had an opportunity to observe the development of skiing there, and envision the possibilities in Vermont. It was not until the depression of the thirties that the dream could be effected. By the establishment of the Civilian Conservation Corps (C.C.C) in 1933 by President Franklin Delano Roosevelt, a camp of 200 youths was established in Waterbury. With this opportunity of available manpower, a side camp was established in 1933 on state land in Smugglers' Notch area. From this camp the C.C.C. youths were immediately put to work on ski trail construction.

Charles D. Lord was employed as an engineer foreman at the camp and with others directed the layout and construction of ski trails and facilities. Other foremen at the camp included Arthur Heitmann, later Commissioner of Forests and Parks; Albert W. Gottlieb, a former state forester; and Warren Warner, later manager and developer of ski developments in other parts of Vermont and New Hampshire.

The first trail named the Bruce, after an old lumberman of the area, was cut on November 1, 1933 from the Ranch Camp up to the Toll Road. The Houston nearby was cleared at about the same time. The Nose Dive Trail was cut in 1936. More trails were cut as time went on. A new type of trail, named Perry Merrill after the Commissioner of Forests and Parks, which started from the Toll Road was cut through a forest glade leaving many of the old growth yellow birch. Later another trail, the Tear Drop, was constructed from summit of Mt. Mansfield down the western side of the Mountain.

As a result of the author's observance of the pleasures of cross-country skiing in Sweden, Charles Lord was directed to lay out and construct a trail from Mt. Mansfield to the Little River Dam in Waterbury. Work was started on this project in 1940. However, the concept of this type of skiing was a bit in advance of the times, so the trail grew up to brush. It was not until about 1970 that cross-country skiing caught on and a number of such trails were built by private organizations on both sides of the mountain, which are well patronized. At other places in the state, cross-country skiing has become quite popular. Such a location is Putney where large numbers participate in cross-country races.

A ski shelter was constructed by the C.C.C. youths at the base of Mt. Mansfield from long spruce timbers cut on state land on the western side of the mountain. The shelter has since been enlarged several times.

Roland Palmedo stated that in the summer and fall of 1934, the first American girls' ski team was organized by Alice Chiaer and himself, and the girls (who included Betty Woolsey, Marion McKean, Clarita Heath, Grace Carter and Nancy Reynolds Cooke) trained abroad. These girls who had raced in Europe through 1937, were brought to Stowe for a race in 1938. In Europe they were used to riding a chair lift to the top of the ski trail. They complained that they were too tired after climbing Mt. Mansfield on skis, and that it was positively primitive. This thought inspired Roland Palmedo and J. Negley Cook, together with Lowell Thomas, to get a lease from the State of Vermont to build a chair lift from the base to the top of the mountain near the Octagon Hut. The lease for the lift was approved by Governor George D. Aiken and the Board of Conservation and Development, which consisted of Donald L. Smith, Chairman; John Keeler, and Samuel Ogden. The demands upon this lift were so great that the Board approved another lease to the Smugglers' Notch Lift Company for a T-Bar type lift to be located southerly from the chair lift of the Mt. Mansfield Company. These two lifts were eventually acquired by a new Mt. Mansfield Company of which Cornelius Starr was the President. Business developed so rapidly that it was soon necessary to construct a double chair lift adjacent to the first one. The next construction followed in a few years with a gondola-type lift which carried skiers to a point just below the Chin.

### *Ski Trains Arrive*

Frank Elkins, the dean of ski writers at the time and editor of the New York Times sport section, did much to publicize Mt. Mansfield. To quote him: "Yet it seems not so long ago, when the village strained itself to accommodate 100 skiers back in 1932, with hotels bulging at the seams .... By 1936, three years after this correspondent had written his first yarn, 'When you think of snow, think of Stowe', the first snow trains arrived at Waterbury, some 700 skiers moved into the area and with only two small hotels, two camps and a few tourist homes. This explains why skiers slept in barns, attics, cellars and some trucks parked in Clyde Chase's garage. The train trip dumped us in Waterbury at 4:30 A.M."

### *Ski Shelters*

During the early part of the winter of 1935-36, Franklin Griffin and Craig O. Burt, Sr. constructed a rope tow in the Mt. Mansfield area at the Old Toll House slopes. Later Mr. Griffin installed a rope tow on a slope back of the present state ski shelter, where the C.C.C. youths had cut the scrubby tree growth. More parking areas were built to meet the demand as more lifts were erected.

Cornelius Starr, who had amalgamated many Far Eastern insurance companies into a great combine, came into the author's office one day to see if he could make arrangements to acquire the leases of the lifts on state land in the Mt. Mansfield area. In 1950 he was successful in acquiring all these companies, which were merged into the present Mt. Mansfield Company. Mr. Starr glanced over one day at the forested mountain side northerly of the Smugglers' Notch road and directed Sepp Ruschp, manager of the Starr ski interests, to acquire that area. For the development and management of the Mt. Mansfield ski area thousands of skiers are indebted to Sepp Ruschp for his foresight, energy and friendliness. These Burt lands were purchased and lifts were built successively thereon, beginning in 1951 with a rope tow. This action was followed the next year with a T-Bar lift and next with a double chair lift, which was completed to the crest of Spruce Peak in 1954.

### *The Mt. Mansfield Ski Patrol*

In order to insure safety on the ski slopes and care for those who were injured it was considered necessary to form a ski patrol. Quoted below is a good historical sketch by Lanou Hudson of Burlington, one of the promoters of the project. "As most skiers know, the basic idea of what we know as the Ski Patrol originated here in Stowe during the winter of 1934-35. It was also in Stowe at the running of the 1938 National Ski Races that C. Minot Dole, later known to thousands of skiers as 'Minnie', conceived the idea of a National Ski Patrol. It was Dole who almost single-handed and with the sacrifice of his time, energy and much of his own money, built the National Ski Patrol into the organization that it is today. In February 1960, the first professional ski patrol examination under the United States Eastern Amateur Ski Association was held in Stowe, where skiers from Vermont and New Hampshire ski areas took part in these examinations."

### *Woodstock - Vermont's First Ski Tow*

Bunny Bertram, fresh out of Dartmouth College, where he was interested in winter sports of snow-shoeing and skiing, built the first rope tow in Vermont in 1934. The tow was constructed on the Gilbert Farm in the town of Woodstock northerly along the road to Barnard. With the aid of David Dodd, a trained and practical engineer, a replica of a ski tow in use at Shawbridge, Quebec was built. It consisted of a model-T Ford engine, which moved 1,200 feet of endless rope through sheaves that pulled the skiers uphill. With Yankee ingenuity Dodd obtained some discarded automobile wheels for sheaves, which were fastened to the top of some cedar posts formerly used for fencing. The first tow in Vermont was made to operate with the use of pieces of scrap lumber and some discarded wire.

Two years later Bunny built two more tows and installed them at "Suicide Six", which was followed later by the first Poma-lift used in this country. Rockwell Stephens of Woodstock was the first ski equipment manufacturer in Vermont.

*Vermont's First Rope Tow, Woodstock*

### *East Corinth Ski Area*

A letter from W. Gilbert Cole of Bradford furnished the following information. "In 1934 a group of young winter sports enthusiasts organized a club known as the Bradford Winter Sports Club. They sponsored a skating rink and open-slope skiing in Bradford village. The interested persons were W. Gilbert Cole, George and Lester Eaton, David Dodd and others. David Dodd, a mechanical genius, agreed to constuct a ski tow from an old Reo station wagon engine, having been successful with a similar project in Woodstock the previous year. The machine was erected on a small slope which was adequate, but it happened to be one of those years when the snow melted in January. In desperation the boys looked for some snow patches."

"In driving along Vermont Route No. 25 beyond East Corinth, we noticed an open field with snow just opposite George Eastman's farm house. Climbing to a higher elevation on our skis we found a fine snow covered area, which opened out into an excellent ski slope."

"'The Rube Goldberg' tow was moved to East Corinth and operated during the rest of the season. The following year an old Dartmouth man, Wes Blake, was intrigued by this hill. He offered to replace our equipment with electric power if he could have the use of the hill. So we set up an electric tow in Bradford village, which operated during the war time. However, Wes Blake's northeast slopes continued to operate during the lean years when there was little snow. Skiers came from Stowe, Waitsfield and Dartmouth. Northeast Ski Tows was organized by local residents when the partnership was ended. This area still has good skiing and is well patronized."

### *Hogback Ski Area*

Harold P. White, who was born in Cuttingsville, Vermont, in the late 1880's, attended the Kimball Union Academy in Meriden, New Hampshire, where he was a drop-out. His father had a store in Ludlow in the basement of which there was a woodworking shop where chairs were made. They began making ash skis which Harold took to KUA in the fall of 1906. In his early days he traveled about Okemo Mountain on skis and snowshoes.

In the early 1930's Mr. White purchased 200 acres of land on Hogback Hill in Marlboro bordering Vermont Route No. 9, with the thought that the area had possibilities for development. In order to learn something about the ski business he took over the concession at the Guilford Ski Area in Brattleboro.

The development of Hogback started in 1931 as a family ski area. In order to develop a well-rounded ski area, it was necessary for him to lease from the State the top of the Hogback in the Molly Stark State Park. The great number of skiers passing this area on their way to Carinthia and Mt. Snow areas were a great potential for his area, which continues to operate successfully today.

### *Big Bromley Ski Area*

In the early 1940's, a big six-footer plus pulled into the state forester's office with an infectious grin that soon won what he desired. Fred Pabst, Jr. wished to lease a part of the Hapgood State Forest on the top of Bromley Mountain in Peru, so that he could extend his chair lift to the summit.

His first interest in skiing dates back to his prep school days at Salisbury, Connecticut, where some transplanted Norwegians had introduced the sport. When the ski fever broke out in the east in 1935, Fred bounced into the thick of it by starting a chain of ski tows and standard ski schools from Maine to Minnesota. In 1935 he started Canada's rope tow at Hill 70 at St. Sauvier in the Laurentians, followed by another on Hill 69.

He devoted the winters of 1939-41 in making the middle west down-hill-ski conscious by organizing the first day ski trains from Chicago and Milwaukee areas to Iron Mountain, Michigan; and Wausau, Wisconsin. In 1937 he built rope tows on Buck Hill,

*Big Bromley Ski Area, Started in 1939*

Minneapolis; Houghton, Michigan; Iron Mountain, Michigan; Lake Placid, New York; and in New Hampshire at Plymouth and Intervale. His last rope tow was in Manchester, Vermont. In 1939 he built the ski area in Peru where he concentrated all his efforts , after selling all of his other ski interests. Big Bromley has developed into a well-known and well-patronized area, thanks to Fred's insight and experience.

### *Killington Ski Area*

In June 1946, about three thousand acres of forest land in the Town of Sherburne was purchased as a state forest for a sum of under seven dollars per acre. The Commssioner of Forests and Parks later had the area surveyed by Sepp Ruschp and Charles Lord to learn of its possibilities as a ski area. In 1954 Preston Smith, a twenty-three-year old youth born in New York City, had a yen to develop a ski area. After looking over the chances of a development on the west side of the Ascutney State Park he came to the office of the Commissioner to learn of the possibilities of getting a lease to a portion of the park. He was advised first to look over the possibilities of Killington by studying the snow fall and depths during the winter. The winter's study convinced him that he should go ahead there. He visited many persons in Rutland with a fine prospectus but sufficient funds there did not seem to be in sight. However, he was able to find the necessary financing in Connecticut.

The 1957 legislature provided funds to build an access road to the area. Development started soon thereafter with the state providing a warming shelter at the base of the chairlift which ran to the summit of Killington. Many trails were cut and other lifts followed rapidly. The last major development was the construction of a gondola lift which operates from near West Bridgewater to Killington summit. As at other ski areas, a snow-making machine was installed since experience showed that at times such a snow maker was necessary. Within the area many motels and condominiums have since been built.

### *Mt. Snow Ski Area*

Reuben Snow peacefully operated his farm in West Dover until money became short in the late forties. From his fifty-acre woodlot, he sold timber to an operator for a minimum price. Having no further use for a cut-over woodlot, he tried without success to sell the lot for $1.00 per acre.

Interest in the development of Vermont ski areas has developed in many ways. Walter Schoenknecht of East Haven, Connecticut, when a young boy became interested in ski jumping. After World War II, he chucked his job with an aviation company and opened the Mohawk Mountain Ski Area at Cornwall, Connecticut.

Since Mohawk was limited in its capacity and possibilities, a man like Walter Schoenknecht started a search for a wider field of operations. While on an air flight, he spotted a high peak Mt. Pisgah (3,000 feet elevation) about twelve miles north of Wilmington, Vermont in the peaceful Dover Valley. He kept winter measurements of the snow depth on the mountain.

He has developed one of the larger ski areas in Vermont with great success. A 5,000 foot long Ski-On bubble-protected gondola has been built.

### *Jay Peak Ski Area*

Interest was shown by many northern Vermont citizens in the development of Jay Peak, as they gathered in 1920 at a picnic in an open field near the base of the mountain. Soon thereafter a Kiwanis Club was formed in North Troy to analyze what could be done at Jay Peak. Field days were instituted and at such a meeting Lee R. Emerson, the Governor, suggested that the first thing to do was to acquire the land on the mountain. At the following session of the legislature, a bill was brought in to authorize bonding for state forest purchases. A legislative committee comprised of Senator Fred Crawford of Newport and Merrill Perley of Enosburg, with others, made a visit during that winter to the area.

Jay Peak Inc. was formed soon after the committee's inspection trip and in 1954 the state acquired 1,700 acres of forest land to be known as Jay State Forest. A strip of land 200 feet wide for a road from the town road in Jay over the mountain pass, to connect with the road from Montgomery was acquired through the efforts of the Commissioner of Forests and Parks, without cost to the state. Soon thereafter the Highway Department constructed the road between the two towns. The Department of Forests and Parks built a ski shelter and parking area, while Jay Peak, Inc. built the ski trails and a chair lift. As funds were raised in the local area more trails were cut and further lifts were installed. The Weyerhauser Company which owned adjoining acreage eventually purchased the interest of Jay Peak, Inc. They enlarged the facilities with the construction of a chair lift to the top of the mountain, built a larger ski shelter and condominium. The area has had great success due to good snow conditions and its nearness to Montreal, Quebec.

### *Shrewsbury Peak Ski Area*

On an 800-acre tract in the Calvin Coolidge State Forest in Shrewsbury, a group of Rutland businessmen installed a rope tow in

1936. Among this group which formed a ski club were Robert Franzoni, Ken Day, Dr. Stuart Ross, Gordon Landon, A. B. Porter, Dr. Earl Johnson and Craigue Perkins. They were given a lease to the area by the Vermont Forest Service. The nearness to Rutland and an area of heavy snowfall gave promise of a successful ski development. The use of the area was thwarted when heavy snowfall occurred on weekends and holidays. Then the Town of Shrewsbury had insufficient equipment to open up the town highways and afterwards plow the approach road to the area for the use of skiers.

### *Pico Peak Ski Area*

The result of the situation at Shrewsbury caused the removal of the ski tow to the Freeman property along U. S. 4 on the approach to Sherburne Pass. The tow was later moved to the present Pico slopes, where eventually chair lifts were installed that carried skiers to the top of Pico Peak with good downhill ski runs. The area has been well patronized and housing developments have mushroomed around the area.

### *Mt. Prospect Ski Area*

In 1939 Alexander B. R. Drysdale of Bennington built a rope tow in the Town of Woodford. The tow extended from a base point with an elevation of 2,000 feet up the mountain to an elevation of 2,800 feet. After the purchase of some 250 acres of mountainside for $500.00; for about $750.00 more, he built a rope tow, 2,400 feet of one-inch manila rope, and old Dodge chassis, and Model-A Ford axles and wheels for pulleys. He built a tarpaper-covered shack as a "base" lodge which was heated by a 55-gallon oil drum constructed into a heater. Mr. Drysdale stated then that "the clothing was not as gay as now but we had fun. And this I mention because in the next fifty years you will see more fantastic growth and change." This area being near Bennington has been developed as prophesied and is well patronized.

### *Okemo Mountain Ski Area*

The 4,200 acre Okemo State Forest lying in the towns of Mt. Holly and Ludlow was acquired by the State in 1935 for the sum of $4.00 per acre. A C.C.C. camp was located there, and the men constructed a highway near to the mountain summit. The chief promoter for a ski development there was the late Judge Ernest E. Moore, who was joined by Donald Ayers, Lindley Robinson, Merrill A. Proctor, Allen Fletcher and Henry Vail. This group formed a company to develop the ski area. The State Highway Department improved the access road from bond funds which were authorized for the construction of roads to a ski area. The Department of Forests and Parks constructed a warming shelter. Warren Warner was employed as the first manager, and he supervised the construction of the ski trails, the installation of the ski lift, and the general operation of the area. From its inception it was a completely-financed Vermont corporation. Over the years more trails have been cut, better shelters built and as a result of a good snow belt the area has had good success.

### *Ski Trains*

In the early days of skiing, the Pennsylvania Railroad in conjunction with the Central Vermont Railway established a ski train, so-called, which was attached to the Montrealer. The train left the Pennsylvania Station in New York at 9 p.m. and arrived in Waterbury at 6:51 a.m. on Fridays. The return trip left Waterbury about 11 p.m. and reached New York in the morning in time for skiers to go to work. Special sleepers were added to the train at other times to take care of the demand. Until passenger train service was discontinued, many skiers used this means of travel to Vermont ski areas. With the gasoline shortage in 1974, again many skiers began to use the Amtrac train which ran at about the same time as the previous Montrealer.

The citizens of Windsor also became interested in getting skiers to their community. In 1936 they interested the Boston and Maine Railroad to run a special weekend train from Boston to a siding just north of Windsor Village, which delivered the skiers to a spot opposite a ski slope. The first train arrived with several cars of enthusiastic skiers from Boston and environs. They brought their lunches with them and left papers scattered about the countryside. The venture did not last long since the restaurant owners and the merchants of Windsor could see little profit from the venture.

At about the same time Brattleboro citizens induced the New York, New Haven and Hartford Railroad to run a ski train from the Hartford environs to Brattleboro. The advertisement for the special ski train called for dining-car service, breakfast, luncheon and dinner at moderate prices, together with a sports service car. The proposed Sunday trips were not run for any length of time.

### *Ski Jumping*

Ski jumping was a winter sport many years before downhill skiing. Fred Harris of Brattleboro was one of the early pioneers in ski jumping. When Fred entered Dartmouth College in 1908, he took a pair of skis with him. Two years later in his junior year he promoted the formation of a ski and snowshoe club. Early in his skiing days he

*The late Fred Harris, 1924, Father of Ski Jumping*

became interested in ski hills and the collection of profiles of ski jumps in many other countries.

The first ski jumping contest at Dartmouth was in the winter of 1910 on a jump built by Fred Harris. In that year Fred had a chance to put into effect on the Brattleboro 70-meter hill some of the practices he had learned. The Brattleboro ski jump has been visited by many national celebrities who have participated, such as the brothers, Sigmund and Birger Ruud, who in 1938 were the F.I.S. world champion jumpers. Many Vermont youths have made their name know nationally. Merrill Barber of Brattleboro also in 1938, at the age of 18 made the longest jump of the day, 198 feet. Walter Malmquist, Jr. of Post Mills, Vermont made outstanding jumps in the winter tryouts of 1974 for Olympic competition.

### *Ski Types*

There has been a great change in skis since the end of the 19th century, when farm boys took a couple of oak barrel staves and some pieces cut from their fathers' harness reins for toe straps, to the expensive modern skis of 1974. Ski lengths have become shorter.

Cross country skis are narrower and longer than down hill skis. James Madden, a former Olympic figure skating champion, is accredited with being the originator of the short ski. Short skis were manufactured in Waterbury, Vermont by William Mason, who also made what were known as "Goon skis", which turned up at both ends so one could slide backwards.

Later, Clifton Taylor, after using the short "Goon skis", decided to merely shorten the standard skis to 3 or more feet. Mr. Taylor advertised that with short skis a person could learn to ski in a day. This development disturbed the ski instructors since they foresaw a day when their jobs would be insecure. They combatted the short ski by advertising courses in the graduated length ski lessons. Some of the first short skis were used by Lowell Thomas at the Hogback Ski Area in Marlboro.

### *Cross Country Skiing*

Cross country skiing in Sweden and other European countries was popular in the early 1900's, since the entire family - regardless of age - could participate. Mention has been made of the trail cut in 1941 on state land from Mt. Mansfield to the Little River Dam, and not used because the fad had not yet taken hold in Vermont. The author, while studying in Sweden, was introduced to cross country skiing which had developed into a cross country race. This was the 51-mile Vasaloppet race which was run from near the Norwegian border to Mora in Darlcarlia. The race was evidently named after old King Gustave Vasa who lived at Mora. Hundreds of racers take part in this race.

Eric Barradale of Guilford, Vermont in 1963 conceived the idea of the first Washington's Birthday Ski Race, which probably ranks as the oldest and largest regularly-run tour race in the United States. The number of competitors has increased from forty during the first year to over 600, who come from all over the Northeastern United States and Canada. The race, managed by the Putney School, is run in the town of Guilford. In 1965 a cross-country race of 24 kilometers was established in the town of Cambridge. The course extends from the Madonna Ski Area's parking lot and ends at the Underhill Center mountain road.

### *Access Roads to Ski Areas*

The first major job of ski access road improvement was done by the Highway Department when it improved Route No. 108 leading from Stowe to the Mt. Mansfield Ski Area. The demand for such roads increased, so the legislature made a special appropriation of $750,000.00 for the purpose. The locations and number of miles built into the areas are: Burke Mountain - 1.92 miles; Jay Peak from Route No. 101 to Montgomery - 12.45 miles; Killington - 4.3 miles; Mt. Snow - 2.08 miles; and Okemo Mountain - .7 mile.

*Early 1900 cross-country skis used by Finnish Pulp Cutters.*

## VERMONT SKI LIFTS

| *Name* | *Town* | *Number Lifts* | *Trails* | *Elevation Feet Base* | *Vertical* |
|---|---|---|---|---|---|
| Bromley Mt. | Peru | 25 | 25 | 1,940 | 1,320 |
| Bolton Valley | Bolton | 4 | 21 | 2,150 | 1,100 |
| Burke Mt. | E. Burke | 4 | 23 | 1,680 | 1,800 |
| Burrington Hill | Whitingham | 2 | 7 | 2,000 | 240 |
| Carinthia | West Dover | 2 | 5 | 2,000 | 800 |
| Dutch Hill | Readsboro | 3 | 7 | 1,900 | 570 |
| Glen Ellen | Waitsfield | 5 | 36 | 1,490 | 2,645 |
| Haystack | Wilmington | 6 | 21 | 2,000 | 1,400 |
| High Pond | Brandon | 4 | Open | 1,100 | 300 |
| Hogback | Marlboro | 4 | 12 | 1,900 | 500 |
| Jay | Jay | 4 | 24 | 1,850 | 2,090 |
| Killington | Sherburne | 12 | 50 | 1,160 | 3,000 |
| Lyndon Outing | Lyndonville | 4 | 20 | 1,600 | 1,985 |
| Mad River | Waitsfield | 4 | 25 | 1,600 | 1,985 |
| Magic Mountain | Londonderry | 8 | 24 | 1,400 | 1,600 |
| Maple Valley | Dummerston | 3 | 9 | 500 | 850 |
| Middlebury College | Ripton | 4 | 10 | 1,500 | 1,100 |
| Mt. Ascutney | West Windsor | 5 | 24 | 800 | 1,475 |
| Mt. Mansfield | Stowe | 21 | 29 | 1,550 | 2,150 |
| Mt. Snow | Dover | 13 | 46 | 1,900 | 1,700 |
| Mt. Tom | Woodstock | 2 | 5 | 700 | 500 |
| NE. Slopes | East Corinth | 1 | Open | 1,300 | 2,150 |
| Norwich University | Northfield | 3 | 11 | 850 | 920 |
| Okemo | Ludlow | 9 | 18 | 1,300 | 2,150 |
| Pico Peak | Mendon | 7 | 30 | 2,000 | 1,967 |
| Pinnacle | Randolph | 2 | 4 | 750 | 550 |
| Prospect | Woodford | 3 | 10 | 2,200 | 650 |
| Round Top | Plymouth | 4 | 10 | 1,300 | 1,250 |
| Snow Valley | Winhall | 2 | 6 | 2,020 | 700 |
| Sonnenberg | Barnard | 2 | | 1,600 | 500 |
| Stratton | Stratton Mountain | 8 | 37 | 2,125 | 1,750 |
| Smuggles' Notch | Cambridge | 3 | 32 | | 2,500 |
| Suicide Six | Woodstock | 2 | 12 | 750 | 600 |
| Sugarbush Valley | Warren | 7 | 27 | 1,625 | 2,400 |

## *WATER RESOURCES*

### *Water Conservation*

The powers of the Public Service Commission over dams other than those which are used for generation of electricity were turned over to the Water Conservation Board by the Acts of 1949.

No person, firm or corporation may build a dam without the approval of the Water Conservation Board which impounds more than 500,000 cubic feet of water in any stream or river within or along the borders of the state where the land in the state is proposed to be overflowed. No dam of the aforementioned size may be remodeled, reconstructed or altered without board approval.

The Fish and Game Department is concerned in the construction of any dam which might impede the propogation of salmon. The department is directed to survey any present dams which impounds over 300,000 cubic feet of water to see that the announced conditions do not prevail on these dams. After hearing with the right of appeal by the owner, such dams may have to be altered.

In order to cooperate with the Federal Government on flood control dams for the state, the state has defined its policy therefore as follows:

(1) No flood control project which contemplates the generation of electricity shall be built without the approval of the Public Service Commission.

(2) No strictly flood control project shall be built which will inundate any village or city in the state.

(3) Adequate compensation shall be made to any town or city which has a loss of tax revenue from strictly flood control projects.

(4) For impoundments which will cover one hundred or more acres of farmland, recreational developments of the state or the economy of the river basin involved may be affected, the Public Service Board may make an investigation and report its findings to the federal authority having such flood control project in charge for its consideration and recognition.

As a result of the Federal Flood Control Act of 1963, the states of Connecticut, New Hampshire and Vermont and the Commonwealth of Massachusetts formed the *Connecticut River Flood Control Compact.* "The principal purposes of this compact are:

(a) to promote interstate comity among and between the signatory states;

(b) to assure adequate storage capacity for impounding the waters of the Connecticut River and its tributaries for the protection of life and property from flood;

(c) to provide a joint or common agency through which the signatory states, while promoting, protecting and preserving to each the local interest and sovereignty of the respective signatory states, may more effectively cooperate in accomplishing the object of flood control and water resources utilization in the basin of the Connecticut River and its tributaries.

"Under the compact the states of Massachusetts and Connecticut agree to reimburse New Hampshire and Vermont for economic damages occurred by the construction of such dams in the state of New Hampshire and Vermont. Each of the signatory states appoints three members to the compact who serve for three years. The apportionment of the costs of the compact are borne as follows: $7,500.00 by Massachusetts; $6,500.00 by Connecticut and $1,000.00 each by New Hampshire and Vermont.

Vermont Statutes Annotated, Title 10, Chapter 29.

## *FLOODS*

The history of floods dates back to the first settlements in Vermont. In March 1839 a major flood was noted on the Connecticut River at Windsor, Connecticut. Specific reference to floods in Vermont did not occur until 1770, when in January of the year major flooding was noted on the tributaries of the Connecticut River. In the fall of 1771 Vermont experienced another flood which caused extensive damage in the central Connecticut River Valley.

According to Zadock Thompson "the year 1811 on the 22nd of July was distinguished by one of the most remarkable freshets known in Vermont. Dark clouds came over from the southwest, and rain soon began to descend in such torrents that every rill was swollen into the magnitude of a river, and foaming cataracts were formed where ordinarily no water was to be seen. The deluge of water rushed onward with such impetuosity that hardly anything could withstand the force.

"The heaviest part of the storm descended upon the counties of Rutland and Windsor, in which counties probably two-thirds of the mills and bridges were swept away and immense other damage done by the destruction of buildings, fences and crops." Thompson reported his remembrance of a stream which ran by his place in Bridgewater, which normally could fill no more than a three-inch pipe, with the freshet, it formed a brook one to two rods wide with a mid-stream depth of four to five feet.

"The 16th, 17th and 18th days of December, 1835, are memorable on account of the cold. The 16th was the most severe day with a piercing west wind. On the morning of the 18th, the thermometer registered from 30 to 40 degrees below zero."

In 1850, 1869 and 1895, severe floods did statewide damage. The 1927 flood of November 2, 3 and 4 caused severe damage throughout Vermont, which is reported under four principal divisions. In recent history the State has experienced three major floods, those of November 1927, March 1936 and September 1938. Of these floods the flood of November 3 and 4, 1927 was by far the most severe, which wrote a chapter in Vermont history, not soon to be forgotten. The greatest rainfall during the 1927 flood, as measured at Somerset, Vt. was 9.65 inches of which 8.66 inches occurred in a period of 24 hours. There were 55 lives lost in the Winooski River basin alone.

The March 1936 flood, a combination of snow melt and heavy rainfall, produced widespread flooding throughout the state, but did not measure up to the 1927 flood. The September 1938 flood produced flows of great magnitude in the southern portion of the Connecticut watershed, while most other parts of the state experienced minor flooding. The summary of other floods of minor nature found in the publication, *Flood Hazards in Vermont.*[1]

Over 690 farms received damage by erosion or by the dumping of huge quantities of gravel and silt on their fields. There was a loss of about $8,000,000.00 due to 1,258 bridges which were destroyed, and to many miles of highways which were either seriously washed out altogether or the road served as a place for a stream bed. Two hundred sixty-four industrial plants were estimated to have received $7,000,000.00 of damage. The losses and damages to municipalities and state property amounted to about $8,000,000.00 and to the railroads and communication companies another $8,000,000.00. There were 82 lives lost because of the flood. The pilot of Herbert Hoover, Secretary of Commerce, was killed in an attempted landing on a farm on Towne Hill in Montpelier. It was about four months before the Central Vermont Railroad could repair a washout at Slip Hill in Middlesex so that train service could be resumed.[2]

## *FLOOD CONTROL DAMS*[3]

The citizens of Barre, Montpelier and Waterbury and other places down the Winooski Valley were much elated when President Franklin D. Roosevelt signed an appropriation act following the Act establishing the Civilian Conservation Corps on March 31, 1933 that brought the Winooski Valley flood control dams into being.

The coordination and implementation of the program was placed in the hands of the following government agencies; Secretary of War, Secretary of Interior, Secretary of Agriculture and Director of Veterans Affairs. Mr. Robert Fechner of Quincy, Massachusetts was selected as director of the corps.

Inasmuch as Vermont had plans already developed by the Corps of Engineers to alleviate flood damage in the Winooski Valley it was not difficult for Governor Stanley C. Wilson to interest the President to authorize the use of C.C.C. veterans in the development of flood control dams in Vermont.

The Sixth District of the C.C.C. included the flood control work in the Valley. The pioneer company, a colored outfit, of Bonus Marchers on Washington detrained at Barre City railroad station on

1. Vermont, *Flood Hazards in Vermont,* (Department of Water Resources, 1972).
2. Vermont, Report of State Forester. 1927.
3. Reports of Sixth District C.C.C. U.S.A. 1934 et reg.

July 3, 1933. They established themselves at Camp Wilson in East Barre followed by ten more companies of 200 each.

The East Barre flood control dam which they built, is 1,200 feet long, 400 feet wide at the base and 85 at the crest. It rises 65 feet above the old river bed.

The first group of veterans arrived in Montpelier on July 7, 1933 and the last contingent on August 6, 1933. As soon as the wooden barracks at Wrightsville were constructed by civilian workers the veterans moved out of tents into the barracks. The Wrightsville dam is 1,500 feet long, width at base 750 feet and at the top 160 feet. 1,115,000 cubic yards of earth and rock fill were required for the dam, which has a height of 90 feet.

Camp McKee, named after Mayor William McKee was established in a corn field on top of a Berlin Hill about a mile out of Montpelier toward Barre. The veterans arrived there on July 10, 1933, and located in tents. They built the Montpelier Clothes Pin dam and worked on river bank ripraping. The tent camp was closed in December when they were moved to Camp Green in Wrightsville.

The State of Vermont acquired about 4,000 acres of land in the Little River Valley so that the dam could be built there. A number of homes had to be wrecked and the road through the valley from Waterbury to Moscow had to be closed. On the plateau westerly as one approaches the dam Camp Smith with over 200 buildings housed the workers who built the dam.

The Little River dam is among the largest earth filled dams in New England. It required over 2,000,000 cubic yards of earth fill to construct the dam which is 2,000 feet long, with a maximum width of 900 feet and a maximum height of 175 feet. The tunnel under the dam is 900 feet long. Ground was first broken on this project in April 1935.

This dam like the others was faced on both sides with rocks laid by hand. All three dams have tunnels under them that will allow no more water to pass through than can be contained in the lower stream banks.

Camp Meade was constructed at the westerly edge of the village of Middlesex. The companies there worked on channel improvement of the Winooski river above Middlesex.

Though there have been heavy rains since the construction of these dams all the communities have been spared from flooding.

A few years after the Little River Dam had been built, the Green Mountain Power Company according to a previous agreement when they sold the land to the state put in the necessary generating equipment to produce electricity.

## *HURRICANES*

"A tornado occurred in August 1788. It was the most destructive of any since the establishment of the town. It swept the town from west to east, leaving scarcely any timber standing on some farms in its course. The day on which it occurred was still and foggy up to the time the heavy wind struck. There was no premonition of its approach. There was no roar heard 'till just as the main force came upturning trees, leaving devastation and destruction in the track of nearly two miles passing in through other towns to the east."[4]

On September 21, 1938, a hurricane swept through Vermont and left in its wake thousands of acres of damaged and windthrown timberlands between the Green Mountains and the Connecticut River. The worst damage and hazard was in the Connecticut River Valley and on adjacent slopes, decreasing in severity westward from the river and toward the northern end of the state. To aid the states in the area of the hurricane, the New England Forest Emergency Project (NEFE) was established by the federal government under the jurisdiction of the United States Forest Service. Under their direction the existing Civilian Conservation Corps (C.C.C.) and two new organizations, The New England Hurricane Damage Organization (NEHD) and the Northeastern Timber Salvage Administration (NETSA), were set up.

On September 21, 1938, a hurricane swept through Vermont and left in its wake thousands of acres of damaged and windthrown timberlands between the Green Mountains and the Connecticut River. The worst damage and hazard was in the Connecticut River Valley and on adjacent slopes, decreasing in severity westward from the river and toward the northern end of the state. To aid the states in the area of the hurricane, the New England Forest Emergency Project (NEFE) was established by the federal government under the jurisdiction of the United States Forest Service. Under their direction the existing Civilian Conservation Corps (C.C.C.) and two new organizations, The New England Hurricane Damage Organization (NEHD) and the Northeastern Timber Salvage Administration (NETSA), were set up.

The work of the New England Hurricane Damage Organization was concerned with the reduction of fire hazard chiefly around buildings, municipalities and along highways. The Works Progress Administration (WPA) - which was at that time using make-work to give labor to the unemployed - furnished up to 700 laborers to aid in this work. The United States Forest Service established two work

4. Hemingway, Abby Maria, *Vermont Historical Gazetteer,* (Montpelier, Vermont Watchman and State Journal, 1882), Vol. V, p. 146.

camps in the Connecticut River Valley and employed about 250 men. With the Depression in existence the blow-down of about 50 million board feet of saw timber and 30,000 cords of pulpwood, the market would have been so depressed if the federal government had not stepped in. Money was borrowed from the Reconstruction Finance Corporation to pay for the purchase of logs and pulpwood which was purchased from the owners at the fair market price. The lumber was sawn and sold, and released gradually over a period of time so as not to depress prices.

Over 500 laborers found employment during this program. The federal government paid over $816,000,000.00 to forest owners in Vermont alone, and over $400,000.00 to Vermont mill owners for sawing the logs under contract. In this operation the government was able to recover all of its costs and aid the forest landowners in the logging and sale of their timber resources.

## *Water Pollution Control*

The deposition of sawdust, shavings or mill waste in certain specified streams and bodies of water was first prohibited by the Acts of 1890 and the Vermont Statutes of 1947 list the locations in certain waters in Franklin County, Washington, Caledonia, Windham and Orange Counties.

In 1902, the legislature passed laws prohibiting pollution of the waters of the Tyler Branch, the Black River in Orleans, the sources of drinking water supplies and the sources of Willoughby Lake. As early as 1892, the polluting of the waters of Otter Creek was prohibited.

Legislation against pollution occurred in 1908 when the deposition of sawdust, shavings or mill refuse in the streams of Lamoille River or its tributaries above Ithiel Falls in Johnson were prohibited.

The Acts of 1912 prohibited any operator or a water, steam, gasoline or electrical power mill erected after August 1913 to deposit such refuse in the waters of any stream of the state.

Vermont passed a Water Pollution Control Act in 1943. Under the act pollution means the placing in the waters of the state by whatever means of any noxious or deleterious substance which renders such waters harmful to animals or aquatic life, or to use for industrial purposes or for recreation. The waters of the state are classified by the Water Conservation Board into four classes.

Class A. Suitable for public water supply. Character uniformly excellent.

Class B. Suitable for bathing and recreation, irrigation and agricultural uses; good fish habitat, good aesthetic value; acceptable for public water supply with filtration and disinfection.

Class C. Suitable for recreational boating, irrigation of crops not used for consumption without cooking; habitat for wildlife and for common food and game fishes indigenous to the region.

Class D. Suitable for transportation of sewage and industrial wastes without nuisance, and for power, navigation and other industrial uses.

In 1965, municipalities were granted assistance from the state to assist in the cost of sewer system separation projects. Public lands lying under public waters, lakes and ponds are to be managed by the state in the public interest. Consolidated sewer districts were authorized for two or more municipalities.

*WATER CONSERVATION POLICY:* "That the water resources of the state shall be protected, regulated and - when necessary - controlled under the authority of the state in the public interest and to promote the general welfare. It is also declared that this policy necessitates the creation of the department of water resources in which there shall be a water resources board."

The board has very broad powers to make studies and recommendations, control flood control structure, levels of lakes and ponds, administer loans and grants to municipalities, make ground water studies, control stream flow by alteration with dams or otherwise, control of dams, classification of waters.

No person shall discharge any waste substance or material into the waters of the state.

The New England Interstate Water Pollution Control Compact was adopted by the Vermont Legislature in 1951. The compact has been approved by all of the New England States and by the Congress of the United States in 1947. The compact relates to New York in regard to waters common to New York and New England. There are three members appointed for a period of six years with the Commissioner of Health as ex-officio members. Vermont appropriates the annual sum of $1,500.00 for its share of the operation of the compact commission.

To implement compliance by Vermont with Article V of the New England Interstate Water Pollution Control Compact, section 996 of Title 10, the legislature hereby declares:

(1) That the waters of all reservoirs, natural or artificial, wholly within this state, used for public water supply and all waters flowing into such reservoirs are to be Class A waters of Vermont; and

(2) That the water of each natural lake and pond, wholly within this state, and having an area of twenty or more acres, and the waters flowing into such natural lakes and ponds are to be Class B waters of Vermont except such lakes and ponds as are used for public water supply; provided, however, that on petition of the

Vermont state water conservation board by ten persons who own property on the lake, or pond so classified, alleging they suffer unjustice or inequity as a result of this classification, the board shall hold a public hearing convenient to such lake or pond. The board may place the waters of such lake or pond, or the waters flowing into it, in a different class. Such waters shall remain in the class fixed by the board until changed by act of the legislature; and

(3) The Vermont state water conservation board is directed under procedure following to determine what degree of purity of the remaining waters of the state should be obtained and maintained in the future to provide the people of Vermont with the maximum of beneficial use and enjoyment of such waters. The board shall make such tests of any such water as it deems necessary for determining its present classification.

Vermont Statutes Annotated, Title 10, Chapter 33, Section 903.

### *Land Drainage*

"When the public good or necessity or convenience of individuals requires the opening of a ditch or watercourse to drain low or swamp lands, to enable owners or occupants thereof to cultivate the same, such owners or operators shall open such ditch or watercourse in proportion to their several interests. (1868)"

Hearings are held in each case and all expenses shall be paid by the parties interested in such proportion as the selectmen shall order.

Vermont Statutes Annotated, Title 10, Chapter 23.

## *GEOLOGY*

### *Board of Geographic Names*

The Board of Geographic Names was established in 1917 to furnish any state or federal publication the proper terminology and spelling of any geographic name in Vermont. The board may advise the United States Post Office Department regarding the proper selection and spelling of the name of a Vermont Post Office or any railroad company regarding the use and spelling of the name of a Vermont station. Names used on maps of the United States geological survey in cooperation with the state shall be spelled in accordance with the recommendation of the board.

The members of the board are the state librarian, the state geologist, an officer of the Vermont Historical Society, a member of the Department of Highways, and a member of the office of the secretary of state.

Vermont Statutes Annotated, Title 10, Sec. 15ln.

### *State Geologist*

The position of State Geologist was established by the Legislature in 1844. The duties of this position are to be curator of the cabinet and select specimens of rocks and minierals therefor. He may give such aid and advice as may be possible to the development and the working of mineral deposits and beds of rock sutiable for building or road making.

Vermont Statutes Annotated, Title 10, Chapter 25.

## *GEOLOGY OF VERMONT BY CHARLES G. DOLL*

The history of Vermont goes back to the remotest of geologic time. Throughout past eons, periods and epochs there have been vast changes in the Vermont landscape, its underlying rocks and the evolving life forms as well.

The earliest rocks are Pre-Cambrian, an age older than 600,000,000 years ago and spanning several billions of years. Rocks of this time are exposed in the core of the Green Mountains from the latitude of Rutland southward into Massachusetts. Because these rocks have been subjected to intermittent disturbances through eons of geologic time, they are highly metamorphosed and little is known of their geologic history.

The rocks of succeeding Cambrian time, which began about 600,000,000 years ago, tell us much more of their history. They reveal inundation of the state by marine waters and the contained fossils attest the widespread marine conditions. This marine environment continued throughout the succeeding Ordovician and Silurian periods and well into Devonian time. During these geologic periods the seas occupied extensive basins known as *geosynclines,* the western Champlain Basin and the eastern Magog Basin. The Champlain Basin sedimentation was accompanied by a relatively stable environment, resulting in the deposition of carbonate and clastic rocks with little or no alteration, while conditions in the Magog Basin were contrastingly unstable, where sedimentation had numerous interruptions during periods of vulcanism. That vulcanism was in great part submarine can be seen in fossiliferous limestones intercalated with lava flows. Marine conditions came to an end in the Champlain Basin in approximately Mid-Ordovician time and in the Magog Basin somewhat later, about Mid-Devonian time, some 330,000,000 years ago.

Crustal movements toward the end of Cambrian time resulted in uplift of the area of the Green Mountains, forming a seascape of islands, of which some were volcanic. During the late Ordovician enormous amounts of rock material slid into the sea adjacent on the west, creating a mountainous pile of metamorphosed and greatly contorted rocks known as the Taconic Mountains. The Taconic Mountains are the home of the long-known commercial marbles and slates.

Unstable conditions in the Magog Basin in Devonian time brought about the final retreat of the marine waters and extensive folding and faulting of the rocks, metamorphosing them in the process. This occured during a period of mountain building known as the Acadian Orogeny, which was intensified by vast intrusions of igneous rocks as exemplified by the dome-shaped prominences in eastern Vermont, one such prominence producing the famed Barre granite.

With the exception of small-scale tabular igneous intrusions that extended into Cretaceous time, there is a long hiatus in the geologic history of the state during which erosion must have been dominant, which brings us to the Pleistocene Epoch, a time of extensive glaciations. In excess of a million years ago thick sheets of ice moved southward from centers of accumulation to the north in Canada. The record in Vermont is confined to the Wisconsinan glaciation, the latest of the Pleistocene ice episodes. Studies have shown that there were three advances of the ice from two directions, the earliest Bennington stade from the northwest, followed by the Shelburne stade from the northeast, which in turn was succeeded by the Burlington stade from the northwest. All three of these ice episodes in Vermont were determined from both erosional and depositional features left behind when the ice receded from the region.

The directions of ice movement of the several Wisconsinan glaciations was determined from erosional features on the surfaces of the bedrock exposures, such as the orientation of scratches and grooves, and the linear aspect of the fabric of the widespread glacial deposits known as till. During the glacial advances erosion was effective in modifying the topography of the state, producing deep, steep-sided, longitudinal valleys, steep-walled amphitheater-like depressions on the sides of some of the higher elevations, called cirques, and many ice-carved basins which were filled with meltwater when the glacier retreated northward.

The largest basin is that containing Lake Champlain which was preceded by two lake stages of Lake Vermont, known as Coveville and Fort Ann stages when the outlets were successively at these two places and with a southerly drainage to the Hudson Valley. The

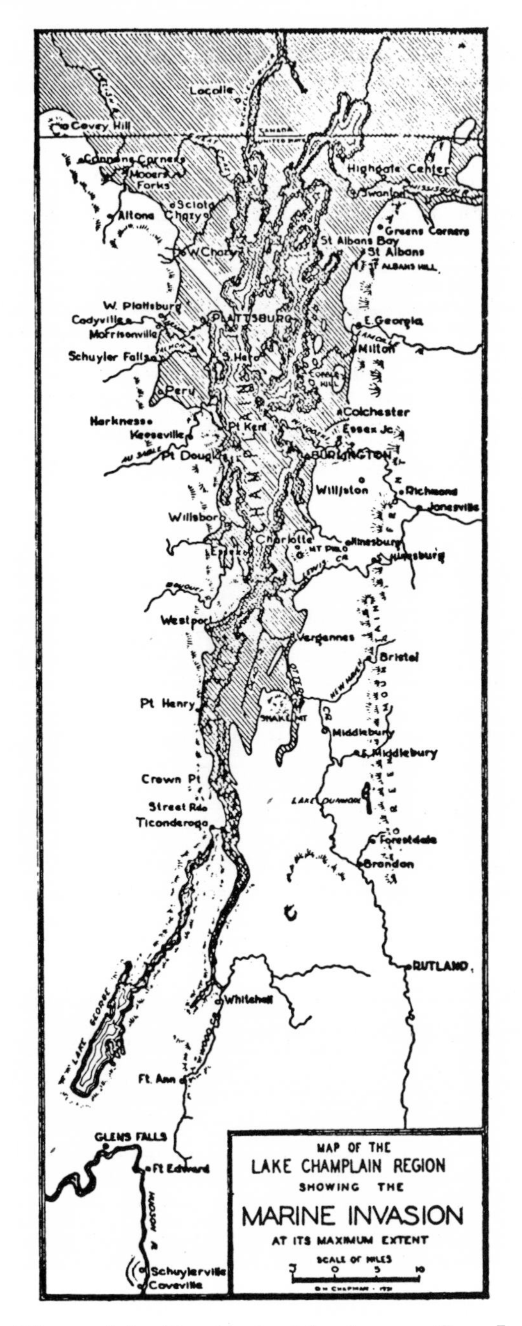


*Lake Champlain Region's Maximum Sea Invasion*

waning ice-front to the north formed a barrier impounding the extensive lake waters. When the terminus of the glacier reached the St. Lawrence Valley the sea water invaded the Champlain Valley, initiating the marine stage which left its mark in fossiliferous shoreline sediments, from which the famous whale specimen was unearthed in Charlotte during construction of the Rutland railroad. This rare treasure is exhibited in the Geology Museum at the University of Vermont.

A slow tilting of the earth's crust to the south gradually elevated a rock barrier in the Richelieu River at St. Jean, Quebec, thus severing connection with the sea, beyond which, in turn, led to the birth of present-day scenic Lake Champlain which is contained in a basin possessing a wealth of geologic history.

Limited space obviously does not permit extended treatment of this fascinating history which may be pursued further in the accompanying references.

### *AGRICULTURE* *SELECTED BIBLIOGRAPHY*

Crockett, Walter Hill, *Vermont The Green Mountain State,* Burlington, Vermont Farm Bureau, 1938.

Janawicz, A. E., Veterinarian Vermont Department of Agriculture, *Personal Interview,* 1974.

Midgley, A. R., *A Promising Forage Plant,* Burlington: University of Vermont, Agronomy Department, 1950.

Stillwell, Lewis D., *Migration from Vermont, 1776-1860,* Montpelier: Vermont Historical Society, Vol. V., No. 2, 1937.

Smith, H. P. and Rann, W. S. ed. *History of Rutland County,* Syracuse: D. Mason and Company, 1886.

Swift, Samuel, *Agricultural History of Middlebury and Addison County,* Middlebury, A. L. Copeland, 1859.

Tremblay, Raymond, H., *Trefoil Seed Production in the Champlain Valley,* University of Vermont, Burlington, 1962.

Vermont, *Biennial Reports,* Montpelier: Department of Agriculture.

Vermont Maple Sugar Makers Association, *History of the Maple Sugar Industry from Indians Down to Present.*

Vermont, *Statutes Affecting Agriculture, 1797-1974.*

Way, Winston, *Trefoil in New England,* Monograph of Summary of a Talk, Stanford Seed Conference, August, 1966.

Vermont, Agricultural Experiment Station, *Apple Growing,* Dec. 1896.

Allen, Ira, *History of Vermont,* Montpelier: Vermont Historical Society, Vol. I, 1870.

Ludlum, David M., *Social Ferment in Vermont,* New York: Columbia University Press, 1939.

### *GEOLOGY* *SELECTED BIBLIOGRAPHY*

Chapman, Donald H., *Late-Glacial and Post-Glacial History of the Champlain Valley,* Report of the State Geologist, Vol. 23, pp. 48-83, 1942.

Kay, Marshall, *North American Geosynclines,* Geol. Soc. Amer. Memoir 48, 143 pp., 1951.
Stewart, David P., *The Surficial and Pleistocene History of Vermont,* Vermont Geological Survey, Bulletin 31, 251 pp., 1969.

# Vermont Historic Sites

The Hubbardton Battlefield Commission composed of A. Vail Allen, Edward Ellis and Perry H. Merrill, as secretary, was authorized by No. 225 of the public acts of 1937. The objective of the Commission was the development of the Hubbardton Battlefield.

The Historic Sites Commission was established by No. 53 of the acts of 1947 and assumed the powers and duties of the previous organization. The commission consisted of the director of the Vermont Development Commission, the director of the Vermont Historical Society and three public persons appointed by the Governor biennially. Under the act the State Forester, the author, serving as executive secretary and the Commissioner of Highways were directed to assist the commission.

The first members of the commission were Vrest Orton, Graham Newell, Burton Smith with ex-officio members Clifton Miskelly, Richard Wood and Perry H. Merrill.

From the inception in 1937 much work has been accomplished in the acquisition and development of state historic sites. The commission has placed markers at the site of private historic sites and homes and graves of important personages.

The sites under the jurisdiction of the commission include in addition to the Hubbardton Battlefield and the Bennington Battle monument, which was built by the state many years ago, the Coolidge Homestead, the Homestead of Uncle John Wilder, the store and birthplace of President Coolidge and other property in the Plymouth Notch region, President Chester A. Arthur's birthplace, the Constitution House, the Hyde Log Cabin, Senator Justin Smith Morrill homestead, Eureka Schoolhouse, Scott Covered Bridge, Mount Independence, Fisher Bridge and Chimney Point, first white settlement in 1690 by Captain DeWarm. The Coolidge Homestead was given to the state by Mr. and Mrs. John Coolidge.

Further information is obtainable from the Historic Sites Commission in Montpelier 05602.

# Transportation

The subject of transportation will be treated under several headings, from the Indian footpaths and canoe routes to today's aviation. Our hardy forefathers who settled Vermont had to encounter a wilderness fraught with Indians and wild animals. The first settlers cut paths through the dense forested areas to reach a homesite.

Many of the early roads followed Indian trails which were gradually improved until by 1791. Vermont roads were widened to accommodate oxcarts; public highways were built to connect Vermont settlements with one another; and stage coaches came into use. Some of the first roads were originally built as military roads such as the Crown Point or Great Road which was constructed from near the mouth of the Black River opposite old Fort Number 4 in New Hampshire northwesterly to Chimney Point, being built about 1776.[1]

The Mount Independence-Hubbardton road was built in 1776 to furnish a shorter new road to Rutland Falls on the Crown Point road, when after taking Fort Ticonderoga, the Continental Congress determined to fortify Mt. Independence. A Hubbardton letter from John Barret to General Gates at Ticonderoga stated, "The party at Work on the Rode have accomplished the cutting of the Rode through from Mount Independence to Otter Creek, and will in a day or two effect the bridging." Later a Hydeville branch of this road of about 8½ miles in length left the Hubbardton Military Road in the northeast corner of Benson and followed southerly along the west side of the shore of Glen Lake to Hydeville, where it connected with a road from Rutland to Skenesborough.[2]

1. Julia R. Kellogg, *Vermont Post Roads and Canals,* (Montpelier: Vermont Historical Society, 1948), Vermont Quarterly, p. 135.

2. Joseph Wheeler and Mabel Wheeler, The Mount Independence-Hibbardton Military Road, (Benson, Bt.: Reprint from History Magazine, 1959.)

The Crown Point Road was built by General Jeffery Amherst in 1759-60 during the French and Indian Wars following his capture of the French Forts at Ticonderoga and Crown Point. Its purpose was to connect the great stone forts at Crown Point, then being built, with Fort No. 4, now Charleston, New Hampshire.

Crown Point was to be the jumping off point in the campaign against the French in Canada. Fort No. 4 was the most northern outpost in the Connecticut River Valley. The new Crown Point Road would thus enable the transportation of troops and supplies from Connecticut, Massachusetts and Rhode Island to the fort at Crown Point. The Crown Point Road was used again during the Revolution, when troops and supplies were sent over the road from Fort No. 4 to support the American army position at Ticonderoga.[3]

The other was the General Jacob Bayley road, built under his direction in 1776 from his home town of Newbury to Canada to facilitate the transportation of troops and supplies for an invasion of Canada. It was built only as far as Peacham, where construction ceased when the Americans withdrew from Canada. Under the direction of General Hazen three years later, the construction of the road was extended some fifty miles further to Hazen's Notch in Lowell, and completed in 1779. That same year the legislature appointed Ebenezer Crafts to survey a route for the road from Greensboro to the Canadian line by the way of Craftsbury and Lowell through Hazen's Notch and Montgomery. The road was laid out in 1791-1792; however, it was not built farther than Hazen's Notch. Of late the entire route has been known as the Bayley-Hazen road.[4]

Colonel Philip Skene, for whom Skenesborough (now Whitehall, N.Y.) was named, built a road from there to Salem, N.Y. in 1786; later others extended it to Bennington. He also built a road from Skenesborough to Poultney, which was later extended to Castleton. The Allens in 1772 cut a road from Castleton to Colchester via Vergennes Falls. The Poultney Turnpike (organized in 1806) was converted later from a primitive road to part of a through route from Albany, N.Y. to Burlington.[5]

One method of financing for highways in the early days was for a town to petition the legislature for permission to assess taxes against real property. The requests ran from one to three cents on the dollar of the grand list of the town. Under the laws of 1797 a peti-

3. Crown Point Road Association, The Crown Point Road, (Springfield: Crown Point Road Association, 1965)

4. Edward Miller and Frederic P. Wells, *History of Ryegate,* (St. Johnsbury: The Caledonian, 1913), p. 70.

5. Julia R. Kellogg, *Vermont Post Roads and Canals,* (Montpelier: Vermont Historical Society, 1948), Vermont Quarterly, p. 135.

tion to assess taxes had to be approved by at least one-half of the town's landowners.

An example of such a petition is one made by the Town of Richford. "There is a necessity of laying out and making roads and building bridges in said Town of Richford for the accommodation of the inhabitants and the public for the promotion of further settlement of said town, the expense of which cannot be borne by a tax on the lands of the township. Therefore your petitioners pray this legislature to lay a tax of two cents under such regulation and direction of the statute, as in duty bound shall ever pray." (Windsor, October 16, 1798)

Another method was for a person or company to be granted a charter to build a road which was usually a toll road between two certain points. Such roads - known as "turnpikes" - had a turnstile through which horses or oxen had to pass. It was actually a pike or hole which turned on an axis to admit passage. In later years swing gates were built in front of the tollkeeper's house, thus we get the name tollgate. Many of the early roads known as turnpikes had a tollgate at either end of the road if it was of some length. Rates charged varied according to the length of the turnpike and type of use. Differing fees were charged for a yoke of oxen, a single horse wagon, a double team and so on.

Some old signs show the charges for wagons, sleighs, cattle, and sheep. The wagon charges depended upon the width of the tires. Narrow tires made deep ruts, whereas wide tired vehicles were charged a lesser fee. Rates varied from one cent for a sheep to one dollar for a four-horse team.

In some locations the local people built bypass roads to avoid the payment of toll. One is reminded of such roads - known as "shunpikes" - when he passes a street sign on U.S. Route 2 in Williston, marked Shunpike Road. About 1812 many studies were made in preparation for the construction of turnpikes between towns, and also from these towns to Montpelier. On some of the turnpikes, the inhabitants along the length of the routes were not required to pay the tolls. The first turnpike corporation was chartered by the legislature to build a road from Bennington to Wilmington in 1812. Many more corporations were granted authority to build turnpike roads; all of these were given the same authority as a town to take land, lay out roads, and build them.

The laws of 1797 allowed towns to elect a surveyor of highways. By the Acts of 1827, five county road commissioners were authorized with powers to lay out or alter roads and assess a tax for the cost thereof. Throughout the first century of Vermont's history as a state, construction and maintenance of highways and bridges was exclusively financed by the towns. In 1892 the legislature authorized the assessment of two cents on the town's grand list which was then apportioned to the towns and cities for local roads.

The only turnpike which collected tolls from automobiles was the one in Peru chartered in 1814. The Rutland Herald wrote of this road in January 1914, "By actual count there are 143 water bars on the six miles of road, mostly of the comb type, on which the low cars of recent years frequently become stalled." Thus when the automobile arrived on the scene there was much complaint about turnpike maintenance. A local representative in the Vermont legislature succeeded in 1913 in getting a law passed to make the Peru Turnpike, the last toll road in the state, made toll free.

On December 1, 1898, the legislature passed a law entitled, "An act to improve the Public Roads and estabish the Vermont Highway Commission." The Commissioner (appointed by the governor with senate concurrence) had supervision through the town road commissioner of the expenditure of permanent highway funds allotted to the towns on a simple per mile basis. Towns were required to assess 20 cents on the dollar of the grand list for town highways.

Passage of the Automobile Act of 1908 provided for the registration of automobiles, revenue from which was appropriated to a maintenance fund for state highways and for assistance to town highways.

## *BRIDGE FUND*

In 1915 the legislature passed a Bridge Fund Act from which monies to pay 25 percent of the cost of building town bridges were allocated to the various towns. No town was to receive over $300.00 for use on bridges four to 30 feet in width. In 1912 a state highway commissioner was given authority to establish a highway patrol system, increasing from ten routes (then) to 100 in 1916.

## *FIRST PAVED ROAD*

The first paved road in Vermont covered a distance of about three miles being built before 1919 with federal funds at Fort Ethan Allen.

## *CONTROL OF HIGHWAYS BY STATE*

It was not until after the 1927 flood (in 1933) that the state took over the control of state highways. This Act stated that, "The State Highway Board at the state's expense, shall construct, maintain and control the state aid highways now or hereafter included in the Federal Highway System, and shall be known as state highways; provided however, such state highways may not include streets and highways where for the space of one-half mile thereon the houses average to stand 100 feet or less apart."

### *FLOOD DAMAGE*

The 1927 flood washed out all or part of about 1258 highway bridges and miles of highways at an estimated loss of eight million dollars. Governor John E. Weeks immediately called a special session of the legislature which speedily appropriated funds to rebuild and repair the highways and bridges.

### *CEMENT OR BLACKTOP*

When Stanley C. Wilson of Chelsea became Governor in 1931, there was a very heated argument in the press as to whether it was better to build cement roads as suggested by Roland Stevens of White River Junction, or blacktop roads as favored by Governor Wilson. Obviously, blacktop roads have been the choice.

### *DIFFICULT TRAVEL*

In the early 1920's, winter travel - especially between Montpelier and Burlington - was occasionally quite difficult. Before the state took over control of the state highways, the Town of Bolton was the only town which either neglected or refused to plow their section of the present US Route 2. The result was that when meeting, with the deep icy ruts formed after a thaw and a freeze, either one driver or the other had to back up to a spot where it was possible to meet and pass. In the spring both state and town roads at times were a mire of mud, due to the absence of drainage and gravel. On such a trip going from Hookerville in the Town of Cabot to Peacham, the writer's Model-T Ford sunk in the mud up to the axle. A rail was pulled out of the adjoining fence and placed on a stone fulcrum near the car. Luckily my wife was with me to sit on the end of the rail when we had raised one of the back wheels out of the mud. The mud hole was then filled with rocks from a nearby stonewall, allowing the completion of the trip.

### *McCULLOUGH TURNPIKE*

The last attempt at a turnpike was made under the Acts of 1933, which authorized A. I. McCullough of Fayston, Earl Hayden and others to build a toll road over the Green Mountains from Fayston to Starksboro. Since sufficient private funds were not raised to build the road, the legislature of 1935 purchased the right-of-way for $7,500.00. With the aid of the Civilian Conservation Corps, the Vermont Forest Service under the direction of the writer was able to build the road to the mountain crest, from where it was later completed and surfaced, down the west side of the mountain by the State Highway Department.

## *GREEN MOUNTAIN PARKWAY*

The late Colonel William J. Wilgus of Ascutney, a prominent engineer and builder of the Grand Central Station, promoted a scenic parkway along the crest of the Green Mountains throughout the length of the state. Three hot hearings were held at the State House and some were held at other places. The subject was much discussed in the Press of the state. Franklin Delano Roosevelt, then President, offered to the state the sum of $18,000,000.00 to build the parkway. The Press of the state took sides with editorials of the Burlington Free Press favoring the project and of the Rutland Herald opposing it. The legislature approved a referendum which was held along with the March meetings of 1936. The proposal was defeated by an approximate vote of 30,000 votes favorable and 42,000 against the project. During Governor Philip Hoff's administration, another parkway was proposed by the federal government which would follow along the side of the Green Mountain range from Massachusetts to Canada. This proposal fell on deaf ears.

## *GRANVILLE GULF ROAD*

The State Highway Department during the administration of Governor Charles M. Smith (1935-37) proposed to straighten the road through the Granville Gulf State Park. The writer as Commissioner of Forests and Parks at that time opposed the project with the support and aid of many of Vermont's prominent citizens. The project was finally settled amicably as stated in a news release of State Highway Commissioner Porter, "I feel that the Board of Forests and Parks and Commissioner Perry H. Merrill are to be commended for their firm stand regarding the project, inasmuch as their protests forced us to use every bit of ingenuity at our command to construct a highway which would meet federal aid standards and yet preserve every inch of undisturbed natural surroundings." The State Highway Department as well as others over the years have proposed straightening the road through Smuggler's Notch. The Commissioner of Forests and Parks again spearheaded the opposition to such action in order to preserve the ecology and scenic beauty of the area of the Notch. The Big Boulders and the steep slopes were left untouched.

## *INTERSTATE HIGHWAY*

A new type of Highway, the Interstate, which has no traffic lights or entrances except at interchanges was adopted by the federal government in 1956. A Highway Trust Fund was created by this act, which in addition to appropriating such funds as it felt necessary, assessed a tax on all sales of gasoline, diesel fuel, motor oils, tires and tubes, trucks and busses.

The Secretary of Commerce determines what percentage of the trust fund shall be used for the Interstate Highway system. In Vermont, the Interstate System comprises I-91 which extends from the Massachusetts line along the Eastern side of the state to Canada and I-89 which extends from its junction with I-91 at White River Junction to the Canadian line via Montpelier, Burlington and Highgate. A section of I-93 extends from the Connecticut River in Waterford to St. Johnsbury. As a rule the federal government pays 90 percent of the cost of the system, which in Vermont has a total length, including ramps, of 321 miles; all of which is expected to be completed by 1978.

## *MOUNTAIN ROADS*

In the 1880's and 1890's there seemed to be a desire to build roads to mountain peaks and construct thereon a resort for summer guests. Again in the 1930's the construction of mountain roads was initiated by the author for recreation purposes in the state parks. These roads were built by the Civilian Conservation Corps, a federal agency set up to aid unemployment.

The Mt. Hunger road was commenced in October 1877 and completed in June 1878. The road, a little over two miles in length, extended from the Middlesex town highway to the summit of Mt. Hunger in Worcester. The upper portion of the road was very steep. Many teams of one to six horses drew carriages of from two to twenty persons to the summit in the summers of 1878, 1879 and 1880. This was a toll road built by Theron Bailey, who was proprietor at the time of the Pavilion Hotel in Montpelier.[6]

## *KILLINGTON MT. ROAD*

In 1879, General Richard D. Cutts of the U.S. Coast Guard and Geodetic Survey was assigned to the region to do triangulation observations. He was persuaded by the local citizens of Rutland to work out a suitable route for a road to the top of Killington Peak. The road was built from the town road to the summit where a substantial

6. Abby Maria Hemenway, *Vermont Historical Gazetteer,* (Montpelier: Vermont Watchman and State Journal, 1882), Vo. Iv., p. 230.

hotel to house 30 to 40 guests was erected with out-buildings for a stable and other uses. The hotel was burned in 1916.[7]

### *LINCOLN MT. ROAD*

In 1899 Joseph Battell of Middlebury - after building the Breadloaf Inn - chose Lincoln Mountain where he owned land, to build a road. He constructed a road up the mountain over an easy terrain to within one-half mile of the barren summit, where due to the steepness the road was terminated. Here he built a story and a half log cabin with a suitable dining room, which was used for a number of years. After long disuse it was finally destroyed by procupines.[8]

### *CAMEL'S HUMP ROAD*

Samuel Ridley Jr., who kept a hotel at Ridley's station in Duxbury in stage coach days, built a carriage road to within three miles of the summit of Camel's Hump, a bridle road to the dizzy peak, and a house at the terminus for the entertainment of those who made the ascent. This building was abandoned to the porcupines in 1867.

In 1894 the legislature incorporated the Camel's Hump Road and Hotel Company of which J. A. and L. J. Durkee of Waterbury were the incorporators. They were authorized to build a road by the most feasible route from the John O'Neil place in Duxbury to the site of the Old Hotel on Camel's Hump and were given the right to manage a hotel and stable thereon.[9]

### *ELMORE MT. ROAD*

In 1892 the legislature incorporated the Elmore Turnpike and Building Company. The plan was to build a road around Lake Elmore and then to the summit of Elmore Mountain.

### *BURKE MT. ROAD*

An old carriage road was constructed about 1910 by the late Elmer Darling to the summit of Burke Mountain in East Burke and later rebuilt in the summer of 1925. The property was turned over to the State as Darling State Park in 1933. A Civilian Conservation Camp was established at the foot of the mountain in 1933 and under the direction of the Commissioner of Forests and Parks, an automobile road was built by the C.C.C. boys approaching the summit. The road was later paved by the State.[10]

7. W. Storrs Lee, *Green Mountains of Vermont,* (New York: Holt, 1955), p. 211.

8. Ibid, p. 267.

9. Childs, *Gazetteer of Washington County,* (Syracuse: Syracuse Journal Co., 1889).

10. Walter O'Kane, *Trails and Summits of the Green Mountains,* (Rutland: Green Mountain Club, n.d.)

## *MT. PHILO STATE PARK*

A one way road with turnouts was constructed to the summit of Mt. Philo by the late James Humphrey who owned the mountain and the hotel and cottages at the base of the mountain. His widow in 1924 gave the mountain to the State. With the aid of the Civilian Conservation Corps, a two-way road following the old road was built to the summit and a one way down road was also built in a new location, both of which were later paved by the State.

## *SNAKE MT. ROAD*

A summit house was built on Snake Mountain in Addison in the early 1880's with a rough road to reach it. The hotel later called the Grand View House had a capacity for 15 guests and was closed in 1925.

## *ASCUTNEY MOUNTAIN ROAD AND PARK*

The Ascutney State Park was acquired in 1933 and contained 1,530 acres. With the aid of the Civilian Conservation Corps a two-way paved road was constructed in the 1930's nearly to the summit where a parking area was built. Another parking overlook was built midway up the mountain.[11]

## *GROTON STATE FOREST*

This forest area had its first purchase in 1919. It lies in Marshfield, Groton and Peacham. To reach the far end of the forest from Marshfield to Groton was over twenty miles by public highway. When the Civilian Conservation Corps arrived on the scene in 1933, two camps of 200 boys each were built, one on the Marshfield end of the proposed road and the other on the Groton end. About ten miles of road was built through the forest which together with the town roads on either end connect U.S. Route 2 with U.S. Route 302. Several miles of forest and recreation roads were built within the forest, which then comprised about 16,000 acres.

## *OTHER STATE FOREST AND PARK ROADS*

Over 100 miles of roads were built by the C.C.C. within and as an access to the State land areas. Such roads were built in Downer, Coolidge and Mt. Mansfield State Forests and Brighton and Brunswick State Parks.

11. Ibid

## *MT. MANSFIELD*

It was not until about 1850, however, that a trail of sufficient width to allow the passage of a man on horseback was cut up the mountain. Then in 1857, William Henry Harrison Bingham, a Stowe lawyer and businessman for whom Bingham Falls was named, induced the Town of Stowe to build a road as far as the site of the old Halfway House, where the woodshed once stood. Those wishing to see a view from the mountain top could ride part way in carriages, refresh themselves with a drink at the spring, and mount horses for the remainder of the climb.

The work of extending the carriage road was begun in 1868 and finished two years later. This road was used until 1920 when, after a new company had taken control, it was decided to reconstruct the road so that horseless buggies could use it. Under the supervision of Craig O. Burt, the present automobile road was completed in 1923 at a cost of some eighty thousand dollars.

In 1858 the first Summit House was built. The timbers were carried on men's backs up the west side of the mountain from Stevensville. The original hotel, twenty four by forty feet, was enlarged in 1923. Until it was closed in 1957 and eventually torn down, the comfortable accommodations for a hundred guests were a far cry from the time when the only habitation on Mt. Mansfield was that housing a caretaker and a few saddle horses at the Halfway House.[12]

## *PLANK ROADS*

Transportation in Vermont has passed through several stages ranging from Indian trails, roads, railroads, canals, plank roads, turnpikes and toll roads to our modern interstate throughways. Each new type of transportation was based upon the need of moving goods and people within and without Vermont as the population increased.

The period of plank roads extended roughly from about 1840 to 1861. It appears that the spurt in railroad building in the 1840's was an incentive which gave many communities the desire to have access to a railroad line. In the railroad charters there was usually a condition that the road should be built within two to four years. Plank roads were classified as one or two track roads with the width extending not to exceed four rods. Authorized capital ran from $7,000.00 to $30,000.00.

Information as to how many of of these plank roads were actually constructed does not seem to be available. However, the La Moille Plank Road Company, which had authorization in 1859 to build a

12. W. Storrs Lee, *Green Mountins of Vermont,* (New York: Holt, 1955), p. 207.

road from Waterbury through Stowe and Morristown to Hyde Park, was built only to Stowe. The tollgate was on the town line. The Vergennes and Bristol Plank Road Companies (authorization in 1850) was further authorized in 1859 to change its name to the Vergennes and Bristol Turnpike Company, with a release which allowed the use of earth and gravel in the road instead of plank. The charter of the plank road was surrendered in 1861.[13]

During 1849, charters for plank roads were granted by the legislature as follows: from somewhere in Montpelier village to some point in the La Moille Valley convenient to connect with the roads in said valley to the towns of Morristown, Wolcott or Hardwick; from St. Albans Bay through the village of St. Albans to the town of Richford, thence to the south line of Lower Canada; the Glastenbury Plank Road was authorized to run from some point in the Searsburg-Waterford turnpike near Knapp's bridge through the town of Woodford to the south line of Glastenbury, thence to some point in the west line of Somerset. The Bellwater Plank Road was to run from the north line of Sheffield near the head of Bellwater Pond in Barton to Sutton Corners. During 1850, the push for more plank roads resulted in the following authorizations: from Hinesburg to some point in the village of Burlington; from some point in Williston to the village of Burlington; from the Williston turnpike at Eagle Hall in Williston upon the nearest route to the "Four Corners" in Jericho; from the railroad in Georgia through Fairfax and Cambridge to Johnson; the Connecticut and Passumpsic Plank Road from some point on the Connecticut and Passumpsic Railroad to St. Johnsbury; from Hinesburg through Charlotte to the Rutland and Burlington Railroad in the village of Shelburne.

These charters of 1850 were extended in 1853 evidently since work had not started or other corporate conditions had not been carried out.

In 1851 the legislature approved further corporation requests; from St. Albans through Fairfield with a single or double track road to the town of Bakersfield; from the Massachusetts line in Stamford to a point on the Deerfield River in Readsboro; from Danville to the Connecticut and Passumpsic Railroads near the McLaren place in Barnet.

By 1852 the plank road fever was dying down since only the following authorizations were granted; The Rutland and Chittenden Plank Road was authorized to run from Rutland to Chittenden with the right to build branches to Pittsford and Mendon; The Glastenbury Plank Road was authorized to extend its road through

13. Edwin Bigelow, *Stowe Ski Capital of the East,* (Stowe: Stowe Historical Society, 1964), p. 111.

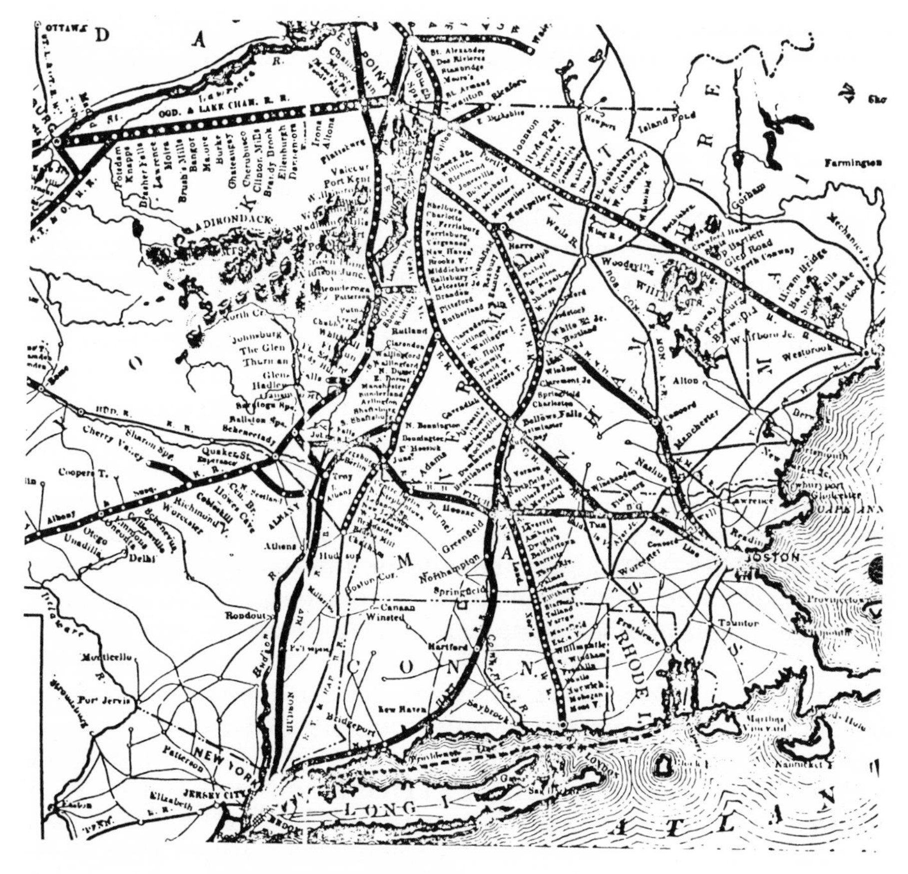


*19th Century Vermont Railroads*

parts of Somerset to some point in Searsburg, to the turnpike near Doane's Mills. A plank road from Brandon to Forestdale was granted in 1853.

By 1859 the maintaining of plank roads had become so expensive that the legislature granted to all plank road companies the right to repair their roads with gravel or to macadamize them, with the stipulation that the repairs had to meet the acceptance of the judge from the county where the road was located.

## *VERMONT RAILROADS*

from John G. Saxe - "Rhyme of the Rail"

Swinging through the forest, Rattling over ridges,
Shooting under arches, Rumbling over bridges,
Whizzing through the mountains, Buzzing over the vale-
Bless me! this is pleasant, Riding on the Rail!

Lack of transportation had been a great problem ever since the influx of early settlers following the War of 1812. Many suggestions had been made for the development of a canal system in Vermont. The building of the Champlain Canal in 1823 opened up markets for transportation of goods from the western part of Vermont into New York. Markets in Boston and southern New England were walled off by the Green Mountain range. With the Construction of the *Great Northern and Erie* and other railroads, interest in canals subsided since financial interests in Boston and elsewhere foresaw a golden opportunity to tie Boston into the stream of traffic both of goods and of people to and from the Lake states and the developing West. Undoubtedly, the greatest political and business war in Vermont was waged in the 1840's and 1850's as a result of the strife following attempts to develop railroad lines.

Realizing the need for more efficient transportation, railroad construction projects were initiated in 1829 and 1830. Ogdensburg, New York was an important center to tap, as it formed an outlet to the Great Lakes traffic. Many citizens in Rutland foresaw a possible expanding future, while businessmen of southern New England were still skeptical of investing in railroad projects.

Meetings were held in Montpelier to interest members of the legislature in approving charters for railroad lines. Among the group of interested persons were: George Parrish of Ogdensburg (one of the wealthiest men in northern New York), Timothy Follett of Burlington (a steamboat operator and merchant), and Charles Paine of Northfield (later to serve as Governor, 1841-43). He was a banker, mill owner and held a vast land acreage. These were a few of the early influential players on the railroad chessboard.

The chief dream of many was to connect Ogdensburg with Boston. Strife developed over that route and who would control the lucrative traffic. To solve the jigsaw puzzle, the legislature of 1835 authorized the incorporation of several railroads, namely the Vermont Central (which was given ten years to complete a quarter of its mileage and 20 years to finish it); the Rutland and Connecticut River Railroad via Ludlow and Cavendish to the west bank of the Connecticut River; and the Bennington and Brattleboro Railroad which was never built; the Bristol and Vergennes Railroad was also then authorized. Another important incorporation was in that same year, the Connecticut and Passumpsic Railroad up the Connecticut River from Vermont's southern boundary to Newport, which would tie together all of the proposed routes. Most of these charters - as well as many later ones - required completion of a railroad by a certain date, so later new charters to parts of the same routes were requested.

The investors of Vermont and nearby states were cautious about investing in railroad enterprises. Even the federal government when asked for aid looked upon the proposition with doubt. About a decade passed before further action was taken in the Vermont legislature. The construction of spiderlike lines in New York State seemed to whet the appetite of Vermonters for further action. In the meantime George Parrish was developing a line from Ogdensburg to Lake Champlain. From Boston, the Fitchburg line was being developed in the direction of the Connecticut River and the Northern of New Hampshire was carving a snakelike rocky route across New Hampshire from Boston to White River Junction. Many of the following charters were only a part of the spider web which would eventually tie the main lines together throughout. Each community in Vermont encouraged its representative to approve a charter for a feeder line.

With the renewed interest in railroading in 1843 railroad barons were able to initiate or renew their charters. These included the Vermont Central Railroad (which charter started at some point on Lake Champlain, up the Onion River and down to some point on the west bank of the Connecticut River) the Brattleboro and Fitchburg which ran southerly to the easterly line of the state, where it would meet the Fitchburg line out of Boston and the Champlain and Connecticut River Railroad, which ran from Burlington through Addison, Rutland and Windsor counties and through either Mt. Holly or Weston to the west bank of the Connecticut River to meet the railroad from Fitchburg. The Connecticut and Passumpsic charter was renewed.

Through the interest of Timothy Follett and others, the New York and Champlain Steamboat Company was chartered to furnish a connection from the Rutland line with Plattsburg, St. Johns and other lake ports. Also, Follett in his wisdom purchased 65 acres of prime Burlington waterfront.

At this time there was also a real question as to whether the Vermont Central Railroad should pass through Barre and Williamstown Gulf to Royalton, or via Northfield and Roxbury. Charles Paine, who had been in the Governor's chair, wielded his power and the Central Vermont of today passes through Northfield. On January 29, 1946, ground was broken at Northfield, this action being the first railroad construction in the state. Just two years later, the first regular passenger train on the Vermont Central, ran the 27 miles from White River to Bethel. It was in the same year that the first telegraph line in Vermont, a necessary adjunct to railroading, began operations. Ground was broken for the Rutland Railroad a year later.

For the next thrity years, over fifty railroad charters were granted. Little had been heard of John Smith, a banker of St. Albans, a man of considerable wealth and influence in Franklin

County. He made his move in 1845 by getting a charter for the Vermont and Canada railroad, which would run from the Canadian line somewhere in Highgate southerly to some point in Chittenden County, to meet with the Champlain and Connecticut River Railroad and the Vermont Central Railroad.

With the construction of the Vermont and Canadian Railroad headed toward the Vermont Central Railroad west of Burlington, Follett was granted a charter for the Rutland Railroad, from Burlington near the head of Malletts Bay, crossing the La Moille River near Manley's Falls on to St. Albans. This branch was never built and this move in defense of the Rutland-Burlington Railroad was short-lived, since the opposition had written an amendment in the act requiring that the road be completed in two years. A "plant" of the Vermont Central was able to get an injunction which prevented the construction to St. Albans, thus delaying the period beyond the two years required.

In 1848 several charters were granted which later played an important role in the railroad chess game. They were the Rutland and Whitehall Railroad, the Windham and Bennington, and the Danville and Passumpsic (none of which were ever built) and the Rutland and Burlington extension at Bellows Falls to connect with the Sullivan line. The entire length of the railroad chartered from the Massachusetts line to Newport was not completed under the charter, so several others were granted for parts of the distance. In 1845 the Western Vermont Railroad from the Massachusetts line to Ruland was chartered. Other charters were for the Cheshire Railroad, Bellows Falls to the Massachusetts line, the Connecticut and Passumpsic-White River to Wells River, and the Montreal and Concord-Wells River to St. Johnsbury. Thus by then, most of the railroad lines which played an important role in Vermont's through traffic had been authorized.

With the construction of the railroad from Ogdensburg to Lake Champlain, John Smith lost no time in getting legislative approval to establish a route for his Vermont and Canadian line from St. Albans to East Alburg and to build a bridge across Lake Champlain. This action was opposed by a New York Central group in the New York legislature, who saw a threat to New York traffic.

John Page of Rutland, Governor of Vermont 1867-1869, controlled the Montreal and Plattsburg Railroad. The construction of the Addison branch from Leicester Junction through Whiting and Orwell and by bridge across the lake to Ticonderoga, gave Rutland access to the Ogdensburg line. With the completion of what is now the Delaware and Hudson from Plattsburg to Whitehall and the leasing of the Rutland and Whitehall line in 1851, the Rutland had through traffic from Ogdensburg to New England points fairly well served.

Business on the O&LC dropped off, so J. Gregory Smith, son of John Smith, made an offer to lease the O&LC line, which offer was pondered due to their contact with Mr. Page. Finally an offer by J. Gregory Smith to lease the line for a term of 20 years for the sum of $8.5 million was too good to be turned down. The O&LC business picked up with traffic via the Vermont Central, the Boston and Lowell and the Portland and Ogdensburg lines.[14]

The Rutland had extended its lines through the Islands with connections at Alburg Junction and Noyon Junction in Quebec. Again the O&LC business took a severe drop in revenue, and after some lawsuits the Rutland was able to buy this line. Revenues were good for a time, with through sleeper car service via the Rutland to Boston. The Rutland eventually came under the control of the New York Central and went into receivership in 1938. A strike of the Rutland employees seemed to seal the fate of the Rutland, since the management would not agree to the employees' terms. When Governor Philip Hoff took over the reins of government in 1963, he proposed a $3.5 million measure to the legislature for the purchase of all the lines in Vermont, but it failed of passage. Finally, the state purchased the Rutland sections, Burlington to Bennington, Burlington to Alburg and part of the Bellows Falls line. The line north of Burlington was disposed of by the state except for a few sections which were considered of value to the state. The rest of the lines were leased to Jay Wulfson and appear to be operated on a sound financial basis.

A number of railroads were chartered in 1851 which included the Woodstock, no longer operating, the Wantastiquet section of this line from Londonderry either to Ludlow or Danby was never developed. In 1880 a charter was granted to the Brattleboro to Londonderry, known as the West River Railroad, which operated until the 1927 flood. At the request of two influential directors, Elmer Melendy of Londonderry (a member of the State Highway Board) and John Ware of Townshend, the legislature appropriated a hundred thousand dollars to put the line back into operating conditon. Operations continued for only a short time until it threw in the sponge and was acquired by the state. Part of the right-of-way in Jamaica forms part of the Jamaica State Park.

The Gallups Mills Railroad which ran from the Maine Central at North Concord to Gallups Mills was begun in 1882 and completed in 1885. Wood was piled along the right-of-way at convenient places for use in the wood burning engines which operated on this line. The road was built primarily to transport out lumber and pulpwood. The

14. Thomas Hawley Canfield, *Papers of Thomas Hawley Canfield about Railroads,* (Montpelier: Vermont Historical Society), Vol. XIV, p. 101.

last trip on the so-called Victory Branch was made in 1917. Mr. O. M. Gallup for whom Gallups Mills was named surveyed the course of the railroad and furnished most of the railroad ties. Many of the early railroads depended upon wood to fire the engines.

The 1927 flood also knocked out the St. Johnsbury and Lake Champlain Railroad, which ran from St. Johnsbury to Swanton. The legislature appropriated a hundred thousand dollars to refurbish this line. Within the past few years, under the operations of Samuel Pinsely to whom it was leased, revenues had dropped and the railroad had not been kept in good running condition. Pinsly asked the federal government for the right to abandon the line, which was approved. The legislature, this year (1974), appointed a committee to see what could be done to keep the line in operation.

The sums of $3,600,000.00 and $75,000.00, respectively were appropriated to the public service board to be used to purchase and rehabilitate the St. Johnsbury and Lamoille County railroad and to pay for administrative expenses connected with railroads. The Commission was granted the right as an agent of the state with the approval of the governor, to sell, transfer or lease all or any part of the property acquired under this act, which would include any other railroad. The railroad was acquired, rehabilitated and leased to a Lamoille county corporation. The railroad was operated from Swanton to Hardwick. No permit has been given by the commission for operation between Hardwick and St. Johnsbury.

It seems that for many years, every community felt it should have a railroad, so many charters were granted to lines which were never developed. Included were such routes as: Montpelier to Bradford; Montpelier to Rutland; Montpelier to Newport; Bennington, Searsburg to Halifax; Woodstock to Rutland; Deerfield R.R. from Halifax through Townshend, Ludlow and Pittsfield, to connect with the Montpelier to Rutland line; and a number of others. One line built the grade from Sheldon Junction to the Canadian line and finished there. Part of that right-of-way, the writer used as a road within the Lake Carmi State Park.

Other short lines now still in operation were built at various times.

## *ELECTRIC RAILWAYS*

During the almost 200 years of Vermont's statehood the means of transportation has changed several times to meet the demands of the public and the availability of new energy sources. It was near the beginning of the twentieth century that public interest brought forth the incorporation of 40 or more electric operated railway companies, of which only about eleven were built and operated. The 1904 report of the Vermont Railroad Commission which was the precursor of the present Public Service Commission stated: - "Fortunately these roads are owned largely by capitalists from outside the state. Vermonters having, for the most part, shrewdly declined to invest in the securities offered them." The Public Laws of 1906 stated: "For the term of five years from and after the date when cars for public traffic or accommodation commenced running on an electric railroad hereafter built, a sum equal to ninety percent of the tax...is hereby annually appropriated to the Railroad Commission."

The *first horse-drawn street cars* in Vermont were authorized to run in Burlington, Winooski, Colchester, Charlotte, St. George and Hinesburg under an 1872 Act which granted a charter to the Winooski and Burlington Horse Railroad Company. Nothing effectual was accomplished until 1885, when a contract was let to A. C. Harris to build and equip a road for the sum of $40,000.00. A three-mile stretch of four feet eight inches width was built. In summer, open air cars were placed on the tracks as they were after the electric line was in operation.[15]

On October 31, 1892, the Burlington Traction Company which took over the name of the previous company, was given a special charter by the legislature to operate an electric line of eleven miles in Burlington and Winooski. Travel was extended to Essex Junction by the formation of The Military Post Street Railway to serve the soldiers at Fort Ethan Allen. The line was later incorporated with the Burlington Traction Company which ceased operation in 1924 when bus operations began.

The Rutland Street Railway (1927)* was incorporated in 1888 and granted authority to extend its line to West Haven in 1896. The Rutland Railway, Light and Power Company, which consolidated the Rutland Street Railway Company, the Chittenden Power Company. The Peoples Gas and Electric Company and the Vermont Internal Improvement Company, were all approved in 1906. The line was extended to Fair Haven, a distance of 15.7 miles, with a 2.5 mile spur from Castleton Corners to Lake Bomoseen.

In 1892, the Bellows Falls and Saxtons River Railway (1927)* was chartered to operate six and one quarter miles of line. Another company chartered this year was the Barre Electric, Light, Power, Manufacturing and Street Railway Company, which by the Acts of 1896 became the Barre and Montpelier Traction Company (1927)* with Frank Corry as President and Edward H. Deavitt as Secretary. The line had a trackage of 9.2 miles which extended in Montpelier on to College Street and to Barre up Washington Street.

The Springfield Electric Railway was chartered in 1894 to

15. W. S. Rann, ed. *History of Chittenden County, 1886,* (Syracuse: D. Mason & Co.), p. 489.

transport freight and passengers between Springfield and Charleston, New Hampshire, a distance of eight and one-half miles. This is the only original electric line which is still in operation; however it has no trolley. The St. Albans Street Railway Company (1923)* incorporated in the same year was authorized in 1898 to extend its line to Swanton. The line went into receivership and was reorganized in 1912 under the name of the St. Albans Traction Company. This line had a spur track to St. Albans Bay where it serviced people coming in on the Lake Champlain steamboats.

In 1894 we see two more electric railways incorporated. The Mt. Mansfield Electric Company (1933)* was chartered to operate from Waterbury through Stowe to Morrisville, Hyde Park, and Craftsbury to connect with the Canadian Pacific at Newport. Only the Waterbury-Stowe section was built, with Craig O. Burt as President. The Bennington Electric Railway Company (1927)* chartered in 1894 was consolidated with the Bennington and Hoosick Valley Railroad Company, a New York corporation, and it was later in 1906 consolidated with the Bennington and North Adams Railway Company. The New York, New Haven and Hartford Railroad had the sole and direct ownership of the stock. The name of the company was changed to the Vermont Company (1927)* in 1923 and included the Berkshire Street Railway chartered in 1910.

In 1906 under a Connecticut charter the Twin State Gas and Electric Company was organized and consolidated with the Brattleboro Street Railway Company, chartered in 1888 to operate to Wilmington; however only the line to West Brattleboro was built. The other companies in the consolidation were the Brattleboro Gas Light Company, the Bennington Electric Company (1927)*, the Dover Gas and Light Company, and the Hoosac Falls Illuminating Company. The capital in back of this company originally came chiefly from outside of Vermont.

In 1892 the St. Johnsbury Street Railway was incorporated to run a line as far as Waterford, but in 1896 an amendment restricted the line to St. Johnsbury and Lyndonville.

It appeared to be the desire of every community in Vermont to be a steam or electric railway line. Many of the Acts passed included the following statement: "by horse, cable, electric or other power, except steam, in the streets and highways." The other lines incorporated by legislative acts which do not appear to have been built were chronologically:

1984 The Hartford Street Railway Company
Manchester Railway and Improvement Company - to Jamaica
Bennington and Woodford Electric Railroad Company

1896 Montpelier and Mad River Valley Electric Traction Company
Orleans and Essex Railroad Company
Richford and Montgomery Electric Railway Company
Western Vermont Street Railway Company

1898 Camel's Hump Light and Power and Railway Company - Richmond-Bristol
Lake Dunmore Power and Traction Company - Salisbury-Rutland
Montpelier and Northern TractionCompany - to Worcester
Hoosac Power and Traction Company - Stamford, Searsburg, Glastenbury
Orange County Electric Railroad Company - Barre to Chelsea
Swanton Electric Railway Company - Swanton and Highgate

1900 Granville and Poultney Railroad
Essex and Mt. Mansfield Electric Railway Company

1902 Wells River and Barre Electric Railway Company
Bennington County Traction Co. - Wells, Manchester to Stratton
Chittenden County Traction Company - Burlington to Vergennes
Essex and Waterbury Traction Company
Franklin County Traction Company - Essex to St. Albans
Grafton and Saxtons River Railway Company
Interstate Railway Company - Rockingham to Newbury
Montpelier and Warren Railway Company
Bennington and North Adams Street Railway Company

In many of these companies the name of J. J. Flynn of Burlington appears as one of the incorporators.

## *BUSES*

In 1922, Fred A. Jewett and Son of Waterbury established the first passenger bus line between Montpelier and Burlington. Using the chassis of an old Cadillac automobile, young Jewett built their first bus which ran for 40,000 miles. Later the Jewetts purchased thirteen White buses which not only served their chartered route but also were used to carry recreation groups from Middlebury College, UVM, Montpelier High School and other institutions upon request.

Evidently the Public Service Commission saw the need for state regulation of this new means of transportation, as many other bus lines - both for passengers and freight - were springing up all around the state.

Under the Acts of 1925 every person, association or corporation which carried passengers, freight or express for hire regularly over a fixed route was declared a common carrier and subject to the jurisdiction of the Vermont Public Service Commission, from which a certificate of public good was required. Jurisdiction over the registration of such vehicles was within the office of the Secretary of State, to which the Motor Vehicle Department was attached.

Under this Act (effective September, 1925) the Jewetts were granted authority to operate bus service between Williamstown and Burlington, but no local passengers were allowed to be carried between Barre andMontpelier since this area was served by an electric line. The line was reactivated after the proceedings and finally folded after the 1927 flood. The electric line went into bankruptcy and the Jewetts obtained their right.

Approximately fifty other motor bus lines have been granted charters under this Act. The Jewetts sold out their franchise to the Vermont Transit System in September 1929. The city of Burlington had granted to William Appleyard of the Burlington Rapid Transit,

*Jewett Bus line, 1925, west of Waterbury, after road cleared of ice flows.*

the right to operate buses on North Avenue and to Queen City Park, an area not then covered by the trolley line. He was given a charter by the Public Service Commission in 1925. Appleyard was interested in the Burlington Rapid Transit (which in 1972 was granted a petition to abandon service due to the small amount of patronage). Seeing the need for transportation of its citizens, some public spirited citizens of the Burlington area in 1973 organized a new bus line service in Burlington and adjoining communities which is subsidized by the areas served. The Vermont Transit System, which operates out of Burlington as both an interstate and state bus line, was granted a charter in 1929.

There were a number of truck lines operating in Vermont previous to the granting of thirteen charters in 1928. At the close of 1972 the Public Service Commission reported that there were then seventeen authorized truck routes operating in Vermont, some of which ran interstate. At the same time there were two express companies, the REA Express and the United Postal Service, Inc., which were authorized to operate in Vermont. When Vermont railroads discontinued passenger trains, the American Express Company began operation of trucks under the name of REA Express.

## *CANALS*

A petition to the Vermont Legislature for a canal around Bellows Falls was granted in November 1781. This action resulted in one of the first canal charters issued in the United States. English capital provided the necessary funds, so the operations on the canal began in 1802. There were eight short locks at Bellows Falls. Shorter canals were constructed at White River and at Water Quechee. The toll at Bellows Falls was $2.80 for each ton carried. It required 25 days to go by flatboat from Wells River to Hartford, Connecticut, and return. The canal was built chiefly to transport pulpwood and logs down the river. In 1792 Dave Anderson was granted by the Legislature the exclusive right to draw goods, wares and merchandise through the Bellows Falls Canal.

In 1807 a company was formed to build locks to make the Quechee River navigable; however due to high costs the project failed.

In 1792 the Northern Inland Lake Navigation Company received a charter from the State of New York to build a canal from the Hudson River near Troy to Whitehall on Lake Champlain. Governor Philip Schuyler of New York wrote a letter to Governor Thomas Chittenden on October 10, 1793 concerning the Hudson-Champlain Canal. Governor Schuyler in 1796 suggested that Vermont help the project by subscribing to 50 shares of stock to be paid over a period of 5 years, to which Governor Chittenden replied that Vermont had considered the request and decided that Vermont did not wish to become a stockholder. However, Vermont passed an act which allowed any Vermont town to vote to tax themselves for this purpose.

The canal was completed in 1823 with a width of 40 feet at the surface and 28 feet wide at the bottom and 4 feet deep. The entire length of the canal was to be 64 miles - 11 miles of which followed the Hudson River, 6½ made use of Wood's Creek and the balance of 46½ miles was to be excavated channel. Six ascending and 11 descending locks were constructed.[16] The first boat to pass through the canal was "The Gleaner" from St. Albans loaded with wheat and potash.

Previous to the opening of this canal about 40 vessels plied on Lake Champlain in commerce with Lower Canada (as it was then called). The main business with Canada was the shipment to Quebec of logs and lumber for transshipment to England and the Continent. The lofty white and red pine were desired for masts for the Royal Navy. The oaks and elms were also used in ship building. The logs were collected at the foot of the falls in Winooski and bound into rafts for floating down Lake Champlain, the Richelieu and St. Lawrence Rivers to Quebec City. The King had forbidden the cutting for personal use of such trees as would be suitable for masts. The Canadian trade fell off with the opening of the Champlain Canal. An enterprising Vermonter built near a wharf, at Benson Landing, on Lake Champlain a warehouse from which quantities of wool, grain, lime and potash were shipped south by the canal.

Ethan Allen once stated, "At some future time, when the long-projected canal from Lake Champlain to the St. Lawrence shall unite those waters, and open up a free navigation between them, in conjunction with a ship canal from the Lake to the Hudson, it will make Champlain one of the busiest thoroughfares on the continent."

In 1825 the Secretary of War transmitted a document No. 154 to the 19th Congress, which reported upon a survey made for a canal along the Connecticut River near Bradford to the Connecticut Lakes Region of New Hampshire. In the same year another report was made by him for a canal route from Lake Memphremagog to the Connecticut River, which was read on April 12, 1836 and tabled. These surveys followed the Valley of the Black River to the LaMoille River, to Joe's Pond and the Passumpsic River to the Connecticut. Another route followed the Barton River, Lake Willoughby and the Passumpsic River to the Connecticut, while a third route surveyed followed the Clyde River Valley to Spectacle Pond, thence passing over the divide to the Nulhegan River and thence descending to the Connecticut.

16. John A. Williams, ed., Vermont, *The Public Papers of Governor Thomas Chittenden,* 1778-1789, 1790-1797, Vol. XVII., 1969. p. 804. Vermont, Statutes of, Specified dates.

In 1825 a canal convention was held in Montpelier, which favored the survey of a canal connecting Lake Champlain with the Connecticut River by one of two possible routes. The routes followed up the Winooski River where they branched; one going by the Wells River and the other by the White River. The United States Army Engineers reported favorably on this project. The state chartered a company known as the Onion River Navigation and Towpath Company to perform this operation. However, many of these plans were abandoned in favor of removing obstacles in the Connecticut River so steamboats could ascend the river as far as Wells River.

The Battenkill Canal Company was granted a charter in 1825 by the state to construct a canal from the east line of New York State in Arlington through Sunderland and Manchester and up the valley of said Battenkill as far as the company shall deem practicable. In the same year the Legislature authorized the incorporation of the Otter Creek and Castleton River Canal Company to improve the navigation of Otter Creek by canals, railways or other streams from the Village of Middlebury to the Village of Wallingford and from the Creek in Rutland to the East Bay or to the line of the State of New York, to intersect with a canal such as may be branched out from the northern canal in the State of New York to the east line of said state.

"In 1826 a charter was granted to the Swanton Canal Company to build a canal from Maquam Bay to Swanton Falls on the Mississquoi River, and for improving said river from said falls to Keyes Falls in Highgate for navigation purposes." In 1832 a charter was granted to Otter Creek and Champlain Canal Company to construct a canal from Middlebury to Lake Champlain. During the following year approval was given for a canal to start at some point in Vernon and extend northerly in the Town of Vernon on or near the banks of the Connecticut River as far north as Barnet, and thence in the most convenient and safe route to Lake Memphremagog, with approval for side canals. The Otter Creek and Champlain Canal Company was chartered in 1832 to operate between Sunderland Falls (Proctor) and Middlebury Falls.

In 1832 a resolution was passed by the Vermont Legislature requesting the governor to open correspondence with the Governor of Lower Canada upon the subject of removing the obstruction at the outlet of Lake Champlain, near St. Johns in the Province of Lower Canada. In 1868 Governor Page promoted the construction of a canal to connect Lake Champlain with the St. Lawrence.

When Vermont was planning for its canal systems much work was authorized by the legislature to remove obstructions in certain streams. These authorizations in 1867, 1869 and 1874 included work respectively on the Wild Branch of the Lamoille, the Gihon Branch and on the Lamoille north of the Hardwick line.

## *BOATS*

The Embargo Act, which President Thomas Jefferson pushed through Congress and signed in December 1807 with the hope of forcing Britain and France to recognize American desire for neutrality, forced economic sanctions which caused the United States to declare war on Britain in June, 1812.

In the beginning, the local customs officers felt that it was permissible to raft logs and ship goods in sleighs. Thus at first the embargo had little effect on our commerce with Canada. However, instructions were soon issued to enforce the embargo and two gunboats were built in Whitehall, New York to patrol the lake.

This action resulted in meetings to see what could be done to prevent suppression of trade with Canada. The militia was called out by Governor Israel Smith and posted at Windmill Point with instructions to let no commerce pass that point. The guard, who was sympathetic to the smuggling, winked an eye at many cases and occasionally arrested some and then let them go free.

Many ruses were used to get merchandise across the border into Canada. With a large portion of Mississquoi Bay in Canada, it was easy to take a boat from the Vermont waters into Canada. Goods were consigned to the border towns of Swanton and Highgate where they were picked up by the Canadians. Many flat boats and barges on Lake Champlain slipped by the internal revenue agents either undiscovered or without any attempt being made to halt them.

The first boat transportation was the use of birch bark canoes by the Indians who traveled from their reservations in Quebec up and down Lake Champlain to points in Vermont and New York. Thence by portage they reached other points in New England. Some traveled by the Winooski River, then via either the Wells River or the White River to the Connecticut, or up Otter Creek and then by portage to either the West River or the Black River to the Connecticut. Before the development of the steam engine, lumber and logs were transported to Quebec by rafts and schooners or sloops under sail. Other merchandise was transported to ports on Lake Champlain.

General Israel Morey, the representative from Orford in 1778, and later from Fairlee, was the father of Samuel Morey. Samuel developed and operated a steamboat in 1792-93, ten years before Robert Fulton constructed his experimental steamboat. Fulton had the benefit of Morey's invention and supplanted him in history.

The legislature granted a permit in November 1781 to build a canal around Bellows Falls. In 1792 Dave Anderson was granted by the legislature the exclusive right of drawing goods and merchandise through the canal. Many of the early settlers, especially the Scotch immigrants to Barnet and Ryegate came by this route.

In 1826 a steamboat, the Barnet, was built in New York for service on the Connecticut River but it never went above Bellows Falls. In 1830 a small steamboat called the John Ledyard was built and taken from Hartford to Wells River. It then headed north and got stuck in the Ammononoosuc shoals. After being freed it returned to Hartford, never to try the trip again. Another boat named the Adam Duncan made a trial trip and then a second one from Wells River on a fourth of July celebration excursion to Hanover. On this trip the boiler burst, which was the end of the boat and the company did not survive the loss.

At a storage house at Wells River, about one-third of the storage charges were for ardent spirits. Return freight consisted mainly of hides, ashes and lumber. There were eight locks at Bellows Falls, where the toll was $2.80 per ton. It required 25 days to go by boat from Wells River to Hartford and return.[17]

In 1836 the Franklin County Steamboat Company was incorporated for the purpose of transporting by steamboat: tow boats, passengers, goods, wares or merchandise on Lake Champlain. In 1843 the Champlain and New York Steamboat Company was authorized to take advantage of the Champlain Canal which was opened in 1823. Transportation by tow boats on Lake Champlain increased rapidly. The writer recalls that in 1904 at least a half dozen such boats could be seen from a vantage point carting produce and goods up and down the lake. Today (1974) the transportation from Montreal to New York City is chiefly newsprint, and from the Hudson River to Lake Champlain ports, the boats carry chiefly gasoline and fuel oil.

In 1826 when the legislature incorporated the St. Albans Steamboat Company, one of the provisions stated that the legislature reserved the right to repeal the Act after 16 years if it saw fit.

In 1868 paper boats were introduced and were rowed by winners in that year.

## *FERRIES*

Before the construction of bridges the ferry was the only means of crossing lakes and streams. The early acts of the legislature gave exclusive rights to persons to operate ferries between certain points for specified periods of time. Many early grants were for the operation of ferries on Lake Champlain either between the mainland and Grand Isle County, or between there and the New York shore. Other ferries operated across the Connecticut River before statehood.

In 1793 Issac Gage was given a permit to build a bridge of temporary nature over Otter Creek in Ferrisburg to be used when

17. Frederic P. Wells, *History of Newbury*, (St. Johnsbury: The Caledonian, 1902), p. 301.

the ferry could not operate. In the same year an exclusive right was given to operate a ferry between Colchester and South Hero. There was no bridge across the Sand Bar until many years later.

1795 - Exclusive right to Alexander Phillips and Israel Jocelin to operate a ferry from Milton to South Hero.

1796 - Exclusive right to operate from Alburg to the western shore of the lake. To Reuben E. Taylor.
- Enoch Hall a ferry right between Isle la Motte and Alburg for 8 yrs.
- To David Maxfield from Georgia to north part of South Hero.
- To Benjamin Bell to operate from So. Hero to Cumberland Head.

1799 - John S. Larabee of Shoreham from Rowley's Point to said Battery in New York.

During the 1800's many ferry authorizations were granted. Today (1974) the Lake Champlain Transportation Company operates ferries between Charlotte and Essex, N.Y., Burlington and Port Kent and between Grand Isle and Cumberland Head. (Plattsburg).

There are two ferries operating between Vermcnt and New York. They are Chipman Point and New York, and Larabee's Point across to Fort Ticonderoga. Other ferrries which operated over the years traversed the lake to the following points: Ferrisburg to Willsboro, West Haven to Dresden, Panton to Westport, across Mississquoi Bay, and across the Onion River at Williston.

## *BRIDGES*

A compact entered into by the States of New York and Vermont enabled the construction of a bridge from Chimney Point to the New York shore, which was opened in 1927. Prior to the construction of this bridge, the only means of summer crossing of Lake Champlain was by ferry, of which there were seventeen.

When Lake Champlain was frozen over it was a long trip by highway via either Fair Haven and Whitehall or through Canada to reach points in northeastern New York. In winter in some years when the ice was solidly frozen, crossing were made over the ice for a few weeks.

Lake Champlain for its entire length of about 120 miles from the Canadian border to Whitehall, New York, constitutes the boundary between New York and Vermont. It had posed a lengthy barrier from early colonial days, thus restricting vehicular travel except for water-borne commerce.

The need for a bridge at the north end of the lake seemed to be imperative. So after the necessary compact between the State of

Vermont and New York had been completed, a bridge was built from Alburg, Vermont to Rouses Point, New York and opened in 1937.

These bridges are operated as toll bridges under the direction of a Bridge Commission. Funds from tolls pay for operation and repair of the bridges.

## *AVIATION COMES TO VERMONT*[18]

The historic flight by a heavier-than-air craft by the Wright Brothers at Kitty Hawk, North Carolina in 1903 gave impetus to early flights in Vermont. Two Vermont youths flew gliders in 1909. Eighteen-year-old George Schmitt made numerous flights from a meadow near his Rutland home and another Vermont boy, Charles H. Grant of Peru, at the age of 15 constructed a glide which crashed. In 1910 he built a new glider with which he flew in 1910 and continued several years thereafter.

Charles F. Willard, taught to fly by Glenn Curtis of the Curtis Exhibition Company, was the first pilot to fly in Vermont at the Caledonia County Fairgrounds. The first flight might have been made at the Rutland Fair a week earlier if misfortune had not befallen two planes which were there.

## *AERONAUTICS*

The extensive use of airplanes during World War I was the forerunner of the important aircraft industry of today. In 1923 the Vermont legislature recognized the need for establishment of uniform state laws for aeronautics by defining lawful and unlawful flights, liability for injury, crimes, torts and wrongs committed, damages and the killing of birds by aeroplanes.

It was in 1929 when the Commissioner of Motor Vehicles was authorized to set a fee annually of $5.00 for residents to operate an airplane. The fee for nonresidents was established at $100.00, except the fee could be waived for specified dates, locations and occasions. Rules and regulations governing the new industry were authorized. Airplanes were exempt from taxation.

James Hartness of Springfield, Vermont, who was elected Governor in 1920, became the holder of Vermont's license number one. After the great flood in 1927 Herbert Hoover (then Secretary of Commerce) sent his secretary to Vermont, landing on Towne Hill, to make a report to him in regard to Vermont's flood situation. Governor John E. Weeks declined to accept any federal funds, saying that Vermont could herself take care of the situation.

As a result of the development of municipal airports at Montpelier

18. Norman E. Borden, Jr., *Aviation Comes to Vermont,* (Montpelier: Vermont Historical Society, 1973), V. 41, p. 206.

and Burlington, airmail and passenger service on regular schedule was initiated in Vermont in 1934.

The legislature in 1935 granted two or more municipalities the right to acquire real property by purchase, lease or condemnation for airfields. A joint resolution was passed by the legislature which directed the governor to appoint a committee of five persons to investigate the advantages to the state of having a centrally located airport. All airmen's licenses were continued at $5.00 under regulations of the Department of Commerce. In 1937 the state would not grant a pilot's license until a license had been obtained from the federal government. A law was passed stating that flying fields must have approval of the commissioner and no flights were allowed from unlicensed fields. All flights were to keep a minimum height of 500 feet above ground and the dropping of object from planes was prohibited. The Governor was authorized to appoint an aeronautics board of three and designate a chairman. The Commissioner of Motor Vehicles was authorized to appoint an inspector-examiner, since the number of private planes were becoming quite numerous.

Vermont municipalities in 1939 were empowered to accept federal aid for the development of airports. The duties of the Vermont Aeronautics Board were defined by the legislature of 1941, which gave the state the right of eminent domain for airports. An appropriation of $65,000.00 was authorized to be used as match money with municipalities for the establishment of airports.

The legislature of 1945 transferred the authority for the control of aviation from the Commissioner of Motor Vehicles to the Vermont Aeronautics Board established under this act.

An interesting statement made by Governor James Hartness in 1921 reads as follows: "There are many more places that may be made suitable for landing fields by the simple removal of a few obstructions. Planes have already landed at Brattleboro, Bellows Falls, Springfield, Windsor, White River Junction, Randolph, Barre, Montpelier, Burlington, St. Albans, Rutland and Bennington. The fields at Burlington and Springfield are already provided with a circular marker that may be seen for a long distance in the air. Coventry and Springfield are provided with hangars. Lake Champlain and even some of the smaller lakes offer natural landing facilities for flying boats."

As of July 1, 1973 the airports in the state are classified as follows:

*State Airports:* Springfield was the first established in 1968, and the others followed soon thereafter; Barre-Montpelier, Bennington, Caledonia County, Franklin County, Island Pond, Middlebury, Morrisville-Stowe, Newport, and Rutland. Basin Harbor Airport is leased to the state.

*Municipal Airports:* Burlington, Fair Haven, St. Johnsbury.

*Private Fields:* Bondville, Champlain, Enosburg, Mt. Snow, North Windham, Post Mills, Warren, Windsor.

*Personal Landing Strips:* Addison (2), Andover, Bloomfield, Bristol, Dorset, Grafton, Ludlow, Monkton, Moretown, Pawlet, Putney, Savage Island.

All airports in Windham, Orange and Grand Isle counties are privately owned, though the policy of the board is to have a regional airport in each county. The following airlines: Executive, Mohawk, Northeast and Northern Airways were serving Vermont in 1968 at Barre-Montpelier, Burlington, Rutland and Newport.

Edward F. Knapp retired as Commissioner of Aeronautics in 1973 after 30 years of service. He began work when the direction of aviation was under the Motor Vehicle Department.

Barre-Montpelier airport site first used after 1927 flood. Dedicated as municipal airport, Oct. 6, 1936.
Bennington - First airplane landed on present site August 1922.
Brattleboro - First aircraft landed 1920, known as airport in 1930.
Burlington - First known as airport 1920, dedicated August 1928.
Rutland - First aircraft landed Wilson Field 1916, developed 1941.
White River Jct. - Known as such 1920. Moved in 50's to Lebanon, N. H.
Swanton - Dedicated July 27, 1930 as "Missisquoi Airport".
Newport - First airport located in Derby in 1920's, present site, 1942.
Middlebury - Old site on Route 7, present site early 1950's.
Springfield - First airport in state 1914-1916? Incorporated 1919.
St. Johnsbury - Dedicated July 1937.

Information by letter of Walter E. Houghton manager state Airports.

## *GREEN MOUNTAIN CLUB*

Number 211 of the Acts of 1892 established a Green Mountain Club which was organized by A. J. Dewey and others of Bennington to build trails in the towns of Glastenbury and Woodford.

The present Green Mountain Club (1975) was organized in 1910 for the purpose of bringing the mountains closer to the life of the people, not only in Vermont but the entire country. James P. Taylor, principal of Vermont Academy at Saxton's River, the father of the Green Mountain Club, called a meeting of mountain lovers which was held in Burlington on March 11, 1910 at which time the Green

Mountain Club was organized. The initial concept was a trail to traverse the entire length of the Green Mountains from Massachusetts to the Canadian line.

The Vermont Forest Service started in trail building to mountain peaks to enable forest fire lookout watchmen to readily approach the mountain summits. Also it was felt that trails extending along the mountain range would enable crews to get from one section to another readily where there were no roads. The Forest Service during 1911 and 1912 blazed out the sections from Killington Peak to Mount Horrid and from Camel's Hump south to Lincoln Mountain. From U.S. #4 the trail to the top of Killington Peak was brushed out at a cost of $20.00 per mile. The work of trail construction was accomplished during wet weather by the fire patrolmen. During 1913 the trail had been completed from Mt. Mansfield to Killington and one to the top of Stratton Mountain, later a lookout site.

The Club locates, builds and maintains the trails throughout the entire length. The Long Trail is divided into sections which are cared for by the local sections of the Green Mountain Club. Overnight shelters have been erected at convenient points for the comfort of the hikers. The sites have been located so that they are not too easily reached from traveled highways.

From the original 23 members assembled at the initial 1910 meeting the Club has increased in size to a membership of several thousand, who come from many states in the Union. On the twenty-fifth birthday of the club fifty-one shelters had been erected.

The Appalachian Trail which extends from Maine to the Gulf follows the Green Mountain section of the Long Trail as far as Sherburne Pass and then branches across country to Norwich, Vermont.

### *TRANSPORTATION SELECTED BIBLIOGRAPHY*

Borden, Norman E. Jr., *Aviation Comes to Vermont,* Montpelier: Vermont Historical Society, Vol. XXXXI, 1973.

Canfield, Thomas Hawley, *Papers of Thomas Hawley Canfield about Railroads,* Montpelier, Vermont Historical Society.

Congdon, Herbert Wheaton, *The Covered Bridge,* New York: A. A. Knopf, 1946.

Haskins, Harold, R., *A History of Bradford,* Littleton, N.H.: Courier Publishing Co., 1968.

Hemenway, Abby Maria, *Vermont Historical Gazetteer,* Montpelier: Montpelier Watchman and State Journal, 1882.

Hill, Ralph Nading, *The Winooski, Heartway of Vermont,* New York: Rhinehart, 1949.

Lee, W. Storrs, *Green Mountains of Vermont,* New York: Holt & Co., 1955.

Melancthon, W. Jacobus, *A Canal Across Vermont,* Montpelier: Vermont Historical Society, 1955.

Miller, Edward and Wells, Frederic P., *History of Ryegate,* St. Johnsbury: The Caledonian, 1913.
O'Kane, Walter Hill, *Trails and Summits of Green Mountains.*
Palmer, Peter S., *History of Lake Champlain, 1609-1814,* New York: Fraser and Lovell & Co., 1901.
Rann, W. S., *History of Chittenden County,* Syracuse, N.Y.: D. Mason & Co., 1886.
Spooner, Charles Forbes, *History of the Vermont Central Railroad System, 1893-1933,* White River Jct.: The Vermonter, C. C. Cummings, ed., 1939.
Wells, Frederic P., *History of Newbury,* St. Johnsbury: The Caledonian, 1902.
Wheeler, Joseph and Wheeler, Mabel, *The Mt. Independence-Hubbardton Military Road,* Montpelier: Vermont Historical Society, 1959.

*Chester A. Arthur birthplace E. Fairfield, Vermont before and after restoration*

# Societies

There are many different types of societies in the state, so only a few of the early and typical ones will be reported.

The *Vermont Historical Society* was incorporated by the legislature on November 5, 1838. In 1859 the legislature passed an act by which a "convenient and spacious room in the State House" was appropriated to this Society, for the preservation of its library and cabinet. Rare papers and most valuable documents and papers belonging to the Society were destroyed when the State House burned in January 1857. When the Pavilion Office building was completed the Society was given office and museum space on its first floor.

The *Vermont Bible Society* was organized on the 28th of October 1812. Its objective was to distribute the Scriptures (without any comment) among the poor and destitute of our own and foreign lands.

The *Vermont Colonization Society* was organized in the year 1818. Its laudable and humane project was to assist the blacks in the United States who desired to return to Africa.

The *Vermont Anti-Slavery Society* was formed at a state convention held in Middlebury in 1834. Its object was to free the slaves by all lawful means.

The *Vermont Temperance Society* as its name implies was organized in Montpelier in 1829.

The *Associated Industries of Vermont* was organized in 1920 with William L. McKee as its President. Mr. E. L. Olney was the first executive vice-president. The present executive Vice-president is James Mereness who succeeded Theodore F. Kane to the office in 1955.

### *THE GRANGE IN VERMONT*

On July 1, 1870 Jonathan Lawrence of Passumpsic, Vermont wrote a letter to the headquarters of the National Grange in Washington,

D.C. He stated that he had read in the New York Tribune recently about an organization of farmers whose headquarters are in Washington, D.C. He stated, "As president of the Caledonia County Farmers' Club, would like to learn more of its objects, etc. Are there any branches or members in Vermont? Please give me such information as you think proper upon the subject and oblige."

Jonathan Lawrence was duly appointed grand deputy of the State of Vermont, by the authorities of the National Grange. His duties, which were to organize subordinate granges in the State of Vermont, met with the farmers of the section in the old Union schoolhouse on Summer Street, St. Johnsbury, Vt., July 4, 1871, to discuss the feasibility of forming a society of the above order.

After fifteen people had signed a charter application, a committee was established to meet with farmers in the neighborhood and make known to them the principles of the order. A permanent organization was formed August 12, 1871 and a full list of officers were elected which included; Joseph Dow as master and F. V. Powers as Secretary. An appropriate name, Green Mountain 1, was chosen.

The Green Mountain Grange 1, the first one in New England, grew rapidly but relinquished some of its members to form granges in surrounding towns. Meetings were held in homes and several halls and in 1891 it moved to St. Johnsbury Center, where during the following year it dedicated its own hall, still its home.

The first anniversary of the founding of the grange was held in the town hall in St. Johnsbury. The same date marked the organization of the Vermont State Grange. The organization was but a temporary one, so at a meeting held on August 21 the permanent state organization was perfected. At this time the number of subordinate granges numbered four.

The first Pomona grange, Chittenden County 1, was organized on January 3, 1876 being second in New England to one in Maine. By 1880 there were seven Pomona granges in Vermont.

The first Juvenile Grange, now known as The Junior Grange, by the name of Ivy, was organized in Plainfield in 1923, ceased in 1927 and reorganized in 1958 and ceased in 1961. A total of 87 junior granges were organized by 1968 and about 57 had ceased operations.

Soon after its organization the grange took up as its idea cooperative buying, which was criticized by many middlemen. The project was later given up due to losses.

Over the years the grange has had as its leaders men of foresight and ability many of them prominent in state affairs; such as C. J. Bell of Walden who held many state offices including that of Governor, Orlando L. Martin of Plainfield, who served as

Commissioner of Agriculture and representative from Plainfield and County Senator and many others who have served their town, county, state and nation in public office and in the high offices of the grange.

The grange has always been in the forefront for progress in the State of Vermont. Some of the projects for which the grange worked hard include the Railroad Commission, now the Public Service Commission, The Patron's Fire Insurance Company, the retention of the State Agricultural College with the University of Vermont, the construction of Morrill Hall as a memorial to Senator Morrill and the establishment of an educational aid fund for boys and girls to get a higher education.

The information in this chapter is taken from the Grange in Vermont, edited by Royal B. Cutts, who has served several terms as a representative of Townshend and a Master of the State Grange.

## *REVEREND A. RITCHIE LOW PROGRAM*

Some years ago Reverend A. Ritchie Low developed a plan to tear down the walls between the blacks and whites. To carry out this plan he contacted Dr. Adam Clayton Powell of the Abyssinian Church in Harlem, New York, who willingly offered his cooperation. The plan was to bring about 85 black boys and girls from New York to Vermont where they would be placed in white families. Vermont families were located and about 79 children were placed the first year and 89 the second year. This was no fresh air project but one to make better understanding between the races.

## *THE VERMONT-NEW YORK COOPERATIVE YOUTH PROGRAM — 1969*

This program was inspired and conceived in response to the findings of the National Advisory Commission on Civil Disorder, and backed by Governor Philip Hoff. It was designed to serve as an experiment in urban-rural partnership, which might be duplicated in other areas of the country. One of the objects was to demonstrate that people of different races and ethnic backgrounds can interact positively as individuals and that a social value structure can be created within which this can take place.

The census of 1790 showed 16 slaves in Vermont; subsequently (and up to 1860) the number was given as 17. Later this was dismissed since free colored were classified as slaves.

Vermont Constitution first state to make voting available to all (not landed gentry alone) and first to disavow slavery.

# Wars and Raids

Come York or come Hampshire, come traitors or knaves;
If ye rule o'er our land, ye rule o'er our graves.
Our vow is recorded - our banner unfurled;
In the name of Vermont we defy all the world!
*John Greenleaf Whittier*

## *FRENCH EXPLORATIONS* [1]

James Cartier, a Frenchman, was the first person to explore the vast continent of North America. In 1534 he discovered the St. Lawrence River, and during the next year's voyage he sailed up the river two hundred leagues until he reached an Indian village by the name of Hochelaga. He traded with the Indians and everything was peaceful and serene. He erected a fort at Montreal which he called Mount Royal and there passed the winter. He named the country New France.

Donnacona, an Indian who conducted him to the heights of Mount Royal, was taken with him on his return to France. The king, convinced of the expediency, ordered Cartier to return to New France in 1540 where he remained for two years. After it was found impossible to establish a colony, the enterprise was given up and for nearly half a century the French made no further attempts to gain a foothold in the New World.

In 1608 Champlain, who had previously joined a fur trader, founded the present city of Quebec. In 1609 Champlain, accompanied by some Indians, made his first trip to discover Lake Champlain and he traveled as far as Lake Sacrement (Lake George). At the same time Hendrick Hudson made his voyage to the north of the Hudson River. The whites did not occupy any portion of the State of Vermont until 1724, though the Dutch had explored at least as far north as Albany in 1613; the English went up the Connecticut in 1635; and the French were in Montreal in 1640.

1. Zadock Thompson, *The Civil History of Vermont,* (Burlington: Chauncey Goodrich, 1842).

When the French under Champlain settled in Montreal, they found the Five Nations engaged in a bloody war with a powerful tribe, the Adirondacks, who were finally driven north of Quebec. Champlain made his first mistake, though naturally, by joining with the Adirondacks.

Champlain on his voyage up Lake Champlain with some Indians encountered about two hundred Iroquois near what is now Ticonderoga. Armed with arquebuses they soon drove off the Iroquois thus causing an implacable war by the Iroquois against the Canadian settlements on the St. Lawrence River. Through the receipt of arms from the Dutch, the Iroquois became equal in gun power, resulting in the complete annihilation of the Adirondacks.

The distress of the French Colony resulted in the sending of two regiments to Quebec under command of Courcelles, named Governor of Canada. In the winter of 1665, the two regiments were sent by way of Lake Champlain to attack the Five Nations. In the snow wastes they lost their way and ended up in the village of Schenectady, which was founded by the Dutchman named Corlear. Through the compassion and with the assistance of food from Corlear, the possible annihilation of the entire party was prevented and the ragged and impoverished remnant returned home.

To retrieve their misfortunes of the previous winter, about twenty companies of militia were sent in the spring of 1666 into the Mohawk country. This expedition into a foreign and heavily-forested country gave advantage to the Indians who hid at the approach of the militia. With both parties wearied with war, but still with great animosity toward one another, they finally agreed upon a general peace in 1667.

During a period of about twenty years there ensued at least a partial cessation of hostilities, during which time the French did everything possible to turn the Indians against the English settlers. The French ingratiated themselves with the Indians, especially with the aid which they gave during King Philip's War when they were known to accompany the Indians' war parties. The Indians continued for some time their raids in New England.

Peace between the French and Indians which had lasted for about ten years was broken in 1687, when the Indians made a devastating attack upon Montreal. The French, greatly surprised by the onslaught, lost a large number of their people, and their villages were ransacked and burned. The Indians occupied several of the French forts which had been abandoned. The inability of the Indians to follow up their attacks on French forts together with no interposition by the English allowed the French to maintain possession of Canada.

France sent strong reinforcements to Canada under old Count de

Frontenac who strived to gain the friendship of the Five Nations. A body of French and Indians made an attack upon Schenectady when everybody was asleep. Dividing themselves into groups, they set fire to the village and killed a large number of the inhabitants. They were very careful not to kill any Mohawk Indians who were in the village. They returned to Canada pursued by a small party of young men who captured a small number of the fleeing attackers.

At about the same time, attacks by the French and Indians were made through Vermont to the frontier settlements of New Hampshire and Massachusetts. The French (who gave premiums for scalps) encouraged the Indians to continue their barbarous trips.

Sir William Phipps, to avenge the atrocities, sailed from Boston to attack Quebec, while it was planned that a combined force of New York and Connecticut soldiers would attack Montreal by way of the Champlain Valley. Over a thousand men under the command of General Winthrop in his march toward Montreal were defeated in this purpose, because the canoes promised by the Mohawks did not arrive. Feeling that the Indians were losing confidence in the English, Captain John Schuyler, with the services of a few whites and over a hundred Indians, made the journey to Canada and destroyed the village of Laprairie, devastated the country around Montreal, and returned in triumph.

The following year (1691) Major Peter Schuyler (brother of John) made an expedition against Montreal at the head of a large number of Indians and some colonial forces. In their retreat, they inflicted heavy losses upon the French and the Mohawks; inspired by the showing of the English, they continued their attacks upon the French. The peace of Ryswick in 1697 terminated for a short period the hostilities between the French and English Colonies.

In a few years, war broke out again in Europe and hostilities again developed in America. The French encouraged the Indians to attack the English settlements in Vermont, New Hampshire and Massachusetts with wholesale scalping, burning, and taking of prisoners. For ten years these forays continued, with New York keeping a neutral attitude, thus enabling the French to concentrate their attacks in New England. (The Indian Raids were discussed in the chapter INDIANS).

As a result of an appeal for aid, the British government dispatched five regiments to Boston under the condition that the colonials raise twelve hundred men together with suitable transports and provisions to make an attack on Quebec. The other colonies were to make an attack upon Montreal by way of Lake Champlain. Everything was in readiness for the attack when word was received from England that the English Army had to be diverted to Portugal to assist their regiment there, so the planned attack through the Champlain Valley was called off.

Encouraged by previous successes against Port Royal, Governor Nicholson visited England in 1710 to explain his plan for the subjugation of Canada. As a result of the adoption of his plan, a fleet of fifteen ships of war and forty transports arrived in Boston with an army of veteran troops. On the trip up the St. Lawrence, foggy weather with angry seas threw so many of the vessels on the rocks that the trip was called off, with the loss of several hundred of their crew of soldiers. The admiral in charge decided to turn back. Nicholson had gone to Albany to direct the advance of his little army against Montreal when he received word of the St. Lawrence disaster. Thus the third attempt to conquer Canada failed.

The Treaty of Utrecht in 1713 resulted in the termination of wars between the French and English for a period of thirty years.

The French, as a result of their raids on Schenectady, Deerfield and Mohawk castles, had learned that the erection of a fort at the south end of Lake Champlain would protect them from English raids. A small fort was built at what is now known as Chimney Point. It was then decided that a more tenable situation with water on three sides was at the location selected on the west side of the lake and known as Fort St. Frederick. The land upon which this fort was erected was claimed by John Henry Lydius, the son of a Dutch preacher, in Albany. (See Chapter 3 on Seigniories)

## *FRENCH VILLAGE AT FORT ST. FREDERICK* [2]

The history of the Champlain Valley during the period of the late 17th and early 18th centuries represents a probing time in which both England and France took the measure of each other. They were both interested in controlling the great inland waterway which extended from Montreal to New York. Both countries realized the value of this control and appraised the cost of such an undertaking.

Peter Kalm, a Swedish scientist who kept a diary of his travels, wrote under the date of July 1, 1749: "At about five o'clock in the evening we arrived at a point of land about 12 English miles from Fort St. Frederick which the English call Crown Point ***" July 2, 1749; "Early this morning we set out on our journey again, it being moonshine *** happily arrived about eight in the morning at Fort St. Frederick which the English call Crown Point ***" July the 6th, 1749: "The soldiers who had been paid off after the war had built houses round the fort on the grounds alloted to them but most of these habitations were no more than wretched cottages, no better than those in the most wretched places in Sweden; with the difference however, that their inhabitants here were rarely oppressed by

2. Guy Omeron Coolidge, *French Occupation of Champlain Valley*, V.H.S. 1938.

hunger, and could eat good and pure white bread. The huts, which they had erected consisted of board, standing perpendicularly close to each other. The roofs were of wood too. The crevices were stopped up with clay to keep the room warm. The floor was commonly clay, or black limestone, which is common here. The hearth was built of the same stone, except the place were (sic) the fire was to lay, which was made of grey sandstones, which for the greatest part consist of particles of quartz. In some hearths, the stones quite close to the fireplace were limestone *** They had no glass in their windows."

## *1759* [3]

Early in 1759 General Amherst commenced preparations to drive the French out of the Champlain Region, but so many difficulties occurred to deter the operations of his army in that unsettled part of the country that the summer was far advanced before he could pass Lake George with his troops and artillery. Aware of the danger of surprise — and not unmindful of the disaster that the British troops had sustained the year before — this able and judicious officer proceeded with the greatest care, leaving nothing to chance, and making provision for every difficulty or opposition that could be foreseen.

Finally in the latter part of July he arrived in the vicinity of Ticonderoga, with his army of regulars and provincials in excellent order and amply supplied with artillery, military stores and provisions. The enemy had observed all his movements with the hope of gaining some advantage; however they did nothing to deter the troops from crossing the lake and landing supplies. After Amherst had reached the shores at the north end of the lake he made preparations for a siege of the fortress. At first it appeared that the enemy was determined to make a stand. However, they soon realized that Amherst was a formidable foe and well-supplied for a siege. Instead of risking the loss of their force by the surrender of prisoners, they began the destruction of Fort Ticonderoga and soon abandoned it for Crown Point. They left a fire burning which did little damage to the fort or the heavy artillery and several sunken boats.

When Amherst arrived, he set about to repair and enlarge the fort, and to repair and improve his boats for an attack on Crown Point. Scouting parties were sent to the vicinity of Crown Point to observe the actions of the French. Reports were brought back that the French had abandoned the fort and retired to Isle Aux Noix at the north end of the lake. Amherst soon set about the erection of new works, strengthened the old ones and began a new fort. The taking of these two forts (which had been in French possession for

3. Ibid.

thirty years) alleviated the raids in the Champlain Valley by which the settlements had been harassed.

Another means of attacking the English was still left open via the St. Francis River to Lake Memphramagog, to the Connecticut River area from whence the Indians had made numerous raids into New Hampshire and Massachusetts. To thwart some of this pillaging Major Rogers of the New Hampshire Rangers was selected and placed at the head of two hundred hardy and resolute fighters.

It was decided that the only practical approach to the Abnaki Village was to sail from Crown Point to the Mississquoi Bay and then proceed overland for the attack on the village of St. Francis. After a trip of seven days down the lake, Rogers reached the Bay. On October 2nd — after fording many streams and passing through swamps — he reached and forded the St. Francis River although it was swollen after heavy rains. On the evening of October 4th, the Village of St. Francis was sighted. Rogers, together with two officers disguised as Indians, reconnoitered the area and found that the Indians were frolicking in an Indian dance which continued until four in the morning.

Just before sunrise Rogers led his troops to an attack on three sides of the village. The Indians were completely surprised and offered little resistance. The cabins were forcibly entered and in the darkness it was impossible to tell the sex of those who attempted to flee. In the early sunlight, the troops observed the scalps of several hundred of their countrymen suspended from poles. This discovery only drove the troops to harder work and by seven o'clock that morning the entire village had been burned, and over two-thirds of the three hundred inhabitants had been slain. All available food was taken, and without delay Rogers and his men marched up the St. Francis River for a rendezvous at Coos on the Connecticut.

They traveled together for about ten days until they arrived at Lake Memphramagog. There they separated, deciding that each group would make the best of their way back to Crown Point. What with fatigue and shortage of food, their sufferings were great. Many dropped out and died before they arrived at Fort Number Four. This attack seemed to convince the Indians that they should be less unrelenting in their enmity and raids.

## *EXPEDITION AGAINST TICONDEROGA*[4]

In the spring of 1775 a plan had been concocted by the Massachusetts Committee of Safety to seize cannon and armament at Fort Ticonderoga. Benedict Arnold who had received orders from the Committee arrived at Castleton on May 3rd to raise a body of men of whom he would be in command for the purpose of capturing

4. L. E. Chittenden, *The Capture of Fort Ticonderoga,* (Rutland: Tuttle Co., 1872)

Ticonderoga. On the 7th of May at a meeting at the Zadock Remington tavern in Castleton headquarters were established. The Committee of the War met at a farm house and formulated a plan of campaign.

Ethan Allen was placed in command of about 140 men, who were to go directly to Shoreham. James Easton was the second in command and Seth Warner was the third officer in rank. Upon the arrival of Benedict Arnold a dispute arose as to who would command the troops. The men had been promised that they would be under the command of their own officers.

Captain James Douglas had been sent to Panton to secure every boat that he could lay his hands on. The party left Castleton traveling by the way of Sudbury and the Old Crown Point Road to the lake shore at Hand's Cove in Shoreham. Captain Douglas arrived soon after with a scow and a few small boats at dusk. There were insufficient boats to take the two hundred odd soldiers across the lake to a point about a half mile from the fort. A guide, the son of a farmer, who had visited the fort many times had been secured to join the party.

Again a dispute arose as to who would command the attack. It was finally settled that the two would enter the fort side by side with Allen in command. With their muskets poised they were led by a lad who lived opposite the fort. With Allen leading the way and Arnold by his side they advanced to the wicker gate, which had been left open. The men rushed through the open gate while some scaled the walls. A sentry raised his gun to shoot but it miss fired. The guard retreated hastily, while another sentry inflicted a slight wound on one of the officers.

The soldiers gave a round of three cheers which aroused the Captain of the Fort, who came out. Allen demanded that the British Captain immediately deliver over the fort. To the Captain's request by what authority it should be done, Allen replied: "In the name of the Great Jehovah and the Continental Congress." With a sword over the head of Captain Delaplace there was no opportunity for successful resistance and the fort was surrendered.

All the men of the garrison were sent as prisoners to Hartford, Connecticut. A large quantity of military equipment and supplies was found in the fortress. The spoils which were sent to Boston included one hundred and twenty pieces of iron cannon, fifty swivels, ten tons of muskets, three cartloads of flints, thirty new carriages, a considerable quantity of shells, a warehouse of boat building material and a large quantity of other stores.

Seth Warner crossed the lake with the rear division and marched up to the fort just after the surrender was made. Warner was immediately ordered to attack Crown Point, which he captured together with a sergeant and twelve men on May 11th. Here were taken about two hundred pieces of cannon, three mortars and sundry howitzers and swivels.

The day after the capture of Fort Ticonderoga Allen notified the Albany Committee of Safety that he had taken the fortress. He also warned them that there was a probability that Governor Carleton of Canada would exert every effort to retake the fort.

Captain Samuel Herrick, who had been ordered to go to Skenesborough with thirty men, before the capture of Ticonderoga was undertaken, reached the settlement and captured Major Andrew Philip Skene, about fifty tenants, twelve negroes and a schooner which was rechristened the *Liberty.* The captured schooner was brought to Ticonderoga and was sailed to Crown Point.

Arnold with thirty men embarked on a small boat for a trip to St. Johns. On the route a British mail boat with several hundred men was captured. The schooner favored by a good wind overtook Arnold's boat and took him aboard. When within thirty miles of St. Johns the wind fell and the vessel was becalmed, so Arnold boarded one of two small boats to make the trip to St. Johns. After hard rowing all night St. Johns was reached early on a Thursday morning. The trip was concluded about a half mile from St. Johns to await the report of a reconnoitering party. After it was learned that they had arrived unnoticed by the British they proceeded briskly for an attack upon the place. The small garrison retreated into their barracks where they surrendered without opposition. Prisoners together with their arms and small stores were taken. The Kings boats were destroyed and a captured sloop was rechristened the *Enterprise.*

Shortly after leaving St. Johns Allen was met enroute to St. Johns with a fair sized complement of troops. Allen was determined to proceed to St. Johns and hold the captured place. With a supply of provisions furnished Allen continued on to a point opposite St. Johns. Allen's fatigued force was overcome by an ambush of two hundred regulars and made his way as rapidly as possible back to Ticonderoga. Arnold had preceded him by a couple of days.

## *LAKE CHAMPLAIN BATTLES* [5]

The *Royal Savage* was built and launched at St. Johns by the British in August, 1775, partook in the defense of the fort there that fall, was sunk in October near the fort, captured by the Americans when St. Johns fell, raised and sailed to Ticonderoga in November, 1775. She was there stripped of her guns which were shipped to Cambridge, Massachusetts, to assist in the siege of Boston, and was refitted in the spring of 1776 to become Arnold's flagship.

5. Zadock Thompson, *The Civil History of Vermont,* (Burlington: Chauncey Goodrich, 1842.

The armament race betwen the Americans and British for the control of Lake Champlain began in May 9, 1776, when Colonel Philip Skene's trading schooner was taken at South Bay near Skenesborough by Samuel Herrick and a small party of Green Mountain Boys and Berkshire men. This event preceded the capture of Ticonderoga by ten hours. Soon after the taking of Ticonderoga, Benedict Arnold captured at St. Johns at six in the morning of May 18th, the King's sloop, *Betsy,* with seven sailors and a captain. Within two hours he had loaded everything of value and was on his way back to Ticonderoga, arriving just two hours ahead of the British regulars from St. Johns.

The British were left devoid of a single boat on the waters connecting with Lake Champlain. The *Betsy* was renamed the *Enterprise,* taken to Crown Point and fitted for military purposes, and sent with Skene's schooner, renamed the *Liberty,* to the north end of the lake to keep watch of the British movements.

It was quite certain that Governor Carleton would not long delay in an attempt to recapture Crown Point and Ticonderoga. Reports were soon received from spies that the British were busy rebuilding their fleet at St. Johns. They were also informed that the Caughnawaga Indians were incensed and ready to join the British.

The American forts were reported by the disgruntled Arnold, and also by Schuyler, to be in a very poor condition which would not withstand heavy attack. It was later reported that the British were building two schooners and a row galley, which later proved to be the *Royal Savage* and the *Revenge.* This report was confirmed by a scouting trip to St. Johns which was ordered by Montgomery.

Remember Baker, the famous Green Mountain Boy, undertook a scouting trip down the lake from the north with orders not to draw any Indian fire. However, when he noted that his beached bateaux were being towed away, he opened fire which was returned and Baker fell dead. This event created bad political relations between the Indians and the Americans.

To stop the British boat construction, Montgomery dispatched two colonels with 1,200 men to Isle Aux Noix. On September 6th they arrived just south of St. Johns where they met a fusillade of gunfire requiring them to move back a couple of miles. During this skirmish, the Americans noticed a British boat afloat and proposed a plan to capture her. On September 15th three hundred-twenty men promptly boarded the boat but later called off their plans. The armed schooner, *Royal Savage,* was hit by a shell and later by several more. The *Royal Savage* was sent after the Americans but to attempt a fight was reconsidered as futile, since the ship could be easily crippled up-stream by the destruction of her masts.

Following a Council of War, it was decided to establish a battery on the east shore opposite St. Johns, which was finally agreed to by Montgomery. The new battery went to work at once and soon the *Savage* was sunk.

On October 3rd the British surrendered at St. Johns and the Americans took over all the naval stores which included the *Savage,* the *Revenge,* and many bateaux and birch bark canoes. The schooner was renamed the *Yankee* and the name *Douglas* was given to the Row Galley. The American boats, soldiers and sailors were taken back up the river in late November with a great quantity of stores and provisions.

### *THE BATTLE OF VALCOUR* [6]

Five American Generals met on July 5, 1776 in an old building at Crown Point to consider the serious situation which faced the American colonies. The group consisted of Horatio Gates who had been given complete power over the northern army by General Washington; Philip Schuyler who was in overall charge of the fighting on the northern frontier; John Sullivan, bemoaning his defeat, sat patiently at the long table; Benedict Arnold, who had a plan of attack against the enemy and was highly esteemed by General Gates. The fifth member of the group was a German who had served under the King of Prussia. Baron de Woedke, considered by the Americans to be a shrewd officer, quieted his own speech to listen further to Arnold's plan for gaining ships and his means of thwarting Burgoyne and Carleton (who was putting together a formidable array of ships and boats in Quebec). It was decided that they must withdraw from Crown Point to Ticonderoga. The decision was also made that the needed navy should be built at Skenesborough which had sufficient flat space near a waterway and was somewhat removed from Ticonderoga.

The bigger problem on Arnold's mind was the recruitment of seamen and soldiers for the new Navy. The necessary men were eventually recruited by General Schuyler's agents from the Atlantic coast as far south as Virginia. They came also from Connecticut, New York, Boston and other points.

Arnold's little fleet, comprised of his command ship, the *Royal Savage,* the *Boston, Connecticut, Enterprise, Liberty, New Haven, Providence* and *Spitfire,* sailed at sunset in mid-August, 1776. On their northward trip they encountered a heavy storm which snapped the mast of the *Connecticut.*

By September 4th, Arnold's fleet had reached Isle La Motte where they were on watch for any movement of the British fleet. Supply ships brought food, repairs and ammunition from Ticonderoga. In the meantime, while awaiting the galleys and gondolas under construction at Skenesborough, Arnold ordered his

6. Ibid.

fleet back up the Lake into a bay on the west side of Valcour Island near the New York shore.

By October 10th, all the rest of Arnold's fleet had arrived, including the *Washington, Trumbull* and *Congress.* Much time was spent in instructing his officers in what to expect from British ships in the line of maneuvers and how to combat this.

General Guy Carleton during the interim was busy in St. Johns building and amassing ships and boats for his campaign against Arnold. On October 11, 1776, under orders of General Carleton the ships, *Carleton, Inflexible* and *Thunderer* set forth.

The British fleet sailed southward using one of their long boats to prove harbors and headlands on their way, lest by chance Arnold's fleet might be found in hiding. Upon nearly reaching the Island of Valcour, the detected a schooner and a tall masted sloop which had been captured by the Americans at St. Johns the year previously. From the deck of the *Lady Maria* in the midforenoon, the *Royal Savage* and the *Enterprise* were observed trying to break out from behind Valcour Island, according to Arnold's plan.

The British hastily approached the *Royal Savage* which had become grounded on the shore, with her mast fallen from the impact. The *Carleton* in hot pursuit let go a broadside which crashed into the wreckage of the *Royal Savage.* With the American ships streteched out in line from the Island to the New York shore the battle was on. A party from the *Carleton* went aboard the grounded *Royal Savage* but after taking a few prisoners were driven off by American gunners.

A battle ensued, and two British longboats, the *Blonde* and the *Isis* appeared and towed the crippled *Carleton* to safety. In the fray not too much damage had been suffered by American ships save for the *Royal Savage* and a gondola which was sunk (and splinters knocked out of another ship's mast). The crew of the *Royal Savage* had escaped to the mainland where they encountered some Indians who had been landed from a British boat. So closed the first day of the battle, as General Carleton, Burgoyne, Pringle, and the crew went at nightfall to dine and wait for another day to follow up the battle.

General Arnold, on board the *Congress* as his flagship, was also dining below with his officers. Here they made a survey of their losses which included the *Royal Savage* - with the General's chest containing all his private papers - and the *Philadelphia* which was sunk by a broadside from the *Inflexible.* After a period of solitude, General Arnold gave orders to the captain of the *Trumbull* to hug the west shore followed by the other ships and head for Ticonderoga through a prevailing heavy fog. The American fleet sneaked away in darkness completely unobserved by the British.

When, on the morning of October 11th, Arnold's fleet had arrived near Schuyler Island about seven miles south of Valcour, he saw that the *Lee* was beached, two gondolas - the *Providence* and the *New York* had to be sunk, they were in such terrible condition - and the *Washington* had a cracked mast. As the fog raised, Carleton observed that Arnold's fleet had left the harbor and were on their way south. Pursuer and pursued continued their southward journey that day without contact being made, but with Carleton planning to take action on the next morning, the 13th. Due to a strong southerly wind, Arnold's fleet had made little headway being perhaps not more than ten miles south of Schuyler Island at this time.

The British, in pursuit of the fleeing American ships, came upon the slow-moving *Washington* and quickly put her out of action with the *Inflexible's* 12-pounders. When the captain of the *Washington,* with 16 men in a bateau, reached their flagship, the *Congress,* they were ordered to make post haste to Ticonderoga with an urgent request to send a fleet of bateau to Crown Point to move the remnant of the American fleet back to the fort.

Arnold, aboard the *Congress,* was closely pursued by the *Inflexible,* the *Carleton* and the *Lady Maria* through the narrows of the Lake. Under oars and heavily pounded by British shells the *Congress* eventually accepted the inevitable and headed into a small bay. Here Arnold ordered the cannon removed from the *Congress,* which was then set afire and was consumed as the crew of the British ships watched from far out on the lake.

Arnold had disobeyed the strategic instructions of General Gates, "not to make a display of his power". Courts martial and reorganizations followed, with Benedict Arnold emerging as a hero of the Battle of Valcour.

However, the sun had not set on the 13th before a courier was dispatched to Point Au Fer to request the rest of the British Army which lay in the area to head for Crown Point. With strong headwinds, it took the fleet six days to reach Crown Point. Here in the narrows of the Lake the British held up for some time, since through the narrows there were no friendly soldiers on shore.

During this period General Gates and Benedict Arnold had made repairs to the fleet and strengthened the defenses of Ticonderoga. While the enemy troops waited at Crown Point, a log boom was built across the lake from a point north of Ticonderoga to the eastern shore of the lake at Hand's Cove, behind which Arnold awaited the enemy with the *Trumbull, Enterprise* and *Revenge.* Other vessels inciuded the *Gates* and the schooner *Liberty,* the *Valcour* and supply ships, all of which were protected by the land batteries in the redoubts, particularly at Mount Independence on the Vermont (eastern) shore.

While the British waited at Crown Point, Burgoyne pushed for making an attack but with the approach of winter Carleton finally decided that further battle was out of the picture. So after a small foray toward Ticonderoga, the British boats on October 28th, 1776, left Crown Point for Canada.

## *BURGOYNE INVASION* [7]

General Schuyler was elected by Congress on May 22, 1777 to have command on the Lake Champlain Valley, which included Ticonderoga, Albany and Fort Stanwix. General Schuyler assigned General Arthur St. Clair to the active command of Fort Ticonderoga, where he arrived on June 12th.

With the expectation that the British would attack the fort during the coming summer, efforts were made to strengthen it as well as Mount Independence which had up to then received the most attention. A floating bridge connected by iron chains was thrown across the channel of the lake between these two sites to impede the passage of the British fleet. Block houses were erected at the principal sites; Mount Hope was fortified; and a breastwork at the foot of Mt. Independence was hastily put together, although Mt. Defiance, a commanding location about seven hundred fifty feet high, was left unfortified.

To command the northern British army General John Burgoyne was chosen in March 1777 over Sir Guy Carleton who was more knowledgeable about the situation in the Champlain Valley.

General St. Clair's two thousand eight hundred American regulars and nine hundred raw recruits were opposed by Burgoyne's four thousand British soldiers, over three thousand hired Germans, with a few Canadians and about 500 Indians. Their equipment consisted of a strong supply of brass artillery.

The British campaign plan was to separate New England and the Hudson Valley area from the rest of the colonies. General Howe was to proceed up the Hudson from New York and Burgoyne was to traverse Lake Champlain and upper Hudson River valleys to meet Howe in Albany.

On June 20th Burgoyne embarked on the *Lady Mary* with full pomp and ceremony, to martial strains and flags fluttering in the breeze. The armada was preceded by Indians in birchbark canoes followed by the *Royal George* and the *Inflexible* with brigades following in regular order. On the morning of June 23rd, Reidesel tried to set forth with the main body of the army but was thwarted by gale winds which held him up for two days.

Colonel Seth Warner was dispatched by St. Clair to New Hampshire to raise troops to hold back the attackers when they

7. Ibid.

arrived. Warner returned to Fort Ticonderoga on July 5th with about nine hundred Vermont militia men.

General Burgoyne on June 24th reached Crown Point with some of his troops. General Riedesel and General Fraser with the main body of troops reached there two days later. The frigates *Royal George* and *Inflexible* were brought into the lake and anchored just out of reach of the guns at the American fortifications. When the British troops advanced, the Americans abandoned Mt. Hope and burned a blockhouse toward Lake George. Evidently St. Clair had no knowledge of the strength of the British Army until June 3rd, when he received word from a prisoner and some deserters. As the fortification of Sugar Hill was considered by the American officers as unimportant, it was allowed to be occupied by the British on July 5th.

A Council of War was called by St. Clair as he began to see the futility of holding the fort. Thus he decided that a retreat should be made as soon as possible. About midnight orders were given to place the sick, the wounded and women on board two longboats. The cannons, provisions and tents were put aboard other boats. So what was left of Arnold's fleet headed for Skenesborough, which was reached at 3 p.m.

The British broke through the bridge, boom and chains and gave pursuit to the fleeing army which arrived at Skenesborough in time to burn or sink their abandoned craft.

The American garrison at Ticonderoga had crossed the bridge to Mount Independence on the morning of July 6th. It was here that General St. Clair had expected to make a stand. The artillery which the British had placed on Mount Independence made this position untenable, however, and a retreat was ordered.

## *THE BATTLE OF HUBBARDTON* [8]

On the retreat from Mount Independence, St. Clair had planned to move his troops over a rough military road through Hubbardton, south through Castleton, thence west to Skenesborough to join with the forces of Schuyler's Army south of Fort Edward. The last of St. Clair's sorry force stumbled out of Fort Independence about four o'clock on the morning of July 6th.

The route over which they traveled was a poor trail which had been slashed through the virgin forest past Orwell and around the swamps at the northern end of Lake Bomoseen and over the hills to present East Hubbardton, there to join the older road leading south to Castleton.

Colonel Ebenezer Francis with his rear guard some 450 strong kept a slow pace due to illness and fatigue of his men. As the forces

8. Ernest R. Dupuy, *Battle of Hubbardton*, Unpublished Manuscript, 1960.

arrived at Sucker Brook in the Valley before East Hubbardton, it was learned that a raiding party numbering about fifty (which had evidently come from Otter Creek a few days before) had reached Hubbardton and gone on to Castleton. This settlement had been deserted upon the approach of the raiders.

St. Clair had waited for his rear guard which was taken over by Colonel Seth Warner, and he finally decided to push on leaving only about a third of his strength behind, consisting of about 1,000 officers and men, many of whom were not fit for duty.

The British were still pursuing the fleeing American army and soon closed in on it at Sucker Brook at East Hubbardton at the foot of Monument Hill where Warner had taken a stand at what appeared to be a good vantage point.

Trees were felled and brush ambuscades were made ringing the hill to resist the expected British attack under General Fraser who had led the rapid pursuit of St. Francis. General Burgoyne had instructed Major General Frederick Von Riedesel to march part of his jagers in support of Fraser and then push on to Skenesborough. Instead, Von Riedesel rushed on ahead which shocked Fraser considerably.

On the following morning from a vantage point Fraser observed a mile away the place known as Mount Zion, and to the left the high ground known as Monument Hill, where Warner had prepared to meet the British. The British Army pushed slowly up Monument Hill, up Mount Zion and to the left. Warner had not considered a flank attack by the way of Mount Zion, so he pulled back his troops to the Military Road just south of the Selleck Cabin, so-called.

The two militia regiments - under St. Clair's aides - who were now two miles on their way to Castleton refused to turn back and join Warner, and instead, upon hearing the firing of guns, fled toward Castleton in a disorganized array.

Fraser's troops pushed on up the hill, finally meeting Warner's forces point blank. As the enemy appeared near the crest of Monument Hill, Francis swung from a column into line and rushed to the brow of the hill. Under heavy fire Fraser's forces were driven back down the slope toward Sucker Brook.

Again the British light infantry slowly pressed their way up the slopes of Monument Hill. They were again thwarted by a counter-attack led by Francis, which threw the British back down the hill. Attacks on Mount Zion had so far not been successful.

After pursuing the enemy down the slope, Francis pulled his men back up the hill behind an ambuscade of fallen trees. For a third time, Fraser threw his infantry with fixed bayonets up Monument Hill. At Francis' right, the Brunswick Jagers had reached the plateau. Francis' troops rushed forward hoping to repel them, but

Francis fell with a bullet in his head. Devoid of their leader, the Americans fled eastward into the woods and over the hills towards Pittsford to keep a rendezvous with destiny at Bennington, just forty days later.

Down at Castleton the frightened riflemen who refused to go to the aid of Warner were booed by the Continentals. St. Clair at Castleton received word within an hour that "all is over".

Fraser on top of Monument Hill now realized that he had won a battle by the skin of his teeth, since he had no supplies left. His ammunition was nearly exhausted. His men had reached the limit of their endurance and he suspected that his enemies might be gathering in the nearby dense forests for another counterattack. Snipers who lingered in the surrounding forests mortally wounded a British officer and other soldiers. At this point, Riedesel, much to the chagrin of Fraser, sent his entire command off to Skenesborough to join with Burgoyne.

Although Warner and Francis were defeated at Hubbardton, it is now considered by many as a victory, since the timetable of the advance of Burgoyne was held up, enabling the Battle of Bennington to develop into success. Another thought prevailed, "What would have been the result if two militia regiments had not fled to Castleton?"

## *BATTLE OF BENNINGTON* [9]

After the Battle of Hubbardton Colonel Warner's regiment, about 140 strong, took post at Manchester. Burgoyne who was at Skenesboro (Whitehall) issued a proclamation on July 10, 1777 to "the inhabitants of Castleton, Hubbardton, Rutland, Tinmouth, Pawlet, Wells and Granville that they should meet Colonel Skene on the 15th, who would communicate conditions upon which the persons and property of the disobedient might be spared."

General John Stark of New Hampshire, who had served with credit and honor in the previous French War and as a Colonel at Bunker Hill, in Canada and under Washington at Trenton, was contacted by the Council of Safety. Stark gathered his troops at Fort #4 and marched forth reaching Manchester on August 7th. Here he met General Lincoln to whom he refused to move his troops to Stillwater as requested by General Schuyler.

General Burgoyne who was delayed on his march from Skenesboro on learning that there was a large military depot at Bennington, which had articles that he needed. He directed Lieutenant Colonel Baum to proceed to Bennington. Baum set forth with his force on the 13th of August. When he reached a small settlement Sancoick on the second morning he learned that there were

9. Zadock Thompson, *The Civil History of Vermont.*

1500-1800 men at Bennington who were supposed to leave at Baum's approach.

General Stark who had gone on to Bennington on the 13th received word from scouts that a party of Indians were at Cambridge followed by a large body of troops with artillery and headed for Bennington. He immediately sent word to Warner at Manchester to bring his regiment and neighboring militia to his support. On the morning of the 14th he assembled his brigade and in company with Colonels Warner, Williams, Herrick and Brush went forth to meet the enemy. He had marched about five miles when he met Gregg in retreat pursued by Baum. Baum halted in a commanding position and Stark withdrew to a more favorable position.

On the night of the 14th after learning of the position of the enemy Stark called a meeting of the Council, consisting of the Council of Safety and others in which a plan of attack was made for the next morning. Due to excessive rainfall the attack was not made, but scouts were sent out and engaged in a successful skirmish. On the morning of the 16th Stark had been joined by Colonel Simonds and some Massachusetts militia men numbering about 1600. The morning of the 16th was bright and clear and Stark prepared to execute the agreed upon plan. Col. Nichols with 200 New Hampshire men later reinforced by 100 was detached to make a wide circuit to the north of Baum's post and come around on the rear. Col. Herrick with 300 men, composed of snipers and Col. Brush's militia was to make a wide southern circuit to the rear of his right, the two parties to meet and make a joint attack on Baum's entrenchments.

Colonels Hubbard and Stickney with 300 men of Stark's brigade were ordered to the enemy's extreme right. While the three detachments were gaining their assigned positions the enemy was concerned by a three headed attack from the front.

About three o'clock in the afternoon Nichols party began firing which was a signal for a general assault. It was at once followed by the detachment under Herrick and that by Hubbard and Stickney, while Stark with his reserves of New Hampshire men and the Berkshires and some Vermont militia assaulted the enemy's breastworks. The engagement became strong and lasted two hours.

The Indians alarmed at being encircled between the parties of Nichols and Herrick fled at the beginning of the fight. Baum with his Germans behind entrenchments fought with great resolution but were overpowered by the militia assaults. They either fled or surrendered as prisoners of war. The fate of Burgoyne and his army was sealed at Bennington.*

*Abby Maria Hemenway, *Vermont Historical Gazeteer* (Montpelier: Montpelier Watchman and State Journal, 1882), p. 14

## *SARATOGA BATTLES* [10]

The defeat of Baum at Bennington caused Johnny Burgoyne to realize that the enemy opposition was greater than he had anticipated. Colonel Heinrich Breymann who arrived too late for the battle found Colonel Frederich Baum dead and his entire force killed or captured.

This victory had encouraged the Americans to gather their troops at Stillwater, New York, where they outnumbered Burgoyne's forces. Burgoyne was now forced to decide whether he should stay and fight or retreat. He finally decided to forge ahead, and with his army forded Fishkill Creek just south of Saratoga. He soon arrived just four miles north of Bemis Heights where General Gates' army was well-entrenched and protected.

Burgoyne ordered an advance through the brush-covered hillsides, where his forces were driven back by the withering fire of sharpshooters, some of whom were in trees. Several officers were killed in this attack. It was decided to withdraw to give the troops a few days of respite from fighting to clear the forest area in their front for the firing of their cannon, and to construct barricades.

A Hessian officer who had been captured at the Battle of Bennington was released and directed to report to Burgoyne that the Americans had occupied Skenesborough and attacked Fort Ticonderoga, which had held out although the Americans had captured many British boats and controlled the entrance to Lake George.

After a wait of several days the Americans made an attack on the British which caused the death of Colonel Fraser a few days later as a result of a bullet that went through his stomach. Burgoyne finally pulled back his troops under cover of darkness. Burgoyne's supplies had been practically exhausted while waiting for Clinton's advance to his aid up the Hudson River. After carefully weighing the situation, he made a proposal to General Gates, which was accepted, that he and his army be given safe passage to Boston. Little did he know at the time that Clinton with two thousand troops was on his way by boat up the Hudson River. Thus the Champlain Valley was freed of war manuevers until the War of 1812.

## *THE BATTLE OF PLATTSBURG* [11]

On October 9, 1812, Lieutenant Thomas MacDonough arrived in Burlington from Portland, Maine to command the American fleet on Lake Champlain under orders from President James Madison. MacDonough at once made a courtesy call upon the distinguished General Henry Dearborn in Plattsburg. He then made an inspection tour of ships and facilities in Skenesborough (now Whitehall) making himself familiar with the lake en route there and back.

10. John E. Goodrich, *Revolutionary War 1775-1783,* (Rutland: Tuttle Co. 1904).
11. Wilbur Lafayette, *History of Vermont,* (Jericho: Roscoe Printing Co., 1899).

On this trip to the southern end of the lake he observed among the many bateaux, gondolas and scows a sailing vessel - the steamer Vermont — tied up at a port due to the difficulties. The United States Government actually had no active naval boats on Lake Champlain when he arrived. After his inspection he found two armed vessels, the six-gun President docked at Shelburne, and the sloop Montgomery which was well armed and under Army control. The Navy owned but two sloops on the lake, the Hunter and the Bulldog, both of which were unfit for active service. MacDonough ordered that these ships be temporarily repaired so that they could be taken to Whitehall for complete repair.

In the spring of 1813 all these ships were brought to the naval dock in Burlington. In April of 1813, MacDonough sailed out with his fleet to which had been added two gunboats and a chartered boat, the Wasp, to serve as a dispatch boat. On the trip the President was grounded on offshore rocks which were covered during high spring water. She was able to be sailed into Plattsburg along with her two sloops.

The Hunter and the Bulldog had been renamed respectively the Growler and the Eagle. On hearing that the British gunboats were on their way up the Richelieu to the lake, these two American gunboats sailed some distance down the river to where it was narrow. Here they were accosted by the fire of three British boats which, after considerable bombardment on both sides, were able to sink the American boats. The crews surrendered as prisoners.

MacDonough, though beaten in 1812, was not dismayed, and in the spring he got busy with the building of a new fleet which would be able to match the British. In the meantime, the British had refloated and repaired the Growler and the Eagle, which they renamed the Shannon and the Broke. MacDonough had refloated the President and sent her along with the two gunboats to Burlington for repairs. The army turned over the 9-gun Montgomery to the Navy, and that ship was also sent to Burlington to be converted for Navy use. He purchased a private ship which he recommissioned as the Preble to be a chase ship. He also chartered a small sloop, the Frances, which was to join the Wasp as supply ships.

MacDonough put out an urgent call for seasoned sailors and was quite fortunate in having at least a hundred sent to him. To match the rumored six thousand redcoats MacDonough had over four thousand soldiers at Burlington.

On July 31st, British troops landed at Plattsburg from the Shannon and Broke along with three gunboats and numerous bateaux. Both private and public property was destroyed by them. In the afternoon the British sent their sloops and some of their gunboats from Plattsburg over to Burlington to draw out a part of the American fleet for a scrap. The Americans were caught unawares and scurried to their stations. The big guns in the present Battery Park belched forth their 24 pounders which fell short of the two British sloops but caused them to retreat.

It was not until September 6th that MacDonough's fleet was ready to sail forth in search of the British fleet. He sighted them north of Cumberland Head but they scurried forth to the Richelieu River before being overtaken. After minor skirmishes with the American gunboats, the British retired for the winter months.

Early in the spring of 1814 MacDonough received word from the Secretary of the Navy that funds had been authorized to build either a full-rigged ship or about 15 gunboats. From his experience with gunboats, he chose a ship to be called the Saratoga. For a protected haven in which to build such a ship, he selected Vergennes on Otter Creek about seven miles from Lake Champlain. His choice of Vergennes stemmed from several factors; it was close to a supply of raw materials and it was the source of a group of necessary industries which would be very helpful to his ship building; eight forges, a blast furnace, a rolling mill, a sawmill, a grist mill and woolen and cotton mills. Within five days from the time his construction crew was at hand, the timbers for his ship had been logged, sawn into planks and hand adzed for use.

During his trips up and down the lake he had observed the steamer Vermont, the second oldest steamer in the state, which was fired by wood fuel. He gave orders to convert at Vergennes the hull of this boat from a steam boat to a two-masted schooner, which he named the Ticonderoga. As the spring season arrived, six large gunboats were built and launched beside the Ticonderoga at Vergennes. With the aid of the two Browne brothers, Adam and Noah, whom he had hired to direct the construction, the Saratoga was completed as they had promised and launched on the morning of April 11th.

MacDonough received word by a scout from Burlington that the British ships were reconnoitering to determine where the American fleet was harbored. In May they discovered that the fleet was evidently headed for Vergennes, so they began firing upon Fort Cassin near the mouth of Otter Creek. After an exhcnage of fire between the British and Americans at Fort Cassin, MacDonough on May 28th brought his fleet into the lake and set sail for Plattsburg.

A new brig from Vergennes, the Surprise, whose name was changed to the Eagle soon joined the fleet at Plattsburg. MacDonough brought his fleet into a practice line at Cumberland Head and again made another dry run. Word was received that the British fleet was located at Isle LaMotte with many of the smaller boats within the Isle LaMotte Passage. A scout boat was dispatched to a station midway between Cumberland Head and South Hero Island to observe and report on the possible advance of the British.

The approach of the British ships was shortly announced by the discharge of a 2-pounder on the watchboat, the smoke of which was visible to the Saratoga. Early in the morning of September 12th, the Americans got their first view of the advance of the British fleet off Cumberland Head. Troops had been sent ahead as far as the Saranac River, expecting on signal to proceed to the Head.

Though the ships were out of range of one another, the British ordered a broadside from the Linnet which hit the deck of the Saratoga with little harm. The British ship Chubb started the battle; after a few rounds from the Eagle in return, she was put out of commission. At the signal of a white flag she was taken as a prize. Since MacDonough's fleet was fitted with kedge anchors, he was able to turn them easily to fire effectively at the enemy. A battle ensued between the Saratoga and the Confiance. The American Preble, though not too severely damaged, withdrew after the British Finch was so severely damaged that she drifted southerly and grounded on Crabb Island where she was taken a prize. Three vessels, the Saratoga and the British Confiance and Linnet continued the battle; each side knowing that the outcome would be determined by the duel between the two frigates. Many sailors were wounded on the decks of the Saratoga and taken to the hospital rooms below. The British Commander Downs on the Confiance was killed in the battle along with many other casualties, which led to the raising of the white ensign. After learning the condition of the Confiance and the number of the dead and wounded on the Linnet, Prig (now Commander) hauled down the British flag in defeat. This act ended the domination of the British on Lake Champlain.

The plan of protecting Plattsburgh was both by land and by water. General Macomb was given the task of the land defense of Plattsburg with 1,500 tired and under disciplined troops. He was faced with an attack by 14,000 veteran British troops from the north. To protect Plattsburg General Macomb built three redoubts on the south side of the Saranac River near to its mouth and protected by a battery. The Saranac river which divided the village of Plattsburg had only two bridges which crossed it.

By the end of August General Macomb had recruited a force which numbered about 3,500. The British land army consisting of three brigades, each led by a general, set out on a march to Plattsburg on September 6th. When the British reached a height overlooking Plattsburg they noted the defenses and decided to await the arrival of the fleet around Cumberland Head. When the fleet came into view the commander Sir George Prevost ordered one brigade and part of another to advance over the two bridges. The attack failed due to the stern resistance of Macomb forces so the British retreated leaving some prisoners. At that time they learned of the defeat of the British navy.

## *VERMONT AND THE WAR BETWEEN THE STATES* [12]

Vermont was represented at the fall of Fort Sumter. The first reconnaisance in force upon Virginia soil by the United States troops was made by the First Vermont Regiment on the 23rd of May, 1861. Vermont regiments called into service included the First Vermont Cavalry and the following regiments of infantry: Second, Third, Fourth, Fifth, Sixth, Ninth, Tenth, Eleventh and Seventeenth and other volunteer regiments, my grandfather fought in the Thirteenth Vermont Infantry together with the general staff.

The last shot of the Sixth Army Corps was fired by the Second Vermont Regiment, April 6, 1865. The last fighting by Vermont troops was done by the Second Regiment at Wheatler, Alabama on April 31, 1865 and the First Vermont Cavalry at Appomattox Court House on the morning of Lee's surrender, April 6, 1865.

The Honorable Redfield Proctor from Vermont was the Secretary of War at the time.

Some of the battles in which Vermont participated were: the Second Battle of Bull Run, Virginia, July 21, 1863; Gettysburg, Pennsylvania, July 3, 1863; Petersburg, Virginia, April 2, 1865; and 25 other battles. No regiment stood higher as a fighting regiment than the Second Vermont Volunteer Infantry. The losses of the Fourth Vermont in Battle, killed and mortally wounded, exceeded those of other brigades in the United States Army, east or west, and the Fourth was famed throughout the nation at that time.

## *RAIDS* [13]

The St. Albans raid of October 1864 was the farthest north battle of the Civil War. Twenty-two rebels arrived at St. Albans by train in twos and threes on different days. They stayed at each of the three hotels. At one of the hotels one of their number read the Bible aloud continuously, so one of the spinsters at the hotel thought that he must be studying for the ministry. The rebels cased the entire city, giving especial attention to the location of horses, the action of the people and the three banks which were located on Main Street.

Just before closing time on the appointed date, two or three entered each of the banks. A few minutes later they made away on horseback with $208,000.00. Only one person, a citizen of New Hampshire. was shot in the frav. They made their way safely into Canada where they were arrested. From the funds recovered, Canada returned nearly a third of the stolen funds.

12. G. G. Benedict, *Vermont in the Civil War,* (Burlington: The Free Press, 1886).
13. Newspapers.

Still another affair, the Fenian Raid, which occurred on June 1, 1866, may not be of great historical importance, yet it is worth relating. Over 1,200 Fenians congregated at St. Albans, many of them arriving by train from the south. They were joined by local county sympathizers in their march through Sheldon and Franklin and then over the Canadian line. Here they were joined by loyal Canadian Irishmen who desired to assist in the establishment of an Irish Republic. Their attempt was short-lived for within twenty-four hours they had been subdued by the provincial authorities.

## *SPANISH AMERICAN WAR* [14]

The sinking of the Battleship Maine on February 16th, 1898, in the Harbor of Havana was the spark required to bring smouldering pubic opinion to the flaming point. Primarily we fought to free Cuba. To avenge the sinking of the Maine was of lesser importance.

On the 24th of April, Spain declared war on the United States. The First Vermont Infantry (which was comprised of companies A through M) was mustered into federal service on May 16th, 1898.

The President of the United States, William McKinley, by proclamation on April 2, 1898 called upon the several states for volunteers to serve for two years in the Army of the United States. On May 2nd Governor Grout under a general order directed the companies of the Vermont National Guard to assemble at the state grounds adjoining Fort Ethan Allen in Colchester, which was christened "Camp Olympia".

On May 16th the regiment was mustered into federal service with 1,080 men. They broke camp on May 21st and arrived at Chickamauga Park in Tennessee on the 24th after a stop over in Washington. After some training they were ordered to go to Puerto Rico; however due to later conditions that promised early cessation of hostilities, they remained at Chickamauga until after the end of hostilities.

Two noted Vermonters served in the Navy during the war. Admiral George Dewey, then a Commodore, assumed command of the Asiatic station in January, 1898, with his ships scattered along the China and Korea coasts. President McKinley ordered Commodore Dewey on May 9th to proceed to the Philippines with the United States Squadron. He defeated the Spanish Navy and took control of Manila Bay and the city, for which shortly thereafter Congress advanced George Dewey of Montpelier to a full Admiral.

Captain Charles E. Clark, another Vermonter, responded as second in command to orders to take the Oregon to the east coast. He left the Golden Gate on March 17th and arrived at Key West on May 26 after a 14,000-mile trip beset with severe storms around the

14. Herbert T. Johnson, *Vermont in the Spanish-American War,* State of Vermont, 1929.

Cape and the passage through Magellan Straits, and trying to evade the Spanish warships which might be in his course northward up the Brazil Coast.

The Oregon arrived in time to take part in the Battle of Santiago Bay where the Spanish Navy was destroyed. Captain Clark was made a Rear Admiral in 1902 as a result of his exploits.

## *MEXICAN WAR*

A statement in the publication, History of Danby by J. C. Williams, reads as follows: "The object of the Mexican War, being the acquisition of more territory in which to extend the institution of slavery, did not arouse the sympathy of our citizens. The government was then controlled by the slave holders who sought to maintain the balance of power, and although by war a vast amount of territory was acquired, the vast resources of which under the reign of slavery would have forever remained undeveloped, populous states and thriving cities have sprung up, the resources developed, and the end of becoming a slave territory, the large portion was consecrated to freedom."

## *WORLD WAR ONE*[15]

With the eruption of war in Europe, Vermont citizens as a whole took little notice since it was far removed from our peaceful abode.

The first call for Vermont troops came on March 25, 1917 although America was not yet officially at war with Germany. War was declared on April 6, 1917 and armed soldiers were used to guard Vermont railroad bridges and utilities. At this time Vermont had only one regiment, the First Vermont Infantry under the command of Fred B. Thomas. The regiment had had considerable experience the preceding summer on the Mexican border at Eagle Pass, Texas.

Pancho Villa, the Mexican outlaw, made his well-known raid on Columbus, New Mexico in March, 1916. A punitive expedition under the command of General John Pershing chased the fleeing brigands for thirty miles into Mexico inflicting serious casualties as they pursued them. The Vermont National Guard was nationalized, and sent to the Mexican border to prevent any further incursions from Mexico. This action, though having no direct connection with World War I, gave the Vermont Guard an opportunity to be ready when war was declared.

The first organization, St. Albans B Company, was, by virtue of the order of the President, the first group of Vermont soldiers to actually bear arms in World War I. This order contemplated "a more perfect protection against possible interference with postal, commercial and military channels and instrumentalities within the

15. John T. Cushing et al, Ed., *Vermont in World War I*, (Burlington: Free Press, 1928).

state of Vermont." A few days later the rest of the regiment was activated and two days before the formal declaration of war, the entire regiment was assembled at the State Camp Grounds just south of Fort Ethan Allen.

Disappointment was great when Army Headquarters ordered the transfer of 1,338 enlisted men and twenty-three officers from the First Infantry Regiment into the newly created 26th Rainbow Division. The men left Fort Ethan Allen in late autumn and found themselves in France destined for a rest camp for further training.

The First Ammunition Train which included 700 enlisted men and six officers of the First Vermont Infantry, National Guard, a part of the Sixth trained at Camp Bartlett, Westfield, Massachusetts. They left the camp and embarked at Hoboken, New Jersey aboard the A. A. Aurania on October 2, 1917, arriving in Liverpool on October 17th after a zigzag trip across the ocean.

The battles in which the Twenty-sixth Division tool part were: Chemin Des Dames Offensive, Yankee Division at Toul, Battle of Chateau Thierry, The Yankees of St. Mihiel, the Battle of Marcheville, the Meuse-Argonne Forest and other small scraps.

The 102 Machine Gun Batallion numbered 215 men and four officers. Admiral Henry T. Mayo of Burlington was Commander in Chief of the Atlantic Fleet. The number of Vermonters in the Navy was 1,838 and 99 in the Marines.

## *WORLD WAR II* [16]

Well will all Vermonters remember the Japanese sneak attack on Pearl Harbor on December 6, 1941, when war was declared. The membership of the State Staff and Detachment, Vermont National Guard were called into active duty, individually, during September and October of 1940. These officers and enlisted men were assigned to Selective Service headquarters by the War Department.

The executive order of the President called into federal service on February 24, 1941 all components of the 43rd Division in the Vermont National Guard, which included a total strength of 148 officers, 1 warrant officer and 1995 enlisted men. This order included the following units: Headquarters detachment of 43rd Division, Headquarters detachment 86th Infantry brigade, 172 Infantry, Headquarters detachment 118th Quartermaster regiment, Medical detachment of the 118th Quartermaster regiment, 1st Battalion of the 118th Quartermaster regiment, Headquarts detachment of the 2nd Battalion of the 118th Quartermaster regiment and Company E, 118th Quartermaster regiment. The 43rd division October 1, 1942 sailed west under the Golden Gate Bridge.

No. 180 of the Public Acts of 1941 provided for the formation of

16. Reginald Cram et al, Ed., *Roster of Vermonters During Second World War,* 1972.

State Guard to function in the place of Vermont National Guard while on active federal service. Thirty companies of State Guard were organized.

The war ended on December 31, 1946 with the signing of a peace treaty on the U.S.S. Missouri in a Japanese harbor.

Major General Leonard Wing of Rutland commanded the 43rd Division. Colonel Reginald Buzzell of Bennington was one of three, who were promoted to become Brigadier Generals. The others were not Vermonters. There were 43,000 Vermonters in active service during World War II.

## *KOREAN CONFLICT* [17]

On August 1, 1950 word was received at Vermont National Guard headquarters that the 43rd Infantry Division was alerted to be ordered into active Federal Military Service on 5 September 1950. On 5 September 1950 the Vermont National Guard unit of the 43rd Infantry Division-43rd Infantry Division (Det.), the 172nd Infantry Regiment and the 206 Field Artillery Division were inducted into federal service.

On February 1, 1951 the 134th Fighter Squadron and the 134th Weather Station of the Air National Guard of Vermont were inducted into service. No. 175 of the Public Acts of 1951, (Vermont) provided for the organization of the State Guard to provide security for the state.

## *VIETNAM WAR* [18]

The 131st Engineer Company (LE) was ordered to active duty on May 13, 1968. This company had been called up in October 1961 due to the Berlin crisis and remained on active duty until August 1962. The 131st Engineer Company (light equipment) Vermont Army National Guard following a year's service in Vietnam, returned to its home station, Burlington, on September 12, 1969. This engineer company was the only Vermont National Guard unit called to active duty during the Vietnam War for the period of 1968-69.

Note there were approximately 16,000 Vermonters in each of these two conflicts.

## *VERMONT FORTS* [19]

The earliest known fort built on Vermont soil was on Isle La Motte. Previous to the building of this fort others had been built by the

17. Information furnished by Adjutant General's Department.
18. Idem.
19. Many sources.

French along the Richelieu River to protect them from the attacks by the Iroquois Indians. In October 1665 Sir Jean Baptiste le Gardeur de Repentigny was sent out to locate the most suitable spot for an advanced post. Late in the fall, a sandy point was selected on the north shore of the first island sighted upon entering Lake Champlain from the Richelieu River.

In the spring of 1666, Sieur de la Motte had at his command a construction crew of 300 men who completed the fort on July 20th. This fort was dedicated to Sainte Anne on the 26th. The design of the fort followed that of others built on the Richelieu as described in Volume II of the Jesuit Relations. Excavations made at the site about 1900 uncovered a building measuring 12 by 16 feet, and others measuring 16 by 32, all of wood.

Eight miles north of this fort, the French constructed a windmill of stone in a small settlement which was later burned by the British. The location in Alburg is today known as Windmill Point.[20]

Forts - or more properly block houses - of the later period were generally built with large squared timbers laid horizontally one above the other in the shape of a square or oblong and locked together with iron spikes (when obtainable). The structures were roofed, and furnished with loopholes on all sides so that an attack by the enemy could be detected and observed. The second story projected out over the lower part and in the floor of the projection loopholes were cut to enable firing down on the enemy when they came near the fort.[21]

In 1724 a block house, Fort Dummer, was erected on the banks of the Connecticut River in the southeastern part of the town of Brattleboro. When the Vernon Dam was constructed, flood waters covered the site. The fort was named after Lieutenant-Governor Dummer of Massachusetts, who directed Lieutenant Timothy Dwight to build the fort. The first white child born in Vermont was born here. The fort was constructed from our native red or Norway pine. A full description of the fort may be found in Benjamin G. Heath's History of Eastern Vermont. This fort was administered under the direction of Massachusetts for some time until it was found that it lay in the New Hampshire grants; then it was turned over to New Hampshire.

One of the most southern forts in Vermont was built in 1740 by Joseph Sartwell and named for him. It was located on the Connecticut River about four miles south of Brattleboro in what is now the town of Vernon. It was taken down in 1838 and a house was built upon the site by a Sartwell Descendant. Orlando Bridgmen built a similar fort in the same year about a half mile south of the

20. Personal letter from St. Anne's Society.

21. H. P. Smith & W. S. Rann, *History of Rutland County*, (Syracuse: D. Mason & Co., 1886).

*Fort Dummer, erected 1724 in Brattleboro*

Sartwell fort. A garrison known as Fort Hill was built in the town of Putney on a location known as the "Great Meadows".[22]

As early as 1740 a settlement was made at Charleston, New Hampshire, better known as Number Four. From this fort many a scouting party followed the Indians' trails across the Green Mountains over the route which became known as the Crown Point road to Lake Champlain.

At the close of the French War (which terminated in the conquest of Canada in 1760) most of the terriotory which is now the state of Vermont was an uninhabited wilderness. Captain Ebenezer Allen and Isaac Clark in the spring of 1778 were assigned to guard the northern frontiers which were exposed to attack from Canada. Captain Allen was ordered to raise men and post them at a fort in New Haven.

Later forts were built to consist of small pickets and a strong block house. Two forts were erected in the town of Rutland for the protection of the settlers during the troublous times of the Revolution. A picket fort like many of the day was located in what was called the "burnt district" of Rutland village. It had a length from north to south of ten rods and a width of eight rods.

Maple pickets were sunk into the ground to a depth of about five feet and extended about fourteen feet above ground. At each corner there was a redoubt or "flanker" about eight feet square. At an effective height and about six feet apart, portholes large enough to take muskets were made. On the inside of the fort there was a small building to house provision and ammunition.[23]

22. Cabot, Mary R., *Annals of Brattleboro, 1681-18*, (Brattleboro: E. L. Hildreth & Company, 1921), p. 112.

23. Benjamin H. Hall, *History of Eastern Vermont*, Vol. 1, p. 385.

The other fort, known as Fort Ranger, at Gookins Falls, Center Rutland, was built in 1778, when it was decided to make Rutland the headquarters for the state troops. This fort was used until 1781 when the presence of the British in large force on Lake Champlain caused the troop removal to a fort in Castleton.

Fort Warren in Castleton was located one-half mile east of Castleton village. The stockage there was an abatis of fallen entangled trees, the limbs of which were sharpened, and a deep ditch was dug around the abatis. This fort was removed in 1781 to a site at Blanchard's Mills in Hydeville, which was additionally protected with a picket enclosure.

Fort Frederick at Crown Point was built in 1731.

Fort Mott, named after Deacon John Mott, was erected on the east bank of Otter Creek in Pittsford in 1777. Soon after the completion of a second fort on higher ground east of Fort Mott, one of the garrison was killed by an Indian.

It is said that Ebenezer Allen vowed vengeance against every Indian that should come within his power. He dashed a bottle of liquor against the fort gate and christened it Fort Vengeance. He had been directed by the Board of War meeting in Arlington in July 1780 to take five men experienced in brick making, to fabricate twenty thousand bricks for chimneys in the barracks at the fort in the north line of Pittsford.

With the approach of the enemy, the citizens of northern Charlotte County felt the need of protection in case of an enemy attack from the north, so two forts were authorized; one, Fort Frederick, on the Onion River below the falls in Winooski and the other on Otter Creek, probably the place to which Captain Ebenezer Allen had been directed to guard the northern frontier.

Raids by the Indians in the Royalton area caused the people to build forts to which they could flee for safety. After the raid on Barnard, Fort Defense was built there followed by Fort Fortitude in Bethel.

## *WARS AND RAIDS*
## *SELECTED BIBLIOGRAPHY*


Allen, Ira, *History of Vermont,* Montpelier: Vermont Historical Society, Vol. I., 1870.

Appleman, Roy Edgar, *The Korean War, 1950-53,* Washington: Department of the Army, 1948.

Ibid, *South to Nakong, North to Yalu,* ibid, 1961.

Bird, Harrison, *Navies in the Mountains, 1609-1814,* New York: Oxford University Press, 1962.

Bowen, A., *U.S. History of War of 1812.*


5. Abby Maria Hemenway, *Vermont Historical Gazetteer,* (Montpelier: Montpelier Watchman and State Journal, 1882), Vol. III, p. 1082.

6. Benjamin H. Hall, *History of Eastern Vermont.*

Cabot, Mary R., *Annals of Brattleboro,* Brattleboro: E. L. Hildreth Co., 1921.
Corinth, Town Committee, ed., *History of Corinth, 1764-1964,* West Topsham: Colby Press, 1964.
Crockett, Walter Hill, *Vermont the Green Mountain State,* Burlington: Vermont Farm Bureau, 1938.
Dupuy, Ernest R., *Battle of Hubbardton,* Unpublished manuscript, Dec., 1960.
Fall, Bernard B., *The Two Viet Nams,* New York: Frederic A. Praeger, 1964.
Ibid, *Viet Nam Politics and Government,* Ibid.
Folsom, William R., *Battle of Velcour Island,* Vermont Quarterly, Vol. XIX, No. I, 1957.
Hall, Benjamin Homer, *Early History of Vermont,* New York: D. Appleton Co., 2 Vol., 1858.
Hall, Hiland, *History of Vermont from Its Discovery to Its Admission into the Union, 1791,* 1868.
Hemenway, Abby Maria, *Vermont Historical Gazetteer,* Montpelier: Montpelier Watchman and State Journal, 1882.
Keller, Allan, *Valcour Island,* American History Illustrated: Vol. 7, No. 4, July 1972.
Ibid, *Lake Champlain Basin and Other Battles,* Illinois: American History Illustrated, 1972.
Waite, Otis R., *Vermont in the Great Rebellion,* Claremont, N.H.: Tracy Chase and Company, 1867.
Wells, Frederic P., *History of Newbury,* St. Johnsbury: The Caledonian, 1902.
Wilbur, James Benjamin, *Ira Allen, Founder of Vermont, 1751-1814,* Cambridge, Massachusetts: Houghton Mifflin, 2 Vol. 1928.
Wilbur, Lafayette, *Early History of Vermont,* Jericho: Roscoe Printing House, 4 Vol. 1899.
Williams, John A., ed., *The Public Papers of Governor Thomas Chittenden, 1969.*
Williamson, Chilton, *Vermont in Quandary,* Montpelier: Vermont Historical Society, 1949.

### *FORT TICONDEROGA MUSEUM PUBLICATIONS*

Ethan Allen Announced Capture of Fort Ticonderoga, V.V. #2, 1939
Champlain Tells About Indian Crops and Forests, V.V. #2, 1939
The Diary of Reverend John Ogilve, 1750-1759, V. X, #5, 1961
Bougainsville's Journal, V. X, #6, 1962
Fraser Takes Indians Up Otter Creek, V. XI, #4, 1964
Journal of Carlton's and Burgoyne's Campaign, V. XI, #5&6, 1965
Peter Kalm Sets out on a Journey, Vo. XII, #1, 1965
Building Royal Savage, V. XII, #2, 1966
Rogers Around Crow Point, V. XII, #6, 1970
The American Champlain Fleet, V. XII, #4, 1968
Aldolphus Benzel's Notes on Lake Champlain, V. XII, #5, 1969
French Colonial Forts at Crown Point Straits, V. XII, #6, 1970
"The Road Not Taken", V. Xiii, #4, 1973

# Women's Suffrage

The Indians as they went about on their hunting trips left their squaws to raise the family food and take care of their offspring. The wives of the early settlers worked in the fields alongside their husbands and sons.

There was one woman in Vermont who was probably the most active in the early days on behalf of the rights of women. *Clarissa Irene Howard,* born in West Townshend, Vermont in 1810, was educated in the local district school and a private school. She taught in public and private schools in Vermont until her marriage which took her to western New York. There she taught at the Brockport Academy and later founded a young teacher academy at Herkimer, New York.

By 1839 she had returned to Vermont, where she began writing for the *Windham County Democrat* of Brattleboro, a standard Jacksonian county weekly. After divorcing her husband - which caused quite an uproar in those days - Clarina married George W. Nichols, editor and publisher of the *Democrat.* Due to his illness, she was forced to take over the editorship of the newspaper. She soon became one of the earliest women in the United States to actively and strongly advocate women's rights. She published several editorials which deplored the legal and property restrictions of married women.

She was successful in influencing the legislature of Vermont to pass a law in 1947 which gave women the right to inherit and bequeath property. Mrs. Nichols continued her campaign in favor of women's rights. The next step gave women the right to insure the life of their husbands for their sole use; and this was later amended to include all moneys and obligations arising from the sale of real estate. Further acts permitted the unmarried woman to place insurance on her father or brother, which would accrue to her upon their decease.

Mrs. Nichols promoted women's rights before the Vermont legislature in a speech in which she claimed for women the right to represent her property and natural interests in her child in overseeing its educational interests. Her stand on women's rights spread far beyond Vermont. At a women's rights convention in Syracuse, New York in 1852, she met *Susan B. Anthony,* who just at the time was beginning her women's rights movement. She encouraged Miss Anthony to increase her activities in the realm of female participation.

Mrs. Nichols became an ardent supporter of the Vermont State Temperance Society, which she represented at National Conventions.

Over a period of a hundred years, women have gradually attained near equality with men before the law, and this has been made possible largely because of the influence of such women as *Clarissa Howard Nichols.*[1]

From 1852 on at nearly every biennial session, laws were enacted giving women in Vermont more rights. Taxes upon unmarried women became chargeable to the husband after marriage; in joint ownership of property, the wife was considered a competent witness; all personal property and rights to property acquired by any married woman during her coverture by inheritance or distribution shall be held by her to her sole and separate use. When any married man abandoned his wife and had not made sufficient provision for her maintenance, the supreme court could on her petition authorize her to sell and convey his real estate and also any personal property which shall at the time have come to the husband by reason of the marriage.

In 1866 the legislature introduced a joint resolution, No. 75, which read, "that laws ought to be in force in all of the United States guaranteeing equal and impartial suffrage without respect to color." This resolution was submitted to our congressmen.

In 1870 a petition was presented to the Constitutional Convention favoring women's suffrage. The petition was signed by 231 names of persons from Brattleboro but was lost without debate since only one person voted for the petition.

In 1880 women received their first voting rights in a school district meeting. The right to be elected or appointed as a trustee of a public library or town treasurer was granted in 1900. In 1919 women could vote if they had paid their poll taxes. Two years later, Vermont passed the constitutional amendment extending the right of suffrage to women. In the same year, the law stated that a person

1. Cabot, Mary R., *Annals of Brattleboro,* (Brattleboro, E. L. Hildreth and Company, 2 Vol. 1921), p. 380.

could not be debarred on account of sex from holding any office of trust under the state, in Congress, or in any county, town, village or city.

In 1921 *Edna Beard* of Orange was the first woman elected to the Vermont House of Representatives and the following year she was again honored by being elected to the Senate. By 1925 there were nearly a dozen women in the House, and this number has been increased in some years since that date to over forty.

*Consuelo Northrup Bailey* served in the House in 1952 and was elected as the first woman Speaker in the following year. She was elected as Lieutenant Governor in 1954 by a majority of over 8,000 votes. She served for several years as National Republican Committeewoman.

A partial list compiled by *Mrs. Vivian Bryan,* Law Librarian, contains many names of Vermont women born before 1900, who have made important advancement and recognition in the fields of arts and science:

Adams, Mary Holden, Manchester, first woman to hold a judicial post in Vermont
Baxter, Martha W., Castleton, a well-known artist
Bolta, Anne C. (Lynch), Bennington, poet
Bradwell, Myra, Manchester, first woman member of Illinois bar
Brungardt, Theresa, Bellows Falls, first Director, Vermont Recreation Department
Brown, Beatrice, South Londonderry, Judge of Probate
Bundy, Gladys, Bethel, Missionary to China and Japan
Cooke, Helen T., Rutland, President of Dana Hall
Cooke, Lucy (Sleeping Lucy), Calais, Clairvoyant for thirty years
Corliss, Arlene Soule, Cambridge, Author of several novels
Eddy, Ethel, Stratton, teacher, school superintendent, legislator
Fisher, Dorothy Canfield, Arlington, author of many books, stories, novels
Gibson, Anna L., Peacham, Hospital Superintendent, pioneer teacher on clinical lab
Gilchrist, Ruth, Bradford, Peacham, writer of books for young people
Gould, Hannah F., Guildhall, poet, two volumes in 1850
Hastings, Mary L., South Shaftsbury, Teaching Supervisor, normal schools in Maine and Massachusetts
Hemingway, Abby, Ludlow, five volumes of Vermont history
Hobson, Sarah, Island Pond, doctor, practiced in Maine and Illinois
Kent, Louise Andrews, Calais, writer and columnist
Luce, Marjorie, Waterbury, teacher, home economist, Vermont Extension Service
Meyer, Lucy Rider, New Haven, founded Chicago Training School for missions
Mills, Susan L., Enosburg Falls, Missionary, founded Mills College
Mould, Ruth G., Morrisville, portrait artist
Pearl, Mary, St. Johnsbury, Director, Nutrition, Maltex Company and radio commentator
Sherman, Ellen B., Montgomery, author, editor, book publisher
Smith, Elva S., Burke, Author children's books

Spaulding, Phoebe E., Westfield, President, Pomona College
Wheelock, Lucy V., Cambridge, founded Wheelock Kindergarten School
Wild, Laura H., Greensboro, ordained Minister, Professor Mr. Holyoke College
Williard, Emma, Middlebury, taught Middlebury, founded Troy, New York female seminary

### *WOMAN SUFFRAGE*
### *SELECTED BIBLIOGRAPHY*

Bassett, T. O. Seymour, *The 1870 Campaign for Woman Suffrage in Vermont,* Montpelier: Vermont Historical Society, Vol. XIV, 1946.

Cabot, Mary R., *Annals of Brattleboro, 1681-1895,* Brattleboro: E. L. Hildreth and Company, 2 Vol., 1921.

Crockett, Walter Hill, *Vermont the Green Mountain State,* Burlington: The Vermont Farm Bureau, 5 Vol., 1938.

# Appendix

## *GOVERNMENT*

### *Legislative Council*

Up until 1965 the duties of the present Legislative Council were vested in and performed by the State Legislative Librarian who was the State Librarian.

The Legislative Council was created by No. 81 of the Acts of 1965, which established a legislative drafting division and a legislative research division.

MEMBERS AND ORGANIZATION The Council consists of the president of the senate and the speaker of the House of Representative together with seven senators and seven representatives, who are appointed respectively by the President of the Senate and the Speaker of the House, biennially in the month of February. Their appointments have to be confirmed by majority vote by each chamber. They are appointed from both political parties in general proportion to the membership of each party in each house, with a minimum of two members from the minority party.

The Council may accept major research and study projects and make recommendations to the General Assembly. It may appoint such committees as may be necessary to accomplish its research and study projects.

The Council appoints an executive director and prescribes his duties and fixes his compensation. The chief legislative draftsman may act in this capacity.

### *COUNCIL OF STATE GOVERNMENT*

The Council of State Government was formed in 1925 with headquarters in Chicago, now in Lexington, Kentucky. There is a commission in each of the fity states as official entities of state government. The purpose of the council is to serve state governmental programs within the individual states, among the states working together and by the states in their relations with the federal government. They provide staff services to the state agencies and serve as a clearing house and draft bills.

The Vermont commission on Interstate Cooperation was authorized in 1937 by joint resolution No. 364 and by No. 217 of the Acts of 1943. The composition of the Vermont Commission is made up of three members of the senate and three members of the house, the attorney general and the administrative heads of two state departments.

The duties of the commission are defined as (1) to encourage all state officials and employees to develop and maintain friendly contacts with those of other states, (2) to advance cooperation by: a) adoption of compacts, b) uniform or reciprocal statutes, rules and regulations.

## *SOME NOTED VERMONTERS*

Early Vermonters were imports from Massachusetts, Connecticut and New Hampshire. Our first 13 governors migrated to Vermont. Since then about 20 were born outside the State of Vermont, and two outside of the United States. Vermonters have played not only an important part in the Vermont Government but also in the government of other states and the federal government. They have also held high position in the fields of education, government, church and business outside Vermont.

### *Two Presidents*

Two of Vermont's honored citizens rose to the Presidency; Calvin Coolidge born in Plymouth and Chester Arthur born in Fairfield. Levi P. Morton born in Shoreham was Vice-President in 1888.

Other men of prominence as President had their fathers born in Vermont. Alfonso Taft, father of President William Howard Taft owned a farm in West Townshend. Nathaniel Fillmore, father of President Milliard Fillmore, moved from Bennington to western New York, where the President was born. Rutherford Hayes moved from Brattleboro to Ohio, where his son Rutherford B. Hayes was born. Both Chester A. Arthur and James A. Garfield taught at different times in a school in Pownal.

### *The Press*

It was a Vermonter, who gave the exhortation, "Go west Young Man". Horace Greeley born in West Haven founded the New York Tirbune. His partner George Jones was the founder of the New York Tribune. The New York World was established by James Spaulding who came from the vicinity of Montpelier. William H. Field, a former owner of the Rutland Herald, founded the New York Daily News. George Harvey of Peacham was editor of the North American Review and a minister to England. Elmer Silver born in Bloomfield established the book publishing company known as Silver Burdett Co.

### *Education*

The following educational institutions had a Vermonter as founder Beloit College, Chicago Divinity School, Marietta College, Negro Schools in Washington, D. C., Newton Theological Seminary, Union Theological Seminary, University of Wisconsin.

Those institutions which had a Vermont born President are: Bowdoin College, Chicago Divinity School, George Washington University, University of Georgia, Iowa State College, John Hopkins University, Kansas University, Mills College, New York Academy of Medicine, North Dakota University, Pacific University, Richmond Virginia College, Tufts College, Vassar College, Wesleyan College, Wabash College, Western College for Women, University of Wisconsin, Yale University, George Washington University.

### *Government*

*Governors* of the states of - Colorado, Indiana, Iowa, Louisiana, Massachusetts, Michigan, Minnesota, New Hampshire (3), Rhode Island, South Dakota.
*Attorney Generals* - Haiti, Iowa, Minnesota, Tennessee, United States.
*U.S. Senators* to - Alabama, Canada, Colorado (2), Illinois, Michigan, Minnesota, North Dakota, New Mexico, Pennsylvania, South Dakota, Wisconsin.
*U.S. House* - Illinois, Indiana, Iowa, Kansas, Massachusetts, Michigan (5),

Minnesota, Missouri, Nebraska, North Dakota (2), New York (2), Ohio (3), Pennsylvania (2), Wisconsin (5).
*Supreme Court Chief* - Arizona, California, District of Columbia, Iowa, Illinois, Michigan, Minnesota, Nevada, Texas, Washington, Wisconsin.
*Member* - District of Columbia, Iowa, New Mexico, Ohio, Philippines, Hawaii, and United States.
*Minister to* - Austira (2), Turkey (2), Portugal, Spain, Siam, Switzerland, Russia, Cuba, France, England, Venezuela, Philippines.

### *RAILROADS*

President, Founder or Builder (B), Chairman of the Board (C) - Chicago and Northwestern (B), New York Central Lines, Terre Haute, Alton and St. Louis, Grand Trunk, Erie Railroad (3), Atchinson Topeka and Santa Fe (5), Union Pacific, Gulf Mobile and Northern, Chicago and Northwestern, Baltimore and Ohio, Atchinson Topeka and Santa Fe (C), Burlington and Cedar Rapids (B), Northern Pacific (2), Illinois (B), New York Elevated (B), Fort Wayne and Chicago, Mexican Railway.

### *RELIGION*

Bishop of Montana, Joseph Smith of Sharon, founder of Mormons, Brigham Young of Whitingham and Heber Kimball Apostles.

### *BUSINESS*

Those in this field are too numerous to mention.

### *GOVERNOR AND COUNCIL REPORTS*

Volume
I. First Constitution, Council of Safety
II. Catamount Tavern, Union of N.H. Towns, New York Towns, Haldimand Correspondence.
III. Massachusetts Claims, Admission to the Union, Windsor Insurrection, Shays' Rebellion.
IV. Amendments to Federal Constitution, Champlain Canal, Northern Frontier, New York Settlement.
V. Vermont State Bank, Canadian Boundary, British Intrigue, State Printer, Domestic Manufacture.
VI. New York Boundary, War of 1812, Vermont and Slavery,
VII. Survey for Canals, Railroads, Lafayette visit,
VIII. Judges of Supreme Court, Indian Claims, New Hampshire-Vermont Boundary, 2nd State House.

### Vermont Statutes

1. Laws of the State of Vermont. Digested and compiled, Published by order of the legislature, Vol. I. and Vol. II., Randolph, Sereno Wright, 1808. 786 pp.
2. The Laws of Vermont, of a Public and Permanent Nature, coming down to and including the year 1824, Compiled by authority of the legislature by William Slade, Jun., Windsor, Simeon Ide, 1825. 756 pp.
3. The Revised Statutes of the State of Vermont, Published by order of the legislature, Burlington, Chauncey Goodrich, 1840. pp. 676.
4. The Compiled Statutes of the State of Vermont, Compiled in Pursuance of

the legislature by Charles L. Williamson, Burlington, Chauncey Goodrich, 1851. pp. 815.
5. The General Statutes of the State of Vermont, Published by the State of Vermont, Cambridge, Massachusetts, Riverdale Press, 1863. pp. 1050.
6. The Revised Laws of Vermont, 1880, Published by authority, Rutland, The Tuttle Company, 1881. pp. 1169.
7. The VErmont Statutes, 1894, Published by Authority, Rutland, Vermont, The Tuttle company, 1895. pp. 1313.
8. The Public Statutes of Vermont, 1906, Published by Authority, 1907. pp. 1302.
9. The General Laws of Vermont, 1917, Published by Authority, Burlington, Free Press Printing Company, 1918. pp. 1370.
10. The Public Laws of Vermont 19033, Published by Authority, Montpelier, Capital City Press, 1934. pp. 1603.
11. The Vermont Statutes of 1947, Published by Authority, 1947. pp. 2160.
12. Vermont Statutes Annotated, Orford, New Hampshire, Equity Publishing Company 9 vol. Titles 1-33 with index and tables. Revised each session.

*STATE BUILDINGS*

| | Date Built | |
|---|---|---|
| Barre Tuberculosis Hospital | 1921 | Sold |
| Brandon State School for Feebleminded | 1912 | |
| Brattleboro State Asylum for the Insane | 1836 | |
| Burlington Correction Center | 1975 | |
| Montpelier First State House | 1801 | Torn down 1836 |
| Montpelier Second State House | 1836 | Burned 1857 |
| Montpelier Third State House | 1859 | |
| Montpelier Addition to State House | 1898 | |
| Montpelier State Library and Supreme Court | 1918 | |
| Pittsford Veront Sanatorium, Gift | 1912 | |
| Pittsford Caverley Preventorium, Gift | 1922 | |
| Rutland State Prison for Women | 1923 | Torn Down |
| Rutland Home for Crippled Children | 1969 | |
| St. Albans Correctional Facility | 1967 | |
| Vergennes Weeks School | 1865 | |
| Windsor State Prison | 1807 | Discontinued 1975 |
| Montpelier Employment Security | 1966 | |
| Montpelier State Office Building | 1960 | Purchased |
| Montpelier Pavilion Office Building | 1971 | |

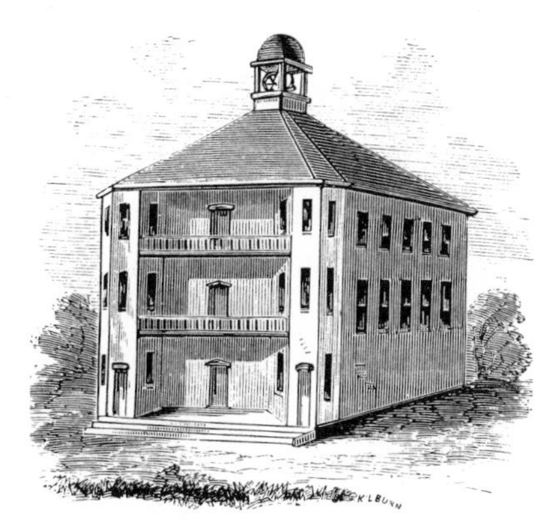

*The First State House*

*The Second State House*

*The Third State House*

## STATE OFFICERS AND TERMS OF SERVICE
**(Since 1778)**

A list of Persons who have held the Offices of Governor, Lieutenant-Governor, Treasurer, Secreatry of State, Auditor of Accounts, Attorney General, Secretary of the Governor and Council, and Secretary of Civil and Military Affairs, since the organization of the State.

### Governors //

Thomas Chittenden ............1778-1789
Moses Robinson ...............1789-1790
‡Thomas Chittenden ...........1790-1797
*Paul Brigham Aug. 25 to Oct. 16, 1797
Isaac Tichenor ................1797-1807
Israel Smith ..................1807-1808
Isaac Tichenor ................1808-1809
Jonas Galusha ................1809-1813
Martin Chittenden ............1813-1815
Jonas Galusha ................1815-1820
Richard Skinner ..............1820-1823
Cornelius P. Van Ness ..........1823-1826
Ezra Butler....................1826-1828
Samuel C. Crafts ...............1828-1831
William A. Palmer .............1831-1835
**Silas H. Jennison ............1835-1836
Silas H. Jennison ..............1836-1841
Charles Paine .................1841-1843
John Mattocks ................1843-1844
William Slade .................1844-1846
Horace Eaton .................1846-1848
Carlos Coolidge ...............1848-1850
Chas. K. Williams .............1850-1852
Erastus Fairbanks..............1852-1853
John S. Robinson ..............1853-1854
Stephen Royce.................1854-1856
Ryland Fletcher................1856-1858
Hiland Hall ...................1858-1860
Erastus Fairbanks..............1860-1861
Frederick Holbrook.............1861-1863
J. Gregory Smith...............1863-1865
Paul Dillingham ...............1865-1867
John B. Page ..................1867-1869
‡‡Peter T. Washburn ...........1869-1870
***George W. Hendee ..........1870
John W. Stewart ...............1870-1872
Julius Converse................1872-1874
Asahel Peck ...................1874-1876
Horace Fairbanks ..............1876-1878
Redfield Proctor ...............1878-1880
Roswell Farnham ..............1880-1882
John L. Barstow ...............1882-1884
Samuel E. Pingree .............1884-1886
Ebenezer J. Ormsbee ...........1886-1888
Wm. P. Dillingham.............1888-1890
Carroll S. Page ................1890-1892
Levi K. Fuller .................1892-1894
Urban A. Woodbury ............1894-1896
Josiah Grout ..................1896-1898
Edward C. Smith...............1898-1900
William W. Stickney............1900-1902
John G. McCullough............1902-1904
Charles J. Bell .................1904-1906

*Lieutenant-Governor, acting Governor on the death of Governor Chittenden.
**Lieutenant-Governor, Governor by reason of no election of Governor by the People.
***Lieutenant-Governor, Governor by reason of the death of Governor Washburn.
†Died August 25, 1797.
‡Died in office, February 7, 1870.
//For a "Note on Political Affiliations and Elections of Vermont Governors, Since 1778," see page 318.

Fletcher D. Proctor .............1906-1908
George H. Prouty ..............1908-1910
John A. Mead ..................1910-1912
Allen M. Fletcher ..............1912-1915
Charles W. Gates ..............1915-1917
Horace F. Graham .............1917-1919
Percival W. Clement............1919-1921
James Hartness................1921-1923
Redfield Proctor ...............1923-1925
Franklin S. Billings .............1925-1927
John E. Weeks ................1927-1931
Stanley C. Wilson ..............1931-1935
Charles M. Smith ..............1935-1937
George D. Aiken ...............1937-1941
William H. Wills ...............1941-1945
Mortimer R. Proctor ............1945-1947
†Ernest W. Gibson .............1947-1950
††Harold J. Arthur .............1950-1951
Lee E. Emerson................1951-1955
Joseph B. Johnson .............1955-1959
Robert T. Stafford ..............1959-1961
F. Ray Keyser, Jr. .............1961-1963
Philip H. Hoff .................1963-1969
Deane C. Davis ................1969-1973
Thomas P. Salmon .............1973-

†Resigned and appointed U.S. District Judge by Pres. Truman, Jan. 16, 1950.
††Became governor when Gov. Gibson resigned, Jan. 16, 1950.

**Lieutenant Governors**

|  |  |
|---|---|
| Joseph Marsh | 1778-1779 |
| Benjamin Carpenter | 1779-1781 |
| Elisha Payne | 1781-1782 |
| Paul Spooner | 1782-1787 |
| Joseph Marsh | 1787-1790 |
| Peter Olcott | 1790-1794 |
| Jonathan Hunt | 1794-1796 |
| *Paul Brigham | 1796-1813 |
| William Chamberlain | 1813-1815 |
| Paul Brigham | 1815-1820 |
| William Cahoon | 1820-1822 |
| Aaron Leland | 1822-1827 |
| Henry Olin | 1827-1830 |
| Mark Richards | 1830-1831 |
| Lebbeus Edgerton | 1831-1835 |

|  |  |
|---|---|
| *Silas H. Jennison | 1835-1836 |
| David M. Camp | 1836-1841 |
| Waitstill R. Ranney | 1841-1843 |
| Horace Eaton | 1843-1846 |
| Leonard Sargeant | 1846-1848 |
| Robert Pierpoint | 1848-1850 |
| Julius Converse | 1850-1852 |
| William C. Kittredge | 1852-1853 |
| Jefferson P. Kidder | 1853-1854 |
| Ryland Fletcher | 1854-1856 |
| James M. Slade | 1856-1858 |
| Burnam Martin | 1858-1860 |
| Levi Underwood | 1860-1862 |
| Paul Dillingham | 1862-1865 |
| Abraham B. Gardner | 1865-1867 |
| Stephen Thomas | 1867-1869 |

|  |  |
|---|---|
| *George W. Hendee | 1869-1870 |
| George N. Dale | 1870-1872 |
| Russell S. Taft | 1872-1874 |
| Lyman G. Hinckley | 1874-1876 |
| Redfield Proctor | 1876-1878 |
| Eben R. Colton | 1878-1880 |
| John L. Barstow | 1880-1882 |
| Samuel E. Pingree | 1882-1884 |
| Ebenezer J. Ormsbee | 1884-1886 |
| Levi K. Fuller | 1886-1888 |
| Urban A. Woodbury | 1889-1890 |
| Henry A. Fletcher | 1890-1892 |
| F. Stewart Stranahan | 1892-1894 |
| Zophar M. Mansur | 1894-1896 |
| Nelson W. Fisk | 1896-1898 |
| Henry C. Bates | 1898-1900 |
| Martin F. Allen | 1900-1902 |
| Zed S. Stanton | 1902-1904 |
| Charles H. Stearns | 1904-1906 |
| George H. Prouty | 1906-1908 |
| John A. Mead | 1908-1910 |
| Leighton P. Slack | 1910-1912 |
| Frank E. Howe | 1912-1915 |
| Hale K. Darling | 1915-1917 |
| Roger W. Hulburd | 1917-1919 |
| Mason S. Stone | 1919-1921 |
| Abram W. Foote | 1921-1923 |
| Franklin S. Billings | 1923-1925 |
| Walter K. Farnsworth | 1925-1927 |
| †Hollister Jackson | 1927-1927 |
| Stanley C. Wilson | 1929-1931 |

*Became Governor during term.
†Drowned November 3, 1927.

|  |  |
|---|---|
| Benjamin Williams | 1931-1933 |
| Charles M. Smith | 1933-1935 |
| George D. Aiken | 1935-1937 |
| William H. Wills | 1937-1941 |
| Mortimer R. Proctor | 1941-1945 |
| Lee E. Emerson | 1945-1949 |
| *Harold J. Arthur | 1949-1950 |
| Joseph B. Johnson | 1951-1955 |
| **Consuelo N. Bailey | 1955-1957 |
| Robert T. Stafford | 1957-1959 |
| Robert S. Babcock | 1959-1961 |
| Ralph A. Foote | 1961-1965 |
| John J. Daley | 1965-1969 |
| Thomas L. Hayes | 1969-1971 |
| John S. Burgess | 1971- |

*Became Governor during term.
**First woman Lieutenant Governor in United States.

### Treasurers

|  |  |
|---|---|
| Ira Allen | 1778-1786 |
| Samuel Mattocks | 1786-1800 |
| Benjamin Swan | 1800-1833 |
| Augustine Clarke | 1833-1837 |
| Allen Wardner | 1837-1838 |
| Henry F. James | 1838-1841 |
| John Spaulding | 1841-1846 |
| Elisha P. Jewett | 1846-1847 |
| George Howes | 1847-1853 |
| John A. Page | 1853-1854 |
| Henry M. Bates | 1854-1860 |
| John B. Page | 1860-1866 |
| John A. Page | 1866-1882 |
| William H. DuBois | 1882-1890 |
| Henry F. Field | 1890-1898 |
| John L. Bacon | 1898-1906 |
| Edward H. Deavitt | 1906-1915 |
| Walter F. Scott | 1915-1923 |
| Thomas H. Cave | 1923-1943 |
| *Levi R. Kelley | 1943-1949 |
| **George H. Amidon | 1949-1965 |
| †Peter J. Hincks | 1965-1968 |
| Madelyn Davidson | 1968-1969 |
| Frank H. Davis | 1969- |

*Resigned to become treasurer of U.V.M., Sept. 6, 1949.
**Appointed by Gov. Gibson, Sept. 6, 1949.
†Died while in office. Mrs. Davidson appointed Acting Treasurer to complete unexpired term.

### Secretaries of State

|  |  |
|---|---|
| *Thomas Chandler | 1778 |
| Joseph Fay | 1778-1781 |
| Micah Townshend | 1781-1788 |
| Roswell Hopkins | 1788-1802 |
| David Wing, Jr. | 1802-1806 |
| Thomas Leverett | 1806-1813 |
| Josiah Dunham | 1813-1815 |
| William Slade, Jr. | 1815-1823 |
| Norman Williams | 1823-1831 |
| Timothy Merrill | 1831-1836 |
| Chauncey L. Knapp | 1836-1841 |
| Alvah Sabin | 1841-1842 |
| James McM. Shafter | 1842-1849 |
| Farrand F. Merrill | 1849-1853 |
| Daniel P. Thompson | 1853-1855 |
| Chas. W. Willard | 1855-1857 |
| Benjamin W. Dean | 1857-1861 |
| **George W. Bailey, Jr. | 1861-1865 |
| ***George Nichols | 1865-1884 |
| Charles W. Porter | 1884-1890 |
| Chauncey W. Brownell | 1890-1898 |
| Fred A. Howland | 1898-1902 |
| Fred'k G. Fleetwood | 1902-1908 |
| †Guy W. Bailey | 1908-1917 |
| Fred'k G. Fleetwood | 1917-1919 |
| ††Harry A. Black | 1919-1923 |

**Died in office.
***Secretary of State first elected by the people.
*Resigned Oct. 8, 1778.
†Resigned September 1, 1917 and Frederick G. Fleetwood appointed on same date.
††Died April 9, 1923.

|  |  |
|---|---|
| †††Aaron H. Grout | 1923-1927 |
| ‡Rawson C. Myrick | 1927-1947 |
| ††Helen E. Burbank | 1947-1949 |
| Howard E. Armstrong | 1949-1965 |
| Harry H. Cooley | 1965-1969 |
| Richard C. Thomas | 1969- |

†††Appointed April 21, 1923. Resigned and Rawson C. Myrick appointed May 2, 1927.
‡Resigned Sept. 1, 1947, and Helen F. Burbank appointed Oct. 15, 1947.
††First woman Secretary of State in Vermont.

Please notify the author at once of any errors or omissions. Some subjects had to be omitted.

# Index

FINIS